Statistics for Social Workers

SEVENTH EDITION

Statistics for Social Workers

Robert W. Weinbach
University of South Carolina

Richard M. Grinnell, Jr.
Western Michigan University

Boston   New York   San Francisco
Mexico City   Montreal   Toronto   London   Madrid   Munich   Paris
Hong Kong   Singapore   Tokyo   Cape Town   Sydney

Series Editor:	Patricia Quinlin
Series Editorial Assistant:	Sara Holliday
Marketing Manager:	Laura Lee Manley
Production Editor:	Roberta Sherman
Editorial-Production and Composition Services:	Progressive Publishing Alternatives
Composition Buyer:	Linda Cox
Manufacturing Buyer:	JoAnne Sweeney
Cover Administrator:	Joel Gendron

For related titles and support materials, visit our online catalog at www.ablongman.com.

Between the time website information is gathered and then published, it is not unusual for some sites to have closed. Also, the transcription of URLs can result in typographical errors. The publisher would appreciate notification where these errors occur so that they may be corrected in subsequent editions.

Library of Congress Cataloging-in-Publication Data

Weinbach, Robert W.
    Statistics for social workers / Robert W. Weinbach, Richard M. Grinnell, Jr.–7th ed.
        p. cm.
    Includes bibliographical references and index.
    ISBN 0-205-48422-0
    1. Social sciences–Statistical methods. 2. Social service–Statistical methods. 3. Statistics.
I. Grinnell, Richard M. II. Title.

HA29.W42 2006
519.5024'362–dc22

                                                                                                2005058678

Printed in the United States of America

10   9   8   7   6   5   4   3   RRD-VA   10   09   08

Contents

8   Correlation

9   Regression Analyses

12   Other Contributions of Statistics to Evidence-Based Practice   249

Preface

As a group and on a general level, social workers continue to be more people oriented than statistically oriented. Nevertheless, over the past two decades, they have developed a greater appreciation for the importance of statistical analyses. In addition, they have also become more sophisticated about the use of statistics by asking challenging questions and requesting more explanations than in the past. The previous six editions of our book as well as this one, all reflect these trends. We have attempted once again to adapt the current edition's contents to the changing needs and demands of contemporary social work practice.

AUDIENCE

This book is written for undergraduate and graduate social work students. It can be used as the primary text in a course on statistics or as a companion text for a social work research methods course. It can also be a useful supplementary text for a course on program evaluation or single-system design.

The book is written so that no background in statistical analyses is required. In fact, we have found that many current social work students have had one or more courses in statistics. They may have been able to crunch the numbers, and get the right answers. However, they may never have understood what they were doing, why they did it, or what it meant. This book will help these students to finally understand the logic of statistical analyses and the theories that underlie them. We have made the book as reader friendly as possible, by choosing simple words and case examples in an effort to help explain difficult concepts. Numbers and formulas have been kept to a minimum.

GOALS

What will this book accomplish? We think it will enable social work students to better understand the logical process of statistical analyses—to see how logic and the laws of probability (both important parts of all social work practice) both play dual roles in their use. It will help students to make correct decisions about when a particular statistical analysis(es) will be helpful for addressing theoretical and/or practice-based problems. It will help them to decide which type of a statistical analysis is most appropriate for a given situation, to interpret results of many different types of statistical analyses, and to present them to others in a form that easily communicates what was learned from the data.

We do not believe that social workers in the twenty-first century need to be mathematicians in order to be competent in the use of any particular statistical analysis. Although a small percentage of them might enhance their understanding of it by entering numbers into a formula and seeing for themselves how the results are obtained, many more do not require this experience. They are perfectly content to let the computer do the math. In writing this book, we have assumed that most contemporary social workers have access to computers and statistical software packages. Questions at the end of chapters serve as a good test of whether key concepts are understood and, in a few instances, they offer the opportunity to perform some simple mathematical operations. However, we believe it is the understanding of the logic of statistical analyses (not the mathematics of it) that separates social workers who comfortably use them in their research and practice situations from those who do not. We believe this book will help readers to understand statistics, and, thus, to take the fear and bewilderment out of it. In sum, we believe this book will help its readers to use statistical analyses as important tools for enhancing their practice effectiveness.

ORGANIZATION

This edition is organized similarly to the previous one.

- Chapter 1 introduces basic concepts and definitions that are necessary to understanding statistical analyses.
- Chapters 2–4 cover descriptive statistics (or data reduction)—methods designed to summarize and display the distribution of a variable within a research sample or population.
- Chapters 5–7 cover the related topics of inference and hypothesis testing with special emphasis on the role of sampling error in statistical testing.
- Chapters 8–11 present a wide array of statistical tests commonly used in social work research studies. Correlation, linear regression, cross tabulation, and *t* tests receive in-depth coverage. Other alternatives (including some popular nonparametric alternatives and multivariate procedures) are briefly presented.
- Chapter 12 discusses how statistical analyses are used in specialized types of research that help to make evidence-based practice possible.
- An Appendix contains two tables that can be used to help in selecting an appropriate statistical test.

WHAT'S NEW IN THIS EDITION?

As in the past, we have made changes in response to comments from numerous students and faculty members who have used earlier editions of the book. Many of the suggestions we have received stressed the need to provide additional clarification in some areas or to add content that might form a necessary linkage between ideas. To the extent possible (while still keeping the book affordable and consistent with the depth of coverage which we have tried to achieve), we have addressed them. What are some of the new features in this edition? They include:

- A section on statistical analyses of qualitative research data
- New figures, tables, boxes, and examples to summarize key concepts
- An added chapter (Chapter 12) that focuses on how statistical analyses contribute to evidence-based practice in meta-analysis, program evaluations, and single-system research
- Additional content on interpretation of findings from *t* tests and ANOVA and the use of planned comparison and post hoc analyses
- Additional content on selection of statistical tests

The publication of the seventh edition of this book would seem to suggest that we have attracted loyal supporters since the book's initial publication two decades ago. It also means that to omit sections might risk its success. Thus, very little is deleted from the previous edition. We chose instead to refine the writing style of most existing content in an effort to make it more crisp and clear. Some of the new tables and figures should also help in this regard.

We once again determined not to include a subsection within each chapter on how to use current statistical software packages (i.e., Excel™, SPSS™) to generate the statistics discussed in each chapter. We continue to believe that instructors who wish to demonstrate how to generate the results of statistical analyses via the use of statistical software packages can easily do so by using the tutorials and self-help content contained in the software packages themselves. In short, Excel™ and SPSS™ are now amazingly easy to obtain, are menu driven, and are of the self-taught genre, that is, discover-as-you-go.

Over the years, we have received a great amount of feedback on how instructors use our book in the classroom. Those who believe that their students should become skilled in using computer software simply supplement the book's content by introducing the basics of either Excel™ or SPSS™, and then provide any needed mentoring as the students teach themselves any additional content. A second group—those who focus on only the conceptual underpinnings of statistics—seem to appreciate the fact that the flow of the book is not interrupted by content that they deem unnecessary at the present time, and that can be readily learned independently at a later date.

ACKNOWLEDGMENTS

The list of people who have contributed to the seven editions of this book is extensive. Literally hundreds of professors and students (many of whom we acknowledge by name in previous editions) have made valuable suggestions for improvement that we very much appreciate. In addition to all of them, four reviewers, Julia F. Hastings, University of California, Berkeley; Peter Allen Lee, San Jose State University; Bibhuti K. Sar, University of Louisville; and Carolyn Turturro, University of Arkansas at Little

Rock provided valuable feedback for this edition. We wish to thank them for their contributions.

This book (along with any shortcomings that it might contain) remains our responsibility. We are gratified by the wide degree of acceptance that it has received over the years and look forward to more suggestions as to how it can be improved. We hope that it will continue to inspire many current students and future practitioners alike to appreciate and use statistical analyses in an effort to help them become more accountable and effective social work practitioners.

Robert W. Weinbach

February 2006   Richard M. Grinnell, Jr.

Statistics for
Social Workers

1

Introduction

This book is about building social work knowledge in a systematic and objective manner using data. The statistical analysis process is used to analyze and make sense of data. The data can come from many sources; they can be taken from a complex and sophisticated research study, or from something as simple as an agency client intake form.

Statistical analysis is a process that helps social workers make practice-related decisions via the use of data. Both the National Association of Social Workers (NASW) and the Council on Social Work Education (CSWE) take the position that contemporary social workers need to understand statistical analyses. There are three interrelated reasons why statistics should be studied:

1. *Social workers conduct research studies.* A knowledge of statistical analyses enhances our ability to design research studies and to draw justifiable conclusions from their findings. Thus, we need to know how to perform statistical analyses in order to collect, sort, organize, and draw conclusions from the data collected.

We contribute to the profession's knowledge base by disseminating the findings of research studies. For our study to have credibility, we must demonstrate that the data we gathered were collected, analyzed, and interpreted according to accepted methodological and statistical procedures. Fortunately, these procedures are based on the same logic that we already use in many social work practice situations.

2. *Social workers rely on others' research findings.* We use the results of others' statistical analyses of their research data to inform our practice decision making. As we read the professional social work literature or attempt to evaluate the vast amount of information now available on the Internet, we must be statistically literate. Unless we know whether a particular statistical analysis was performed correctly, we cannot know whether the findings that were derived from the study are credible. Understanding the results of a statistical analysis increases the likelihood that we will use the most effective and efficient practice interventions with our clients and helps us avoid those that lack adequate statistical support.

3. *Social workers need to evaluate their practice effectiveness.* We evaluate the effectiveness of our individual practice methods and our social service programs not only for our own feedback, but also to justify that we are accountable in the use of the resources we receive to carry out our work. To do this, we must rely on more than our own personal insights, past experiences, intuitions, or feelings that we are or are not being effective. Increasingly, both single-system designs and program evaluations rely on statistical analyses to <u>determine</u> whether an individual intervention and/or program is accomplishing its objectives.

As should be evident by now, an understanding of statistics is essential to a goal that social workers strive to achieve—evidence-based practice (EBP). **EBP** entails regularly using the best available evidence to guide us in our practice decision making. However, EBP requires that we be selective in what we allow to influence our decisions. We encounter many reports of research studies in our professional practice. They may take the form of research monographs reporting on major studies funded by the federal government or private foundations, articles in professional journals, summaries of program evaluations, or the graphs used in our own single-system studies of our individual practice effectiveness. We cannot and should not integrate all of their findings and recommendations into our practice decision making. But which ones are useful and trustworthy and which ones are not? Unless we have a <u>solid</u> <u>grounding in statistics</u> (and in research design), we cannot make <u>judicious use</u> of the many products of research that we encounter, and thus we will be hindered in our goal of becoming evidence-based practitioners. Understanding and using a statistical analysis correctly guarantees neither the generation of "true knowledge" by a research study nor positive client outcomes in practice interventions. However, it can increase the likelihood of these two events and, at the same time, helps us move toward the goal of becoming evidence-based professional social work practitioners.

USES OF STATISTICS

Whether we are evaluating our own practice effectiveness or conducting a research study to generate new knowledge, a good statistical analysis is of great assistance, for example, when we select, design, evaluate, and fine-tune our data-collection instruments. It can also help us make decisions about how large a research sample we need for a given research study or whether a measurement instrument is likely to produce valid and reliable data.

Once data are collected, a statistical analysis can help us:

- Summarize the characteristics of a specific research sample or population
- Estimate the characteristics of the population from which our sample was drawn

- Determine if any patterns of relationships found within a research sample can safely be generalized back to the population from which the sample was drawn

STAT ANAL
USEFUL :
when SND.
METHODS FOR
MEASUREMENT +
DATA COLLECT.
have been USED.

A statistical analysis can produce useful information only when sound methods for measurement and data collection have been used. To put it another way, even a good statistical analysis can be useless or, worse yet, misleading if the data that were collected to answer a research question or to test a research hypothesis were flawed in some way.

METHODOLOGICAL TERMS

Many terms used in the research enterprise have specific meanings. Eight of the most important ones are (1) **data,** (2) **information,** (3) **variables and constants,** (4) **conceptualization,** (5) **operationalization,** (6) **reliability,** (7) **validity,** and (8) **research hypotheses.**

Data

In the previous pages, we have used two terms: data and information. Although these terms are sometimes used interchangeably in everyday conversation, in this book, an important distinction is made between them. The term **data** refers to the measurements (numbers, scores, and so forth) collected in a research study before they have been analyzed in any way. (*Data* is the plural; the singular is *datum.*) For example, the group of scores obtained by administering a client satisfaction scale to 100 clients is *data.* (An individual client's satisfaction score on the same measuring instrument is referred to as *datum.*)

In conducting a research study (and in our day-to-day practice), social workers engage in many types of data-gathering activities and data-collection methods. We conduct in-depth interviews, content analyses, participant observations, and planned observations of behaviors in natural settings. We also conduct surveys, group experiments, case experiments, meta-analyses, historical research, and so forth.

Data usually consist of measurements that we take ourselves, but they may also be measurements taken previously for some other purpose, (such as, by other researchers seeking to answer another research question or by other practitioners for client record-keeping purposes). When data collected for some other purpose are statistically analyzed, we refer to the process as **secondary data analysis.**

Whatever method is used to acquire data, measurements must be as accurate as possible. Conclusions based on a research study's findings are never any better than the quality of the data that formed the basis for those conclusions.

Information

Data, when analyzed, produce information. **Information** is the interpretation we give to collected data after we have analyzed them. The research conclusion based on a data analysis that "Treatment Intervention *A* is more successful than Treatment Intervention *B* in reducing substance abuse among research participants" is information. Similarly, if the outside temperature measured by a thermometer is 102 degrees Fahrenheit, the 102 degrees is *datum.* The interpretation that it is very hot is *information.*

Variables and Constants

There is always a limit to how much data we can collect and use in any given research or practice situation. Like a social work practitioner conducting an intake interview, a social work researcher does not need to know everything about the phenomenon being studied. Thus, we limit data-collection activities to measuring only what is believed to be essential and useful for the specific research study, that is, certain variables.

What exactly is a variable? A **variable** is a characteristic or attribute that differs in quantity or quality among the people (or objects) studied. All research studies focus on variables. Among human beings, examples of variables are educational level, gender, sexual orientation, ethnicity, motivational level, stress level, and self-esteem level. The list is practically endless.

Constants, in comparison to variables, are traits or characteristics that do *not* differ in quantity or quality among people (or objects). An example of a constant among all human beings is mortality. Life expectancy, on the other hand, is a variable, as it differs among human beings.

Researchers often wish to determine and describe the degree to which people vary in relation to some variable. But they may also want to learn why these variations occur among people (or objects) and what other variables may relate (or not relate) to these variations in some way. We may study, for example, a sample of female adolescents addicted to crack cocaine. We would attempt to learn how some other variables, such as educational level and *income level*, might relate to different patterns of drug addiction within the sample. In this example, adolescence, gender, and addiction to crack cocaine are constants (characteristics of all research participants), but the research participants' different educational and income levels, along with their patterns of drug-use addiction, are variables.

Value Categories and Values. The different measurements that a variable can assume can be expressed in words (e.g., homeless, not homeless) or in numbers (e.g., 1, 2, 3). When measurements are expressed in words, they are called **value categories** and simply describe different forms that the variable can take. The variable *gender,* for example, can be measured by classifying people into two value categories that can be expressed in words—male and female.

When the different measurements of a variable are expressed in numbers that reflect some quantifiable difference, they are called **values** and reflect more precise measurement than value categories. We can measure the variable *age,* for example, by using actual numerical values (e.g., 23, 35, 67) to reflect the actual ages of people on their last birthdays.

Frequencies of Value Categories and Values. More often than not, a given value category or value occurs more than once in a group of people (or objects). The number of times that it occurs within a group of cases is called its **frequency.** Frequencies for the different value categories or values of variables tend to vary within data sets. Within a research sample of 48 agency clients, for example, the frequency for the value category *female* might be 26 for the variable *gender,* while the frequency for the value category *male* might be 22.

The following example of a questionnaire item can be used to summarize the relationship between a variable, its value categories, and the frequencies of each value category.

What is your highest social work degree completed? (*variable*)

Value Category	Frequency
Associate degree	90
BSW	220
MSW	190
PhD/DSW	30
Total	530

In the above example, the variable *highest social work degree completed* has four value categories (i.e., Associate degree, BSW, MSW, PhD/DSW) and each value category has a frequency (i.e., there are 90 people who have an Associate degree, 220 people who have a BSW, 190 people who have a MSW, 30 people who have a PhD/DSW).

Conceptualization

Sometimes, when a research study begins, we may not know which variables will need to be measured and which will not. We need to narrow down the list of potential variables by identifying those that must be measured in an attempt to arrive at answers to our research question. But this is only the first step in an important three-step process known as **conceptualization,** which takes place with the help of a thorough review of the available professional literature. The steps in the conceptualization process are:

1. Select the most important variables to study.
2. State exactly what is meant by each variable.
3. State the value categories or values that each variable can assume.

After we have selected the variables to measure, we need to define exactly what each one means. Let us say, for example, that we wish to see if there is support for our belief that, among 3-year-old children who are diagnosed as autistic, Treatment Intervention *A* will decrease autistic behavior more than Treatment Intervention *B*. In order to examine the relationship between the two treatment interventions used and their relationship to the rate of decrease in the autistic behavior of 3-year-old children, we must clearly state the meaning of both variables (the type of intervention and the amount of autistic behavior). We must also state the value categories or values that each variable can assume as well as the nature of the relationship that we believe to exist between them.

What exactly constitutes autistic behavior? What exactly are Interventions *A* and *B*? Without first delineating the meaning of all variables, it would be futile to attempt to establish a relationship between or among them. Note that age and a diagnosis of autism are constants—they do not vary among the children we are studying. Of course, the severity of autism would vary among the children. It would constitute a third variable that we also might decide to measure so that we can better understand the relationship between the two variables of primary interest, type of intervention and reduction of autistic behavior. If so, we would also have to conceptualize what exactly we mean by severity, magnitude, or intensity of autism.

Operationalization

Specifying exactly how we are going to measure the variables we have conceptualized is called **operationalization.** Many different indicators may be used to measure the same variable. For example, the variable assertiveness might be operationalized as specific client behaviors observed by medical staff in an inpatient setting, as a subjective diagnosis of clients by the social worker, as self-analyses by clients, or as clients' responses on a standardized self-administered measuring instrument that is believed to measure assertiveness.

More often than not, we need to measure variables by multiple indicators—not one indicator. We might measure, for example, the written and physical responses of research participants to specific stimuli. Suppose we wanted to determine the extent to which computerization in a particular human service agency has affected the job satisfaction of the social workers employed there. The variable *level of job satisfaction* of the social workers could be measured with the use of several different indicators both before and after the computerization takes place. Methods of measurement might include directly asking workers about their current level of job satisfaction and also having them complete a standardized job-satisfaction measuring instrument. We could also measure their behaviors, such as job absenteeism, which previous research studies have indicated is directly related to job satisfaction. Each of the three indicators would serve as a kind of check on the other two, thereby increasing the likelihood that our measurement will be valid and reliable (more on this later on).

The specific indicators of a given variable as well as the methods used for measuring it may differ from place to place, time to time, person to person, and study to study. Specifying exactly how a variable is to be operationalized is just as important to good measurement as conceptualization. If, for example, we want to learn something about the relative effectiveness of two different treatment interventions— individual treatment and group treatment—for people who are clinically depressed, we need to state clearly (1) how we will determine which of the two different types of interventions was used and (2) how we will measure level of depression. Will we operationalize depression level as clients' appearances as reported by staff? We would select this indicator only if there is strong evidence in the professional literature of a relationship between depression levels and personal appearance. Even if there were, when used alone to measure depression levels, staff observations of appearance would not be expected to yield valid measurements because appearance is a subjective judgment. Another, better indicator might be each person's score on a standardized self-report measurement instrument that has been shown to measure the variable *clinical depression.*

However we decide to operationalize the variable *clinical depression,* we would hope that a pattern would emerge from our measurements. Perhaps clients who received individual treatment would appear to be less depressed than clients who received group treatment. However, solely on the basis of an apparent pattern of this nature, we should not conclude that treatment effectiveness and treatment methods are related. To come to such a conclusion would require a good statistical analysis of the data. For example, the result of statistical testing could help us to determine if it was the type of treatment or something else that might have produced different depression levels. The value of any conclusions drawn from statistical testing depends on the accuracy of the measurements. Statistical tests perform mathematical operations with data; they have no way of knowing whether the measurements that produced the data were reliable and valid.

Reliability

Two terms are used to describe the quality of measurement of variables—reliability and validity. In the simplest of terms, **reliability** is the degree of consistency of a measurement. Reliability answers the question: To what degree does the measurement of a variable produce consistent results? There are several different types of reliability and several different ways they can be determined. They rely heavily on the concept of correlation (Chapter 8).

Few, if any, measuring instruments can be said to possess perfect reliability. But some are more reliable than others. For example, a measuring instrument that proposes to measure the variable *clinical depression* may produce very consistent measurements among individuals in a wide variety of situations. Therefore, it can be considered to be relatively reliable. On the other hand, another measuring instrument that also claims to measure depression may be more easily influenced by who is performing the measuring, where the individuals are being measured, the time of day or year that the measurement takes place, and so on. Thus, this second measuring instrument would be considered less reliable than the first one.

Validity

Even if a measuring instrument has a high degree of reliability, it does not guarantee that the procedure(s) used to measure the variable is (are) a good one. A measuring instrument can be very consistent in producing the same measurements, but the measurements can be consistently wrong. In other words, the measurement lacks **validity.** This means that the measuring instrument is not measuring what it is believed to be measuring. Only valid measurement of variables produces data that, when statistically analyzed, can generate valuable knowledge about the variables and the possibility of relationships between and among them.

A reliable measuring instrument, or measurement procedure, may be biased or distorted in some way. A measuring instrument believed to measure the variable *clinical depression,* for example, may produce consistent results when measuring the depression level of the same group of people in a variety of research or practice situations. But if the measuring instrument really is measuring some variable other than depression (e.g., self-esteem, energy level, physical health), it is not producing an accurate measurement of depression and is not an appropriate instrument for measuring the variable *clinical depression.*

If measurement of a variable is both reliable (consistent) and truly measuring what it is believed to be measuring, then the measuring instrument is said to be valid. There cannot be validity without reliability. As we have seen, however, there can be reliability without validity. Thus, reliability can be regarded as a necessary but not sufficient indication of the presence of validity.

There are several different indicators (often referred to as types) of validity. Demonstrating that one or more of them was present in the measurement of a variable is critical to the credibility of a research study's finding S. Thus, researchers often report on the face validity, the content validity, the predictive validity, the concurrent validity, or some aspect of the construct validity of their measurements. A detailed discussion of each of these terms is beyond the scope of this book; they are discussed in basic social work research methods texts.

Research Hypotheses

A **research hypothesis** is a statement of a relationship between or among variables. It is often stated in the future tense because it predicts what will be found when the data derived from the research study are collected and analyzed. It expresses what we believe will be found to be true.

A carefully worded research hypothesis expresses more than just a belief in a relationship between or among variables—it also conveys the nature of the predicted relationship. The relationship may be either causal or noncausal. In a **causal relationship,** the values of one variable are believed to actually produce the different values of the other variable. Demonstrating support for a causal relationship between variables requires a rigorous research design such as the classical experiment. In the experiment, there is random selection and random assignment to experimental and control groups and introduction or manipulation of one variable to study its affects on the other variable.

There are two types of **noncausal relationships** expressed in research hypotheses, relationships in which there are identifiable patterns but there is no reason to believe that one variable directly causes the measurements of the other variable. One, **association,** simply states that certain value categories of one variable will be found with certain value categories of the other variable. For example, it might predict that males will be found to drive one type of car and females will drive another type of car. In no way would it suggest that being male or female will cause people to drive certain cars.

If the variables in a research hypothesis can be measured with more precision (discussed later in this chapter), the relationship between them might be described as one of correlation. In **correlation,** there is a predicted pattern in which high values of one variable are found with high values of the other variable and vice versa (known as a positive correlation) or high values of one variable are found with low values of the other and vice versa (a negative correlation). For example, we might predict a high positive correlation between undergraduate grade-point average and grades in graduate school. As with association, the presence of a correlation is not, in itself, sufficient evidence of a cause–effect relationship. Correlation (and the statistical methods used for identifying it) will be discussed in detail in Chapter 8.

The way a research hypothesis is stated allows it to be supported—or not supported—by a statistical analysis. We might state a research hypothesis about the two variables *clinical depression* and *sleep patterns,* for example, as follows:

> *People who are depressed will have different sleep patterns than people who are not depressed.*

We can see if there is support for this hypothesis by measuring the sleep patterns of people who are diagnosed as depressed and compare these patterns with those people who are not depressed. Sleep patterns could be operationalized in relation to sleep phases or simply as number of hours of sleep.

This research hypothesis proposes a relationship of association between two variables—*sleep patterns* and *clinical depression.* If we find statistical support for the research hypothesis that the two variables are related, it doesn't tell us whether depression influences sleep patterns or sleep patterns influence depression, or neither. It could simply mean that the two variables *co-vary*—that certain measurements of one variable tend to be found with certain measurements of the other.

Suppose that, based on a review of the professional literature, we had stated our research hypothesis in a slightly different way; one expressing a belief in a causal relationship:

> *Disturbed sleep patterns cause depression.*

To better understand what this research hypothesis conveys, we need to discuss the difference between two labels that are applied to variables within research hypotheses, independent and dependent.

Independent Variable.   If one variable is predicted to influence the other variable. The variable that is predicted to do the influencing is called the **independent variable.** If we wanted to see whether disturbed sleep patterns cause depression, for example, we could disturb the sleep patterns of a number of people in an experimental group to see if they became depressed. (In reality, there are ethical reasons why we would do nothing of the sort.) Theoretically, however, sleep patterns would be the independent variable—the one that is manipulated.

Dependent Variable.   In the above research hypothesis the second variable, *clinical depression,* is the dependent variable. A **dependent variable** is believed to be influenced by the independent variable: People's depression levels are believed to be influenced by their sleep patterns. The research hypothesis could be turned around:

> *Depression causes disturbed sleep patterns.*

Here, depression is believed to do the causing (or at least influencing) and is therefore the independent variable. What is being influenced—sleep patterns—is the dependent variable. Of course, unless the researcher employed the kind of design rigor seen in true experiments, proving a causal relationship may be impossible. Other variables, such as drugs taken to treat depression (called *confounding* or *extraneous* variables), may help cause the variation in the dependent variable or may affect the relationship between the independent and dependent variables in many different ways.

Independent Variables and Dependent Variables or Predictor Variables and Criterion Variables.   The terms independent variable and dependent variable are nothing more than convenient labels to aid in the communication process. They are used to indicate the presumed direction of influence between or among variables, based on logic, time sequence, and so forth. They generally are used in reference to research hypotheses that suggest that one variable (the independent one) is believed to influence the other (the dependent one); that is, it produces (or at least contributes to) its variation.

Social work researchers often wish only to find support for the belief that two variables co-vary. They often do this so that they might be able to predict the value of one variable by knowing the value of the other variable.

When demonstration of covariance between variables is our study's main goal, two other terms are used to describe the relationship between or among them. The variable that is used for prediction is called a **predictor variable.** The variable whose values we hope to predict is called **an outcome variable** (sometimes called a criterion variable). To make it easier for the beginning student of statistics, and to be consistent with how other books have used the terms, we use predictor variable and outcome variable in discussing statistical analyses that do not imply influence or causality but rather focus on covariance (Chapters 8 and 9). We use independent variable and dependent variable throughout the rest of the book.

MEASUREMENT LEVELS

The conceptualization and operationalization processes provide a necessary and orderly method for selecting and measuring variables. Formulation of research hypotheses and identification of the variables within them as independent, dependent, predictor, or outcome provide further clarification of our study's focus and purpose. Before a statistical analysis can occur, however, we need to make another determination: We must judge how precisely all of our variables within our study have been measured.

Some variables are difficult to measure with a high degree of precision. Others can be measured precisely, but, through choice or accident, they are measured in a way that provides less precise data than could have been produced. We generally want to select a measuring instrument that yields the highest level of precision possible. But, sometimes, this is neither desirable nor necessary because of either ethical or practical concerns. For example, we may elect to provide income intervals for research participants to check rather than to directly ask them their exact earned income for the previous year. We would do this in the interest of confidentiality and in order to increase the likelihood of a higher response rate.

TABLE 1.1 Measurement Levels and Numerical Value Requirements

Level	Numerical Value Requirements
Nominal	None: uses value categories.
Ordinal	Values must preserve rank order.
Interval	Values must preserve rank order and unit differences.
Ratio	Values must preserve rank, unit differences, and fixed zero point.

Determination of a variable's level of measurement (along with other factors discussed in Chapter 6) provides direction as to the most appropriate type of statistical analysis to use. A variable can assume four levels of measurement: (1) **nominal,** (2) **ordinal,** (3) **interval,** and (4) **ratio.** Table 1.1 provides a brief summary of each level of measurement and the requirements that must be met for each level.

Nominal

The first, and least precise, level of measurement is the **nominal** level. Its value categories are discrete—which means that they are distinct from each other. The nominal level categorizes variables into discrete subclasses—nothing more, nothing less. The different value categories it uses reflect only a difference in kind. There is no implication of a quantifiable difference among the value categories; therefore, no rank ordering of the value categories is possible. Variables, such as gender, race, ethnicity, referral source, diagnosis, occupation, sexual orientation, marital status, and political party affiliation, are considered by their very nature to be at the nominal level of measurement, since the value categories used with them tend to be little more than simple labels reflecting qualitative differences. The following is an example of a question that produces nominal level data:

> *Do you believe the government should provide national health care insurance?*
> **1.** Yes
> **2.** No
> **3.** Undecided

A nominal level variable must have two or more value categories, and the value categories must be distinct, mutually exclusive, and mutually exhaustive. This means that each case (each research participant or object studied) must appropriately fit into only one of the value categories and that there must be an appropriate value category for each case. There are only two value categories, for example, for the nominal level variable *life status*—living or deceased. These two value categories are clearly exhaustive and mutually exclusive, as every person can be classified into one of the categories (exhaustiveness), but only one (exclusiveness).

In nominal level measurement, numerals (e.g., 1, 2, 3) or letters (e.g., A, B, C) are sometimes assigned for convenience. Suppose we have divided the nominal level variable *type of treatment intervention* into three value categories: individual treatment, group treatment, and family treatment. We could assign numbers to the three types of intervention, but the numbers would be just labels for value categories. For example:

1. Individual treatment
2. Group treatment
3. Family treatment

The numbers serve only to classify—to reflect a difference in kind. We could have also assigned letters to the three types of intervention:

A. Individual treatment
B. Group treatment
C. Family treatment

Nothing would change. It would be incorrect to say that the value category of 1 (or A) is more or less treatment than 2 (or B) or 3 (or C), or to make any other statement that implies that the three value categories have any quantitative meaning.

Ordinal

In **ordinal** level measurement, not only do variables assume different value categories (and, sometimes, values), but the different value categories or values also have some quantitative meaning. With ordinal measurement, it is possible to rank-order a variable's value categories or values in such a way that they range from high to low or from most to least. Examples of variables that often are measured at the ordinal level are social class, occupational prestige, educational degrees received, ratings of client change, ratings of treatment effectiveness, ratings of clients' satisfaction with treatment, and rankings of problem severity. Below are some of the more common groupings of value categories that usually suggest that a variable is at the ordinal level of measurement:

1. Considerable
2. Some
3. Little
4. None

1. High
2. Moderate
3. Low

1. Very effective
2. Somewhat effective
3. Somewhat ineffective
4. Very ineffective

1. Very severe
2. Severe
3. Mild
4. Very mild

The following are examples of research questions that would produce ordinal measurement:

How would you rate the services you have received from our agency? (Circle one number below.)

1. Very good
2. Good
3. Fair
4. Poor
5. Very poor

How satisfied are you with the services you have received from our agency? (Circle one number below.)

1. Very satisfied
2. Somewhat satisfied
3. Somewhat dissatisfied
4. Very dissatisfied

It is important to note that these value categories do not indicate absolute quantities or assume equal intervals between them. We might, for example, ask all social workers in North America who hold a social work degree to answer the following question:

What is your highest social work degree completed?

1. Associate degree
2. BSW
3. MSW
4. PhD/DSW

Because the intervals between the four value categories are not equal, we cannot say that the difference between a person who has an Associate degree and a person with an MSW is exactly the same as the interval between a person with a PhD/DSW and a person who has a BSW. If we could say this, we could claim that the variable *highest social work degree completed* meets the criteria for the next level of measurement, interval level measurement.

Interval

Like ordinal level measurement, **interval** level measurement also makes it possible to rank order different measurements of a variable. It also has one important added criterion—it places the values for the variable on an equally spaced continuum. Thus, unlike ordinal measurement, interval measurement has a uniform unit of measurement, such as one year or one degree of temperature. Therefore, the values indicate exactly how far apart one value is from another. With an interval level variable, we can say that a research participant has more or less of a given variable than another participant, and we can specify exactly how many units more or less.

With equal distances between the values, a measurement of 1 for a variable will be the same distance from a 4 ($4 - 1 = 3$) as a 6 is from a 9 ($9 - 6 = 3$). On a measuring instrument that is designed to measure intelligence, which is generally assumed to be an interval level variable, the difference between IQ scores of 100 and 105 ($105 - 100 = 5$) should reflect the same difference in intelligence as between IQ scores of 115 and 120 ($120 - 115 = 5$). On another test, two individuals with achievement scores of 60 and 50 respectively should differ from each other in achievement as much as two other individuals with scores of 90 and 80 respectively.

Interval level measurement does not have an absolute zero point. This means that we cannot identify a point at which *no* quantity of the variable exists. Thus, we cannot say that a 2 is twice as much as a 1—only that it is 1 unit more. Because a reading of 0 degrees on a Fahrenheit thermometer does not coincide with the absence of heat, a temperature of 60 degrees does not mean that it is twice as hot as a temperature of 30 degrees.

Ratio

The existence of a fixed, absolute, and nonarbitrary zero point constitutes the only difference between interval level and **ratio** level measurement. Therefore, values at the ratio level of measurement indicate the actual amount of the property being measured. With such measurement, we can say not only that one person has so many units more or less of a variable than a second person, but also that the first person has so many times more or less of the variable. Examples of variables that can be measured at the ratio level are birth, death, and divorce rates; number of children in a family; and number of times that a client attended group treatment over a 6-month period.

The absolute zero point in ratio measurement permits all arithmetic operations— addition, subtraction, multiplication, and division. It also allows for the valid use and meaningful interpretation of ratios formed by two or more measurements. It would be correct to say, for example, that a country with an average birth rate of 4 children per couple has twice as high a birth rate as a country with an average birth rate of 2 children per couple.

One way to test for the existence of ratio measurement is to think about the possibility of negative values for the variable being measured. If negative numbers can logically be assigned (e.g., a temperature of –25°F), then the measurement of the variable cannot be considered to be more than interval.

MEASUREMENT LEVELS AND DATA ANALYSIS

Determining if a variable is at the ordinal, interval, or ratio level can be difficult. There is an ongoing debate, for example, about whether certain measurement instruments produce data that should be regarded as ordinal or interval. A few people suggest that certain measurement instruments (for example, Likert scales) should be regarded as interval for purposes of data analyses. Others strongly disagree, insisting that only standardized measuring instruments that have undergone the most rigorous methods or development have any claim at all to interval level measurement.

Often, when using a single item or question to measure a variable, the way that it is worded can determine the level of measurement that is produced. For example, when measuring employment status we might ask:

Nominal: *Are you currently employed? Yes/no*
Ordinal: *What is your employment status?*
  Unemployed _____
  Employed part-time _____
  Employed full-time ($37\frac{1}{2}$ − 40 hours) _____
  Employed over 40 hours _____
Ratio: *How many hours a week are you employed?* _____

For statistical purposes, the distinction between interval level and ratio level is usually not an important one. Because of this, it is common practice where appropriate to simply describe a variable as "interval/ratio" level. However, as we shall see, the distinction between nominal and ordinal is important, and the distinction between ordinal level and either interval level or ratio level is often critical in deciding which type of statistical analysis can be used.

Because of the way some variables are measured, they may appear to be at the interval or ratio level, but should be treated as ordinal. Suppose, for example, we are measuring the variable *driving skill.* We can operationalize, or measure, driving skill by recording the number of traffic accidents that people have had over the past 10 years. Should driving skill be regarded as ratio? No, even though the number of traffic accidents has a true zero point and equal intervals, the underlying variable, *driving skill,* lacks measurement precision. We cannot say that the difference in driving skill between a person who had four accidents and a person who had three (4 − 3 = 1) is exactly the same as the difference between a person who had one accident and a person who had none (1 − 0 = 1). When data are analyzed, it might be best to form grouped values for the number of traffic accidents (e.g., 0–2 accidents, 3–5 accidents), to treat the variable at the ordinal level of measurement, and to select a statistical analysis created for use with ordinal level data.

Making a judgment about the variable's level of measurement is important in determining what form of statistical analysis to use. As discussed in later chapters, sometimes even if we conclude that we have, say, an interval level variable, that in itself may not be enough to justify the use of a certain form of statistical analysis. Most analyses require other assumptions about variables and the way in which their values are distributed (see Chapter 7). If these assumptions cannot be met, statistical analyses normally designed for higher levels of measurement (interval or ratio) should not be used. Statistical analyses designed for use with ordinal or even nominal data should then be substituted.

While it may be necessary to use a statistical analysis designed for lower-level data, we generally cannot move in the other direction. For example, if a variable is measured in a way that produces only nominal level data, the variable cannot be treated as if it were at the ordinal level. It would be equally incorrect to use a statistical analysis intended for use with interval level or ratio level variables with nominal level or ordinal level data unless the nominal or ordinal variables are first converted into one or more dummy variables (to be described later).

ADDITIONAL MEASUREMENT CLASSIFICATIONS

Like the levels of measurement discussed above, other classifications of variables also guide the selection of the most appropriate statistical analysis to use when analyzing data.

Discrete and Continuous Variables

Discrete variables can take on only a finite number of values, such as the number of correct answers on the Scholastic Achievement Test (SAT) or the number of siblings a person has. Note that there are only a limited number of SAT scores that people can receive. They can score 1000 or 1010, but not 1002.5. Also, people can have 2 or 3 siblings but not 2.16 siblings. By contrast, **continuous variables** can theoretically take on all numerical values. Height of social work students and grade point averages are examples of continuous variables. If we take any two measurements of a continuous variable, it is theoretically possible that there could be one or more other measurements between them. The number of different values a continuous variable can take is unlimited, assuming that we can use measuring instruments capable of measuring the values with ever-increasing precision.

Dichotomous, Binary, and Dummy Variables

A **dichotomous variable** is a specific type of discrete variable that only has two value categories. Examples are gender (male or female) or the result of an election (win or lose). We could take a more precisely measured variable—such as age of voters, which is at the interval or ratio level—divide its range of values into two groups (top half and bottom half), and convert it into a dichotomous level variable with value categories of older voters and younger voters. However, such an activity would be wasting the precision of measurement that is available for the variable age.

A special type of dichotomous variable is a **binary variable.** With binary variables, we assign numerical value categories of 1 or 0 to indicate the presence (1) or absence (0) of the variable. For the variable car ownership, for example, we could assign a value category of 1 for people who own a car and a value category of 0 for those who do not own a car.

Another special type of dichotomous variable is called a **dummy variable.** Suppose, for example, we wanted to take the variable gender, a nominal level dichotomous variable, and make it more quantitative in order to perform a statistical analysis that requires more precise measurement. We could convert the variable *gender* into one of two binary variables—either *femaleness* (female = 1; not female = 0) or *maleness* (male = 1; not male = 0). There would be no need for both dummy variables, because both males and females would be represented in either one of them. The number of dummy variables that can be created from any variable is always the number of value categories in the original variable, minus one.

Why would we ever want to create dummy variables? Of what use are they in statistics? Because when we convert a variable such as gender into a dummy variable, we have transformed it. In our previous example, *gender* was previously a nominal level variable; it is now a ratio level one. In addition, if the original variable has more than two value categories (for example, religious affiliation), all of the dummy variables created will be dichotomous. These changes can be very useful—they allow us to include a variable like gender or religious affiliation in certain types of statistical analyses that require that variables be interval/ratio level or, in some cases, dichotomous. Unless the transformation to one or more dummy variables occurs, that would not be possible.

CATEGORIES OF STATISTICAL ANALYSES

There are as many ways in which statistical analyses can be categorized as there are people willing to categorize them. Two of the most common ones are the number of variables being analyzed and the primary purpose of the analysis.

Number of Variables in an Analysis

Statistical analyses can be categorized into three categories: univariate, bivariate, or multivariate:

1. **Univariate analyses** examine the distribution of value categories (for nominal and ordinal level data) and values (for interval and ratio level data) for a single variable.
2. **Bivariate analyses** examine the relationship between two variables.
3. **Multivariate analyses** examine the relationship among three or more variables.

Primary Purpose of the Analysis

We can also group statistical analyses into two broad categories, descriptive and inferential. These two categories simply reflect the purpose, or use, of the analysis.

Descriptive Analysis.   After data are collected, the large number of measurements or scores (called **raw data**) frequently is overwhelming. A way must be found to summarize and communicate the most important, salient characteristics of the data set. We can use certain forms of descriptive analyses to accomplish this. They are described in the early chapters of this book.

A descriptive analysis summarizes the actual measurements of the variables within a data set. Our concern does not extend beyond the particular research sample (or population) studied. Descriptive analyses generally consist of compiling graphs, tables, and descriptive summaries of measurements, which are easier to comprehend and interpret than a long list of data reporting the results of measurement of each variable for every case.

Descriptive analyses are also known as **data reduction.** Their purpose is to reduce large amounts of data into simple and more understandable forms without distorting or losing their overall meaning. Of course, of necessity all summaries sacrifice some detail. Descriptive statistical analyses are no exception to this rule.

Data may have been collected from a **population**—that is, all individuals or events that meet certain criteria. Such a population, for example, might be all full-time students currently enrolled in accredited schools of social work in North America in 2007. Descriptive summaries of the measurements of populations are called **parameters.** Descriptive analyses also are used to summarize the measurements taken of certain variables within research samples. When samples are used, the summaries of their measurements are called **statistics.**

Often descriptive statistical analyses are preliminary to other types of statistical analyses (inferential). However, in some types of research studies—surveys and some qualitative research designs, for example—a descriptive analysis is the primary product of the data analysis.

Inferential Analysis.   Inferential analyses are used when we have access to only a sample drawn from a population rather than to the total population. Inferential analyses refer to a group of procedures for determining how safe it is to make generalizations about the distribution of measurements of variables within a population (parameters) based on the measurements taken of the variable within a sample drawn from that population (statistics). Sample statistics are merely estimates of population parameters; they thus can be more or less accurate.

Unless specifically indicated, our discussion of statistical analyses in the pages that follow assumes that the tasks of constructing a study's research design have been performed well and the study has generated valid and reliable measurements of the study's variables.

ANALYSIS OF QUALITATIVE DATA

Statistical analyses are an important part of all quantitative research studies. The number crunching that characterizes the field of statistics is often the last step in determining whether or not support can be claimed for a research hypothesis. But what if the data are not in the form of numbers — they consist of words, as is often the case in more qualitative approaches to knowledge building? Can statistics still be used to help to interpret them? Yes, it sometimes can. Although qualitative research is often interpretative and subjective, some data may be analyzed with the use of the methods described in this book. However, special caution should be exercised in drawing conclusions from analysis of qualitative data. Qualitative studies are not generally designed to test hypotheses (they are more likely to produce them) or arrive at other definitive conclusions. If we are not careful, we can use statistics to make too much of the data.

Data derived from qualitative research studies often are in the form of notes, audiotapes, or videotapes resulting from such data-collection methods as in-person interviews, focus groups, or the researcher's own observations. They must be transcribed. Meaningful content may be embedded in a considerable amount of noise, superfluous words such as the exchange of social greetings or ice breakers. It must be isolated, identified, and quantified to the degree possible. This entails the use of processes such as content analysis and coding, an in-depth discussion of which is beyond the focus of this book. However, a few examples of how this might work can illustrate the point that statistical analyses can be used to examine qualitative data, once they are transformed.

Suppose data consist of videotaped 1-hour personal interviews with older people who have recently become addicted to prescription medication. How could these data be transformed so that they would be suitable for at least some forms of statistical analysis?

- A content analysis of the tapes could reveal the number of times that each person uses the word "depression" or a synonym over the course of the interview (an interval/ratio-level variable).
- Three clinical social workers could independently view the tapes and determine whether each person appeared to be "severely depressed," somewhat depressed," or "showing no sign of clinical depression." Level of depression could then be assigned if at least two judges were in agreement (an ordinal level variable).
- Answers to the interviewer's question, "When did you first acknowledge that you had this problem?" could be grouped into several time intervals (an ordinal level variable).
- Descriptions of methods for coping with the addiction could be coded with the use of predetermined category labels and then assigned numbers (a nominal level variable).

Once data have been thus transformed into quantitative variables, statistical analysis could be used to analyze them with the use of both descriptive and (less frequently) inferential methods. Of course, there would be severe limitations regarding any conclusions that could be drawn, either about people who did not participate in the study or, especially, about relationships between variables. Why? The original data are likely to have come from a relatively small, nonrandom sample of research participants using nonstandardized methods. They also were likely to have been influenced by the person or persons who collected them in one or more important ways.

CONCLUDING THOUGHTS

This chapter emphasized the relationship between good measurement and meaningful statistical analyses of research data. It reviewed some of the basic terms that are especially important to understanding the statistical analyses of data.

As suggested in this chapter and demonstrated in the chapters that follow, statistical analyses involve methods for gathering, organizing, summarizing, and evaluating data. They are not a mysterious mathematical process. In fact, a statistical analysis is little more than the application of the same logic and common sense that are applied elsewhere in good social work practice.

STUDY QUESTIONS

1. Discuss why good measurement is essential to a meaningful statistical analysis. Use an original example in your discussion.
2. Discuss how a variable differs from a constant. Provide an original example of each in your discussion.
3. In a research hypothesis, what do we call the variable whose variations we are most interested in explaining? What do we call the variable that we believe may affect these variations? Which other terms are substituted if we are primarily interested in studying only their covariance or in predicting the value category (or value) of one variable through knowing the value category (or value) of the other? Provide original examples to illustrate your understanding of these terms.
4. What characteristic does a valid measuring instrument possess that an instrument that is merely reliable does not?
5. Suggest three different possible indicators of the variable *motivation to attend a graduate school of social work.*
6. What does the term *value category* mean when referring to a nominal level variable? What does the term *value* mean when referring to an ordinal, interval, or ratio level variable? Provide one original example of each in your discussion.
7. What additional criterion must be met for a variable to be considered ordinal that is not a requirement for nominal level measurement? Provide an original example in your discussion.
8. What is required for ratio level measurement that is not required for interval level measurement? Provide an original example in your discussion.
9. Operationalize the variable *educational level* so that its measurement would produce nominal level measurement, ordinal level measurement, interval level measurement, and ratio level measurement.
10. In your own words, discuss the differences between descriptive statistical analyses of data and inferential statistical analyses. Describe some social work research situations where the use of each would be appropriate. What do inferential analyses attempt to determine that descriptive analyses do not? What other methods are used to classify different types of statistical analyses?
11. Construct a research hypothesis with one nominal level independent variable and one nominal level dependent variable. Explain how you would measure the dependent variable to produce the desired level of measurement.
12. Construct a research hypothesis that has one nominal level independent variable and one ordinal level dependent variable. Explain how you would measure the dependent variable to produce the desired level of measurement.
13. Construct a research hypothesis that has one nominal level independent variable and one interval level dependent variable. Explain how you would measure the dependent variable to produce the desired level of measurement.
14. Construct a hypothesis that has one nominal level independent variable and one ratio level dependent variable. Explain how you would measure the dependent variable to produce the desired level of measurement.

15. What level of measurement is the variable *highest social work degree received?* Justify your response. What other ways of operationalizing the variable would produce different levels of measurement? Explain.

16. Find a research-based article in a professional social work journal that is of some interest to you. Answer the following questions in relation to the article:

    a. How much of the article is a report of statistical analyses per se (as opposed to theory, ideas, implications, research design, sampling, data collection, and so on)?

    b. Was the study conducted using a sample or population? If a sample was used, how was it selected? Do you believe the findings generated by the sample can be generalized to the population from which it was drawn? Why? Discuss.

    c. Do you feel the author conceptualized the study's key variables correctly? Why? How could the author have conceptualized them differently? Provide examples.

    d. Do you feel the author operationalized the dependent (or criterion) variable correctly? Why? How could the author have operationalized it differently? Provide examples.

    e. What were the study's independent (or predictor) and dependent (or criterion) variables? What level of measurement were they? Justify your response.

    f. What methods of statistical analyses were used in the article? Did each appear to be descriptive or inferential?

    g. Do you think the measurements of the study's key variables were reliable and valid? Why?

    h. Did the author use a standardized measuring instrument to measure the dependent (or criterion) variable? If so, which one was used? Do you feel the instrument measured what it was supposed to measure? Why?

17. Could statistical analyses be used to analyze recordings of your classroom discussion? Why would any conclusions drawn from it have limitations?

2

Frequency Distributions and Graphs

Before any type of data analysis begins, data (really raw data at this stage) can take many forms. They may exist in the form of a large stack of completed questionnaires or several hundred sheets of paper assembled from what was found in an agency's case records. If the goal of the study was to evaluate the effectiveness of a social worker's own practice effectiveness in working with a client or client system, data may be a series of repeated measurements of a behavior, attitude, and so forth, taken at regular intervals. If the researcher was seeking to evaluate a social work program at some stage of its development, data may consist of demographic descriptions of clients participating in the program, descriptions of staff, budget data, success rates to date, or most anything else that might suggest the value of a proposed or existing program.

No matter what type of study was conducted, the researcher is likely to be confronted with more data than can be used or understood, at least in their current form. A frequent question is, "How do I begin to make sense of all these data?" A corollary question is, "How can I communicate to others (often, the readers of a research report) what I found so that they can understand it?" The answer is simple: The data must be summarized, "boiled down" in such a way that it is possible to begin to comprehend and visualize them.

Two simple formats are used to begin the summarization process: (1) frequency distributions and (2) graphs. Both formats are helpful in visualizing the distribution of the measurements of variables within a data set drawn from a research sample or population. Frequency distributions and graphs may also begin to show trends in a data set, which can then be analyzed more extensively (to be discussed in later chapters).

Even when another, more sophisticated type of data analysis is used, frequency distributions and graphs may be appropriate to include in research reports. They can provide clear and dramatic evidence of a point made less effectively in words or in the numerical results of a statistical analysis.

FREQUENCY DISTRIBUTIONS

One of the first questions often asked after data have been collected relates to how many persons or objects fell into each value category or value for the variables that were measured. We want to know how the research sample or population broke—that is, we want to know the *frequency* of each value for each variable. *Frequency distribution* tables are designed to help us answer this question. They also provide additional information on the distribution of values of variables.

If a variable is at the nominal level of measurement, frequency distributions are constructed directly from the raw data set. If data are at the ordinal level of measurement or higher, however, it is necessary to first arrange the data into an array based on a ranking of their values. An **array** is an ordering of every value that occurred within the raw data set from the lowest or smallest to the highest or largest.

Suppose that a social work agency administrator, Sharon, wonders whether her agency is truly serving older residents of the community, which the agency has operationally defined as residents 50 years of age or older. Sharon decides to record the ages of all new clients who apply for services during the month of October. Twenty clients apply for services, and Sharon obtains their ages from the agency's intake form. The first new client was Rashad, who was 32 years of age; the second client was Rosina, 27 years of age; and so on. Sharon lists the raw data for these 20 clients in a table (Table 2.1).

Sharon's next step is to place the raw data into an array, which is shown in Table 2.2. Note that the array displays the data set from the lowest value (21) to the highest value (69). Every client is represented by a value or number—his or her age. Table 2.2 shows that 2 of the 20 clients were 21 (low) years of age (Chuck and Tony) and only 1 was 69 (high) years of age (David).

TABLE 2.1   Raw Data: Clients' Names and Ages

Name	Age	Name	Age	Name	Age
Rashad	32	David	69	Clarisse	37
Rosina	27	Herb	26	Karen	26
Brad	26	Vincent	31	Elwin	49
Chuck	21	Rosemarie	37	Tony	21
Shanti	37	Marguerite	49	Leon	27
Kathy	31	Raquel	31	Mario	31
Antoinette	32	Peter	27		

TABLE 2.2 Array: Clients' Names and Ages

Name	Age	Name	Age	Name	Age
Chuck	21	Leon	27	Shanti	37
Tony	21	Kathy	31	Rosemarie	37
Brad	26	Vincent	31	Clarisse	37
Herb	26	Raquel	31	Marguerite	49
Karen	26	Mario	31	Elwin	49
Rosina	27	Rashad	32	David	69
Peter	27	Antoinette	32		

The data in Table 2.2 provide a beginning answer to the research question about the age of clients served. Only one client, David, meets the agency's operational definition of "older." Table 2.2 makes it much easier for us to eyeball the data than Table 2.1. If the data set had consisted of 250 cases instead of just 20, for example, an array would have been even more helpful.

Having formed an array, Sharon can now construct frequency distribution tables in order to make the data even more comprehensible. Simply put, frequency distribution tables consolidate data taken from arrays.

Absolute Frequency Distributions

To construct an **absolute frequency distribution** table (also known as a *simple frequency distribution*), we count the number of times each value occurred and place this total next to the name of that value. An absolute frequency distribution may be constructed for data at any level of measurement.

The absolute frequency column on the right side of Table 2.3 indicates the number of times each value occurred. For instance, Chuck and Tony were 21 years of age, and

TABLE 2.3 Absolute Frequency Distribution Table: Clients' Names and Ages

Name	Age	Absolute Frequency
Chuck + Tony	21	2
Brad + Herb + Karen	26	3
Rosina + Peter + Leon	27	3
Kathy + Vincent + Raquel + Mario	31	4
Rashad + Antoinette	32	2
Shanti + Rosemarie + Clarisse	37	3
Marguerite + Elwin	49	2
David	69	1
Total		20

TABLE 2.4   Cumulative Frequency Distribution Table: Clients' Names and Ages

Name	Age	Absolute Frequency	Cumulative Frequency
Chuck + Tony	21	2	2
Brad + Herb + Karen	26	3	5
Rosina + Peter + Leon	27	3	8
Kathy + Vincent + Raquel + Mario	31	4	12
Rashad + Antoinette	32	2	14
Shanti + Rosemarie + Clarisse	37	3	17
Marguerite + Elwin	49	2	19
David	69	1	20

as a group they constitute a frequency of 2—that is, the absolute frequency for the value 21 is 2. Similar data are given for each of the other 7 ages that occurred. The clients' ages range from 21 (Chuck and Tony) to 69 (David), and the value most frequently reported is 31 (Kathy, Vincent, Raquel, and Mario). Absolute frequency distributions sometimes are seen in research reports, but, more commonly, they appear as just one column within one of the other frequency distributions discussed next.

Cumulative Frequency Distributions

A **cumulative frequency distribution** table, such as Table 2.4, can be constructed if the data generated for a variable are at least at the ordinal level of measurement (i.e., if an array can be formed as in Table 2.2). As Table 2.4 shows, 2 clients were 21 years of age, and 3 clients were 26. Thus, the cumulative frequency of clients' age 26 and under is 5 (2 + 3). A total of 17 clients (2 + 3 + 3 + 4 + 2 + 3) were 37 years of age and under. In a cumulative frequency distribution, the last number in the cumulative frequency column is the same as the total number of cases, indicating that all case values have been included.

Percentage Frequency Distributions

A third type of frequency distribution table, the **percentage frequency distribution** table, displays an absolute percentage column on the far right-hand side (see Table 2.5). Because there are 20 clients in the sample, each client represents 5 percent of the sample (100%/20 = 5%). The number in the percentage column for each age that occurred within the sample of clients represents the absolute percentage of the entire sample. As Table 2.5 indicates, 2 people (Chuck and Tony) were 21 years of age, and together they represent 10 percent of the total number of clients (5% for Chuck + 5% for Tony). Similarly, Brad, Herb, and Karen together represent 15 percent of the total sample (5% for Brad + 5% for Herb + 5% for Karen). Of course, the total for all the clients should equal 100 percent.

If the number of cases in a data set is not a number that can be divided cleanly into 100 to obtain the percentage that each case represents, the percentages in the

TABLE 2.5   Percentage Frequency Distribution Table: Clients' Names and Ages

Name	Age	Absolute Frequency	Absolute Percent
Chuck + Tony	21	2	10
Brad + Herb + Karen	26	3	15
Rosina + Peter + Leon	27	3	15
Kathy + Vincent + Raquel + Mario	31	4	20
Rashad + Antoinette	32	2	10
Shanti + Rosemarie + Clarisse	37	3	15
Marguerite + Elwin	49	2	10
David	69	1	5

row alongside a value may have to be rounded up or down to either whole numbers or numbers containing decimals. When this is done, the total for all cases may not be exactly 100 percent. It may be slightly more or less than 100. A notation at the bottom of the table is then used to explain why the total is something other than 100 percent.

Cumulative Percentage Frequency Distributions

A fourth type of frequency distribution table is the **cumulative percentage frequency distribution** table. It combines features of the cumulative frequency and percentage distribution tables, by displaying a column that reports cumulative percentages for each value. In Table 2.6, two clients (Rashad and Antoinette) are 32 years of age. Together, they represent 10 percent of all clients (5% for Rashad + 5% for Antoinette). Additionally, 70 percent ($14/20 = .7 = 70\%$) of all clients (including Rashad and Antoinette) are 32 years of age or younger.

TABLE 2.6   Cumulative Percentage Distribution Table: Clients' Names and Ages

Name	Age	Absolute Frequency	Absolute Percent	Cumulative Percent
Chuck + Tony	21	2	10	10
Brad + Herb + Karen	26	3	15	25
Rosina + Peter + Leon	27	3	15	40
Kathy + Vincent + Raquel + Mario	31	4	20	60
Rashad + Antoinette	32	2	10	70
Shanti + Rosemarie + Clarisse	37	3	15	85
Marguerite + Elwin	49	2	10	95
David	69	1	5	100

GROUPED FREQUENCY DISTRIBUTIONS

Sometimes it is difficult to interpret frequency distribution tables because of the unequal spread of the values. In the example, the variable age is distributed in such a way that there are differently sized gaps (e.g., 21 to 26, 27 to 31, 49 to 69). It is sometimes easier to visualize and comprehend the meaning of values that are distributed this way if they are condensed into a smaller number of groupings of values (e.g., 20 to 29, 30 to 39, and so on). These groupings could then be displayed using any of the frequency distributions, such as Table 2.3 to 2.6 or using only those columns from Table 2.6 that are of special interest.

In creating a **grouped frequency distribution**, we can use age groupings in the first column instead of using the clients' actual ages. We then adjust the numbers in the other columns accordingly. Table 2.7 is an example of a **grouped cumulative percentage distribution** table. It does not contain the actual frequency for any exact age, but it nevertheless provides a good overview of how the data are distributed.

Grouped frequency distributions are especially useful when there are too many different values to individually list each one of them. This often occurs when there are a large number of cases with many different values and when forming frequency distributions for variables that are at the interval or ratio levels of measurement. The number of miles driven to class by students in a school of social work, for example, would make for a lengthy list, especially if the miles were measured in fractions or tenths of a mile. Transforming the data into meaningful groupings makes it easier for the reader to visualize the distribution of the variable, *miles traveled.*

What is a meaningful grouping? It is a grouping that reduces the number of values to a reasonably small number that can be easily understood while not losing any more measurement precision than is necessary. When the values are fairly evenly distributed, it is desirable to have groupings that each encompass an equal number of potential case values. If the values are not evenly distributed, the groupings should be set up to reflect homogeneity. This means that the groupings should use value intervals of a size that allows cases within them to be similar. In grouping students based on the number of miles they travel to class, for example, five meaningful value groupings could be as follows:

1. 3 miles or less
2. 4–10 miles

TABLE 2.7   Grouped Cumulative Percentage Distribution Table: Clients' Ages

Ages	Absolute Percentage	Cumulative Percentage
20–29	40	40
30–39	45	85
40–49	10	95
50–59	0	95
60–69	5	100

3. 11–50 miles
4. 51–100 miles
5. 101 miles or more

What makes the previous value groupings homogeneous? Note that all students in the 3 miles or less category share a similar characteristic—they all live close to the university. Those in the 4–10-mile grouping live fairly close, but they may not walk to class or ride bicycles, may not feel they are a part of the university community, and so forth. Those commuting more than 100 miles may be involved in some form of distance education, may have extreme difficulty participating in student social activities on campus, and so on.

There is a logic to the groupings—students within a specific grouping share some similarities with the other members and are likely to be different in important ways from students in the other groupings. Obviously, the students cannot be similar to others in their grouping in all respects. Which characteristics matter the most? Here we must rely on judgment and a review of professional literature to suggest areas where homogeneity should be taken into consideration when forming groupings.

Every case should fall cleanly into one and only one grouping; the grouping should be mutually exclusive and exhaustive. In the above five groupings, a consistent method would have to be devised for assigning those students on the edge of the different value groupings (e.g., 10.6 miles) into a group. It would entail rounding up and rounding down. A customary way to do this, for example, is to consider 11 miles as really representing the interval 10.50 to 11.49 miles. Thus a student who drives 10.6 miles would fall into the grouping 11 to 50 miles, as would a student who drives 50.4 miles.

USING FREQUENCY DISTRIBUTIONS TO ANALYZE DATA

Frequency distributions can be very revealing if properly constructed. Cumulative percentage distributions are especially useful when we are interested in knowing approximately where a particular value falls relative to the other values in the data set. Suppose, for example, that an administrator of a large social service agency, Jennifer, wants to study the problem of unauthorized staff absenteeism. She would like to identify whether there are seasonal patterns that could possibly be reduced by creating new vacation and annual leave policies. A cumulative percentage distribution table might reveal such patterns.

Table 2.8 shows that in April there were 30 instances of absenteeism, or 15 percent of the total absenteeism in the 4-month period. Another 40 instances (20%) occurred during May. In all, only 70 instances (35%) occurred during (April and May), while the other 130 instances (65%) occurred during June and July. The table seems to suggest that there is a seasonal pattern of absenteeism; absenteeism increases in the summer months.

Cumulative percentage distributions also can be helpful for comparing measurements taken from two different groups or two different data sets. If the measurements differ somewhat (e.g., if the actual ages were recorded for one data set and age ranges were recorded for the other one), grouped distributions can be used to make the different data sets comparable.

TABLE 2.8   Cumulative Percentage Distribution Table: Staff Days Lost by Month at XYZ Agency (N = 200)

	Monthly Totals	
Month	*Absolute Frequency*	*Cumulative Percentage*
April	30	15
May	40	35
June	60	65
July	70	100

An example will illustrate how cumulative percentage distributions can be used to compare two groups or two different data sets. Sue, a social worker, developed a state merit examination study guide. She wished to get a preliminary indication of whether it was effective. She decided to compare the respective scores of people who used the study guide (experimental group) with those of people who did not use it (control group).

Cumulative percentage distribution tables displaying the differences between the results for the two groups are shown in Tables 2.9 and 2.10. Of the people in the experimental group (Table 2.9), 40 percent scored between 70 and 79 on the examination, and 50 percent scored 79 or lower. Table 2.10 shows that 40 percent of the people in the control group scored between 70 and 79 on the examination, and 60 percent scored 79 or lower.

Cumulative percentages also make it possible to calculate approximate percentile ranks for individuals within the two groups. **Percentile ranks** indicate the percentage of cases within a group whose value falls below a particular value. Suppose that Clarice, a member of the experimental group, scored a 90 on the merit examination after using the study guide. A review of Table 2.9 would indicate that she scored higher than at least 80 percent of all people in the experimental group, meaning that she scored at approximately the 80th percentile. Percentile ranks thus enable us to put an individual value in perspective relative to the other values in a group.

Also notice that the two groups contained different numbers of cases—300 in the experimental group and 200 in the control group. Using percentages (rather than

TABLE 2.9   Grouped Cumulative Percentage Distribution Table: Experimental Group's Scores (N = 300)

Scores	Absolute Percentage	Cumulative Percentage
50–59	0	0
60–69	10	10
70–79	40	50
80–89	30	80
90–100	20	100

TABLE 2.10   Grouped Cumulative Percentage Distribution Table: Control Group's Scores ($N = 200$)

Scores	Absolute Percentage	Cumulative Percentage
50–59	5	5
60–69	15	20
70–79	40	60
80–89	35	95
90–100	5	100

frequencies) facilitates comparing two or more groups of unequal size. It puts groups of different sizes into the same framework; all percentages are based on "out of 100". This is helpful if two research samples are of unequal size.

MISREPRESENTATION OF DATA

From a statistical perspective, the two groups of 200 and 300 in the previous illustration were fairly comparable in size. Percentage comparisons drawn from them would be appropriate, since they would make the data easier to interpret. But a word of caution is in order: The practice of drawing comparisons between or among groups of vastly unequal sizes can distort rather than clarify data. The following example demonstrates how this can happen.

Example: An Administrator's Efforts to Hire More Women.   Emma, a social service agency administrator, proudly reported to the board of directors that the results of her efforts to hire more women during the last two years were "highly successful." Using the data from Table 2.11, she noted that in five of the six job classifications (A, B, C, E, and F), she had hired a higher percentage of women applicants than men. Emma was able to make this statement because she was using percentages with value

TABLE 2.11   Hiring Data Broken Down by Gender

	Males		Females	
Classification	*Number*	*Percent*	*Number*	*Percent*
A	3 of 6	50	4 of 6	67
B	1 of 3	33	1 of 2	50
C	0 of 1	0	1 of 10	10
D	85 of 100	85	2 of 40	5
E	2 of 3	67	2 of 2	100
F	3 of 7	43	4 of 7	57
Totals	94 of 120	78	14 of 67	21

groupings of very different sizes. The actual data she summarized presented a very different picture. In fact, Table 2.11 actually shows that Emma hired 78 percent of all male applicants but only 21 percent of all female applicants.

More often than not, misrepresentations are not deliberate. Emma may have made an honest mistake based on inadequate understanding of the importance of using comparably sized groups when making comparisons using frequency distributions. There is a way to avoid giving the impression that we are attempting to distort the facts in such situations. The actual numbers on which percentages are based can be reported along with the percentages for all groups, as presented in Table 2.11.

Percentages help people comprehend large numbers, especially when they are used to report research findings based on odd numbers. For example, 35.5 percent is more easily understood than 146 out of 411. Percentages are generally meaningless, however, if not misleading, in reporting data from small samples. There is little reason to report, for example, that 60 percent of the graduates of an intensive job training program found employment if the 60 percent really means three of five completed the program and found a job (3/5 = .60 or 60%). With a small number of cases, it is best to report only the numbers.

Statements that describe findings based on small numbers are comprehensible by themselves. Why not simply report that three out of five graduates found work? Reporting findings based on small numbers as percentages can be misleading. Percentages convey the impression that findings were based on a larger numbers of cases (100 or more).

GRAPHS

Sometimes it may be difficult to grasp the bigger picture of the distribution of values by using frequency distribution tables. A graph, on the other hand, can often communicate the "bigger picture" almost immediately.

Graphical representations generally sacrifice detail in an effort to improve communication. This sacrifice is justifiable and even desirable in many situations. If the intended audience of a research presentation or report is not "research astute," the audience may become impatient with the tabular presentation of vast amounts of data. Graphs are more likely to hold everyone's interest. Also, if it is essential to get a point across quickly and dramatically, graphs do the job effectively. They allow readers to obtain a comprehensive picture of the distribution of the values without having to focus on unnecessary detail.

Like all methods of displaying data, graphs can also produce misleading statements. It is possible to lie with graphs, just as with other types of statistical analyses. We need to be alert to the dangers inherent in the use of graphs and ask whether they are communicating the findings of a research study accurately. But the possibility of their misuse should not preclude their use; they can be effective communicators.

Several types of graphs are commonly used to display how many cases have the various measurements of a variable. Both the measurement level of the variable and clarity requirements of data displays determine which of the various graphical options is best.

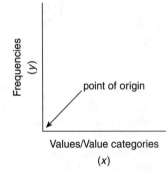

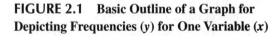

FIGURE 2.1   Basic Outline of a Graph for Depicting Frequencies (*y*) for One Variable (*x*)

Most graphs are drawn (usually using computer software) with *x* and *y* axes. The vertical line, or **y axis,** is called the **ordinate,** and the horizontal line, or **x axis,** is called the **abscissa.** The point at which the *x* axis and the *y* axis meet (see Figure 2.1) is called the **point of origin.** In a graph used to present the distribution of values or value categories of one variable, the values or value categories are displayed along the *x* axis. The *x* axis may extend to the left beyond the *y* axis if the data set contains negative values. The *y* axis is used to display the frequencies for each value or value category.

Bar Graphs and Line Diagrams

One method of displaying the distribution of frequencies for the value categories of a nominal level variable is a **bar graph,** also called a bar chart. Bars of equal width (one for each value) are displayed in any order, because the value categories reflect only qualitative, not quantitative, differences. The bars are not allowed to touch. The height of each bar reflects the frequency of the value category. A comparison of the frequency for different value categories is implicit. In other words, if a bar of one length represents the frequency of a value category, a bar twice as long represents a frequency twice as large for another value category. Figure 2.2a is an example of a simple bar graph.

If lines are used rather than bars, they are drawn so that their length reflects the frequencies with which given value categories occur. We refer to this type of graph as a **line diagram.** Line diagrams may be constructed so the lines run horizontally, with different nominal value categories placed along the *y* axis and frequencies reflected in the length of the lines parallel to the *x* axis, as in Figure 2.2b. Bar graphs and line diagrams are used interchangeably.

Pie Charts

If a variable is only at the nominal level, we can use a **pie chart,** also called a pie graph, to represent the distribution of its value categories. Although pie charts are used primarily to display the distribution of nominal level variables within any given data set, they can also be used with variables that are measured more precisely.

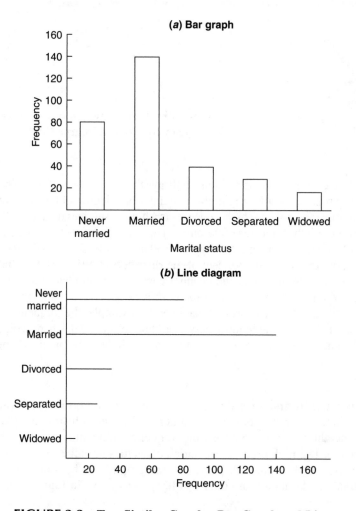

FIGURE 2.2   Two Similar Graphs: Bar Graph and Line Diagram Portraying the Marital Status of Active Clients in XYZ Agency

Traditionally, pie charts are constructed to look like pies—that is, as circles divided into two or more wedges, each representing the frequency for a different value or value category. With today's computer software graphic programs, many other pictorial representations of the distribution of a variable are now possible. A pie chart can look like a cartoon figure or almost any object. For example, if we want to show how a client's family budget is divided into expenditures for food, shelter, clothing, recreation, and so forth, the total budget could be displayed as a pie. Portions of the pie could be drawn proportionally to reflect the portion of the total budget represented by each budget item. Or we could portray the same family budget as a cash bag or a paycheck divided to represent the percent of the budget that is spent for each budget item.

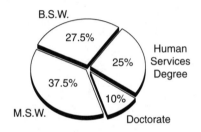

FIGURE 2.3   Distribution of Social Workers at XYZ Agency by Highest Degree Held ($N = 100$)

Figure 2.3 is an example of a pie chart that portrays the percentages of staff who work at XYZ Agency, broken down by the highest social work degree obtained. Note, for example, that staff members whose highest degree is a human services degree (25% of all staff) occupy one-fourth the total area of the circle. The angle in the center of the circle for the human services degree segment is 90 degrees (360 degrees $\times$ .25 = 90 degrees).

Pie charts allow rapid visual appraisal of the distribution of values or value categories. Their main limitation is that they cannot easily accommodate many different categories of a variable without becoming too complicated, large, or illegible. Figure 2.3 is comprehensible, but a pie chart that displays, for example, the frequencies of all the academic majors within a large university would be impractical. There would have to be many different slices of the pie, some of them so thin as to be barely visible.

Histograms

A **histogram** is a useful graph for displaying ordinal, interval, or ratio level data. Histograms look like bar graphs, but the bars touch each other. A histogram, like a bar graph, uses the height of the bar to reflect the frequency of a value or value category for a given variable. The rank order of the variable's values or value categories determines the sequence of the values displayed in the graph. The bars of a histogram displaying ordinal level data are of equal width, such as those in Figure 2.4, which

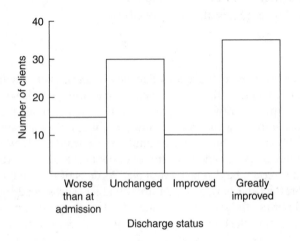

FIGURE 2.4   Histogram: Frequency of Discharge Status at XYZ Agency during February

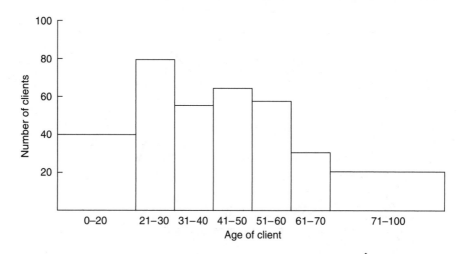

FIGURE 2.5   Histogram: Ages of Clients on Record in XYZ Agency during October

displays four categories of outcome data derived from a review of February case records at XYZ Agency.

When displaying the frequencies for interval or ratio level data, and when grouped frequencies of unequal value intervals are used, the bars may be constructed so that their different widths correspond to the size of the different intervals. Figure 2.5 illustrates this variation. The graph accurately portrays frequencies by showing bars of different heights, intervals, and widths. To do this, there must be a degree of measurement precision not present within nominal or ordinal level data.

Frequency Polygons

After constructing a histogram with interval or ratio level data, we can convert the histogram into a frequency polygon. A **frequency polygon** is a shape that reflects the distribution of values for a variable. If we were to take a pencil and mark a dot in the middle of the top of each vertical bar in a histogram and then connect the dots with a straight line, we would have a frequency polygon. Lines usually are drawn at each end of the distribution of values to connect the first and last dot with the horizontal axis, thus completing the polygon. Figure 2.6 is an example of a frequency polygon displaying data collected by XYZ Agency at intake.

The data displayed in Figure 2.6 were at the ratio level of measurement when first made. (They were the actual dollars and cents of income reported on clients' most recent federal income tax returns.) When they were grouped into income intervals to reduce the number of value groupings, some sacrifice of accuracy (measurement precision) occurred. The data were transformed into ordinal level measurement. In Figure 2.6, the numbers along the *x* axis are the midpoints of the income groupings that were used. As Figure 2.6 demonstrates, it is possible to plot a frequency polygon for data that are only at the ordinal level of measurement. However, this should be

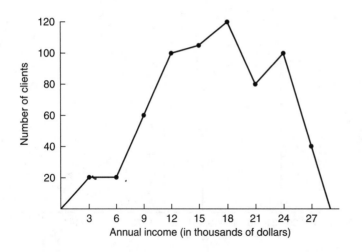

FIGURE 2.6   Frequency Polygon: Annual Income of Families Receiving Family Counseling at XYZ Agency (Rounded to Nearest Category)

done only when the data are inherently at the interval or ratio level of measurement and have been transformed into ordinal level data.

Stem-and-Leaf Plots

Another graph that is easily generated by computer software packages is the **stem-and-leaf plot.** It makes it possible to display all of the actual case values in the distribution of a variable.

Figure 2.7 portrays the distribution of the ages of the residents of an extended-care facility. The age of a resident is displayed as a stem in the middle column (in this case, the first one or two digits of the age) and a leaf in the right-hand column (in this case, the last digit of his or her age). Thus, a resident who is 77 years of age would be represented by one of the sevens in the row where the seven appears under the leaf column. The sample contains two residents who are 66 years of age, one who is 80, four who are 84, and so forth. The two oldest residents are 95 and 103. If we were to rotate the graph 90° counterclockwise, with the frequency column on the bottom, and connect

Frequency	Stem	& Leaf
1	5	9
2	6	24
6	6	566889
4	7	1144
16	7	5577777777788999
6	8	014444
3	8	558
1	9	5
1	10	3

FIGURE 2.7   Stem-and-Leaf Plot: Ages of Residents at XYZ Residential Care Facility ($N = 40$)

the top of the columns of numbers, we would have a frequency polygon for the variable *age of residents.*

A COMMON MISTAKE IN DISPLAYING DATA

As computer graphics become more user friendly, there is a temptation to display larger and larger amounts of data. Some graphs can become so complex that they are hard to interpret.

Even relatively simple ways of displaying data, like bar graphs and histograms, can be made complicated. The horizontal bars in bar graphs, for example, may be extended to the left and to the right simultaneously. Figure 2.8 displays data about client problems in a social service agency. It illustrates the percentage of clients who reported problems within one or more of three nominal level categories of presenting problems—environmental, psychological, and social. A given client may have reported one, two, or all three types of problems. It takes quite a bit of study to be able to understand the data presented in this graph. The *x* axis represents the percentage of clients reporting each problem area (right side) and the percentage not reporting it (left side). Thus, the total number of clients reporting and not reporting each problem equals 100 percent. Figure 2.8 shows that 30 percent of all clients reported psychological problems and 70 percent did not; 50 percent reported social problems; the other 50 percent did not; and so forth. The data in Figure 2.8 could have been communicated more clearly with the use of three simple bar graphs, one for each type of client problem.

The computer technology that created Figure 2.8 is a mixed blessing. It allows us to communicate more information on a single graph, but it may sacrifice clarity in the process. As we are tempted to use more complex and creative frequency distributions and graphs, we must ask ourselves whether they will really help the reader understand our data set. Or will they have the undesirable effect of confusing the reader? Communication is the goal of frequency distributions and graphs. If they confuse the person who is trying to understand how the data were distributed, they have failed to achieve this goal.

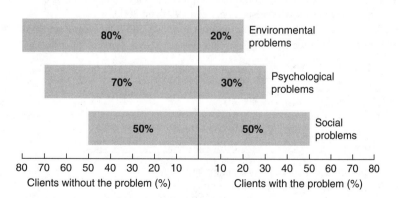

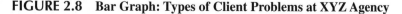

FIGURE 2.8   Bar Graph: Types of Client Problems at XYZ Agency

CONCLUDING THOUGHTS

This chapter briefly examined some of the most basic ways of organizing and displaying the distributions of value categories and values of a variable—frequency distributions and graphs. It examined how we can take simple frequencies and convert them into tables that portray the percentage of the whole that a given frequency represents. It also introduced the concept *percentile* and its relationship to cumulative frequency distributions.

The chapter examined a few of the most commonly used graphs, in what situations they are appropriate, and how they are constructed. It discussed some of the dangers inherent in the overuse of computer-generated graphs.

STUDY QUESTIONS

1. Discuss how an array differs from raw data. Provide an original example in your discussion.
2. What information is conveyed in a cumulative frequency distribution that is not present in an absolute frequency distribution? Provide an original example in your discussion.
3. What type of frequency distribution would tell us what percentage of the clients of a child protection agency have fewer than four children?
4. In a study attempting to relate type of counseling to success in seeking employment, why would it be inadvisable to group the variable *number of interviews* as 1–10, 11–20, and more than 20?
5. Why is it misleading to report a 50 percent success rate in a treatment program for alcoholics when there were only eight people in the treatment program? Explain in detail.
6. How does a bar graph differ from a histogram? Provide an example of each.
7. If an agency with an $800,000 annual budget allocates $160,000 for travel expenses, what portion (percentage) of a pie chart would be reserved for the travel segment? How many degrees would the angle at the center of the pie chart contain for the travel segment?
8. Why are frequency polygons an accurate portrayal of data only if data are at the interval or ratio level of measurement?
9. When selecting a graph to display data, why is simplicity a goal?
10. Describe several ways that we could use graphs to display changes in the ethnic composition of an agency's professional staff between 1999 and 2000.
11. At the University of Twin Peaks, the number of males and females in various major fields of study are as follows:

Major	Males	Females
Social Work	20	80
Humanities	40	40
Business	60	50
Education	90	90
Nursing	10	90

    a. What percentage of social work majors are female?
    b. What percentage of the total student body are male?
    c. Construct a five-slice pie chart for the different female majors. Do the same for the males.

   d. Construct a bar chart like Figure 2.2a for all males, broken down by major.
      Do the same for the females.
   e. What level of measurement is the variable major? Justify your response.
12. The dean of your school of social work has asked you to organize and present data from a one-question (one-variable) survey to determine students' satisfaction in the social work program. There are 220 students in the program; 55 of them (25 percent) were randomly selected to receive the survey. The research question was "How satisfied are you with the social work education you are currently receiving?" Possible responses were

   1. Very satisfied
   2. Satisfied
   3. Somewhat satisfied
   4. Somewhat dissatisfied
   5. Very dissatisfied

   a. At what level of measurement is the variable *satisfaction?*" Justify your response.
   b. Is the variable an independent variable or a dependent variable? Justify your response.
   c. The raw data for the variable were as follows:

   1, 4, 5, 3, 2, 1, 4, 5, 5, 4, 2, 5, 1, 1, 2, 3, 4, 3, 3, 3, 3, 4, 5, 4, 3, 3, 2, 2,
   1, 3, 4, 2, 2, 2, 4, 2, 1, 1, 2, 3, 4, 5, 4, 3, 2, 1, 1, 2, 2, 3, 2, 2, 1, 1, 3

   d. How many students completed the survey? Should these students be considered a research sample or a population? Why?
   e. Construct an absolute frequency distribution to display these data.
   f. Construct a cumulative frequency distribution to display these data.
   g. Construct a percentage distribution to display these data.
   h. Construct a cumulative percentage distribution to display these data.
   i. Do you believe that, overall, the students were satisfied with the social work education they were receiving? Justify your response.
   j. The dean took the results to the vice president and said that the social work students were very pleased with their education. Was the dean correct in saying this, given the results of the survey? Why?

3

Measures of Central Tendency and Variability

Sometimes we wish to do more than simply display data in tables or graphs as presented on the previous chapter. For example, we may wish to summarize the characteristics of the distribution of a variable within a data set by reporting on what was found to be a typical value and how much the degree to which the values of a variable tended to cluster around that typical value. The methods for summarizing the characteristics of data that are discussed in this chapter are useful for providing a summary description of the people (or objects) that were studied. As we shall see in later chapters, they are also key elements in more sophisticated forms of data analyses.

MEASURES OF CENTRAL TENDENCY

In everyday speech, we tend to use the word *typical* rather loosely. We speak of a typical client or a typical starting salary for MSW social workers, often without stating exactly what is meant by the term typical. In analyzing a data set, the search for the typical represents an attempt to find a single number, or a series of numbers, that is most representative of the distribution of values for a variable within a data set. In a data set (e.g., Table 2.1 in Chapter 2), a typical case is the one that best represents all cases within the data set.

Three terms, the **mode, median,** and **mean,** are used to describe what is meant by typical within a data set. They are grouped under the general category of *central tendency*. These terms are not interchangeable; they have specific meanings that differ in important ways. They must be used correctly to avoid confusion and to avoid misrepresenting the characteristics of a data set.

The Mode

The **mode** is the value (in a distribution of values) within a data set that occurs most frequently. In the ages of the sample of clients presented in the array below, 42 is the mode because it occurs more frequently than any of the other values—in this case, four times more frequently.

Ages of clients (n = 15):

28, 31, 38, 39, **42, 42, 42, 42,** 43, 47, 51, 54, 55, 56, 60

Sometimes, more than one value will occur more frequently than all the other values within a data set. If we were to draw a histogram of the distribution of the values, it would have two distinct peaks. When this situation occurs, we report both values as the mode for the data set and describe the distribution of the variable as **bimodal.** In the following example, the values in the bimodal array of years of prior social work experience among all 22 social workers in a family service agency contain two modes—0 and 7. Both values occur five times each.

Years of prior social work experience (N = 22):

0, 0, 0, 0, 0, 1, 2, 2, 3, 4, 5, 5, 6, **7, 7, 7, 7, 7,** 8, 9, 11, 14

When data are available in grouped form, the mode can be reported in one of two ways. We may simply report the grouping that had the largest frequency as the mode, or we can report the actual midpoint of the interval with the highest frequency. Table 3.1 portrays the grouped job-satisfaction scores of 50 social workers. For these data, the mode could be reported as the value interval containing the largest frequency, which is 48–50, which includes the values 48, 49, and 50. This three-number range occurred seven times. The mode could also be reported as 49, since the midpoint for the interval 48–50 is 49.

Of the three measures of central tendency, the mode is the most unrestricted—that is, it has the fewest requirements for its use. It can be used with all four levels of measurement (i.e., nominal, ordinal, interval, ratio). The mode, however, is not used as often as the other measures of central tendency, as it may not do a good job of describing what is typical in the distribution of a variable. As can be seen in Table 3.2, the most common or frequent value of a distribution of scores is not necessarily the most accurate portrayal of a typical value. The mode is clearly not in the center of the distribution; rather, it is toward the high end of it (the 57–59 group). When data are at the ordinal, interval, or ratio level of measurement, we can usually obtain more accurate and representative descriptions by using one or both of the other two measures of central tendency.

The Median

If data can be formed into an array—that is, if they are at least at the ordinal level of measurement—the median can be used to report central tendency. The **median** divides an array of values into two equal halves; it is a value above and below which

TABLE 3.1   Grouped Cumulative Frequency Distribution: Job Satisfaction Scores for Social Workers

Scores	Absolute Frequency	Cumulative Frequency (High-Low)	Cumulative Frequency (Low-High)
81–83	3	3	50
78–80	1	4	47
75–77	5	9	46
72–74	6	15	41
69–71	1	16	35
66–68	5	21	34
63–65	4	25	29
60–62	1	26	25
57–59	1	27	24
54–56	4	31	23
51–53	3	34	19
48–50	7	41	16
45–47	1	42	9
42–44	4	46	8
39–41	2	48	4
36–38	2	50	2

half the values in an array fall. The example in Distribution *A* on the following page presents an array of 21 values for the variable *number of treatment sessions attended*. The median is 9 sessions because 9 coincides with the point that divides the 21 values into two identical parts. There are just as many values, or cases (10), above 9 as there are below 9.

TABLE 3.2   Grouped Cumulative Frequency Distribution: Job Satisfaction Scores for Social Workers

Scores	Absolute Frequency	Cumulative Frequency (High-Low)	Cumulative Frequency (Low-High)
57–59	10	10	33
54–56	6	16	23
51–53	7	23	17
48–50	3	26	10
45–47	2	28	7
42–44	1	29	5
30–41	4	33	4

Distribution A: Number of treatment sessions attended (N = 21):

2, 2, 2, 3, 3, 4, 5, 5, 7, 8, **9,** 10, 11, 11, 14, 14, 15, 16, 18, 20, 41

If there had been an even number of values, the median might be the average of the two most central values as in Distribution B below. Here the median is 4.5.

Distribution B: Number of treatment sessions attended (N = 24):

1, 1, 1, 1, 1, 1, 2, 2, 3, 3, 3, 4, 5, 6, 6, 7, 8, 11,
11, 13, 14, 15, 17, 20   ↑
                                                         median

Unlike the mode, the median does not always coincide with an actual value in the distribution. In Distribution *B* it cannot, because with an even number of cases there is no case that falls at exactly the midpoint. This observation underlines a point that is important to understanding the median. Contrary to a common misconception, the median is not synonymous with the value of the middle case in an array of data (although it sometimes works out that way, as in Distribution *A*).

The median may be a whole number, a fraction or decimal, or a mixed number that coincides with no actual case value. That happens because the formula used to compute the median takes various conditions into consideration, such as case values with a frequency of 0 near the center and others with a frequency greater than 1 that occur near the center of the array (but are not centered around it). When these conditions exist, computation involves viewing values as intervals, as in the discussion in Chapter 2 of assignment of cases within grouped frequency distributions. Fortunately, whatever situation exists, statistical computer software packages can compute a median in a matter of seconds once the raw data have been entered.

If we look at Distribution *A*, we see that one client had been seen many more times than any other—41 times. This atypical value is known as an **outlier.** If a histogram were created for the variable, this value would lie outside the area where most of the other values are found (in Distribution *A*, between 2 and 20). The frequency polygon that could be formed by connecting the tops of the bars in the histogram would be distorted by the value 41. It would be asymmetrical, or skewed. (We will discuss skewness in more detail in Chapter 4.)

Of the three most common measures of central tendency, the median is affected the least by the presence of outliers, such as the client who was seen 41 times. Remember that the median coincides with the midpoint of the values in an array. In finding the midpoint, the client seen 41 times is "canceled out" by the first client, who was seen only 2 times and is the counterpart at the extreme other end of the array. The client seen 29 times similarly is canceled out by the second client seen only 2 times, and so on. It would not matter whether the client seen the most times was seen 41 times, 100 times, or 410 times—the median would treat any of these values as simply the highest value in the data set.

The Mean

When a variable within a data set is at the interval or ratio level of measurement, another measure of central tendency can be used to represent a typical value of that variable. It is the most easily understood, the best known, and the most useful of the three measures of central tendency. The **mean** is nothing more than the sum of all the values in a distribution divided by the total number of values—what we refer to in everyday speech as the average.

A mean can be computed for any interval level or ratio level variable. It cannot be computed with nominal level variables. It also should not be computed with ordinal level variables, even if numbers have been used for values, as in the case of rankings. For example, students may be assigned rankings based on their grades in each class they are taking. A student may rank number 3 in one class, number 4 in another, and number 2 in a third class. Although a mean ranking could be obtained mathematically (the student's mean rank would be 3), to report this could be misleading. A ranking, while it is a number, is still a rather imprecise measurement of student achievement. A mean rank thus might not provide an accurate description of overall student performance relative to that of other students. A student with a mean ranking of 3 could actually be performing less well academically overall than a student with a mean ranking of 3.1! When we see that the mean is used as an indicator of central tendency, we should be able to assume that the measurement of the variable was at least at the interval level.

Another issue must be considered when deciding if it is appropriate to use the mean. Unlike the median, the mean uses all the values within a data set in its computation, not just some of them (the ones near the center of an array). This characteristic of the mean can promote accuracy or distortion when it is used as a measure of central tendency, depending on the degree to which a distribution of values is symmetrical or skewed. Even one or two outliers can easily distort the mean (skew it badly) if the total number of cases is small. With larger data sets, a few outliers cause less distortion.

The Trimmed Mean.   A variation of the mean, the **trimmed mean** is designed to minimize the effect of a few extreme outliers. It combines the best features of both the mean and the median. It still uses most of the actual case values in its computation, but, like the median, it allows extreme values on either end to cancel each other out. It works like this: First a small percentage (usually, the top 5% and the bottom 5%) of values in an array are thrown out. Then, the remaining 90 percent of values are averaged. This average is the trimmed mean.

Even when a mean can be computed, the presence of a few extreme outliers may distort it so that it can no longer be considered a typical measurement of variable. Then the trimmed mean, the median, and/or the mode should be considered.

The Weighted Mean.   There is still another variation of the mean that is used in social work research and practice. Sometimes, it is necessary to compute an average for values that are not equally weighted (or of equal importance). Then we should compute a **weighted mean.** Computing a weighted mean entails the "weighting" of numbers in order to arrive at a value that is more meaningful for the data set than either the arithmetic mean or the trimmed mean.

For example, RuthAnn, a social worker working on a case-management team in a hospital, was being criticized by her boss for her team's lack of productivity. She decided to compare her team's number of successful hospital discharge placements with those of a widely Praised case-management team within the hospital in order to demonstrate that her team had been equally productive during the past week. Unlike RuthAnn's team, all five members of the other team were full-time employees. RuthAnn used the arithmetic mean to determine the other team's mean rate of success. She simply added together all of the workers' successful placements for the previous week and then divided by five to get the mean number of successes (per worker). The other team produced a total of 35 successful placements during the past week, so the mean number for members of the other team was 7 (35/5 = 7).

Computing a comparable indicator for RuthAnn's team was a bit more complicated. Unlike the other team, her team has six workers. Two (including herself) are full-time (5 days per week); three work half-time; and one works one-fourth time. Their number of successful placements for the week were (respectively): 8, 8, 3, 2, 4, and 2. RuthAnn could not simply add the number of successes together and divide by six. (The result would be 4.5, suggesting an unfair and unfavorable comparison.) Because most of the workers on her team are part-time, she needed to compute a weighted mean in order to get a fair description of their success.

How did RuthAnn compute a weighted mean for her team? She set up her data as follows:

Worker Name	Employment Status	No. Placed Successfully	×	Weighting Factor	=	Score
RuthAnn	Full	8		1		8
Ralph	Full	8		1		8
Joaquim	Half	3		2		6
Jerry	Half	2		2		4
Ricky	Half	4		2		8
Simeon	Quarter	2		4		8
Total						42

RuthAnn used a weighting (multiple) for all six team members, based on the time that each worker actually worked. For team workers employed full-time, she used the weighting of 1 (really, equivalent to no weighting). For workers employed half-time, she used the multiple of 2; for the one worker employed one-quarter time, she used the multiple of 4. When she multiplied the workers' actual number of successful placements for the week by their respective weightings, she produced the number of cases that (theoretically) they would have successfully placed if they had been employed full-time and had continued at the same rate of productivity.

RuthAnn then added the scores for all six workers to get a total of 42, the number of placements that (theoretically) would have been made if all six workers had been employed full-time. Dividing by six, the mean worker success rate was 7 discharges, exactly the same as that of the other team.

Weighted means have a variety of uses. Teachers use them to compute final grades of students when averaging scores on assignments and examinations that are given different weights. If Joetta, for example, received a 90 on her midterm exam (¼ of the final grade), 80 on her final exam (½ of the final grade), and 100 on her term paper (½ of the final grade), her three scores could not simply be added up and divided by 3. (That would produce an arithmetic mean of 90.) Because the graded assignments were not of equal importance, a weighted mean would need to be computed as follows:

Exercise	Score	×	Weighting Factor	=	Points
Midterm	90		.25		22.5
Final	80		.50		40.0
Paper	100		.25		25.0
Course grade (weighted mean)					87.5

As the previous two examples clearly demonstrate, a weighted mean (rather than the arithmetic mean) should be used in those situations where not all measurements are of equal weight, or importance. It allows for fair comparisons.

Which Measure of Central Tendency to Use?

With nominal level variables, the mode is the only measure that should be used. With ordinal level measurement, it is sometimes helpful to report where the median (midpoint) of a distribution fell (along with the mode). It is not always easy to decide which measure of central tendency to use when describing a distribution of values at the interval or ratio level. The final decision is often more a question of judgment and of ethics than of rules. Judgment relates to the issue of what outliers might distort the mean and whether the median or trimmed mean should be used instead. Ethics are involved because we have an ethical obligation as researchers and practitioners to represent our data as accurately as possible. As with frequency distributions and graphs, we want to use measures of central tendency to provide our readers with an accurate mental image of our data set—a shorthand description of what our data really look like. Yet, in some situations no single measure of central tendency would accurately represent a data set. If so, accuracy dictates that we should report more than one measure of central tendency. An example using data from records of closed cases in a social service agency will help illustrate this point.

An agency administrator wishes to see if the agency really is using short-term crisis intervention treatment, as stated in its mission statement. Data are collected and analyzed for cases closed during the month of December (Table 3.3). Figure 3.1 is a frequency polygon that presents the data from Table 3.3 with the mode, median, and mean indicated.

The variable *number of interviews* is at the ratio level of measurement, and there are a large number of cases ($N = 1290$). These conditions suggest that the mean might be the best measure of central tendency to report, but what about outliers? The shape of the frequency polygon indicates that the presence of outliers may produce a distorted mean—it is rather badly skewed.

The mean number of interviews in Table 3.3 is actually 4.37, primarily because of the fairly large number of cases (outliers) that were seen 10 times ($n = 35$). A trimmed mean (5% off both ends) would be a little lower, about 4.24. Yet, it is apparent from Figure 3.1 that a client interviewed 4 times (rounding down) would not really be a typical client within the agency in some respects. There are actually two other

TABLE 3.3   Frequency Distribution: Number of Interviews for Cases Closed at XYZ Agency during December ($N = 1290$)

Number of Interviews	Number of Cases	Total Number of Interviews (Column 1 × Column 2)
1	55	55
2	35	70
3	55	165
4	40	160
5	25	125
6	15	90
7	10	70
8	20	160
9	5	45
10	35	350
Totals	295	1290

values, both lower (i.e., 1, 3), that occurred as frequently as or more frequently than 4. Because they are both well to the left of the mean, the mean or trimmed mean appear to be too high to reflect a typical value for the distribution.

If the mean or trimmed mean would not be representative portrayals of the data, what about the median? It falls between the values of 3 and 4, very close to one of the most common values (3). As a choice for a single measure of central tendency to

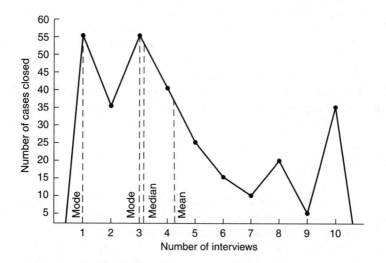

FIGURE 3.1   Frequency Polygon: Number of Interviews for Cases Closed at XYZ Agency During December

represent the data, it is fairly good. It does not, however, even hint that a fairly sizable group of clients ($n = 35$) were interviewed 10 times, a fact that may be useful to the administrator of an agency whose mission is to provide short-term crisis intervention. It also does not confirm the more predictable finding that a large number of clients ($n = 55$) were interviewed only once. In short, the median may be better in some ways than either the mean or the mode for presenting what is typical, but it has its own problems.

The distribution in Table 3.3 is bimodal, with the two modes falling at 1 and 3 interviews. But if we were to use only the mode, we would be suggesting that either 1 or 3 interviews (both small numbers) is representative of the typical client when, in fact, fewer than half of all clients were seen 4 times or less. As is true of the median, the mode alone provides no hint of the possibility that a sizable percentage of crisis-intervention cases were interviewed a fairly large number of times. Besides, the mode is really most appropriate for nominal and ordinal level data. It treats different value categories of a variable as if they were differences of kind only. It would not take into account the fact that the value categories in our example reflect quantitative differences, which is critical to an accurate interpretation of the data set.

In our example, as in many data sets, no single measure of central tendency would adequately summarize the distribution of values for the variable *number of interviews*. Any one measure of central tendency has the potential to mislead. Yet, the mode, the median, the trimmed mean, and the mean all would help to describe how the data looked. The fact that the data set was bimodal, with modes at 1 and 3 interviews, indicates that short-term treatment occurs quite often within the agency. The median suggests that short-term treatment may not be as typical of the agency as one might believe from reading the agency's mission statement. If the mean or the trimmed mean is also reported, the fact that either is over 4 is even stronger evidence that a sizable number of clients clearly are not the recipients of short-term crisis intervention services.

As we have said before, knowing only one measure of central tendency can be misleading. When in doubt about which measure of central tendency to use, a good rule is to report all that would be helpful in visualizing the data set. If the mode, median, and mean (and/or trimmed mean) are all reported, an experienced reader of research reports, or even one with just a good understanding of central tendency, will be able to compare them and piece together a reasonably accurate picture of how the data were distributed for a particular variable. Of course, the inclusion of a graph (e.g., Figure 3.1) would make the picture even clearer.

MEASURES OF VARIABILITY

Measures of central tendency can tell us much about the distribution of the values of a variable. They can fall short, however, of giving us a complete picture of what a data set looks like. For example, they cannot easily tell us if most values tend to cluster around a typical value or, if not, how widely they vary from the typical value. To provide a more accurate description of the distribution of the variable, we need to add a summary descriptor called *variability,* which gives us an indicator of the degree of variation among values or value categories that occurred. Variability is also called *dispersion.*

Why is an understanding of variability so important? Suppose that there are two class sections of a graduate social work research course. The ages of the 15 students in each of the sections are as follows:

Ages; Section 1:

21, 22, 24, 24, 26, 29, 30, 31, 32, 33, 36, 38, 38, 40, 41

Ages; Section 2:

27, 28, 28, 29, 29, 30, 30, 31, 32, 32, 33, 33, 34, 34, 35

If we were to report only the mean and median for the variable *age* for each section, both measures of central tendency would be identical. The mean (31) and median (31) are the same for both sections. Only the sections' modes would give us any hint that the distribution of ages within them are quite different.

If a student who was 23 years of age were to register late for the class, the student might feel more comfortable in Section 1 than in Section 2. A student who is 34 might feel more comfortable in Section 2. Neither student would know this based only on central tendency data. If the two students had one or more measures of variability for the two sections, however, they could anticipate how comfortable they might feel in registering for one section or the other.

If a variable is at the nominal or ordinal level of measurement, variability can be communicated best in a frequency distribution or graph, such as a bar chart. If a variable is at the interval or ratio level of measurement, however, measures of variability can help describe the distribution of values. There are five measures of variability: (1) range, (2) interquartile range, (3) mean deviation, (4) variance, and (5) standard deviation.

The Range

The **range** is the distance that encompasses all values within a data set. Expressed as a formula, the range is computed as follows:

Range = maximum value − minimum value +1

The formula above differs slightly from the way we use the word *range* in common English usage. Why is the range not simply the difference between the maximum value (the value of the case with the largest value of the variable) and the minimum value (the value of the case with the smallest value of the variable)? We add 1 to the difference so that the range reflects the total number of values of the variable that it encompasses.

In a distribution of the variable *age*, for example, with a maximum age of 35 and a minimum age of 30, the range is 6 (35 − 30 + 1 = 6). That is because there are potentially 6 different ages (or values) that are included within the range: 35, 34, 33, 32, 31, and 30. Even if we think of values as reflecting equal intervals (Chapter 1), the range would still be 6, because it would include the distance from the lower limit of the interval for 30 (29.50) and the upper limit of the interval for 35 (3.49).

The range for Section 2 in our previous example is 9 ($35 - 27 + 1 = 9$). There are potentially 9 different ages included in the data: 27, 28, 29, 30, 31, 32, 33, 34, and 35. The range for Section 1 is 21 ($41 - 21 + 1 = 21$). The larger range in Section 1 indicates a greater variation in the students' ages.

The range can be computed quickly and easily. Calculating the range also suggests the number of intervals to employ in creating grouped frequency distributions (Chapter 2) as well as the most appropriate interval size. Like the mean, however, the range is easily distorted by the presence of outliers. One outlier at either end of an array can greatly increase the range of a data set and suggest much more variability than is actually present. Let us suppose that the student who is 41 years old in Section 1 drops out of the research course and is replaced by a student who is 64. The distribution of values would now look like this:

Ages; Section 1:

21, 22, 24, 24, 26, 29, 30, 31, 32, 33, 36, 38, 38, 40, 64

Although only one value has changed, the range for Section 1 has jumped from 21 to 44 ($64 - 21 + 1 = 44$). A student considering enrolling in Section 1 who was told that the range for the students' ages is 44 would mistakenly assume that the ages of the students are much more diverse than they really are.

The vulnerability of the range to the influence of outliers is an undesirable characteristic, especially when comparing the ranges of two distributions of the same variable. The presence of outliers in one distribution and not in the other can give a misleading impression about the degree of dissimilarity of the two distributions.

The Interquartile Range

One way to handle the problem of outliers is to use another measure of variability. Instead of using the maximum and minimum values to obtain a range as previously discussed, variability can be reported as the distance (in whole numbers and decimals) between the 75th and 25th percentiles. This distance is known as the **interquartile range.**

As we have discussed before, the median falls at the midpoint, or 50th percentile of an array, where half the values fall above it and half the values fall below it. In such an array, the 25th percentile theoretically would fall at the point where one-fourth of values in the array would have lower or smaller values and three-fourths would have higher values. The 75th percentile would fall at the point where three-fourths of values in the array would have lower or smaller values and one-fourth would have higher values.

Once an array has been formed and the 75th and 25th percentiles have been determined, the interquartile range is found by subtracting the 25th percentile from the 75th percentile. The interquartile range is a more stable measure of variability than the range for the same reason that the median is a more stable measure of central tendency than the mean. Outliers cannot distort the interquartile range as they distort the range because their actual values are used only in the first step of its computation, forming an array. Once an array is formed, their specific values are not used for computation.

Like the median, the interquartile range is difficult to compute. It is often not a whole number, as it would be with any of the examples of distributions that we have previously used. With the use of computers to analyze data, however, this presents few problems, and computation takes only a few seconds once the data have been entered.

Another, less widely used measure of variability that is a variation of the interquartile range is the **semi-interquartile range.** It is simply the interquartile range divided by 2. Thus, it is a distance that is one-half the distance (in whole or fractional values) between the 75th and 25th percentiles in an array of values for a variable.

The Mean Deviation

The range, interquartile range, and semi-interquartile range present accurate descriptions of the variability of values for a variable. They are all useful in certain situations. However, the fact that they do not use every case value in their final calculations sometimes results in a distorted picture of the data set. The **mean deviation,** however, is derived from computations involving all the values in a given data set.

The mean deviation is the average amount that the values of a variable differ (or deviate) from the mean. Like other measures of variability, it describes only the amount of variation among values of a variable, not their absolute values. That is the work of frequency distributions and graphs, as presented in Chapter 2.

Table 3.4 lists five values (i.e., 1, 2, 3, 4, 5), their mean (3), and the deviation score of each (i.e., -2, -1, 0, 1, 2), which is the difference between each respective value (i.e., 1, 2, 3, 4, 5) and their mean (3). The formula for the mean deviation is

$$\text{Mean deviation} = \frac{\text{Sum of deviation values (ignoring sign)}}{\text{Number of cases}}$$

To compute the mean deviation for the data in Table 3.4, we would proceed as follows:

$$\text{Mean deviation} = \frac{2 + 1 + 0 + 2 = 6}{5}$$
$$= 1.2$$

TABLE 3.4   Deviations from the Mean for Five Values (population) for a Variable

Value − Mean = Deviation from the Mean

Value	−	Mean	=	Deviation from the Mean	
1	−	3	=	−2	} add to −3
2	−	3	=	−1	
3	−	3	=	0	} sum always = 0
4	−	3	=	1	} add to +3
5	−	3	=	2	

Although the mean deviation is relatively easy to compute and interpret, it is rarely reported in professional literature. We have chosen to discuss it because the process of subtracting raw scores (values) from the mean is an important step in computing two other, more widely used measures of variability, the variance and the standard deviation.

Variance

Obtaining the variance of a set of values for a variable requires:

1. Subtracting the mean of the distribution from each value (getting the mean deviation as previously discussed)
2. Squaring each difference
3. Dividing the sum of the squared differences (called the *sum of squares*) by either the total number of values minus one (for sample data) or simply the total number of values (for population data)

To compute the variance for the population data in Table 3.4, we would proceed as follows:

Variance = sum of squared deviations from the mean divided by the number of cases

Substituting values for words, we get the following:

$$\text{Variance} = \frac{(-2)^2 + (-1)^2 + (0)^2 + (1)^2 + (2)^2}{5}$$

$$= \frac{4 + 1 + 0 + 1 + 4}{5} = \frac{10}{5}$$

$$= 2$$

The variance sometimes is computed merely to describe (in shorthand fashion) the variability of a variable within a data set. It also is a critical component of some of the formulas for other types of statistical analyses discussed in later chapters of this book. It is mainly used to obtain a more useful type of variability, standard deviation.

Standard Deviation

The **standard deviation** is simply the square root of the variance. It appears frequently in quantitatively oriented reports. It is useful for describing the variability of a data set (when certain conditions are met), and it is used in many other types of statistical analyses as well.

Like the mean deviation and the variance, the standard deviation requires interval level or ratio level data. It is most appropriately used with a fairly large number of cases within a sample or population and with variables that, if graphed, would produce a frequency polygon that is relatively symmetrical and bell shaped (described in Chapter 4). It is not appropriate when the distribution of a variable is badly skewed within a sample or population.

Like the mean deviation and the variance, the standard deviation uses all case values in its computation. It tells us to what degree the values cluster around the mean, which makes it extremely useful. As we shall see in Chapter 4, when used with the mean in appropriate situations, it allows us to determine where a given value falls relative to other values (its exact percentile) and to reconstruct the distribution of all the values of a variable for any given data set. For the moment, we will concentrate on how the standard deviation is computed from a set of values for any variable at the internal or ratio level.

Computing the standard deviation involves eight steps, those discussed in relation to the variance, plus one more (determining the square root of the variance). A convenient way to compute a standard deviation is to construct a table like Table 3.5:

1. List the values for the variable in column *a.*
2. Compute the mean of the values in column *a.*
3. List the mean in column *b.*
4. Subtract the mean from each value in column *a,* and place this value in column *c.*
5. Square each value in column *c,* and place this value into column *d.*
6. Compute the sum of the squares in column *d.*

TABLE 3.5 Determining the Standard Deviation of Years of Employment for Agency A (population)

Step 1 (*a*) Value	−	Step 3 (*b*) Mean	=	Step 4 (*c*) Deviation from Mean	Step 5 (*d*) Squared Difference from Mean
5	−	6	=	−1 ⎫ −2	1
5	−	6	=	−1 ⎭	1
6	−	6	=	0	0
6	−	6	=	0	0
7	−	6	=	+1 ⎫ +2	1
7	−	6	=	+1 ⎭	1
		Total		0	Step 6 = 4
					Step 7 = $\frac{4}{6}$
					= .67 (Variance)
					Step 8 = $\sqrt{.67}$
					= .82 (Standard deviation)

7. Divide the sum of squares in column *d* by the total number of values minus one (for sample data) or simply the total number of values (for population data) in column *a*.
8. Compute the square root of the number computed in Step 7 (the variance). The result is the standard deviation of the values in column *a*.

The data in the distribution below give the number of years of employment of the six social workers (the population) who work in Agency *A*:

Years of Employment; Agency A:

5, 5, 6, 6, 7, 7

Using the data, we can compute the standard deviation with the use of the eight steps described above (see Table 3.5).

Now suppose that Agency *B* also has six social workers, but their years of employment are as follows:

Years of Employment; Agency B:

1, 2, 4, 8, 10, 11

Again, we can compute the standard deviation for the variable *years of employment* (see Table 3.6).

The distribution of years of employment in Agency *B* shows more variation than does the distribution for Agency *A*. This is also reflected in their respective standard

TABLE 3.6   Determining the Standard Deviation of Years of Employment for Agency B (population)

Step 1 (*a*) Value	−	Step 3 (*b*) Mean	=	Step 4 (*c*) Deviation from Mean	Step 5 (*d*) Squared Difference from Mean
1	−	6	=	−5	25
2	−	6	=	−4	16
4	−	6	=	−2	4
8	−	6	=	2	4
10	−	6	=	4	16
11	−	6	=	5	25
		Total		0	Step 6 = 90

$$\text{Step 7} = \frac{90}{6}$$

$$= 15 \text{ (Variance)}$$

$$\text{Step 8} = \sqrt{15}$$

$$= 3.87 \quad \text{(Standard deviation)}$$

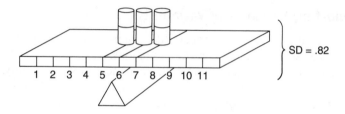

FIGURE 3.2 Variability of Years of Employment for Agency A (from Table 3.5)

deviations—3.87 for Agency *B* and only .82 for Agency *A*. This demonstrates an important point: In comparing two distributions of measurements of the same variable, larger standard deviations reflect more variation, and smaller standard deviations reflect less variation. (The same is true for all of the other measures of variability discussed in this chapter—larger measures of variability correspond to more variation among values, and smaller measures correspond to less variation.)

A pictorial representation of the above data will further demonstrate the meaning of standard deviation. Figures 3.2 and 3.3 each show how the data on length of employment in the two agencies would look if displayed as weights on a scale. Note that Figures 3.2 and 3.3 both balance on 6 years, reflecting the fact that both distributions have a mean of 6 (years of employment). Notice, however, how much more variation is shown in Agency *B* (Figure 3.3) than in Agency *A* (Figure 3.2). This is a graphical portrayal of the greater variability among values of the variable in Agency *B* as reflected in its larger standard deviation.

Although adding or subtracting a fixed amount to all values of a distribution will affect the mean by increasing or decreasing it by that amount, it will not affect the standard deviation for that distribution. A standard deviation reflects variation, and the amount of variation does not change. For example, if every employee in the agency in our example above received a $2,000 annual raise, the mean annual salary would increase by $2,000, but its standard deviation (and its range and interquartile range) would remain exactly the same. Similarly, if we were to repeat our measurement of years of employment 1 year later with the same employees in either agency, the mean would now be 7 years, but the respective standard deviations would be the same as they were a year earlier. The same phenomenon would occur in relation to the other measures of central tendency and variability that we have discussed. The measures of central tendency would change, but the measures of variability would remain the same.

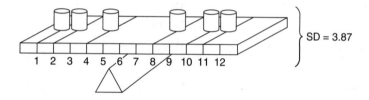

FIGURE 3.3 Variability of Years of Employment for Agency B (from Table 3.6)

Reporting Measures of Variability

Like measures of central tendency, different measures of variability are most appropriate for certain research and practice situations. Also like measures of central tendency, it often is desirable to report more than one measure of variability.

The range is generally reported (as a single number) within the text of a research report. Interquartile ranges, semi-interquartile ranges, variances, standard deviations, and, when they are reported, mean deviations can be reported in tabular form, especially when there are many to report.

Because the standard deviation represents the distance between the mean and a certain point on a frequency polygon, it is only natural that the mean is commonly reported along with the standard deviation. Where one is appropriate, the other generally is also. Reporting the two together enables the reader of a research report to get a fuller picture of how the values of a variable were distributed around the mean.

When the interquartile range or semi-interquartile range is used instead of the variance or standard deviation because of the presence of a number of extreme outliers within an interval level or ratio level data set, it is often reported along with the median. Again, this is logical as both of these measures are designed to counteract the distorting effect of outliers. Table 3.7 summarizes the most common measures of central tendency and variability and when each is used.

To provide an even more complete image of the distribution of the measurements of a variable, we sometimes report what is referred to as a *five-number summary*. It consists of the minimum value, the 25th percentile, the 50th percentile (median), the 75th percentile, and the maximum value.

A graph known as a **box plot** is also sometimes used to display the central tendency and dispersion of the distribution of a variable. In a box plot such as Figure 3.4 (a representation of the ages of the extended-care facility residents described in Chapter 2), we can identify the 25th percentile, the median, the 75th percentile, and outliers. The box in the figure contains all cases between the 25th and 75th percentiles (those within the interquartile range). The horizontal line within it is the median. The

TABLE 3.7   A Guide to Selecting Measures of Central Tendency and Variability

Level of Measurement	Central Tendency	Variability
Nominal	Mode	# of value categories
Ordinal	Mode Median	Range
Interval/ratio (no outliers)	Mean	Standard deviation Variance
Interval/ratio (outliers)	Median, trimmed mean	Interquartile range Semi-interquartile range

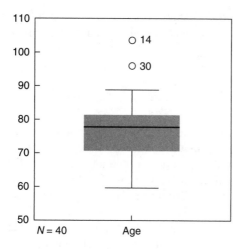

FIGURE 3.4 Box Plot: Ages of Residents at XYZ Residential Care Facility (*N* = 40)

short horizontal lines outside the box (above and below a vertical line extending from the box) represent the largest values that would not be regarded as outliers. Values above or below these lines would be regarded as outliers. Their case numbers (14 and 30) appear near the top of the graph alongside the values (ages in this case).

OTHER USES FOR CENTRAL TENDENCY AND VARIABILITY

Central tendency and variability are extremely important to our understanding of statistics. They are used in two different ways:

1. *They describe the overall distribution of a variable within a research sample or population.* This helps the reader of a research report to get a reasonably complete summary picture of how the variable is distributed.
2. *They make other types of statistical analyses possible.* They do this in several ways. For example, we could use them to:
   a. Compare the distribution of some variable within a research sample with the distribution of the variable within another research sample (for example, a control group).
   b. Compare the distribution of some variable within a research sample with the distribution of the variable within the population from which the sample was drawn.
   c. Compare the distribution of some variable within a research sample with the distribution of some other variable within the sample.
   d. Compare simultaneously the distributions of several variables within a research sample or population.

The first usage has been the focus of this chapter. In the chapters that follow we will see much more of central tendency and variability as we move into a discussion of the latter.

CONCLUDING THOUGHTS

This chapter briefly discussed basic ways to summarize the distribution of values of a variable within any given data set. We discussed one group of measures that is used to describe what is typical of a data set (central tendency) and another group that is used to summarize the degree to which values differ from each other (variability). We suggested when each measure is most appropriate to use and noted their respective limitations.

As in Chapter 2, this chapter emphasized the importance of honest and clear communication. Frequently, using a single measure of central tendency or a single measure of variability will not accomplish this objective. This is especially true when the distribution of a variable is skewed—that is, it contains outliers that tend to badly distort the distribution. Thus, we should include as many measures of central tendency and dispersion as are necessary to ensure that the distribution of a data set can be fully visualized.

STUDY QUESTIONS

1. What does a frequency polygon look like when its distribution is described as bimodal? Provide an original example in your discussion.
2. Why is the median more likely to be an accurate description of interval level data than the mode? Explain.
3. Discuss why the median is a more stable measure of central tendency than the mean. Provide an original example in your discussion.
4. Why do we generally consider the mean to be a more precise measure of central tendency than either the median or the mode?
5. How does a trimmed mean combine the best features of both the median and the mean?
6. In what situations is it necessary to compute a weighted mean? Provide an original example.
7. Why may only one measure of central tendency be an inadequate description of a data set? Provide an original example in your discussion.
8. Discuss why the range is an especially unstable measure of variability and when the interquartile range may be preferable if the distribution of a variable is skewed.
9. Which measures of variability consider all values of a variable in their computations? When is this better than using only some of the values in a distribution? When is it not? Explain in detail.
10. How would an extreme outlier tend to distort the mean deviation of a data set?
11. How would a data set containing the values of a variable with a mean of 50 and a standard deviation of 3 compare with another data set containing the same variable but a mean of 50 and a standard deviation of 12?
12. How would adding the number 10 to each of the values of a variable affect its mean and standard deviation? Provide an example.

13. Fifteen students were registered in Section 1 and 15 in Section 2 of a research course. They took the same midterm exam, and their exam scores were distributed as follows:

Section 1: 89, 56, 45, 78, 98, 45, 55, 77, 88, 99, 98, 97, 54, 34, 94

Section 2: 77, 88, 87, 67, 98, 87, 55, 77, 45, 44, 88, 99, 69, 67, 98

   a. Calculate the mode, median, mean, range, variance, and standard deviation for both sections.

   b. Which section did better overall on the exam? Fully justify your answer using the concepts presented in this chapter.

14. Locate an article in a professional social work journal that uses one or more of the measures of central tendency and variability presented in this chapter. Answer the following questions in relation to the article.

   a. Do you feel the author reported the data accurately when referring to the data set used in the research study? Why?

   b. What other measures of central tendency and variability would you have liked the author to report? Why would they have been helpful?

15. Discuss why a mean should not be used with ordinal level variables. Justify your answer.

16. For each of the following, indicate the measure of central tendency that would be most appropriate, and indicate why.

   a. An income distribution in which 97 percent of the cases are in a range of $20,000 to $50,000 and a few cases are between 0 and $5,000.

   b. Data reporting the religious preferences of 100 social work students.

   c. A grouped frequency distribution of the variable *age* that has an open-ended interval of over 65 years of age.

17. The measures of central tendency have been reported for three different social service agencies for the variable *number of years employed in the agency* as follows:

Agency A: mode 16, median 17, mean 16

Agency B: mode 4, median 7, mean 10

Agency C: mode 1, median 3, mean 6

Use the measures of central tendency to describe and compare the staff of the three agencies.

18. What is a box plot, and what does it portray?

4

The Normal Distribution

Chapter 2 presented various ways that tables and graphs can portray the distributions of values (and value categories) of a variable within any given data set. The following chapter illustrated the methods that can be used to summarize two important characteristics of a variable's distribution within a data set—central tendency and variability. This chapter will demonstrate how this knowledge and other knowledge can be used to present a more complete description of the distribution of an interval level or ratio level variable.

SKEWNESS

A frequency polygon can assume a variety of shapes depending on where the values of an interval level or ratio level variable tend to cluster. Some variables contain relatively large numbers of low values and thus, when displayed on a frequency polygon, a large percentage of the area of the polygon is on the left side, where lower values of the variable are displayed; others reflect the opposite pattern.

Suppose, for example, a hospital administrator, Sue, wished to study changes in admission diagnoses over a 6-year period. She wanted to substantiate her impression that the hospital was experiencing a decline in some diagnoses and an increase in others. The data might look like those in Table 4.1 for a diagnosis such as emphysema.

Just by glancing at the data contained in Table 4.1, it is easy to see that the number of emphysema patients admitted to the hospital over the 6-year period has declined

TABLE 4.1   Cumulative Frequency Distribution: Emphysema Patients Admitted to XYZ Hospital by Year ($N = 210$)

Year	Absolute Frequency	Cumulative Frequency
2002	60	60
2003	50	110
2004	40	150
2005	30	180
2006	20	200
2007	10	210

over time. This trend is even more apparent when the data are placed in a histogram, such as the one in Figure 4.1.

The midpoints of the bars in the histogram in Figure 4.1 are connected via a line. The continuous line joining them to form a frequency polygon is called a curve. Distributions like the one shown in Table 4.1 and reflected in the frequency polygon in Figure 4.1 are referred to as skewed, a term we introduced in the previous chapter when we were discussing the presence of outliers (i.e., extreme values) in the distribution of a variable. As we noted then, a *skewed distribution* is asymmetrical—that is, its ends do not taper off in a similar manner in both directions. Note that the frequency polygon in Figure 4.1 has a "tail" on the right side (where, normally, the largest case values are displayed). A curve like the one in Figure 4.1, which has a tail to the right, is called a **positively skewed distribution.**

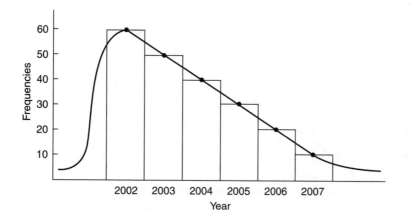

FIGURE 4.1   Positively Skewed Frequency Polygon: Emphysema Patients Admitted to XYZ Hospital by Year (From Table 4.1, $N = 210$)

TABLE 4.2 Cumulative Frequency Distribution: HIV-Positive Patients Admitted to XYZ Hospital by Year (N = 210)

Year	Absolute Frequency	Cumulative Frequency
2002	10	10
2003	20	30
2004	30	60
2005	40	100
2006	50	150
2007	60	210

Trends in admissions of HIV-positive cases over the same 6-year period in the hospital might reflect the exact opposite pattern from those with emphysema admissions. Table 4.2 and Figure 4.2 illustrate this point.

The distribution in Figure 4.2 is also skewed, but this time, the outliers and thus the tail of the frequency distribution are on the left. A curve that is skewed to the left, where the smallest case values are displayed, is called a **negatively skewed distribution.**

KURTOSIS

Skewness is the degree to which a distribution of a variable (and the frequency polygon portraying it) are not symmetrical. But suppose a distribution of a variable is symmetrical. A second way to describe the distribution of a variable, kurtosis, is still needed to complete its description. **Kurtosis** is the degree to which a distribution is peaked, as opposed to relatively flat. Or, to describe it another way, it is the degree to

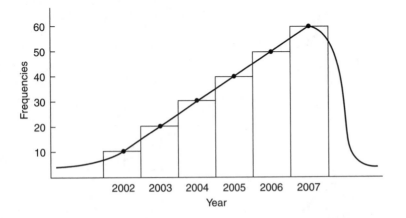

FIGURE 4.2 Negatively Skewed Frequency Polygon: HIV-Positive Patients Admitted to XYZ Hospital by Year (From Table 4.2, N = 210)

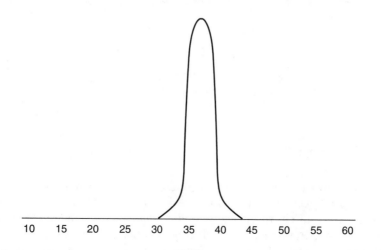

FIGURE 4.3   **A Leptokurtic Distribution of Caseloads in Agency A.**

which measurements cluster around the center, as opposed to being spread out into its end points (tails).

A distribution that has a high percentage of case values that cluster around its center (the mean), thus giving the appearance of peakness is described as **leptokurtic.** Figure 4.3 portrays a frequency polygon that is leptokurtic. Notice how it differs from Figure 4.4. which contains case values that are widely spread out into its tails. It is described as **platykurtic,** or more flat.

NORMAL DISTRIBUTIONS

Some distributions of interval- or ratio-level variables are symmetrical and contain no or relatively few outliers. Measurements closest to the mean are the most common. But the frequency of measurements of the variable "taper off" in a consistent, gradual pattern among values as they get farther and farther away from the mean (either above or below it). These distributions are neither leptokurtic or platykurtic; values would be neither bunched in the middle or widely spread out. They are bell-shaped or **mesokurtic.**

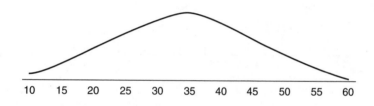

FIGURE 4.4   **A Platykurtic Distribution of Caseloads in Agency B.**

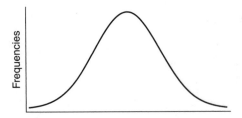

FIGURE 4.5   The Normal Curve

When such a distribution occurs, it can be referred to as a **normal distribution.** In a frequency polygon reflecting it (such as Figure 4.5) the curved line of the polygon is referred to as the **normal curve.** A distribution of scores on a standardized test are supposed to reflect the pattern of a normal distribution, that is, if we were to graph the scores of all people who take the test as a frequency polygon, the curved line of the polygon would be a normal curve.

Distributions of all interval or ratio level variables that tend to be normally distributed share the same properties. In addition to being symmetrical and bell shaped, in a normal curve, the mode, median, and mean all occur at the highest point and in the center of the distribution, as in Figure 4.6. Note that in skewed curves, the mode, median, and mean occur at different points, as in Figure 4.7*a* and *b.*

The ends of the normal curve extend toward infinity—they approach the horizontal axis (*x* axis) but never quite touch it. This property represents the possibility that, although the normal curve contains virtually all values of a variable, a very small number of values may exist that reflect extremely large or extremely small measurements (or values) of the variable (outliers). It also reflects the fact that at a higher level of abstraction, a total population of cases (or the universe) is never static because it is always subject to change as cases are added or deleted over time. Thus, populations are always evolving.

The horizontal axis of a normal curve can be divided into six equal units—three units between the mean and the place where the curve approaches the axis on the left side, and three units between the mean and the place where it approaches the axis on the right. These six units collectively reflect the amount of variation that exists within virtually all values of a normally distributed interval or ratio level variable. In a normal

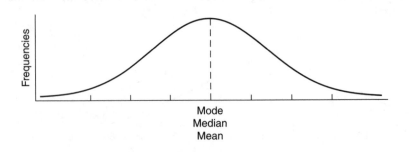

FIGURE 4.6   The Normal Distribution

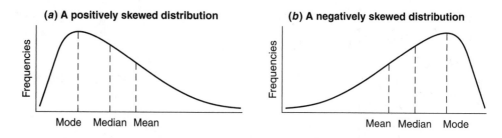

FIGURE 4.7 **Skewed Distributions**

distribution of any variable, virtually all values (except for .26%) fall within these six units of variation. The larger the units (the more variation among values in the data set), the flatter the curve. The smaller the units (less variation), the higher the curve.

Each unit corresponds to exactly 1 standard deviation. Thus, exactly how much variation a unit represents within a frequency polygon portraying the distribution of measurements (i.e., values) of a given variable is determined by using the standard deviation formula presented in the previous chapter.

Figure 4.8 displays a typical normal curve with 3 units of standard deviation to the left of the mean and 3 units to the right of the mean. Note that the units are labeled to reflect the number of standard deviations (SD) that each falls from the mean. Units to the left of the mean (where values are smaller than the mean) use the minus sign (i.e., $-1SD$, $-2SD$, $-3SD$), and units to the right of the mean (where values are larger than the mean) use the positive sign (i.e., $+1SD$, $+2SD$, $+3SD$) or no sign at all.

The term *standard deviation* can be a little misleading. *Standard* refers to the fact that once the standard deviation for measurements of a variable has been computed, it becomes a standard unit that reflects the amount of variability that was found to exist. But remember, a standard deviation (or a mean) is specific to a given variable within a given data set. Standard deviations (and means) differ from one variable to another and from one data set to another (even when the same variable has been measured). They differ based on the measurements that were taken and how much they vary from each other. The mean and standard deviation for test scores for males, for example,

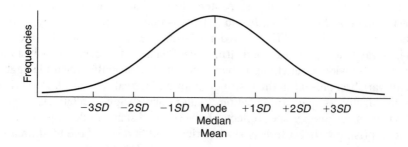

FIGURE 4.8 **The Normal Distribution with Standard Deviations Illustrated**

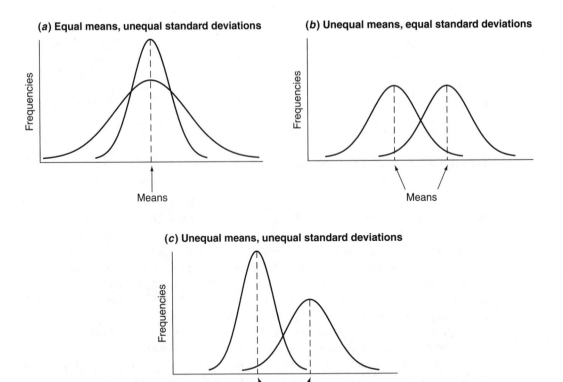

FIGURE 4.9   Variations in Normal Distributions

might be different from the mean and standard deviation for test scores of females who take the same examination. Or the mean and standard deviation computed from test scores of people who took the examination in 2007 might be different from the mean and standard deviation computed from scores of people who took the examination in 2006.

Different normal curves, therefore, tend to have different means and different standard deviations. Figure 4.9*a, b,* and *c* demonstrate how this occurs by comparing three pairs of normal curves. They also demonstrate the fact that normal curves can be drawn in a way that they reflect the distribution of data; that is, curves may be high and narrow, low and wide, or anything in between. They are usually drawn to suggest the degree of variation present in the distribution of an interval- or ratio-level variable— that is, the size of its standard deviation. Flatter curves suggest relatively large standard deviations, and higher ones reflect relatively small standard deviations.

Not surprisingly (because it is symmetrical), 50 percent of the total area of the frequency polygon formed by a normal curve falls below the mean, and 50 percent falls above it. Other segments of the frequency polygon similarly reflect standard

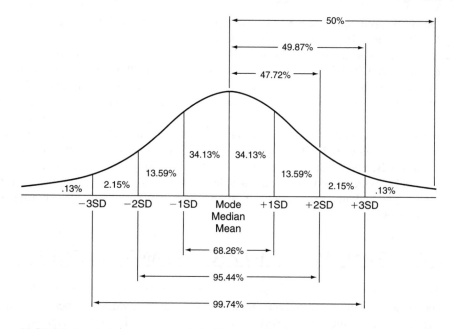

FIGURE 4.10   Proportions of the Normal Curve

percentages of its total area. Figure 4.10 displays the percentage of the normal curve that falls between the mean and the point referred to as +1 standard deviation, between +1 standard deviation and +2 standard deviation, and so forth.

By looking at Figure 4.10, we can see that the area of a normal curve between a point on the horizontal axis (e.g., −2SD) and the mean is equivalent to the area of the curve between the comparable point on the other side of the mean (e.g., +2SD) and the mean. This makes sense because, as we have already noted, a normal curve is symmetrical. If we add up all the percentages within each of the segments of the frequency polygon between −3SD and +3SD, they equal 99.74 percent of the curve. Thus, almost all the area of the frequency polygon (99.74%) lies between the points −3SD and +3SD. We could also add together other segments of the normal curve to learn that, for example, 47.72 percent of it (34.13% + 13.59% = 47.72%) falls between the mean and −2SD and another 47.72 percent falls between the mean and +2SD, or that 68.26 percent (34.13% + 34.13% = 68.26%) falls within ± 1SD of the mean.

Now let us look at Figure 4.10 from a different perspective. Up to this point, we have viewed the numbers in the figure as areas or portions of a frequency polygon. But these numbers are also something else. They are also the percentage of values (measurements of persons, cases, or objects) that fall within the respective distances from the mean of a normally distributed interval or ratio level variable. If, for example, Figure 4.10 were a frequency distribution of a normally distributed variable, such as height of female social work students, the figure would tell us that the height of 47.72 percent of all female social work students (34.13% + 13.59% = 47.72%) falls between the mean and $-2SD$; the height of 68.26 percent of them ($34.13\% + 34.13\% = 68.26\%$) falls between $-1SD$ and $+1SD$ from the mean, and so on.

If we know that the height of female social work students tends to form a normal distribution (which it probably does), we could compute the mean and standard deviation for their heights and then make very precise statements about the distribution of values of the variable. We could assign actual heights to correspond to the various mean and standard deviation points in Figure 4.10 and make statements like 68.26 percent of the heights of female social work students fall between _____ inches tall and _____ inches tall. Understanding that the percentage of the area under a normal curve is also the percentage of values that fall within a certain area of a normally distributed interval or ratio level variable is critical to understanding the material in this chapter and other parts of our discussion of statistics that rely on the normal distribution of values.

CONVERTING RAW SCORES TO *z* SCORES AND PERCENTILES

When we encounter values of an interval or ratio level variable based on measurements taken from two different samples or populations, we are sometimes unable to make direct comparisons between them. Suppose we have two friends, Rita and Miriam, who are in two different sections of a social work practice course. Both take their midterm exams. Rita's raw score is 21, and Miriam's is 85. Who did better on her midterm? Without additional information, we would have no way of knowing.

If we could learn the maximum score that each could have received on her respective examination, it would help a great deal. Perhaps, Rita's score of 21 was out of a maximum of 25—that would be 84 percent correct. And Miriam's score of 85 was out of a maximum of 100—85 percent correct. Can we thus assume that Miriam is doing better at midterm than Rita? Maybe, maybe not. Perhaps we would learn that Miriam's 85 percent was the lowest grade in her course section and Rita's 84 percent was the highest grade in her section. That might cause us to rethink our initial assumption.

We could conduct a meaningful comparison of our friends' scores if we had a more comprehensive picture of how each score compares with the scores of other students in the respective course section. We can do this by converting the two raw scores, or values (i.e., 21, 85), to a common standard.

It is possible to use a common standard to compare values of an interval or ratio level variable taken from two different samples or populations only if the variable is normally distributed within both samples or populations. Let us assume that the scores in both sections are normally distributed (a pretty big assumption). Now we can use *z* **scores** (also known as standard scores), which are raw scores converted to standard deviation units. Every raw score in a normal distribution has a corresponding *z* score that reflects how many standard deviation units it falls above or below the mean. Once two raw scores are converted to *z* scores, each *z* score (even if the scores were taken from two different normal distributions) can be compared directly with the other. Or, the *z* scores can be converted to percentiles, and the two percentiles can be compared by seeing where each score fell relative to all other scores in their respective distributions. Remember, a percentile is a point below which a certain percentage of the distribution of values lies. Thus, each *z* score corresponds to both a certain *z* score and a certain percentile rank.

For example, suppose that Axel received a raw score of 75 on a research methods exam. By converting his raw score first to a *z* score and then to its corresponding percentile we might determine that approximately 82 percent of his class received a score below his score. Suppose Durshka's score on a research methods exam in a different section was also 75, but by converting her score first to a *z* score and then determining its percentile we might learn that 92 percent of students in her class did not receive as high a score as Durshka. It is now possible to compare Axel's and Durshka's scores (even though they took different exams in different course sections) and conclude that Durshka did better on her exam (at least in one respect) than Axel did on his.

To convert a raw score into a *z* score, the following formula is used:

$$z \text{ score} = \frac{\text{raw score} - \text{mean}}{\text{standard deviation}}$$

Remember, any given value's *z* score is the number of standard deviation units that the value falls from the mean of the distribution that contains the value. Thus, a value above the mean has a corresponding positive *z* score; a value below the mean has a corresponding negative *z* score. The mean of all the *z* scores of a normally distributed interval or ratio level variable is 0.00. To put it another way, if we were to take all the *z* scores of a normally distributed interval or ratio level variable and place them into a frequency polygon, that polygon would have a mean of 0 and a standard deviation of 1.

Once we have determined the mean and the standard deviation of a distribution from which any raw score is obtained, we can compute its *z* score. A figure such as Figure 4.10 could also quickly tell us the corresponding percentile for a raw score that turns out to have a *z* score that is a whole number such as $z = -2.0$ or $z = 3.0$. As we observed earlier and can see from Figure 4.10, 34.13 percent of the area of the curve falls between the mean (the 50th percentile) and +1 standard deviation. Thus, a score with a corresponding *z* score of 1.0 would fall at approximately the 84th percentile $(50 + 34.13 = 84.13)$. A raw score with a *z* score of −1.0 would fall at approximately the 16th percentile $(50 - 34.13 = 15.87)$. A raw score with a *z* score of 2.0 would fall at approximately the 98th percentile $(50.00 + 34.13 + 13.59 = 97.72)$; a raw score with a *z* score of −2.0 would fall at approximately the 2nd percentile $(50.00 - 34.13 - 13.59 = 2.28)$, and so forth.

As we might expect, *z* scores usually do not turn out to be whole numbers. More typically, they are fractions or mixed numbers, which we express in the form of decimals, such as $z = -2.11$ or $z = -2.24$. We have to use a table like Table 4.3 to convert fractional *z* scores into percentiles. Table 4.3 shows the area of a normal curve (and the corresponding percent of values) within any normal distribution that falls between a whole or fractional *z* score and the mean.

In Table 4.3, the whole number and the first decimal of a *z* score are found in the left-hand column. The second number to the right of the decimal in the *z* score is found in the column headings that run across the top of the table. The area of the normal curve

TABLE 4.3   Areas of the Normal Curve

z	.00	.01	.02	.03	.04	.05	.06	.07	.08	.09
0.0	00.00	00.40	00.80	01.20	01.60	01.99	02.39	02.79	03.19	03.59
0.1	03.98	04.38	04.78	05.17	05.57	05.96	06.36	06.75	07.14	07.53
0.2	07.93	08.32	08.71	09.10	09.48	09.87	10.26	10.64	11.03	11.41
0.3	11.79	12.17	12.55	12.93	13.31	13.68	14.06	14.43	14.80	15.17
0.4	15.54	15.91	16.28	16.64	17.00	17.36	17.72	18.08	18.44	18.79
0.5	19.15	19.50	19.85	20.19	20.54	20.88	21.23	21.57	21.90	22.24
0.6	22.57	22.91	23.24	23.57	23.89	24.22	24.54	24.86	25.17	25.49
0.7	25.80	26.11	26.42	26.73	27.04	27.34	27.64	27.94	28.23	28.52
0.8	28.81	29.10	29.39	29.67	29.95	30.23	30.51	30.78	31.06	31.33
0.9	31.59	31.86	32.12	32.38	32.64	32.90	33.15	33.40	33.65	33.89
1.0	34.13	34.38	34.61	34.85	35.08	35.31	35.54	35.77	35.99	36.21
1.1	36.43	36.65	36.86	37.08	37.29	37.49	37.70	37.90	38.10	38.30
1.2	38.49	38.69	38.88	39.07	39.25	39.44	39.62	39.80	39.97	40.15
1.3	40.32	40.49	40.66	40.82	40.99	41.15	41.31	41.47	41.62	41.77
1.4	41.92	42.07	42.22	42.36	42.51	42.65	42.79	42.92	43.06	43.19
1.5	43.32	43.45	43.57	43.70	43.83	43.94	44.06	44.18	44.29	44.41
1.6	44.52	44.63	44.74	44.84	44.95	45.05	45.15	45.25	45.35	45.45
1.7	45.54	45.64	45.73	45.82	45.91	45.99	46.08	46.16	46.25	46.33
1.8	46.41	46.49	46.56	46.64	46.71	46.78	46.86	46.93	46.99	47.06
1.9	47.13	47.19	47.26	47.32	47.38	47.44	47.50	47.56	47.61	47.67
2.0	47.72	47.78	47.83	47.88	47.93	47.98	48.03	48.08	48.12	48.17
2.1	48.21	48.26	48.30	48.34	48.38	48.42	48.46	48.50	48.54	48.57
2.2	48.61	48.64	48.68	48.71	48.75	48.78	48.81	48.84	48.87	48.90
2.3	48.93	48.96	48.98	49.01	49.04	49.06	49.09	49.11	49.13	49.16
2.4	49.18	49.20	49.22	49.25	49.27	49.29	49.31	49.32	49.34	49.36
2.5	49.38	49.40	49.41	49.43	49.45	49.46	49.48	49.49	49.51	49.52
2.6	49.53	49.55	49.56	49.57	49.59	49.60	49.61	49.62	49.63	49.64
2.7	49.65	49.66	49.67	49.68	49.69	49.70	49.71	49.72	49.73	49.74
2.8	49.74	49.75	49.76	49.77	49.77	49.78	49.79	49.79	49.80	49.81
2.9	49.81	49.82	49.82	49.83	49.84	49.84	49.85	49.85	49.86	49.86
3.0	49.87									
3.5	49.98									
4.0	49.997									
5.0	49.99997									

Source: The original data for Table 4.3 came from *Tables for Statisticians and Biometricians,* edited by K. Pearson, published by the Imperial College of Science and Technology, and are used here by permission of the Biometrika trustees. The adaptation of these data is taken from E. L. Lindquist, *A First Course in Statistics* (revised edition), with permission of the publisher, Houghton Mifflin Company.

between a given z score (obtained by using the z score formula) and the mean would be the number in the body of the table where the appropriate line and column intersect. Note that the number alongside 1.0 in the left-hand column is 34.13, the area of the normal curve between the mean and either $-1SD$ or $+1SD$ (see Figure 4.10) and the percent of cases that fall between the mean and either -1 or $+1$ standard deviations. Also, the number alongside 2.0 in the left-hand column is 47.72, the sum of the numbers 34.13 and 13.59 in Figure 4.10. The 47.72 represents the percentage of values in any normal distribution that falls between the mean and either $-2SD$ or $+2SD$.

To find the area of the curve between a raw score and the mean when, for example, the raw score's z score computes to 1.55, we would first go down the left-hand column in Table 4.3 to 1.5. Then we would move right across the table to the .05 column (to pick up the second decimal). The number 43.94 appears at the intersection of the 1.5 line and the .05 column. That means that the area of the curve between our raw score and the mean would be 43.94 or, viewing it another way, that nearly 44 percent of all values (or cases) fall between that raw score and the mean.

For positive z scores (those to the right of the mean) we would add the area of the curve found in the body of Table 4.3 to 50.00 (corresponding to the area of the curve below the mean) to find the percentile rank where the raw score fell. In our example (using a z score of 1.55), we would add 43.94 to 50.00 (the percentile of the mean) to get 93.94. The raw score corresponding to a z score of 1.55 would fall at approximately the 94th percentile. It is logical to add 50.00 to the number found in Table 4.3, because we know that the raw score fell above the mean—it would thus have to fall above the 50th percentile. With a z score of 1.55, all scores below the mean (50% of them in a normal distribution), plus the other 43.94 percent between the mean and the score, fell below it.

As in our earlier example using whole-number z scores, for negative z scores (those to the left of the mean), we would subtract the area of the curve found in the body of Table 4.3 from 50.00 (the percentile of the mean). If the z score in our example had turned out to be -1.55, we would subtract 43.94 from 50.00 to get 6.06. The raw score corresponding to a z score of -1.55 would fall at approximately the 6th percentile. Table 4.4 provides additional examples of z scores and their corresponding areas and percentiles.

TABLE 4.4   Examples of z Scores and Their Corresponding Areas and Percentiles

z Score	Row	Column	Area Included between Mean and z Score	Percentiles
.12	0.1	.02	04.78	54.78
1.78	1.7	.08	46.25	96.25
−2.90	2.9	.00	49.81	.19
1.15	1.1	.05	37.49	87.49
−1.15	1.1	.05	37.49	12.51

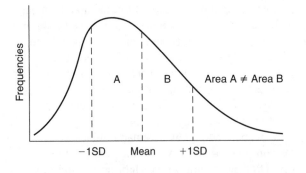

FIGURE 4.11   Comparing Areas of the Curve of a Skewed Distribution

It is appropriate to use z scores only with interval or ratio level variables that form normal distributions or at least approximate the normal curve. When a distribution is badly skewed, the areas between, for example, $-1SD$ and the mean and between $+1SD$ and the mean are not likely to be the same. Then, a z score cannot be used to produce a standardized proportion of the distribution from which it was computed. The distribution in Figure 4.11, for example, is positively skewed. Area A is clearly not equal to area B.

Practical Uses of z Scores

When used with a normally distributed variable, z scores make it possible to take any raw score and gain an accurate understanding of where it falls relative to the other scores. By converting raw scores to percentile ranks, we can put raw scores into perspective. A student receiving a raw score of 57 on a first exam, for example, may become quite alarmed, but learning that the score fell at the 96th percentile among scores in her class would be of considerable comfort, especially if the instructor has promised to "grade on a curve."

In fact the process of grading on a curve is a dubious one, especially in course sections that are not very large. Scores on examinations are often not normally distributed. Because of this and because of the frequent presence of outliers (extremely high or low values), assigning grades based on, essentially, how many standard deviations scores fall from the mean can produce grades that may seem unfair.

Treating scores as if they are normally distributed might lead an instructor to award an A to exam scores that were in the top 16 percent (above $+1SD$) or an F to exam scores below the 2nd percentile (below $-2SD$). Is this fair? What if the class was especially knowledgeable, and the 2nd percentile corresponded with a raw score of 97 out of 100? Should an individual who received a 97 get a letter grade of F, even though mastery of most of the content was demonstrated? Or should a student who answered only 35 percent of questions correctly get an A on an exam, just because all scores were extremely low and the 35 fell at $+1SD$ for the class?

Grading on a curve may be desirable if it is unknown whether an exam is too easy or too difficult. It guarantees the distribution of letter grades among class members in a way that not "too many" (whatever that is) will get any one grade, but it is unnecessary if an instructor can create a fair and rigorous exam and knows what constitutes exceptional, average, or poor performance on it.

A common and more statistically justifiable use of normal distributions can be seen in standardized tests, such as IQ tests or the Scholastic Achievement Test (SAT). Over the years, these tests repeatedly have been refined to the point that the scores of the large numbers of persons taking them tend to fall into patterns with consistent means and standard deviations. In other words, their scores now form normal distributions.

SAT scores were originally designed so that combined verbal and math scores for large numbers of students would form a normal curve with a mean of 1000 and a standard deviation of 200. In addition, all scores would fall between $-3SD$ and $+3SD$ from the mean. The lowest possible score would be $3 \times 200 = 600$ below the mean, or 400. (This is the 400 that one is rumored to get for just showing up or signing one's name.)

The highest possible (or perfect) score (the 100th percentile) would be 1600. SAT scores declined considerably during the 1980s and early 1990s, however. Although scores of 400 and 1600 still occurred, the mean dropped to around 920. In 1994, a decision was made to adjust future test scores upward so that they would again have a mean of approximately 1000, which in turn would better approximate a normal curve.

The results of various IQ tests tend to form normal distributions. They generally have a mean of 100 and a standard deviation of either 15 or 16, depending on the test. If we understand the principles and characteristics that relate to normal distributions, it is possible, given these data, to convert any raw IQ score to its corresponding z score and then to a percentile using Table 4.3. A score with a z score of 1.00 (115 or 116, depending on the test), for example, would fall at about the 84th percentile.

Even when we have little or no knowledge of a standardized measurement instrument other than its mean and standard deviation, we can put a raw score derived from it into a meaningful perspective. Or we can compare a score derived from it with another score on a measuring instrument with which we are more familiar.

Example: Student Anxiety.   Deborah is a social worker in a student health center. She leads a treatment group of college students diagnosed as experiencing chronic anxiety. In the past, group members have been selected for treatment on the basis of their scores on Anxiety Scale *A*, a standardized measuring instrument given to all students as a part of intake screening at the center. The measuring instrument has a mean of 70 and a standard deviation of 10. Only students scoring over 80 on Anxiety Scale *A* are eligible to join Deborah's group.

A vacancy occurred in the group. Deborah checked the files of active cases and noted that the highest score among potential group members was 78 (Gina). Deborah, however, had just received a referral from a family service agency stating that one of their former clients (Tom) had just enrolled at her university and needed further assistance with his anxiety problems. The referral letter indicated that Tom had received a score of 66 on Anxiety Scale *B*. The letter further stated that Anxiety Scale *B* has a mean of 50 and a standard deviation of 12.

Both standardized measuring instruments (Anxiety Scales *A* and *B*) are considered to be valid and reliable when used with college students. Based on her knowledge

TABLE 4.5   Comparative Data: Two Indices and Clients' Scores

Data	Anxiety Scale A (Gina)	Anxiety Scale B (Tom)
Raw score	78	66
Mean	70	50
Standard deviation	10	12

of normal distributions and the information received in Tom's referral letter, Deborah saw no need to have Tom take Anxiety Scale *A*. She decided to use *z* scores to determine whether Gina or Tom was a better candidate for the group vacancy. To simplify her decision, Deborah constructed Table 4.5.

Deborah then computed the *z* score for both potential group members, which allowed her to compute their percentile rank.

$$z \text{ score(Gina)} = \frac{\text{Raw score} - \text{mean}}{\text{Standard deviation}}$$

Substituting values for letters, we get:

$$z = \frac{78 - 70 = 8}{10} = .80$$

.80 (corresponds to area of 28.81; see Table 4.3)

Area between raw score and mean = 28.81 +
Area left of the mean = 50.00
= 78.81
= 79th percentile (Scale *A*)

$$z \text{ score (Tom)} = \frac{\text{Raw score} - \text{mean}}{\text{Standard deviation}}$$

Substituting values for letters, we get:

$$z = \frac{66 - 50 = 16}{12} = 1.33$$

1.33 (corresponds to area of 40.82 in Table 4.3)

Area between raw score and mean = 40.82 +
Area left of the mean = 50.00
= 90.82
= 91st percentile (Scale *B*)

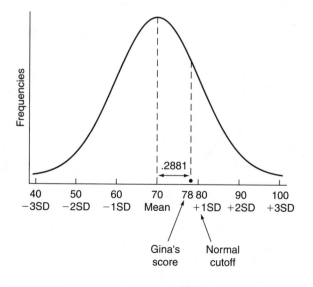

**FIGURE 4.12   Distribution of Scores on Anxiety
Scale A (Mean = 70; Standard Deviation = 10)**

Based on her comparative analysis using z scores, Deborah chose Tom for the group. His relatively higher level of anxiety (based on the measuring instrument that was used for him) made him more appropriate for the group than Gina, whom she assigned to individual counseling.

Figures 4.12 and 4.13 illustrate the comparison that Deborah was able to make with the use of z scores. Note that the score of 80 (cutoff point on Scale *A*) is comparable to a score of 62 on Scale *B*, because both fall at the point $z = +1$ (the 84th percentile). Tom's score was above this point (Figure 4.13) and Gina's (Figure 4.12) was below it.

DERIVING RAW SCORES FROM PERCENTILES

Although the most common use of z scores is to gain a better perspective on the meaning of a raw score by determining its percentile, there are occasions when social work practitioners and researchers use them to derive a raw score from a percentile as well. This entails reversing the steps. For example, suppose a social worker, Lauren, wishes to form a treatment group of college students with high anxiety levels using Anxiety Scale *B* that tom used (mean = 50; standard deviation = 12). However, she wants to include only those who are very high in anxiety, which she operationalizes as being in the top 10 percent of all students measured by Scale *B*. She will need to know who to admit or not admit to her group. Lauren can use the z-score formula to find what she is seeking—the cutoff point (the raw score) that would best coincide with the 90th percentile. Only students who scored at or above that raw score would be admitted to her group.

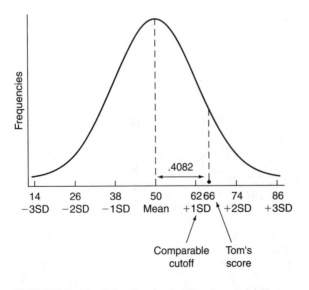

FIGURE 4.13   Distribution of Scores on Anxiety Scale B (Mean = 50; Standard Deviation = 12)

Lauren would begin by subtracting the percentile of the mean (50.00) from 90.00 to determine the area of a normal curve that would fall between the 90th percentile and the mean. It is 40.00. Then she would go to the body of a table such as Table 4.3 to find the area that is closest to 40.00. Note that 40.00 falls between two numbers in the table, 39.97 and 40.15. It is closer to 39.97, which corresponds to a z score of 1.28, so the raw score that Lauren would be seeking had a corresponding z score of about 1.28. Now the z score formula could be used, but this time Lauren would be solving the algebraic equation for the raw score (x) since she already knows the other three parts of the equation, the z score (1.28), the mean (50), and the standard deviation for Scale B (12). The equation would look like this:

$$\frac{1.28\,(z\,\text{score}) = x\,(\text{raw score sought}) - 50.00\,(\text{mean})}{12\,(\text{standard deviation})}$$

Solving for x algebraically, Lauren would remove the denominator on the right-hand side of the equation (12) by multiplying the z score on the left-hand side by it ($1.28 \times 12 = 15.36$). Now the equation would read:

$$15.36 = x - 50$$
$$x = 50.00 + 15.36$$
$$= 65.36$$

Because the z score was positive (and the percentile was greater than 50.00), Lauren would expect to get a raw score larger than 50.00, which she did (65.36). To play it safe, she would probably round up in this instance, using a raw score of 66 or higher as her cutoff point. Only college students with an anxiety score of 66 or higher on Anxiety Scale *B* would be admitted to her treatment group.

CONCLUDING THOUGHTS

This chapter focused on the different shapes that a frequency distribution of a variable can assume, especially the normal distribution. We described in detail what normal distributions are and some ways that they are useful for the social worker.

When the values of an interval or ratio level variable form a normal distribution, it is possible to determine where a given value (raw score) falls relative to other values. Using a simple formula, we first convert the raw score into its *z* score. Then, using a table of areas of the normal curve, we can learn the score's percentile rank. The percentile rank tells us approximately what percentage of scores falls above or below the raw score.

This procedure is especially useful to the social worker practitioner for interpreting the results of standardized testing, a commonly used diagnostic tool in many medical and psychiatric settings. Even if all we know about a standardized test are its mean and standard deviation and the fact that it is believed to provide a valid and reliable measurement of an interval or ratio level variable, it is possible to take a client's individual score and put it into meaningful perspective. By using *z* scores, we can even compare two scores drawn from two different data sets with different means and/or different standard deviations. Or, we can reverse the procedure and find the cutoff score (the raw score) that corresponds to any percentile that we wish to select.

This does not conclude our discussion of normal distributions. We will examine other ways in which they are used for analysis of data in the following two chapters.

STUDY QUESTIONS

1. How does a positively skewed distribution differ in appearance from a negatively skewed one? Provide examples of social work variables that tend to be positively skewed or negatively skewed.
2. Discuss the characteristics of a normal, or bell-shaped, curve.
3. In a frequency polygon for the variable *number of times married* within the general population, is the distribution likely to be normal, positively skewed, or negatively skewed? Explain.
4. In a positively skewed distribution, where is the median relative to the mean?
5. With a variable that is normally distributed, approximately what percentage of all scores falls within one standard deviation of the mean?
6. What is the *z* score for a score of 79 when the mean score of all persons who complete a depression scale is 89 and the standard deviation is 5? Is a person with a score of 79 more or less depressed than most other people who complete the scale?
7. In a normal distribution, how frequently would a score occur that is more than 3 standard deviations above or below the mean?
8. On an IQ test with a mean of 100 and a standard deviation of 16, at approximately what percentile will an IQ of 104 fall?

9. Which z score corresponds to a higher value within a distribution of values, -1.04 or 1.00? Explain.

10. If an individual falls at the 16th percentile for weight and the 48th percentile for height, would that individual be considered underweight or overweight? Explain.

11. Discuss several ways in which a social worker can use z scores in social work practice.

12. Assume that a distribution has a mean of 12, a median of 14, and a mode of 13. Should a distribution with these central tendencies be considered normally distributed? Why?

13. Use Table 4.3 to find the following:
    a. The area of the normal curve above a z score of 1.71.
    b. The area of the normal curve between the mean and a z score of -1.34.
    c. The z score that marks the lower limit of the 38 percent of the curve immediately below the mean.
    d. The z scores that mark the upper and lower limits of the middle 42 percent of the normal curve.

14. Explain how to find the raw score that corresponds to the 75th percentile using the formula for the z score.

5

The Basics of Hypothesis Testing

The previous chapters presented ways to organize, display, and summarize the distribution of the values of a variable. Sometimes this is the only type of analysis that we need—our only intention is to accurately describe the distribution of the values of a variable within a sample or population. This would likely be the case in a research study that is primarily descriptive. But, more often than not, we want to learn more from the data. For example, we may want to determine the likelihood that two variables that appear to be related within our research sample are truly related within the population from which the sample was drawn. This requires different methods of data analyses—the topic of this and the chapters that follow.

Research samples are used for reasons of efficiency. It is much less expensive and more feasible to study samples than to study an entire population. Researchers study samples in order to attempt to learn something about the population from which they were drawn (often, a relationship between or among variables). However, samples, even random ones, are likely to differ from their populations. Thus, relationships between variables can:

1. Exist in research samples, but not in their populations.
2. Not exist in samples, but exist in their populations.
3. Exist in both samples and their populations.
4. Exist in neither samples nor their populations.
5. Exist in both samples and populations, but to a different degree.

As noted in Chapter 1, the issue of how safe we might be in generalizing findings from a sample to the population from which it was drawn brings us to the concept of

inference. Inference requires us to assess the degree of confidence we have when we say that the relationship (or nonrelationship) between two variables that we observed within a research sample is a real one that probably also exists among the other cases within the population from which the sample was drawn.

ALTERNATIVE EXPLANATIONS

Suppose the distribution or values for two variables within a sample of cases drawn from a population indicates that they are related. We can only be certain that they are really only related within the sample. In order to make inferences about the relationship between the same two variables within the population from which the sample was drawn, we have to be reasonably confident that what we found to exist about the two variables within the sample cannot be attributed to alternative explanations, that is, other reasons that might account for the relationship between the two variables.

Many alternative explanations to a true relationship between variables might be proposed. Three likely suspects are (1) **rival hypotheses** (2) **design flaws,** and (3) **sampling error.**

Because rival hypotheses and design flaws are both related to problems of research design, they are best addressed well before the data are collected. Social work research methods texts generally devote considerable space to discussing strategies designed to minimize their existence. Once data are collected, it may be possible to conduct statistical analyses to estimate the amount of effect that they had, or to statistically "control" them in some way. But this is not nearly as desirable as a proactive approach that uses methods to eliminate or at least reduce their effects before data are collected.

Rival Hypotheses

Rival hypotheses are one theoretical explanation for the possible relationship between the independent and dependent variables in a research sample. Rival hypotheses really refer to "other variables." They are a recognition of the fact that some other variable(s), unknown to us, may have caused the independent and dependent variables to be related in our sample or made them appear to be more strongly or less strongly related in the sample than they really are in the population from which they were drawn.

In a research hypothesis, we often predict that the independent variable will be found to have produced or at least influenced the values of the dependent variable. But, if in our literature review, we did not identify one or more other variables that, either individually or in concert, help produce the variations within the dependent variable, we could be led to a false conclusion about the "true relationship" between the independent and dependent variables. Some other variable, for example, may have caused both the independent and dependent variables to co-vary, or it may have produced the relationship between the independent and dependent variables in some other, more complicated way.

Research Design Flaws

A wide range of design problems also can produce an erroneous impression about the relationships between two variables found within a sample. Two of the most common design flaws are (1) **measurement error** and (2) **sampling bias.**

Measurement Error.   What appears to be the relationship between variables in data collected from a research sample may be the result of measurement error. Poor measurement of variables can lead to the erroneous conclusion that two variables are related to each other when they are not really related at all. Or, it also can mislead us into either overestimating or underestimating the strength of a relationship between variables.

There are two different types of measurement error—**systematic error** and **random error.** Systematic error sometimes occurs because researchers mistakenly assume that what is measured can be assumed to be synonymous with the variable that they are seeking to measure. For example, a researcher might wish to measure how people respond to increased airport security following terrorist attacks by asking, them, via brief face-to-face interviews, a series of questions about their beliefs for the need for enhanced security. Their beliefs may reflect a high level of tolerance for security. However, when they are actually confronted with security procedures in an airport their behaviors may reflect impatience, anger, resentment, or other emotions that reflect a much lower level of tolerance.

Systematic measurement error also occurs in another, related way. An accurate measurement of *some* variable may occur. However, the measuring instrument does not measure the variable that the researcher wants to measure. For example, the researcher may have sought to measure assertiveness, but because of the way that questions were worded, the variable aggressiveness may have been measured instead. The measurement of what was believed to be assertiveness may have been quite reliable (consistent), but not valid (it didn't measure what it was supposed to measure).

Measurement that is reliable but not valid is biased in some way. **Measurement bias** often enters in during the process of data collection. It may be blatant and even deliberate. For example, asking the question, "Should people who are not physically disabled be supported by those of us who work for a living?" is almost certain to elicit mostly negative responses. Or, the biasing may be unintentional and subtle. If, for example, the researcher nods or otherwise shows pleasure when respondents answer in a way that is consistent with his or her hypothesis, respondents may be more inclined to say what they think is what the researcher wants to hear rather than to describe what they really believe or what they really do.

Some people also just naturally tend to be agreeable, and will agree with most all statements a researcher makes (the **acquiescent response set**), without regard to their content. Then there is the related, **social desirability bias.** It entails giving answers that make respondents look good or that are politically correct, even if they are not truly representative of them. If, for example, a social work researcher were to attempt to measure the attitudes of social workers toward affirmative action, capital punishment, or gay and lesbian adoptive parents, the responses received would most likely reflect how they think that they *should* respond (consistent with the NASW *Code of*

Ethics and position statements). Yet their true feelings and beliefs may be somewhat different.

In cross-cultural research, there is also the possibility that **cultural bias** can produce systematic measurement error. If a data-collection instrument must be translated into another language, for example, certain terms and concepts may "not translate" or can easily be mistaken for something else. Even if the researcher and respondents speak the same language, certain words may connote something different to one than the other and may thus produce measurement error. A frequently discussed form of cultural bias relates to standardized tests (such as IQ tests or the SAT) or certain diagnostic instruments (for example, those that purport to measure clinical depression, family violence, or substance abuse). Those claiming that they produce biased measurement suggest that standardized tests give an "advantage" to some people because of their life experiences. In the case of the diagnostic instruments, it is often argued that they fail to recognize and adjust for the influence of cultural norms within certain subcultures.

Random error is measurement error that does not occur in any particular pattern (unlike systematic error). There are many different sources of random error, only a few of which will be mentioned at here. A common reason for random error is changes in the mood, health, or fatigue of respondents. For example, respondents completing a long, tedious questionnaire may eventually "just put anything down" or answer every item in the same way just to finish completing it. Distractions during measurement (for example, noise, interruptions, or the presence of a video camera) may affect the responses of some people (but not others). Another reason for random error is simple carelessness on the part of the researcher in data collection, for example, in recording data or in entering them into the computer. Or, random error can occur because the terminology used in a data-collection instrument is ambiguous or just unfamiliar to those completing it. They may respond to what they *think* it means or simply just randomly agree or disagree with statements.

Measurement error (especially random error) often goes undetected—the researcher cannot be sure whether it occurred or not. If it is believed to have occurred and depending on how much it occurred, the data may be "questionable." In this case, no statistical analysis will be useful. Any findings of relationships between variables where the data were believed to be questionable, would lack credibility.

Sampling Bias.   A second form of design flaw, **sampling bias,** refers to the systematic distortion of a sample drawn from a population. It prevents the sample from being representative of its population in one or more important respects. It can result from such factors as an inappropriate sampling method or the time and place when and where the sample was drawn. A biased sample is characterized by either overrepresentation or underrepresentation of certain values of variables relative to the population from which it was drawn. Simply stated, the sample is not "typical" of the population in some important ways.

How can we be reasonably certain that sampling bias is not the real explanation for a relationship between variables that occurs within a research sample? Selecting the cases in a sample at random (use of a simple random sample) helps eliminate the potential for sampling bias. Other specific sampling methods that rely on randomization (e.g., cluster sampling, stratified sampling) also help ensure that every case within a population has an equal likelihood of being selected as part of the research sample. We also can pay special attention to how, when, and where a sample is selected.

A true experimental design provides good control of a special kind of sampling bias through random assignment of cases to experimental and control groups. In an experiment, the researcher often hopes to demonstrate that the presence of the independent variable in the experimental group produced a different measurement of the dependent variable than that found in the control group. Random assignment to experimental and control groups relies on the laws of probability (discussed later in this chapter) to equalize the groups, making them comparable to each other in relation to a wide variety of variables, even some that a literature review failed to identify as important. Other methods (e.g., matching) also are helpful when two or more samples are used. They also increase the likelihood that the samples (experimental and control groups) will be comparable in relation to certain matched variables.

No matter what sampling method is used, it is sometimes possible to analyze data in a way that determines whether sampling bias is present. At the point that data have been collected, however, it may be too late to eliminate the negative effects of sampling bias on the quality of a study's findings. Then, all the researcher can do is report the presence of sampling bias (as a possible limitation) within the research report.

Sampling Error

Sampling error is a third alternative explanation to a true relationship between variables. The term *chance* is sometimes used to describe this phenomenon. *Chance* and *sampling error* mean the same thing, but we prefer to use the latter term because we think it is more easily understood. **Sampling error** is the natural tendency of any sample, especially a small one, to differ from the population from which it was drawn. Thus, a sample may not be really representative of the population from which it was drawn. It follows then that any relationship between variables within the sample may be just a fluke, a result of sampling error, and the variables may really not be related (at least not to the same degree) at all. As we shall see, sampling error is likely to be relatively large in small samples and smaller in larger samples. Chapter 6 presents exactly how sampling error works and how the extent of its effect on the representativeness of a sample can be estimated.

We can never totally rule out sampling error as the explanation for an apparent relationship between variables within a sample. The only way we could guarantee that sampling error would not exist at all would be to study an entire population. But then, the concept of inference would be irrelevant. To whom would we be able to generalize our findings?

Sampling error also is commonly referred to as the **null hypothesis.** The null hypothesis says, in effect:

> The relationship between variables within the research sample is just a fluke. The relationship occurred because of sampling error, the natural tendency of samples to differ from their populations. The sample was just atypical.

A researcher must convince the skeptical consumer of a research report that sampling error probably did not produce a relationship between the variables within a research sample in order to be able to claim that the relationship is probably a real one that exists within the population from which the sample was drawn. This is accomplished by providing mathematical proof that sampling error was highly unlikely to have produced it.

Solid research designs cannot prevent sampling error from occurring whenever samples are used. However, it is possible to assess the likelihood that sampling error could have produced any relationship between variables that existed within a sample. We can do this by using various types of inferential statistical analyses. They rely heavily on the laws of probability.

PROBABILITY AND INFERENCE

Probability theory is based on the mathematical likelihood of an event occurring. It relies on certain laws. One basic law of probability, for example, states that the likelihood of any one event occurring can range only from 0 (never) to 1.0 (absolute certainty).

One assumption is central to all probability theory. It is that although certain patterns of events can be seen to exist in many repeated observations over time, individual or short-term observations tend to differ somewhat from these overall long-term patterns. If we flip a fair coin in the air, for example, it has a mathematical probability of 50 percent (.50, or 1 out of 2) probability of landing on heads. It also has a 50 percent probability of landing on tails. But these are only theoretical probabilities. They are the percent of heads (or tails) that would occur in an infinite number of flips of the coin, when the law of averages has had an opportunity to take effect. It is not an accurate prediction of what might occur if we flip a coin only a small number of times. The law of averages suggests that in the long run, things will balance out and events will unfold as they theoretically should.

In reality, we know that if we flip a coin only 10 times, we will probably get a different result from the one that is theoretically expected to occur—that is, five heads. We would not be surprised if we obtained four, six, or even three or seven heads. We would simply blame it on sampling error and assume that in the long run, if we repeated the coin tossing many more times, the percent of heads would eventually approximate 50 percent.

What if the 10 coin flips produced eight or nine heads? At this point, we might suspect that something was wrong. The results seem to be so unlikely that they "defy the laws of probability." How could these results have occurred? Could the coin be defective? Could the way in which the coin was tossed have influenced the results? What is going on here? Another way of stating these questions might be, "Is something else (some other phenomenon besides sampling error, perhaps some other variable) influencing the results (the number of heads)?"

The laws of probability can be applied in many areas of life. They have been developed to determine the theoretical likelihood of an event's occurrence. Some of the laws are simple; others are more complicated. They tell us, for example, that the probability that a student will guess correctly on a multiple-choice question with four alternative answers is 25 percent (.25, or 1 out of 4). That is pretty obvious. One law, the multiplication law, states that the likelihood of guessing correctly on two consecutive questions on a multiple-choice exam with four possible responses is .25 × .25 or 6.25 percent (.0625, or 1 out of 16). That may seem less plausible. Still another law, the addition law, states that the mathematical probability of getting only one answer correct is 37.5 percent (.375, or 6 out of 16) and of getting one or both correct is 43.75 percent (.4375 or, 7 out of 16).

We can use these various laws of probability to determine what should happen in various situations, that is, what would happen in the long run (with an infinite number of events). Of course, in the short run strange aberrations can and do occur. For example, we could flip a perfect coin 10 times and get all 10 heads. Or on a single examination, a student might guess on four questions and get all four or none of the four correct.

How do these phenomena relate to sampling error and our study of inference? Unusual, short-run situations occur in coin tossing, guessing test answers, and an almost infinite number of other life situations, including the drawing of research samples. In all of them, unlikely (but not impossible) events sometimes occur, even though most of the time (in the long run) it would not happen that way.

Variables may appear related based upon their distributions within a research sample. Often, this can be attributable to the same phenomenon that produces unlikely results in tossing several coins or guessing test answers—sampling error. However, sometimes the relationship between two variables is so strong that sampling error is a highly unlikely explanation for it. By using statistical analyses, we can determine the mathematical probability that sampling error might have produced the relationship between two variables.

Probability theory is an integral component of inferential statistical analyses. No matter which inferential statistical test we choose, probability plays a role. It is used to determine the probability that sampling error may have produced an apparent relationship between variables within a sample of a given size. In this way it helps us know how safe it is to generalize, that is, to assume that a relationship between variables found within a sample also exists within the sample's population.

REFUTING SAMPLING ERROR

There are actually two methods for demonstrating that an apparent relationship between variables within a sample was unlikely to be the result of sampling error. They are (1) **replication** and (2) **statistical analyses.**

Replication

Suppose that we work in an extremely large state hospital system that employs 100 medical social workers. We observe among the 18 medical social workers in our particular unit that female workers have higher levels of job satisfaction than male workers. Is our impression conclusive evidence of a relationship between the two variables (i.e., gender, job satisfaction) among all the other medical social workers in the system? Certainly not.

But how can we demonstrate that the apparent relationship between the two variables does not exist only within our small nonrandom sample? After all, we have no reason to believe that the 18 social workers in our unit (what might be regarded as no more than an "availability" or "convenience" sample) are typical of the other medical social workers elsewhere in the system.

In an ideal world with unlimited research resources, we could use replication to determine if the relationship is more than just a fluke. **Replication** entails repeating a research study one or more times using the same methods but different research samples to see if the same findings are produced. To use replication, we could simply use another group (sample) of medical social workers (the staff of another unit) and see if the same relationship between job satisfaction and gender is present.

But even if it were, that might not be enough evidence to dismiss sampling error as the reason for the apparent relationship. Perhaps we could draw a sample of 18 social workers 100 times and each time determine if the same relationship exists. Then if, e.g., the relationship occurred at least 95 times out of 100, we might conclude that the relationship probably is a real one.

Of course, in the real world, repeated replication is impractical. Obtaining resources and access to data even once is often difficult, so how could we ever be able to conduct our research study 100 times? Some replication occurs in social work research, however. Replication usually is used to see if a relationship between variables that was identified in a previous research study will be found to still exist at a different time or with a different sample of research participants. Replication is used far less to demonstrate initial support for the existence of a relationship between variables.

Although the cost of repeated replication makes it impractical, other methods for determining whether an apparent relationship exists between variables employ some of the principles of replication. Later in this chapter we shall discuss how the concept of "95 times out of 100" is applied in making decisions while using statistical analyses of data collected in a single research study.

Statistical Analyses

There is another, less expensive way, to gain support for the inference that there is a true relationship between job satisfaction and gender—statistical analyses of data drawn from a single study. Suppose we had made an educated guess (prediction) that we would find a relationship between job satisfaction and gender among our sample of 18 medical social workers.

Suppose that we had arrived at this prediction through the process of synthesizing existing qualitative and quantitative knowledge (a literature review) on gender differences and job satisfaction among medical social workers. We used our own observations and experiences in working with medical social workers as well as the writings of scholars in the profession and many other sources, such as unpublished documents and interviews with persons who "ought to know." We even learned enough about the characteristics of medical social workers as a group (their demographic characteristics) to conclude that the 18 social workers in our convenience sample do not appear to be unusual in any obvious or important ways. Based on what we learned, we hypothesized the following:

Female medical social workers will have higher levels of job satisfaction than male medical social workers.

The fact that the two variables appeared to be related within our sample, exactly as we predicted they would be, would not be enough evidence to claim support for our prediction. It would help, but we would need to do more. First we would have to rule out the alternative explanations for an apparent relationship (rival hypotheses and design flaws). Even if we were satisfied that they did not produce the apparent relationship between job satisfaction and gender that existed in our sample, the relationship still might have been produced by sampling error.

Our small sample of 18 medical social workers may have differed from the population of all medical social workers within the system in some important ways just because of the phenomenon of sampling error. We would have to demonstrate that the data we examined are so impressive, so clearly and strongly in support of our research hypothesis, that the apparent relationship is unlikely to have been the work of sampling error, that it is most likely a real relationship that exists within the system's population of medical social workers. That could be accomplished through statistical analyses (often called, simply, *statistical testing*).

MORE ABOUT RESEARCH HYPOTHESES

We introduced the concept of research hypotheses in Chapter 1. As suggested in the previous example, hypotheses are generated in many different ways. They may evolve as the product of someone else's research study. This occurs most frequently when a qualitative research study inductively identifies and labels variables and then suggests possible relationships between them for subsequent, more rigorous, studies to examine.

Hypotheses may also evolve from our own observations and reviews of the professional literature. Among other things, we use the literature to narrow or refine a general research question. Frequently, as the evidence in the literature starts to accumulate, we think we may have an answer to that question. We then try to express our tentative impressions, or our conclusions, in the form of a hypothesis.

A research hypothesis, also called a substantive hypothesis or experimental hypothesis, is a statement that expresses what we believe to be the relationship between or among variables. A research hypothesis can take on three different forms:

1. It can state that variables are related and predict the direction of their relationship (a **one-tailed** or directional research hypothesis).
2. It can state that variables are related but not predict the direction of their relationship (a **two-tailed** or nondirectional research hypothesis).
3. It can state that two variables are unrelated (a "no relationship" research hypothesis, often called a **null research hypothesis**).

This third form of a research hypothesis should not be confused with *the* null hypothesis. It is unfortunate that these terms are so similar. But as we noted earlier and will explain in more detail later, *the* null hypothesis is the belief that sampling error caused unrelated variables to appear to be related in a research sample when in fact they are not related in the population from which the sample was drawn. It does not address the possibility of rival hypotheses or design flaws.

The One-Tailed Research Hypothesis

A *one-tailed research hypothesis* states that there is a specific relationship between variables. It also predicts which values of one variable are to be found with, or are associated with, which values of the second variable. Continuing with our previous example, a one-tailed research hypothesis might be as follows:

> *One-Tailed Research Hypothesis:*
>
> Female medical social workers will have higher levels of job satisfaction than male medical social workers.

Suppose our observations and the literature review had led us to believe just the opposite. Then our one-tailed research hypothesis might be as follows:

> *One-Tailed Research Hypothesis:*
>
> Male medical social workers will have higher levels of job satisfaction than female medical social workers.

It is important to note that a one-tailed research hypothesis predicts a relationship and also the direction of a relationship between two variables, which is why it is sometimes called a directional hypothesis.

The Two-Tailed Research Hypothesis

A *two-tailed research hypothesis* (also referred to as a nondirectional hypothesis) states only that there is a relationship between two variables. Unlike the one-tailed research hypothesis, it does not predict which values of one variable will be associated with which values of the second variable. The following is a two-tailed research hypothesis for our example:

> *Two-Tailed Research Hypothesis:*
>
> Among medical social workers, gender is related to job satisfaction level, or females and males differ in their job satisfaction levels.

This two-tailed research hypothesis does not predict whether males or females (gender) will be found to have higher levels of job satisfaction, as the one-tailed research hypothesis did.

The "No Relationship" Research Hypothesis

The third form of research hypotheses states the belief that variables are not related. In our example it would be this:

The "No Relationship Research" Hypothesis:

Among medical social workers there is no relationship between gender and job satisfaction.

Such research hypotheses are rare. They are sometimes used to try to dispel false beliefs when we wish to gain support for our own belief that two variables that are generally believed to be related really are unrelated.

In the past, for example, we sought to disprove the stereotype that people of one nationality are less ambitious than people of another nationality. We did so by finding statistical support for the research hypothesis that nationality and ambition are not related. Similarly, we sought to demonstrate that people from certain backgrounds are no more likely than others to commit certain crimes. In situations like these, we set out to find support for the research hypothesis; that is, we set out to prove that there was not a relationship between those backgrounds and crime rates.

TESTING THE NULL HYPOTHESIS

We never refer to a one-tailed or two-tailed research hypothesis as proven or not proven; we state only that we found support for it or that we did not. This conclusion is based on whether, using our knowledge of research design and statistical analyses, we feel that all other explanations for an apparent relationship between variables (besides a true one) are highly unlikely. We also never test a one-tailed or two-tailed hypothesis directly. Instead, we test its null form. It states that the variables are really unrelated and that any apparent relationship between them in a sample was caused by sampling error.

As was suggested earlier, determining if there is sufficient support for a one-tailed or two-tailed research hypothesis is a process of elimination. To gain support for a one-tailed or two-tailed research hypothesis that two variables are related, we must first be reasonably certain that nothing else caused the variables to be related within our sample.

As also suggested earlier, we try to eliminate rival hypotheses and design flaws as possible explanations by utilizing good research designs. But that still leaves us with sampling error as a possible explanation, the null hypothesis. Before we can claim support for a one-tailed or two-tailed research hypothesis, we also have to demonstrate, with the use of statistical analyses, that the null hypothesis is a highly unlikely explanation for a relationship between the two variables within the research sample. If we can do this, we would be reasonably safe in rejecting the null hypothesis. Only then would we be able to claim support for our one-tailed or two-tailed research hypothesis, because we now would be left with only one possible explanation—a true relationship probably exists between the two variables within the population from which the sample was drawn.

What if we wanted to demonstrate support for a "no relationship" research hypothesis? Let us assume that rival hypotheses and design flaws have been adequately controlled. There might still appear to be a weak relationship between the two variables in the sample. Does that mean the research hypothesis was incorrect and that the variables really are related in the population from which the sample was drawn?

Not necessarily. We could still gain support for our research hypothesis through statistical analyses. We could attempt to demonstrate that the relationship between the two variables in the sample is really so small or weak that it is fairly likely to have been produced by sampling error. In other words, we would hope to show that there is not strong enough evidence to reject sampling error (the null hypothesis) as the explanation for the apparent relationship between the two variables. If we could do this, we would then have demonstrated support for our research hypothesis.

In the previous example, and after a thorough literature review and based upon our own observations, we decided that we had justification for stating the following one-tailed research hypothesis:

One-Tailed Research Hypothesis:

Female medical social workers will have higher levels of job satisfaction than male medical social workers.

Now we will restate our one-tailed research hypothesis in its null form:

Null Hypothesis:

There is no relationship between the gender of medical social workers and their levels of job satisfaction.

If we were really seeking support for the one-tailed research hypothesis, we might draw a simple random sample (rather than a convenience sample) of 18 social workers from all 100 medical social workers in the entire hospital, thus reducing the likelihood of sampling bias. We also probably would not just trust our impressions of the job-satisfaction levels of the 18 medical social workers in our sample. In addition to noting each social worker's gender, we would administer a standardized measuring instrument to all of them that provides a reliable and valid measurement of job satisfaction (the dependent variable). As we analyzed the data, the scores of males and females might seem to provide a reason to reject (or not to reject) the null hypothesis, particularly because the number of social workers is small, and it would be easy to identify any differences in the distribution of job satisfaction scores between the two genders. If, for example, the female group and the male group each had a mean job-satisfaction level of 60, we would not reject the null hypothesis because, even within the sample, there is no difference between the mean job satisfaction levels for males and females.

On the other hand, if the females were found to have a mean job-satisfaction level of 90 and the males had a mean job-satisfaction level of 10, we would feel that we had pretty strong support for the rejection of the null hypothesis. Such a clear pattern of a relationship between variables is rare. If it exists, we probably already know about it. But what if (as often occurs) there is a difference in the mean job-satisfaction levels of the two groups, but it is not so dramatic? What if the mean job-satisfaction level was, say, 70 for females and 50 for males? How likely is it that our observed relationship within our small sample is a real one that represents a relationship between the two variables within the larger population medical social workers within the entire hospital.

Could we infer, based on these central tendency data alone, that as a group, female medical social workers (including those not in our sample) possess a higher mean level of job satisfaction than males? Such a conclusion would seem a little premature, even if we had carefully designed and implemented the research study so that we were fairly certain that rival hypotheses and design flaws could be ruled out as alternative explanations for the apparent relationship. But what about sampling error? Any relationship between the two variables found in our small sample could still be the work of sampling error (the null hypothesis). After all, a sample of 18 research participants is relatively small (considering that there are 100 medical social workers in the hospital).

Inferential statistical analyses in the form of statistical tests could tell us the likelihood that sampling error might have produced the difference in the mean job satisfaction levels between the female and male social workers. They could determine the mathematical probability that a relationship between the predictor and outcome variables within our sample data could have occurred as a result of sampling error. Thus, they can help us determine if an apparent relationship between variables within our sample data is a real one—that is, one that exists in the population from which our sample was drawn.

In attempting to gain support for a research hypothesis, we can never totally eliminate sampling error as the explanation for an apparent relationship between variables. After all, even if females did have a mean job satisfaction level of 90 and males had a mean job satisfaction level of 10 in our sample, we theoretically could have drawn a highly unusual sample of 18 in which females might differ by that much from males, even if the two variables really are unrelated within the population from which our sample was drawn. Although we never can be 100 percent certain that what we found was not the work of sampling error, we generally are convinced if we can be "reasonably certain" that what we observed was not a fluke occurrence caused by sampling error. But, what is "reasonably certain?"

We do not want to report a relationship between variables that appears to be real when it is not. At the same time, we do not want to be so rigid or so unreasonable that we will not claim support for a relationship between variables just because there is a very remote possibility that sampling error may have produced it. If we did that, few, if any, research findings would ever see the light of day. Thus, we need guidelines to help us to know when to reject the null hypothesis and conclude that there is enough statistical evidence that variables really are related, and when not to reject the null hypotheses. Fortunately, they are available.

STATISTICAL SIGNIFICANCE

Continuing with our example, it would be nice if it had been possible to repeat the research study with 100 different samples of 18 medical social workers within the hospital system (replication). We could then have seen if females showed somewhat higher levels of job satisfaction than males in most of the samples (say, in at least 95 percent of them). Usually, however, we get only one shot at doing a research study.

Within a single research study and with only one research sample, we need some evidence that a relationship between the variables is a real one. Statistical analyses can provide it.

At what point can we be sufficiently certain that the relationship between variables we find in our sample cannot simply be dismissed as the work of sampling error? When using statistics, we rely on mathematics, the laws of probability, common sense, and convention. We also use two very important and related concepts: **p values** and **rejection levels.**

p Values

All statistical tests of inference that are discussed in this book (and many more that we will not be discussing) have something in common. They produce a p value. A **p value** is the mathematical probability that a relationship between variables found within a sample may have been produced by sampling error. (It is important to note that the p value tells us nothing about the likelihood that rival hypotheses or design flaws might have produced it.) In theory, a p value can range from 0.00 (would never occur because of sampling error) to 1.00 (definitely the work of sampling error). All p values fall somewhere in between these two theoretical extremes, just like the mathematical probability of any event occurring.

In a sense, a p value is the bottom line in all statistical analyses. (In fact, it often is found on the last line in the results of a computerized data analysis.) However, software packages differ in the ways that p values are reported. Even within a given software package, the results of one test may be reported one way and the results of another test may be reported a different way. An actual p value may be provided (e. g., .07, .11, or .29) or p may simply be reported as *NS* (not statistically significant) or *S* (statistically significant) based on whether the p value was greater than or less than .05 (discussed below). When a p value is very low, it may appear as .00, which is theoretically impossible, because we can never say that there is absolutely no possibility that sampling error produced some relationship between variables within a research sample. When .00 appears, it should be interpreted as meaning the same as *S* (statistically significant).

Even when the actual p value is provided, it may be the value for a two-tailed research hypothesis; the p value for a one-tailed one may not be given. When this occurs and the research hypothesis was one-tailed, it is possible to simply divide the p value provided by two, but only if the direction of the relationship was the same as that which the hypothesis predicted. Remember, we cannot claim "credit" for a finding opposite to that which we predicted.

Different statistical analyses use different formulas, but the p value that each produces is interpreted exactly the same way. Thus, it is possible to know the exact mathematical probability that sampling error produced a relationship between variables within a sample (the p value) even if we do not fully understand the statistical analysis that produced the p value. However, this can be dangerous. Unless we have a good understanding of the way in which a p value was produced (and that it was produced using the appropriate statistical analysis), it is possible to misunderstand the importance of it.

Rejection Levels ("Alpha")

As noted earlier, the decision to reject the null hypothesis does not totally rule out sampling error as the explanation of an apparent relationship between variables. It simply means that we have been able to demonstrate that there is a small likelihood that sampling error caused the relationship between the variables in a sample.

How small is small? Over the years, we have settled on the 95 percent certainty level as the point at which we are sufficiently confident to be able to reject the null hypothesis. Expressed another way, we feel safe in rejecting the null hypothesis if a statistical analysis demonstrates that there is less than a 5 percent probability that sampling error may have produced an apparent relationship between the variables (the *p* value produced by a statistical analysis is less than .05). That much risk of mistakenly concluding that sampling error did not cause an apparent relationship between variables (when it really did) is considered acceptable in most research situations. This is referred to as the **.05 rejection level.** Rejection levels also are called **alpha levels,** or **significance levels.**

There is nothing sacred about the .05 rejection level. Although it is the most widely used cutoff point for rejecting null hypotheses, other rejection levels also can be used. The decision to use rejection levels other than .05 is based on our assessment of the possible consequences of either mistakenly rejecting the null hypothesis or mistakenly failing to reject it. A more demanding proof of a relationship between variables, such as a .01 rejection level, might be used when we wish to allow only a very small possibility that we might erroneously reject the null hypothesis and conclude that a relationship exists between variables. These more stringent rejection levels allow for even less likelihood that sampling error is the reason for an apparent relationship between the two variables than does the conventional .05 level. The .01 rejection level means that the probability of erroneously rejecting the null hypothesis is less than 1 out of 100.

In research studies in which the consequences of mistakenly rejecting the null hypothesis might be less problematic than mistakenly concluding that a relationship between variables was probably the work of sampling error (when it was not), we occasionally consider a higher rejection level such as .10 as acceptable. A .10 rejection level allows for twice the possibility of mistakenly concluding that variables are related in the population when they are related in the sample only because of sampling error as does a .05 level. Sometimes a less demanding rejection level, such as a .10, is used as evidence of a relationship between variables if the research design includes at least one replication. While achieving one .10 rejection level may be viewed as inconclusive support for a relationship between variables, achieving it two or more times in succession may lead to the conclusion that the null hypothesis can be rejected. Why? Because achieving two or more successive .10 levels starts to defy the laws of probability.

Although some flexibility is allowed in selecting the threshold at which sampling error is reasonably eliminated as the explanation for an apparent relationship between variables, the choice of a rejection level should not be viewed as casual. Convention states that the .05 rejection level should be used unless we develop and state a compelling rationale for the use of another rejection level. The selection of a rejection level must always be made before the data are collected. It would be unethical to change the level afterward. The decision could be construed as an effort to manipulate the study's findings, generally to gain support for the study's one-tailed or two-tailed research hypothesis.

When reporting the findings of a statistical analysis of data, the rejection level that was used as a cutoff to reject the null hypothesis is always reported. Usually, this is done using wording like: "The mean annual salary for females was $29,000, and for males it was $31,000. This $2,000 difference is statistically significant at the .05 level." This can also be reported as "$p < .05$." The p is in lowercase italics and stands for probability. It usually is followed by a less-than sign ($<$); however, if statistical significance is not achieved (the probability that sampling error might have produced the salary differences was, for example, .06 or .07), the greater than sign ($>$) can be substituted in front of the rejection level that was used: "$p > .05$."

ERRORS IN DRAWING CONCLUSIONS ABOUT RELATIONSHIPS

Of course, as we have already indicated, whenever we reject (or do not reject) the null hypothesis, we run the risk of being wrong. The two possible errors that we can make are referred to as **Type I** and **Type II errors.**

A Type I error occurs when we reject the null hypothesis and conclude that a relationship between variables in a sample exists in the population from which it was drawn, when in fact it really does not. Conversely, a Type II error occurs when we fail to reject the null hypothesis and conclude that a relationship between variables does not exist in the population from which it was drawn, when in fact it really exists. Neither type of error is inherently better than the other. Both can mislead and misinform social work practitioners and researchers. Table 5.1 summarizes the difference between Type I and Type II errors.

Type I and Type II errors can result from many causes. Even though the probability of doing so was very low, we may have simply drawn a very nonrepresentative sample, one in which the relationship (or nonrelationship) between variables that we observed in the sample is atypical of the population. Type I and Type II errors also can result from the use of inappropriate analyses of data. If, for example, we incorrectly use a statistical test that requires certain conditions that are not present, an error of one type or the other can occur. If the appropriate statistical test is not used within the conditions for which it was designed, we can either falsely conclude that a true relationship between variables exists (Type I error) or a true relationship may remain

TABLE 5.1   Type I and Type II Errors

	Our Decision	
Real World	*Reject Null Hypothesis*	*Do Not Reject Null Hypothesis*
Null hypothesis false	No error	Type II error
Null hypothesis true	Type I error	No error

unidentified (Type II error). Chapter 7 discusses the factors to be considered in selecting the most appropriate statistical test for any given data set.

We must ultimately decide which error, Type I or Type II, is more acceptable to us, should it occur. This is largely an ethical decision that requires a knowledge of social work practice and the consequences of committing one error over the other. Usually, the consequences of making an error in deciding whether to reject the null hypothesis in social work research are not grave. The possibility of committing either a Type I or a Type II error should not preclude us from taking reasonable risks in interpreting research findings and drawing conclusions and implications from them. This is how we make progress in becoming knowledge-based social work practitioners.

Avoiding Type I Errors

No matter what we ultimately decide about whether or not to reject the null hypothesis, we can never totally eliminate the possibility of committing an error of one type or the other. Traditionally, researchers have been most fearful of committing a Type I error, that is, concluding that sampling error did not produce a relationship between variables when it actually did produce it.

How can we at least decrease the likelihood of making a Type I error? We might select a smaller p value than the traditional .05, such as .01 or even .001, so that we can be even more confident (if that level is achieved) that sampling error did not produce the relationship between variables within the research sample. But, that may not be desirable because, although it would result in less likelihood of a Type I error, it would increase the likelihood of committing a Type II error, that is, mistakenly failing to reject the null hypothesis. (Conversely, if we try to avoid committing a Type II error by selecting a larger p value such as .10 or .25 instead of .05, we increase the likelihood of committing a Type I error.)

There are, however, two ways to reduce the possibility of making a Type I error while simultaneously reducing the likelihood of making a Type II error. First, we can use larger sample sizes. As samples get larger, there is less sampling error. (We will discuss this more in the next chapter.) When larger samples are used, the laws of probability take over, and the samples tend to look very similar to their populations—any relationships between variables within the samples are probably real ones that also exist within the population.

We can also decrease the likelihood of making a Type I error and a Type II error at the same time by replicating a research study. If the findings of the second study agree with those of the first study (that is, both suggest that the variables either are or are not related), either conclusion is more likely to be correct. A fluke sample may have been selected the first time, but one is unlikely to have been drawn two times in a row. However, replication and the use of larger samples are not always feasible. In agency-based research, there may not be administrative support for repeating a study a second time. Or, the only sample available may be a small one that cannot be made larger. Both methods also can add considerable cost to a research study. Sometimes they cannot be considered because of funding realities.

Although a concern with committing a Type I error has been the primary focus of analyses of research data in the past, Type II errors also can cause a different set of problems for researchers and practitioners. We will discuss ways to reduce the probability of their occurrence in Chapter 7.

STATISTICALLY SIGNIFICANT RELATIONSHIPS AND MEANINGFUL FINDINGS

The word *significant* is widely and loosely used in our profession and elsewhere to emphasize the importance of something, such as when we refer to a social worker's significant contribution to the passage of social legislation or the role of a significant other in the decision of a client to return to school. As with many other words that we use daily (e.g., value, relationship), it is best to set aside the everyday meaning of the word in order to understand its specific meaning in the field of statistics.

Statistical significance is the demonstration, through the use of mathematics and the laws of probability, that the relationship between variables in a sample is unlikely to have been produced by sampling error (Figure 5.1). A relationship that is declared to be statistically significant is one in which the p value (the mathematical probability that sampling error produced the relationship) is less than the selected rejection level— usually, $p < .05$. For us, this is the only relevant meaning of the words *statistically significant* or *significant;* we must be careful to use the terms in this sense, and only in this sense.

The presence of a statistically significant relationship between variables may be dismissed as the result of rival hypotheses and/or design flaws. The results of inferential statistics, as suggested earlier, are useful only if the effects of other variables were controlled in some way, if the data that produced them are valid and reliable, and if those data were obtained from a representative sample correctly drawn from a population. What if these possible explanations for the existence of a real relationship between variables can be successfully dismissed? In that case, does the presence of a statistically significant relationship demonstrate that sampling error is a very unlikely explanation for the apparent relationship between the two variables? Yes. The relationship probably

---

Statistical significance *is*: evidence, based upon mathematics and the laws of probability, that the relationship between variables in a research sample is *very unlikely to have been* produced by sampling error.

Statistical significance *is not*:

- proof that the relationship was not caused by the influence of some other variable.
- proof that the relationship was not caused by design flaws.
- proof that the relationship is necessarily a strong one.
- proof that the relationship is a valuable, meaningful, or previously unknown one.
- proof that the relationship absolutely could not have been produced by sampling error.
- proof that the variables are related to the same degree within the population from which the sample was drawn (or are related at all).

FIGURE 5.1   Understanding Statistical Significance

is real; the variables probably really are related in the population from which the sample was drawn.

But is the relationship between them a strong one? Is it necessarily a *surprising relationship* between variables? Is it a *meaningful relationship* between variables, or as some books describe it, substantive—that is, is it of practical value to the social worker? We must be careful to evaluate every statistically significant relationship between variables in the context of the question, "So what?" In social work practice, every statistically significant relationship is not a meaningful finding that cries out for immediate implementation.

Assessing Strength of Relationships (Effect Size)

Suppose we find that there is a statistically significant relationship between type of treatment and treatment success at the .05 rejection level and that the relationship between gender and treatment success is statistically significant at the .01 rejection level. Can we then state that the relationship between gender and treatment success is five times as strong as the relationship between type of treatment and treatment success? No. All we can say is that, with type of treatment and treatment success, we have demonstrated that sampling error would produce the relationship less than 5 percent of the time; with gender and treatment success, we have demonstrated that sampling error would produce the relationship less than 1 percent of the time.

In fact, in an absolute sense, some statistically significant relationships are so weak as to be meaningless. Virtually all variables are related to all other variables to a greater or lesser degree. Some types of statistical analyses can and do identify relationships that are so weak (especially when overly large samples are used) that they are worthless in a practical sense, even though the relationship is statistically significant (probably not the work of sampling error).

There are certain types of statistical analyses that (among other things) determine the strength of relationships between variables. Some of them are discussed later in this book. They are what statisticians refer to generically as **measures of association,** and they produce an indicator of the strength of a relationship between variables, usually referred to as the **effect size.** (One example is Pearson's product moment correlation, discussed in Chapter 8.) Their statistical formulas produce a positive or negative number between 0 and 1.0 (a *correlation coefficient*) that can simply be squared to produce the effect size. How is this then interpreted? The squared number is the amount of variation in the outcome variable that is related to the predictor variable. For example, if .5 is the number produced by the formula, we can square it so that the squared number (.25) is the amount of variation (25 percent) in the outcome variable that is related to the predictor variable.

One other simple statistical procedure, which actually is called effect size (or simply ES), is especially helpful in clinical experiments in which the effectiveness of an intervention is examined by offering it to research participants in an experimental group but not to those in a control group. It uses a simple formula:

$$ES = \frac{\text{experimental group mean } - \text{ control group mean}}{\text{control group's standard deviation}}$$

The formula may look familiar. It is similar to the formula for the *z* score introduced in Chapter 4. In fact, ES can be interpreted with the use of the table that we used to convert raw scores to *z* scores and then into percentiles (Table 4.3).

Suppose that a social worker, Kelly, wishes to examine the effectiveness of a new type of assertiveness training (the independent variable). She randomly assigns 30 clients to an experimental group (that receives the treatment) and another 30 to a control group (that does not receive it). After the treatment, all 60 research participants take a standardized assertiveness test (the dependent variable). The mean score in the experimental group is 82, and the mean score in the control group is 78, with a control group standard deviation of 4. Using the appropriate test of statistical significance, the difference is found to be statistically significant (*p* < .05). But this still does not tell Kelly much about the strength of the relationship between treatment and assertiveness level. Perhaps the relationship between the independent and dependent variables was real, but relatively weak. How much effect did the intervention really have on assertiveness? Most importantly, the presence of statistical significance does not allow Kelly to compare the treatment's effectiveness with that of other, established methods of assertiveness training. So she computes the ES as:

$$ES = \frac{\text{experimental group mean} - \text{control group mean}}{\text{control group's standard deviation}}$$

$$ES = \frac{82 - 78}{4}$$

$$= \frac{4}{4}$$

$$= 1.0$$

The mean assertiveness score in the experimental group was 1.0 standard deviation (the ES) higher than the mean assertiveness score of the control group. Using Table 4.3, we can now put this into perspective. The average (mean) assertiveness score of those people in the experimental group was higher than 84.13 (50.00 + 34.13) percent of those people in the control group. This finding can now be used to help Kelly to understand something about the strength of the association between her variables (presence or absence of treatment and assertiveness scores). She can compute effect sizes for other similar studies of the effectiveness of traditional assertiveness training in her agency or elsewhere and then compare the results with her finding to determine if her treatment was more or less effective than the other treatments. This can be accomplished even if the other studies used another measure of association to compute effect size than the one Kelly used. Thus, like a *z* score, an effect size is a kind of common denominator that, among its other benefits, helps in the comparison of different data sets. Of course, we must always be careful in comparing research studies that may have used different instruments for measuring variables or research designs that may reflect different levels of rigor. We might still end up comparing apples and oranges.

Is the Relationship Surprising?

Other relationships, while fairly strong as indicated by measures of association, are already so well known that the discovery of them within a research study is of little or no value. How valuable would it be to learn at this time, for example, that among people there is a statistically significant relationship between the presence or absence of prenatal care and infant health, or between alcoholism and spouse abuse? Previous research studies have adequately demonstrated both of these relationships. We would be surprised (and the finding might be valuable) only if it were found to be otherwise.

Still other relationships between variables that could be found to be statistically significant would not be surprising. They are just logical to assume. For example, the "finding" that students who do not study at all do less well on a statistics exam than students who study at least 10 hours would be pretty much worthless. It is so logical that it would be totally expected.

Complex Interpretations of Statistically Significant Relationships

Attempting to decide whether a statistically significant relationship between variables is a meaningful finding (one that promises to improve the effectiveness of social work intervention) often is a complicated process. It may entail both an examination of effect size and an assessment of how surprising the finding is. It may involve other considerations as well. For example, it may require an administrator to make a judgment about whether she or he can justify the cost of retraining staff to use an intervention that has proven to be more effective than one currently being used in light of service delivery time lost during training or the need for the money elsewhere in the agency. Or it may require a social worker working in the community to assess the political effect of using an intervention that previous research studies have demonstrated to be effective but that may antagonize key supporters of the agency.

The existence of a statistically significant relationship between variables can be determined by statistical testing, which is based on the laws of probability. The determination of whether a finding is meaningful or not, however, requires judgment; it entails the use of insight into many different aspects of the social work practice milieu. Researchers now often report indicators of the actual strength of the relationship between variables (effect size) as well as other relevant information (such as the size of the research sample on which a statistical analysis was based). This additional information allows the reader to begin to make a more informed decision about the meaningfulness of a finding of statistical significance.

Of course, ideally, we would like any conclusion about relationships between or among variables to be a correct one. When this occurs, both social workers and their clients stand to benefit from the finding. For example, if we correctly identify a relationship between variables, it might help us to better understand some form of human behavior and/or to decide how best to intervene in working with some problem. Or, if we correctly conclude that two or more variables are unrelated, the finding might help to dispel some myth or harmful stereotype or allow us to identify and eliminate a service or program that is ineffective.

CONCLUDING THOUGHTS

This chapter examined the underlying logic of statistical testing for relationships between variables. Statistical analyses tell us the mathematical probability that an apparent relationship between variables may have been produced by sampling error, the natural tendency of a sample to differ from the population from which it was drawn. Thus, statistical testing really tests the null hypothesis and only indirectly tests a one-tailed or two-tailed research hypothesis. We have emphasized what statistical significance means—that sampling error is unlikely to have produced a relationship between variables found in a research sample. We also emphasized what it does not mean.

When we reject the null hypothesis and conclude that the relationship between variables is statistically significant, we run the risk of a Type I error. If we fail to reject the null hypothesis, the relationship may in fact be a real one (a Type II error). In deciding whether to reject the null form of a research hypothesis, we must consider the ethical implications of making either a Type I error or Type II error.

If we correctly reject the null hypothesis and conclude that the two variables probably are related in the population from which a sample was drawn, we still must address the issue of the value of such a finding. Even if we have statistical support for the likelihood of a true relationship between variables (in the form of statistical significance), the relationship may still be very weak, well known, or otherwise meaningless. We examined some ways to begin to evaluate these possibilities. Decisions about the value of a relationship between variables should always be made with reference to their potential to benefit or to harm those served, our clients.

STUDY QUESTIONS

1. Before we can claim a true relationship between variables, what alternative explanations for an apparent relationship must be eliminated?
2. Which one of the alternative explanations does statistical testing examine?
3. What alternative explanations are controlled primarily by the design of a research study?
4. What are some other terms for sampling error that are sometimes used?
5. What is the difference between a Type I and a Type II error? How does reducing the likelihood of committing one affect the likelihood of committing the other when the rejection level is adjusted either up or down from .05?
6. What is the null form of a statement (the null hypothesis) for a directional hypothesis about the relationship between the variables *age* and *political party preference?*
7. What is the relationship between the null hypothesis and sampling error in hypothesis testing?
8. Does a statistically significant relationship between variables mean that there is no possibility that the variables are unrelated? Explain.
9. When might we use a rejection level other than the conventional .05 to conclude whether statistical support exists for a research hypothesis? Provide examples from potential social work research studies.
10. Which rejection level, .01 or .10, suggests a greater likelihood of a true relationship between variables? Explain.
11. Discuss the advantages and disadvantages of implementing the results of a study that found a statistically significant 10 percent mean difference in job-performance level between the female and male social workers who work for an employee assistance program. Discuss what additional information you would want before taking action on the study's results. Justify any assumptions or recommendations.
12. Discuss what you would do with a research study's finding that there was a significant difference ($p < .05$) between the mean client hospital readmission rate for those workers who used Treatment *A* and those who used Treatment *B*. How would you use the fact that

Treatment *A* had a mean client readmission rate of 15 percent and Treatment *B* had a mean client readmission rate of 17 percent? Or the fact that Treatment *B* requires 25 percent more staff than Treatment *A*? Justify your answer. Does statistical analysis help us make an ethical decision in this situation? Why?

13. As an administrator of a local United Way agency, your job is to allocate funds for agencies that request them. Two agencies (*A* and *B*) require money from you so that they can stay in operation next year. Both offer the same services, but you have enough money to fund only one. Agency *A* states that its clients had a mean treatment success score of 42 on a standardized measuring instrument that measures client functioning ($N = 1,000$). Agency *B*, using the same measuring instrument, states that its mean treatment success score was 44 for the same period. Agency *B* also had 1,000 clients. You take these data and calculate the appropriate statistic to determine whether sampling error played any role in the difference in scores. Your statistical analysis produces a finding of $p < .25$. Will you be able to use your statistical analysis to decide which agency to fund? Why? Discuss what additional information you would want before taking action on the study's results. Justify your answer.

14. You are an administrator in a very large family service agency. There are two treatment techniques (*A* and *B*) that your workers use to help parents whose children have school truancy problems. Half your workers use Treatment *A*, and the other half use Treatment *B*. You conduct a research study to determine which treatment is more effective in reducing truancy. When they first applied for services, all children in the study were truant a mean of 5 times per month. After treatment, the parents who received Treatment *A* reported a mean of 2 instances of truancy per month, and the parents who received Treatment *B* reported a mean of 3 instances of truancy per month. The difference of 1 is statistically significant at the 0.05 rejection level. How could you use these findings?

6

Sampling Distributions and Testing the Null Hypothesis

Ideally, we would like to be able to draw a research sample that is perfectly representative (in every respect) of the population from which it was drawn. Then we could identify any relationships between or among variables within the sample and safely infer that they also must exist within the population. Unfortunately, it is not that easy. Even drawing a random sample from a population in no way assures its representativeness.

Because of sampling error, samples tend to differ from their populations. For example, if we draw a random sample of ten names from an active list of hospice patients their mean and standard deviation for the variable *years of employment* is unlikely to be exactly the same as that for all active patients. Similarly, two samples drawn from the same population tend to differ from each other. For example, two samples of ten patients each would be unlikely to have the same mean and standard deviation for years of employment. Because of sampling error, a sample is, at best, an estimate of what its population looks like.

In order to safely infer either that a relationship between or among variables in a sample is a real one that exists within its population, or that the differences between two samples is a real one, it is necessary to determine the probability that sampling error might have produced it. In this chapter, we introduce the concept of sampling distributions and the important role that they play in inferential statistics.

SAMPLE SIZE AND SAMPLING ERROR

In Chapter 5, we noted that smaller samples tend to differ more from their populations than larger samples and thus are more likely to contain more sampling error than larger samples. The way that sample size relates to sampling error can easily be demonstrated. Imagine a research class of 30 students. We could collect data on each student's overall grade point average (GPA) and compute an overall mean GPA for the entire population of students ($N = 30$). Let us say that the mean GPA for the entire class of 30 students is 3.0, with a standard deviation of .5. The population's mean and its standard deviation (which would not contain sampling error) would be known respectively as its **true mean** and its **true standard deviation.**

If we were to draw a single random sample of three students ($n = 3$) from the entire class of 30 students and determine this sample's mean GPA and standard deviation, we would not expect them to be exactly the same as the population's mean and standard deviation. In fact, we probably would expect the mean and standard deviation to be different, perhaps quite different, and we would be surprised if they were exactly the same as the true mean and true standard deviation. The sample's mean GPA and standard deviation would almost certainly differ from the population's mean GPA and standard deviation—that is, it would contain a considerable amount of sampling error.

With the above in mind, now suppose that we draw a single random sample of 10 students from the same class of 30 students. We still would not expect the sample's mean GPA and standard deviation to be exactly 3.0 and .5 respectively. We would predict, however, that the sample's mean and standard deviation are likely to be closer to the population's mean and standard deviation than was the case with the 3-student sample because sample sizes of 10 are closer to "the long run" (see Chapter 5) than sample sizes of 3. Thus, the law of averages is more likely to take over with larger samples than with smaller ones. What do we mean by this? Suppose that the first 3 cases drawn for a sample of 10 are among the lowest GPAs in the class. This pattern is unlikely to continue as the sample size approaches 10. Why? Because 3 of the lowest cases have already been selected, there are now a disproportionate number of higher GPAs left from which to draw. Thus, later selections are quite likely to be those with higher GPAs. The higher GPAs will help balance out the lower ones, and the mean for the sample of 10 will look closer to the true mean than it did with the smaller sample of only 3. With a sample of only 3, if the 3 cases drawn have very low GPAs, there would be no opportunity to balance them out with subsequent selections. A very low sample mean will result. Because of the same phenomenon (really a matter of probability), a sample of 10 is also theoretically more likely to have a standard deviation that is closer to the true standard deviation (.5) than a sample of 3. Of course, as we know, what is theoretically more likely to happen does not always happen, especially if only one sample is drawn. Although unlikely, a sample of 3 *could be* more representative than a sample of 10!

Let us now take this example to its extreme. If we were to draw a random sample of 29 students, we still might expect the sample's mean GPA and standard deviation to differ a little from the population's mean GPA of 3.0 and standard deviation of .5, but the difference would probably be very small, much less than with a sample size of 3 or even 10. There would be very little room for sampling error, because only 1 case in the population would not be included in a sample of 29. (Of course, we would be highly unlikely to study a sample of 29 students out of 30. At that point, we might as well study the entire population of 30 students so that there would be no opportunity for sampling error.)

When a sample is selected, we want it to be representative of the population from which it was drawn. That makes it possible to generalize a finding from a sample to its population. To summarize, could a sample of 3 cases be perfectly representative of a population of 30, that is, have the same mean and standard deviation? Theoretically, yes, but this would happen very rarely in drawing many samples of 3 and replacing cases each time before drawing the next sample. Most samples would look quite different from the population and from each other.

If many samples of 10 are drawn from the same population, there might be a few more of these samples that would be perfectly representative of the population—the samples as a group would look more like the population than the samples of 3 cases. They would also be more similar to each other than the samples of 3 cases.

With samples of 29, even more might be perfectly representative and, among those that were not, their means and standard deviations would still be very close to the true mean and standard deviation. The samples also would be very similar to each other.

It should be clear by now that smaller samples are more likely to contain more sampling error and thus to be less representative of their populations than larger samples. Although it is theoretically possible to draw a small representative sample, it will happen much less frequently in many repetitions than if larger samples are drawn.

SAMPLING DISTRIBUTIONS AND INFERENCE

Samples tend to vary from their populations—we can never assume that a sample's characteristics (statistics) are the same as those of its population (parameters). We can assume, however, that there is some degree of similarity between a sample and its population. (If this were not the case, why would we study a sample in the first place?)

A good estimate of the amount of sampling error within a sample would help us know to what degree we might be safe in inferring that a characteristic of a sample is also true of its population. Let us say, for example, that we observe a relationship between *political conservatism* and some other variable, such as *gender,* within a sample of cases. It would be helpful to know how accurate an estimate the mean conservatism score of the people in our sample is of the mean conservatism score of people in the population before we infer that the relationship within the sample really exists within the population. Or, how closely its mode, median, interquartile range, or standard deviation approximate their counterparts within the population. This is why we need sampling distributions. **Sampling distributions** are social constructs that take into consideration the size of a sample and how much sampling error it theoretically may contain. They are a third (hypothetical) distribution (along with the distribution of a variable in a sample and the true distribution of that variable in its population). They are the necessary link between the other two that makes inference possible.

Comparing an Experimental Sample with Its Population

An estimate of the similarity of a sample to its population helps us gauge to what degree a drawn sample is sufficiently representative of its population in relation to one or more variables—usually dependent variables. If we can determine that a sample is sufficiently representative of its population, for example, we can then use this sample to introduce an independent variable and observe its effect on the dependent variable. Because the sample was assumed to be representative of its population, we can then infer (within limits, that is) that the effect on the dependent variable for the sample would also have occurred on that dependent variable if we had introduced the independent variable to the entire population.

Let us use another example of how an estimate of sampling error might be helpful in analyzing research findings. Suppose we wanted to evaluate the effectiveness of a new intervention designed to improve self-esteem among clients. We could draw a random sample of 25 clients ($n = 25$) previously identified as having low self-esteem and offer them our intervention. The intervention would not be offered to the rest of the population. (Our sample could thus be considered an experimental group.) We could then compare the people in the sample with the population from which they were drawn in relation to the dependent variable *self-esteem*. We could attempt to find support for a one-tailed research hypothesis:

> The experimental group will have a higher mean self-esteem level than the population's mean self-esteem level.

We can find support (or nonsupport) for this one-tailed research hypothesis by testing its null form. The null form of the above hypothesis would be:

> There will be *no difference* between the experimental group's mean self-esteem level and the population's mean self-esteem level.

Let us say that the mean self-esteem score for the people in the experimental group (after receiving the intervention) was 69, and the mean score for the population was 64 (higher scores = higher self-esteem). The null hypothesis contends that any difference between the two means is due to sampling error. Specifically, in our example, it would suggest that the 5-point average difference in self-esteem between the experimental group and the rest of the population is explained by the fact that they were not comparable in self-esteem levels to begin with—the experimental group may have been higher in self-esteem before receiving the intervention just because of sampling error. In determining how safe it would be to reject the null hypothesis, we would have to know what percentage of the time, in drawing an infinite number of samples of 25 cases each, a sample would have a mean that is at least 5 points higher than the population, based only on sampling error.

Comparing a Non-Experimental Sample with Its Population

For either ethical or practical reasons, we may not be able to introduce or manipulate an independent variable within a specific research sample to study the independent variables effect on the dependent variable. Or we may simply wish to study a specific category of people (or objects) contained within a population (a sample) to see if they differ from the general population in some way. For example, we might be able to identify a sample of 35 people ($N = 35$) who know they are HIV positive and ask them to complete a standardized self-report measuring instrument that measures the variable *self-esteem*. We could then compare the self-esteem level of the people in our sample with the general population's mean self-esteem level, with the use of a data-collection instrument (such as a scale) that has been "normed" on the general population. We could then test the following one-tailed research hypothesis:

> People who know that they are HIV positive have a lower self-esteem level than the general population's self-esteem level.

We would seek support for the above one-tailed research hypothesis by testing its null form:

> People who know that they are HIV positive have the same self-esteem level as the general population.

Let us say that the mean self-esteem score for the 35 people in our sample was 61, and the mean score for the population was 64 (higher scores = higher self-esteem). The null hypothesis contends that any difference between the two means (i.e., 61, 64) is due to sampling error. In determining how safe it would be to reject the null hypothesis, we would have to know what percentage of the time, in drawing an infinite number of samples of 35 cases each, would a sample have a mean that is at least 3 points lower, ($64 - 61 = 3$) than the population, based only on sampling error. That would help us determine whether we should reject the null hypothesis by telling us that the difference did or did not occur because of sampling error.

At this point it might be a good idea to reiterate that the null hypothesis is only a statistical hypothesis related to the laws of probability. Rejecting it does not in itself provide adequate support for the research hypothesis. Since our sample of 35 people was not randomly drawn to begin with (it was, of necessity, more of a convenience sample), we may still want to try to determine whether our sample was biased in some way before concluding that we have support for our research hypothesis that states people who are HIV positive have lower self-esteem levels than the general population. Perhaps, for example, our 35 sample members were identified from files of people actively seeking counseling and thus are not truly representative of all people who are HIV positive. That may make them atypical—they may have lower self-esteem than those people who are HIV positive who feel no need to seek counseling or who seek other forms of help.

SAMPLING DISTRIBUTION OF MEANS

Because a sampling distribution is a social construct, it does not exist in reality and is only theoretical. Specifically, it is based on the theoretical results of drawing an infinite number of samples of a certain size from a population. We could, for example, theoretically construct a sampling distribution of the means for samples of 25 students for the variable *SAT scores* (combined verbal and math) among BSW students enrolled in accredited departments and schools of social work in North America in the current year (a specific population at a specific time). Let us also assume that these scores form a normal distribution within the population with a mean of 1,000 and a standard deviation of 200. To create a sampling distribution of the means for samples of 25 students, we would (theoretically) have to randomly draw an infinite number of samples of 25 students from this population, replacing cases each time before the next sample is drawn. We would then compute the mean SAT score for each sample. A frequency polygon for the means of all of these samples would have three interesting characteristics:

1. It would be a normal distribution.
2. Its mean would be the same as the population mean (1,000).
3. Its standard deviation is called the *standard error of the mean.* It is not the same as the standard deviation of the population. It is computed as:

$$\frac{\text{the standard deviation (population)}}{\text{square root of the sample size}}$$

It should not be surprising that the mean of a sampling distribution is the same as the mean of the population from which it was constructed. Means of individual samples vary from the population's mean and from each other. But because any sampling distribution (of any size sample) is based on an infinite number of samples of SAT scores, the law of averages (the long run) eventually prevails. Samples with lower means and those with higher means cancel each other out when they are averaged together. Thus the **mean of the means** is exactly the same as the true mean (the mean of the population), no matter what sample size produced the sampling distribution.

Similarly, we expect that the frequency distribution to be a normal distribution. In sampling distributions of samples of any size, most sample means are relatively close to the true mean, and increasingly fewer would occur as we move farther below or above the true mean.

The third characteristic of a sampling distribution of means may be a little more surprising, at least until we think about it. The **standard error of the mean** is not simply the standard deviation of the population. Why not? Sample size (and thus sampling error) must be factored in. Recall that we demonstrated earlier that smaller samples are more likely to have more sampling error than larger samples. Remember also that as larger samples are drawn, the probability of drawing either all small values or all large ones decreases. The formula for the standard error of the mean (whose origins are beyond the scope of this text) takes this into account—it adjusts for sample size.

In our example above, the standard error of the mean is:

$$\text{standard deviation (population)} = \frac{200}{\text{square root of the sample size (5)}}$$
$$= 40$$

We could now add the standard error of the mean to the frequency polygon. We could determine that any given sample's mean was a certain distance—that is, units of standard error or z scores—above or below its true (population) mean. Finally, we could take the z score of that sample mean and use a table of the normal curve (i.e., Table 4.3) to determine the percentile that corresponds to that specific z score (as we did in Chapter 4). This percentile will tell us what percent of all samples will have a mean at or below the mean of our sample. We will see how valuable this can be for testing hypotheses in the next section of this chapter.

When drawing samples from a given population, there is a different sampling distribution of means for each sample size. The size of their respective standard deviations (their standard error of the mean) will vary depending on the size of the sample on which they are based. Sampling distributions constructed from smaller samples will have larger standard deviations than sampling distributions constructed from larger samples.

Returning to our example, if we draw an infinite number of samples of only 4 students and compute the mean SAT score for each individual sample size, the means of all samples will vary widely from one another. Some samples might (theoretically) consist of the four highest scores; that is, they will have very high means. Other samples might consist of the four lowest scores, which will produce very low means. It would be impossible to produce a sample with a mean at either extreme with our earlier sample of 25 students. Even if we somehow selected the top 25 scores (or the bottom 25 scores), the mean of the sample would still be closer to the true population's mean. Thus, there would be less variation overall (standard error of the mean) in the larger samples than in the smaller ones. Let us confirm this logical conclusion mathematically. For samples of 4, the standard error of the mean would be:

$$\text{standard deviation (population)} = \frac{200}{\text{square root of the sample size (2)}}$$
$$= 100$$

Figure 6.1 is a sampling distribution for sample sizes of 4. Note how its standard error differs from the sampling distribution for samples of 25 as presented in Figure 6.2.

Notice too that in both sampling distributions there is no y axis containing numbers (frequencies). The actual frequencies for any given sample mean cannot be calculated, because a sampling distribution is based on an infinite number of samples of a given size.

There are two other factors that determine what a theoretical sampling distribution for a given variable might look like—the shape of the distribution of the population

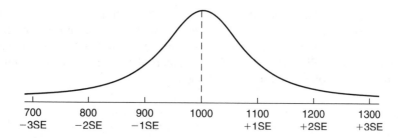

FIGURE 6.1   **Sampling Distribution of Mean SAT Scores:**
$N = 4, SE = 100$

and whether its true mean and distribution are known. However, these factors are not as important as it might be logical to assume.

Samples Drawn from Normal Distributions

If our variable of interest, usually the dependent variable, is normally distributed within its population, it is possible to combine our knowledge of normal distributions with the contents of this chapter to determine if there is support for research hypotheses.

To do so, can use what is generally referred to as the *z* **test** frequently, we conduct research studies to see if a treatment intervention makes a difference. We may wish to know, for example, if a particular type of group experience seems to improve clients' appreciation of diversity.

Let us say that client appreciation of diversity scores on a particular standardized measuring instrument is normally distributed among 1,000 clients in an agency with a known mean of 50 (standard deviation = 5). Higher scores (values) indicate greater appreciation of diversity than lower scores. We then randomly select a sample of 16

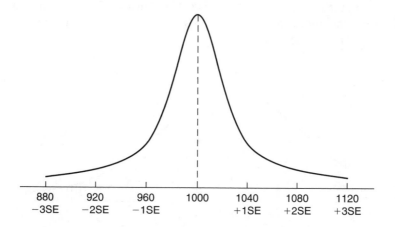

FIGURE 6.2   **Sampling Distribution of Mean SAT Scores:**
$N = 25, SE = 40$

clients from the population of 1,000, provide a group treatment intervention to this sample (an experimental group), and calculate the experimental group's mean appreciation of diversity score (e.g., 60) to see if it is significantly higher than its population's mean appreciation of diversity score of 50 (standard deviation = 5). We could write this assumption as a one-tailed research hypothesis:

> The mean appreciation of diversity score of the experimental group will be higher than the mean appreciation of diversity score of the population.

To test the null form of our one-tailed research hypothesis, we need to compare data drawn from our 16-member sample with a table of the areas of the normal curve (i.e., Table 4.3). We thus compare our sample's mean appreciation of diversity score with the score that we might expect to get from simply drawing a random sample (of a given size) from a population and offering no intervention to those clients.

By using the concepts of rejection regions and the standard error of the mean, we can determine just how typical or atypical our experimental group (or sample) is in relation to how appreciation of diversity scores are distributed within the population ($N = 1,000$) from which our sample ($N = 16$) was drawn. The term **rejection region** refers to two specific regions of a normal curve (see Figure 6.3). When one of the rejection regions contains a measurement from a sample, this suggests that it is safe to reject the null hypothesis. In order to understand the concept of rejection regions, we rely heavily on the use of normal distributions and z scores as presented in Chapter 4.

Rejection Regions for Two-Tailed Research Hypotheses.

The rejection region for statistics that test the null form of research hypotheses depends on (1) the rejection level selected and (2) whether the research hypothesis is one tailed or two tailed.

In the above example, we hypothesized that our group experience intervention would increase the appreciation of diversity of experimental group members (a one-tailed research hypothesis). However, what if our research hypothesis had been two tailed? In a two-tailed research hypothesis, we would just say that our group intervention will affect the appreciation of diversity of our experimental group, but not whether it would raise or lower it:

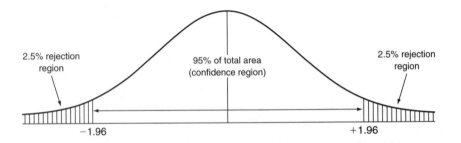

FIGURE 6.3   The Normal Distribution Showing the 95% Confidence Region and the Two 2.5% Rejection Regions for Two-Tailed Research Hypotheses

The experimental group's appreciation of diversity scores will be different than the population's appreciation of diversity scores.

For two-tailed research hypotheses, the z scores of the two rejection regions (the point where they begin) are located using procedures similar to those discussed in Chapter 4 (and Table 4.3) that are used to locate a raw score's corresponding z score. The steps for locating the two rejection regions for two-tailed research hypotheses are:

1. Divide the selected rejection level by 2.
2. Subtract the derived value from .50, and multiply by 100.
3. Locate the derived proportion in the body of a normal distribution table (i.e., Table 4.3).
4. Determine the z score that corresponds to that proportion.

If we are using the conventional .05 rejection level, for example, the calculations for the preceding four steps would look like this:

1. .05/2 = .025.
2. (.50 − .025) × 100 = 47.50 (1/2 of 95.00).
3. Find 47.50 in the body of a normal distribution table (i.e., Table 4.3).
4. The z score corresponding to 47.50 is +1.96 or −1.96.

How do we interpret the results of these calculations? When a rejection level of .05 is used, the rejection regions for a two-tailed research hypothesis are the areas at or above $z = +1.96$ and at or below $z = -1.96$. Such a result must be achieved in order to reject the null hypothesis for a two-tailed research hypothesis. Figure 6.3 provides a graphical illustration of this concept.

If we had used a two-tailed research hypothesis, the experimental group's mean appreciation of diversity score would have to be at least 1.96 standard deviations higher than (i.e., + 1.96) or at least 1.96 standard deviations lower than (i.e., −1.96) the population's mean appreciation of diversity score of 50. As we know, the standard deviation of the sampling distribution of the means (more correctly referred to as the standard error of the mean or just standard error) that we use to test the null hypothesis is not simply the standard deviation for the population. The standard deviation that we use must be specific to the size of the sample, in our example 16. It is the standard deviation of the parent population (in this case 5) divided by the square root of the sample size (in this case 4). In our example, 5 divided by 4 equals 1.25.

Thus, to feel reasonably safe in rejecting the null hypothesis for our two-tailed research hypothesis, our experimental group's mean appreciation of diversity score would have to be

at least 1.96 × 1.25, or 2.45 points, *higher* than 50, or at least 52.45

or

at least 1.96 × 1.25, or 2.45 points, *lower* than 50, or less than 47.55

It should be noted that $+1.96$ or -1.96 is the required z score for all two-tailed research hypotheses that use the .05 rejection level, not just the one in our example. Only the standard deviation for the sample (the standard error of the mean) will vary within the equation, based on the sample's size and its square root.

Rejection Regions for One-Tailed Research Hypotheses.   Now let us return to our original one-tailed research hypothesis:

> The appreciation of diversity scores of the experimental group will be higher than the appreciation of diversity scores of the population.

Now where would the rejection region lie for this one-tailed research hypotheses? Because it predicts the direction of a relationship between two variables, there is a simple variation in the above procedure for obtaining its appropriate rejection region—the selected rejection level is *not* divided by 2. Thus, the .05 rejection region for a one-tailed research hypothesis is derived as follows:

1. $.50 - .05 = .45 \times 100 = 45.00$
2. Find 45.00 in the body of a normal distribution table (i.e., Table 4.3).
3. The z score corresponding to 45.00 is $+1.65$ or -1.65.

How do we interpret the results of this calculation? When using a one-tailed research hypothesis and a rejection level of .05, the calculated z must be at least $+1.65$ or -1.65 in order to reject the null hypothesis. We would use only one or the other, because a directional hypothesis, by definition, would predict not only the existence of a relationship between variables but its direction as well. Which cutoff point would we use in our example—the $+1.65$ or the -1.65? In order to claim support for our one-tailed research hypothesis, the experimental group's mean appreciation of diversity score would have to be at least $+1.65$ standard deviations *higher* than the population's mean score of 50. That is because we hypothesized that our experimental group would have *a higher* mean appreciation of diversity score than is found within the population from which it was drawn. If, instead, we had hypothesized that our experimental group's mean appreciation of diversity score would be lower than that of the population, we would have used the $z = -1.65$ cutoff point.

Because our sample size is still 16, the standard error of the mean for our sampling distribution would be the same as when we had a two-tailed research hypothesis—1.25. With a one-tailed research hypothesis, however, our experimental group's mean appreciation of diversity score would now have to be at least $1.65 \times 1.25 = 2.0625$, rounded off to 2.1 points, higher than 50 for us to reject the null hypothesis.

Thus, our experimental group's mean appreciation of diversity score would have to be at least 52.1 for us to be reasonably certain (95 percent) that there really is a predicted association between the treatment intervention and our experimental group's relatively higher levels of appreciation of diversity when compared to the population from which our sample was dream.

Figure 6.4 graphically portrays the rejection region ($z =$ at least $+1.65$) for a one-tailed research hypothesis where the upper tail is specified as the rejection region.

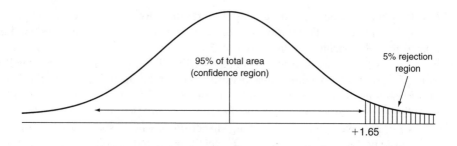

FIGURE 6.4   **The Normal Distribution Showing the 95% Confidence Region
and the One 5% Rejection Region for an Upper One-Tailed Research Hypothesis**

Likewise, Figure 6.5 provides an illustration of the rejection region ($z =$ at least -1.65) for a one-tailed research hypothesis where the lower tail is specified. Unlike Figure 6.3, that contains true rejection regions, Figure 6.4 and 6.5 contain only one rejection region, the one that reflects the direction of the one-tailed research hypothesis.

When using a normal distribution to test a one-tailed research hypothesis, only z scores that fall within the specified rejection region allow us to reject the null hypothesis. A sample statistic (in this instance, the mean) in the region suggests that the probability that sampling error produced the relationship between the two variables in our sample is less than .05. We could conclude that by selecting an infinite number of samples of 16 and offering no intervention, we could expect to draw a sample with a mean appreciation of diversity score that differs from the mean of its population by at least 1.65 standard deviations in the predicted direction less than 5 times out of 100. So, we would be able to claim that sampling error is unlikely to explain the relationship between our experimental group's intervention and the appreciation of diversity scores. We could state that the relationship between the variables was found to be statistically significant.

By glancing at Figures 6.3, 6.4, and 6.5, it can be observed that a one-tailed research hypothesis has certain advantages. As can be seen, it moves the critical rejection regions closer to the mean of the sampling distribution, thus improving the probability of rejecting the null hypothesis. This is only logical; when we predict the

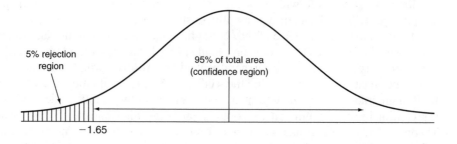

FIGURE 6.5   **The Normal Distribution Showing the 95% Confidence Region
and the One 5% Rejection Region for a Lower One-Tailed Research Hypothesis**

direction of a relationship with a one-tailed research hypothesis, we should get "extra credit" if support for the relationship between two variables and the predicted direction of the relationship is found. As noted in the previous chapter, using a one-tailed hypothesis (if it can be justified) can decrease the likelihood of making a Type II error (missing a true relationship between variables). A relationship in which the direction of the relationship was predicted and then found to exist is less likely to be the work of sampling error than one in which the direction was not predicted in advance.

Note, however, that if the wrong direction has been specified in a one-tailed research hypothesis—that is, if we incorrectly predicted the direction of the relationship—the probability of the rejection of null hypothesis is zero. There simply is no rejection region on the other side of the distribution. As noted in the previous chapter, we are given no prediction credit for results that were the exact opposite of what we predicted in the first place. Thus one-tailed research hypotheses should not be used unless the direction of a relationship can be confidently predicted.

Samples Drawn from Skewed Distributions

Although many variables are normally distributed within their populations the distributions of many other variables are skewed, as illustrated in Figure 4.7. What would the sampling distribution of the means look like for a variable when its a sampling distribution is skewed? In other words, what would be the shape of a frequency polygon of means from an infinite number of "same-size" samples randomly drawn from a population in which the variable is not normally distributed? Actually, it will approximate a normal distribution if the size of the sample is fairly large. This fact is based on what is called the ***central limit theorem,*** which states that if the size of the sample is large, the sampling distribution of means created from a variable that is skewed within its population will be approximately normal. It will be more normal (bell shaped) for very large samples than for smaller samples. The standard deviation (standard error) of large samples is computed the same way as with normally distributed variables.

How large is large enough to produce a sampling distribution that is normally distributed? It depends on the shape of the distribution within the population—that is, its amount of skewness. In most skewed distributions, a sample of 30 is usually large enough to produce a sampling distribution that is essentially a normal one, as portrayed in Figures 6.1- 6.5 in addition to Figures 4.5, 4.6, and 4.8. Sometimes, if the distribution of a variable within its population is only slightly skewed, even smaller sample sizes will produce normal sampling distributions.

To indicate the importance of the central limit theorem, we will use an example to which we all can relate. The scores on a standardized statistics test administered to all MSW students in North America generally would not form a normal distribution. They tend to be negatively skewed within the student population, with most students getting fairly high grades and a small number (outliers) getting quite low grades. What does the central limit theorem tell us about a sampling distribution of this variable? Theoretically, we could take the scores of all MSW students and randomly draw an infinite number of samples of 30 students, replacing each student's score before each subsequent sample is drawn. We could then compute the mean for each sample of 30. We could take all of the sample means and create a histogram and a frequency polygon, as described in Chapter 2. According to the central limit theorem, the frequency polygon created from these samples would approximate a normal curve, even though the scores within the population are negatively skewed.

ESTIMATING PARAMETERS

With what we have learned so far, we can now produce a reasonably accurate estimate of a variable's parameter (a characteristic of a population) from the variable's statistic (a measurement of a variable taken from a sample). This procedure is called **parameter estimation.**

To understand parameter estimation, we need to introduce two related terms—confidence interval and confidence level. A **confidence interval** is a range into which we would estimate a population parameter to fall based on a sample statistic. A **confidence level** is an estimate of the probability that the true population parameter lies within the confidence interval. Together, a confidence level and its corresponding confidence interval form an estimate of the true parameter based on a statistic. Thus, in conducting a parameter estimation, we seek to fill in the three blanks in the following statement:

> Based on measurement of variable *x* within our sample (a statistic), there is a ____ percent probability that the true mean of variable *x* within the population from which it was drawn (a parameter) is between ____ and ____.

In the above statement, the first blank is the confidence level. The second and third blanks are the lower and upper limits of the confidence interval. How would we arrive at the correct three numbers to fill in these three blanks? We set the first blank's number to reflect how confident we wish to be that the true population mean falls within our confidence interval (second and third blanks). If we want to be 95 percent confident that it will (the conventional level comparable to .05), we use the 95 percent confidence level; if we want to be 99 percent confident, we use the 99 percent confidence level; and so on.

What about the two remaining blanks that deal with the confidence interval? How do we arrive at the correct numbers to place in them? By applying logic, we can see that finding the lower and upper limits of a confidence interval is easier than we might think. Suppose we want to estimate the client satisfaction scores of all 2,000 (population) active clients in a large public social service agency. It might be impractical to administer the standardized client satisfaction measuring instrument to the entire population of 2,000. We can, however, estimate the population's mean client satisfaction score, by simply asking 100 randomly selected clients drawn from this population to complete the measuring instrument and then computing this sample's mean client satisfaction score.

Let us say that our sample's mean client satisfaction score is 40. Perhaps we believe that the variable *client satisfaction* is normally distributed in the population from which it was drawn. But whether it is or is not is not important, because our sample is considered sufficiently large (well over 30). Thus, the standard error of the mean will be the same either way (a conclusion based on the central limit theorem). This fact is important to an understanding of how we arrive at confidence intervals.

The true parameter (the population mean) can be thought of as the mean of the sample, plus or minus some amount of sampling error. We can never exactly determine how large this error is, but there are some things that we can determine. First, we can determine the probability distribution of all possible errors in an infinite number of samples of 100 cases—the sampling distribution of these errors. Because the sample is fairly large, we already know that the distribution will be normally distributed.

Second, we can determine the standard error of the mean. Our standardized client satisfaction measuring instrument has a known mean of 50 and a standard deviation of 5. Using the formula presented earlier, the standard error of the mean (standard deviation of the sampling distribution) is the standard deviation of the population (5) divided by the square root of the sample size ($N = 100$). So the calculation would be $5/10 = .5$ (the standard error). We know that a probability distribution of the sample means in an infinite number of random samples of 100 drawn from a population would form a normal distribution with a standard error of .5, or one-half point.

Constructing a 95 Percent Confidence Interval

Suppose we want to be 95 percent confident that the true client satisfaction score of all active clients falls between two scores (the confidence interval) of our sample's mean of 40. Remember that 95 percent of a normal distribution lies between the points $z = -1.96$ and $z = +1.96$. This can be verified with the use of Table 4.3; it is also illustrated earlier in this chapter (see Figure 6.3). We now can arrive at our confidence interval as presented below:

Lower limit ($N = 100$):

$$
\begin{aligned}
\text{sample mean} &= 40.00 \\
-1.96 \times .5 \text{ (standard error)} &= \underline{-.98} \\
&= 39.02
\end{aligned}
$$

Upper limit ($N = 100$):

$$
\begin{aligned}
\text{sample mean} &= 40.00 \\
+1.96 \times .5 \text{ (standard error)} &= \underline{+.98} \\
&= 40.98
\end{aligned}
$$

Now we can fill in the blanks and state the following:

Based on measurement of client satisfaction within our sample ($N = 100$), there is a *95 percent* probability that the true mean of client satisfaction among clients in the agency is between *39.02* and *40.98*.

Constructing a 99 Percent Confidence Interval

Using the same data, we also could have produced a confidence interval reflecting a 99 percent confidence level. With the use of Table 4.3, we could learn that over 99 percent of the distribution would fall between the z scores -2.58 and $+2.58$ more than 49.50 percent of a normal distribution falls between a z score of ±2.58 and the mean). Instead of using $z = +1.96$ or -1.96 this time, as we did to find the confidence interval for a 95 percent confidence level, we would now use $z = +2.58$ or -2.58 instead:

Lower limit (N = 100):

$$\begin{aligned} \text{sample mean} &= 40.00 \\ -2.58 \times .5 \text{ (standard error)} &= \underline{-1.29} \\ &= 38.71 \end{aligned}$$

Upper limit (N = 100):

$$\begin{aligned} \text{sample mean} &= 40.00 \\ +2.58 \times .5 \text{ (standard error)} &= \underline{+1.29} \\ &= 41.29 \end{aligned}$$

Now we can state the following:

Based on measurement of client satisfaction within the sample ($n = 100$), there is a *99* percent probability that the true mean of client satisfaction among clients in the agency is between *38.71* and *41.29*.

Note that whether we use the 95 or 99 percent confidence levels, the confidence interval each one contains may seem quite small—it encompasses just a few points. This is because a sample of 100 cases is quite large in the absolute sense. We would expect that any sample of 100 would have a relatively small sampling error, because a sample of 100 would begin to approximate "the long run."

Let us take the same example to illustrate how decreasing the size of a sample affects the upper and lower limits of a 95 percent confidence interval. This time we will use a sample size of 25 instead of 100. Remember, the square root of 25 is 5, so the standard error for a sampling distribution of samples of 25 is now $5/5 = 1$.

Lower limit (N = 25):

$$\begin{aligned} \text{sample mean} &= 40.00 \\ -1.96 \times 1 \text{ (standard error)} &= \underline{-1.96} \\ &= 38.04 \end{aligned}$$

Upper limit (N = 25):

$$\begin{aligned} \text{sample mean} &= 40.00 \\ +1.96 \times 1 \text{ (standard error)} &= \underline{+1.96} \\ &= 41.96 \end{aligned}$$

Now we can state the following:

Based on measurement of client satisfaction within our sample ($N = 25$), there is a *95* percent probability that the true mean of client satisfaction among clients in the agency is between *38.04* and *41.96*.

The 95 percent confidence interval using a sample size of 100 ranges from 39.02 to 40.98 (a range of 1.96 points). The sampling interval for a sample size of 25 ranges from 38.04 to 41.96 (a range of 3.92 points). Thus, the smaller the sample, the larger the range of the confidence interval, and the larger the sample, the smaller the range of the confidence interval. This should not be surprising, because we know now that a sample of 100 should contain less sampling error than a sample of 25.

CONCLUDING THOUGHTS

This chapter expanded on the preceding one by presenting the theoretical underpinning of sampling distributions and how they relate to inference. The chapter examined how our knowledge of normal distributions, when integrated with the concept of sampling distributions, is used to answer two related questions that are integral to inference: (1) How well does the sample serve as an estimate of the population from which it was drawn? and (2) How confident can we be that the true mean of the population falls within a certain range of values? The first question is answered through the use of rejection regions. The latter question is answered through the use of confidence levels and confidence intervals.

The methods of statistical analyses presented in Chapters 8 through 12 rely heavily on the concepts and ideas presented in Chapters 5 and 6. An understanding of sampling distributions is critical to understanding how researchers use statistical tests to determine whether it is safe to conclude that they have support for their research hypotheses.

STUDY QUESTIONS

1. Discuss how sample size is directly related to sampling error. Use an original example to demonstrate your understanding.
2. Discuss how sampling distributions are used for inference.
3. What exactly is a sampling distribution of means? Explain in detail how a sampling distribution of means is used in constructing the rejection regions for one-tailed and two-tailed research hypotheses.
4. Discuss how a sampling distribution of means derived from numerous large samples drawn from a skewed population will form a normal distribution.
5. Discuss the concept of parameter estimation. How is it useful for social workers?
6. What is a rejection region? What is a confidence level? What is a confidence interval? Discuss how the three concepts are related to each other. Provide original examples throughout your discussion.
7. Discuss how the standard error of the mean is calculated. Is the standard error of the mean smaller or larger in samples of 12 than in samples of 24? Why?

7

Selecting a Statistical Test

The two previous chapters presented a general discussion of how we use statistics to decide if we have support for research hypotheses. They described how, using the laws of probability, it is possible to determine the likelihood that sampling error may have produced a relationship between variables within a sample that was drawn from a population. Assuming that rival hypotheses and design flaws (i.e., measurement error, sampling bias) have been adequately controlled we are now in a position to estimate how safe it would be to conclude that the relationship between variables contained in our sample is a real one—that is, that the relationship actually exists in the population from which the sample was drawn.

There are many different statistical tests that can be used to see how safe it is to claim support for a one-tailed or two-tailed research hypothesis. All of these tests rely on the principles presented in Chapters 5 and 6. This chapter completes our discussion of hypothesis testing and presents basic issues that need to be addressed when selecting the most appropriate statistical test to use, given the level of measurement and distribution of the variables.

THE IMPORTANCE OF SELECTING THE CORRECT TEST

The manner in which a research study is conducted has the potential to enhance—or to harm—the credibility of the study's findings and, thus, the recommendations made from the study's data. Relying on literature that presents only one side of an issue, for example, or choosing to use a measuring instrument that may not be valid with the research participants being studied, using a sampling method that may not produce a representative sample, or using a data-collection method that may influence the data themselves can introduce biases into the study's findings and may cause the reader to doubt the study's credibility.

Even if all the other research tasks have been completed well, that is, the study was well designed and implemented, the credibility of the findings still can be jeopardized by an additional error—the selection of an inappropriate statistical test of inference. A critical reader of a research report always asks, "Was the appropriate data-analysis method used to seek support for the study's research hypothesis?" If not, the study's findings may produce only skepticism at best.

Where Can We Go Wrong?

Why are inappropriate statistical tests sometimes chosen when appropriate ones are available for almost any type of data analysis? Frequently, it is because of the principle referred to as the **rule of the instrument.** This means that people often see the solution to any problem as requiring what they know and/or do best—that is, that with which they are most comfortable and familiar. There are many examples of this principle. Take, for example, the responses of different groups of people to fatal shootings within American schools. Many social workers suggest hiring more school social workers to identify and counsel young people who may feel alienated from their peers. Corrections professionals may think the money might better be spent on metal detectors or placement of armed guards within the schools. Politicians may believe the problem can best be addressed by passing tighter gun-control laws. Religious leaders may see the solution as better moral education, and so forth. In short, both the problem and its solution can easily be defined from one's own perspective or vantage point.

How might the rule of the instrument affect the selection of a statistical test? Many of us, particularly those of us who received our social work education quite some time ago, did not receive extensive training in data analyses. Our knowledge is often confined to familiarity with only one or two statistical tests. Facing the necessity of choosing a test to analyze the relationship between or among variables, we may have a tendency to turn to the one with which we are most familiar, rather than explore the possibility of using a lesser-known or more recently developed one.

In the past, there has also been a tendency to turn to statistical tests that require only relatively simple mathematical calculations and to avoid those that have more complex formulas. There may have been some justification for this when calculations had to be done by hand or calculator—using difficult formulas was time-consuming and the potential for making mathematical errors was great. However, with the current availability of computers and statistical software, there is now no excuse for using anything but the best, that is, the most appropriate test. In fact, once data have been entered, it takes no more than a second or two longer to use a highly complicated test (for example, a multivariate one) than a simpler one. And, there will be no mathematical errors.

There also is a widely held misconception that because statistical tests have so much in common, it makes little difference which one is used. After all, they all rely on the same principles and the same laws of probability. So, why not just use a test that is widely known and understood by both the researcher and the potential consumers of a study's findings? Why bother to seek out one that may be more appropriate but is less widely known or would require additional study?

There are two responses to these questions. First, as suggested earlier, using an inappropriate statistical test will result in a loss of credibility for a study's findings among those who are knowledgeable about data analyses. Second, and perhaps more importantly, those who are not knowledgeable may just assume that the statistical test that was used was the correct one. Thus, they may fail to question a study's findings when the findings should have been challenged or disregarded all along. Assuming that a study's findings represent new knowledge, social workers may apply these findings in a manner that has the potential to harm their clients.

There are literally hundreds of statistical tests available. How do we determine which one(s) to use? This decision is relatively complicated, and several factors need to be considered. This chapter examines some of the factors and provides information about how to get help in identifying which test to use.

FACTORS TO CONSIDER

Ideally, planning for the analysis of a data set begins early in the research process, at about the same time that decisions are made about what data collection instrument(s) will be used to measure variables of interest—that is, when the variables are operationalized and sampling issues addressed. Questions about how variables are to be measured and the size and methods of acquiring research samples are closely related to how data are subsequently analyzed. They help determine which statistical test(s) should and should not be used.

Are such decisions final? Generally, yes—it is customary to select a statistical test prior to data collection. Sometimes, no—it is not especially unusual to encounter problems in a research study that may change either the way data are collected, from whom, and/or the level of precision with which variables realistically can be measured. For example, after data are collected and examined, the distribution of values of a variable may necessitate grouping the values of an interval level variable, such as age, into ranges, so that the data must now be regarded as being at the ordinal level of measurement. When something like this occurs, it is considered both ethical and absolutely essential to select statistical tests different from those that were prespecified in the original research design.

Whenever the final choice of a statistical test(s) is made, five considerations most directly influence that choice:

1. The sampling method(s) used
2. The distribution of the variables within the population
3. The level of measurement of the independent and dependent variables
4. The amount of statistical power that is desirable
5. The robustness of the tests being considered

There are sometimes other issues to consider in the decision-making process that may determine which test is (or is not) used to test a research hypothesis. For example, if one of the variables is at the nominal or ordinal level of measurement, we may need to consider the number of value categories (different measurements) of the variable. If the variable is dichotomous (e.g., yes/no, older/younger), some tests are appropriate. But if there are three or more value categories for the variable (e.g., yes/no/undecided, young/middle-aged/older), other tests must be used. Similarly, whether a variable is discrete or continuous (Chapter 1) may help to determine which test is most appropriate.

Sampling Method(s) Used

Ideally, we would like to be able to draw a simple random sample from a known population. However, this is often not possible in social work research. Such factors as time, money, or the lack of a clearly defined population from which to draw a sample may produce a situation in which the only available sample is a nonrandom one. Ethical constraints may also preclude the use of a random sample. For example, we might wish to select a random sample of clients to participate in an experimental program, but we cannot ethically justify including clients who we believe have little potential to benefit from the program just because they have been randomly selected, or excluding other clients who we believe would really benefit from the program, just because they were not selected.

There are important consequences of using nonrandom samples. The possibility of the presence of sampling bias (and, thus, of spurious findings) is greatly increased. Without random samples, the range of statistical analyses that can be used is also reduced. Unfortunately, some of those statistical tests that must be eliminated are also some of the best ones for drawing conclusions from research data.

We must be fully aware of the kind of sampling method used in a research study in order to select the most appropriate statistical test. Below are some of the questions that need to be addressed:

1. Did the sampling method use a single sample or more than one sample? If so, how many?
2. How large a sample(s) was (were) drawn?
3. If more than one sample was used, do the samples reflect sampling independence? Were they independent of each other, or were they related in any way? For example, were they matched in regard to certain variables to assure that they were comparable?
4. Were the cases within each sample drawn independently? For example, did the selection of one case in any way increase or decrease the likelihood that any other case within the population would also be selected?
5. Was a probability sampling method used (one in which the exact probability of any one case being selected could be calculated)? If so, was the probability of being selected the same for every case, or were cases selected disproportionately from one or more subsamples?

Answering these five questions allows us to begin to narrow the search for an appropriate statistical test. It eliminates a majority of the existing tests because of their inappropriateness for the particular sampling method that was employed. It is only one step, however, in the process of elimination that is used in selecting a test.

Distribution of the Variables within the Population

A second major consideration in selecting a statistical test is the way in which the primary variables of interest (usually the dependent variables) are distributed within the population from which the sample was drawn. Are they normally distributed? Some of the most common statistical tests require the variables that are to be subjected to a statistical analysis to be normally distributed.

As seen in Chapter 3, a seriously skewed distribution of an interval level or ratio level variable usually precludes the use of the mean as a measure of central tendency or the standard deviation as a measure of variability. Unless the dependent variable (or outcome variable) at least approximates a normal distribution, many potentially useful tests that contain the mean and/or standard deviation in their formulas must be eliminated from consideration for research hypothesis testing.

Many times, full descriptive data for a dependent variable in a population do not exist. So, how do we know if the distribution is a normal one? The decision about whether the distribution of a dependent variable in a population is normal enough to be considered normally distributed is often a judgment call. It requires, among other things, a knowledge of the robustness of the test being considered, a concept discussed later in this chapter.

Level of Measurement of the Variables

A third factor to consider in selecting a statistical test is the level of measurement of the variables of interest. Were they measured in a way that they can be considered nominal, ordinal, interval, or ratio? Well-planned construction and use of measuring instruments help generate the highest possible level of measurement of a variable (given ethical and practical constraints). If we are not careful, however, we can end up settling for less measurement precision than might have been available. We may permit a variable that could have been measured at the interval or ratio level of measurement to be measured at only the nominal or ordinal level. We might, for example, ask supervisors to rate a staff member's job performance as outstanding, average, or below average when using an existing standardized measuring instrument instead might have produced interval level data. As noted in Chapter 1, once measurements have been made in such a way that they produce lower-level measurement, it is impossible to achieve the higher level of measurement precision that was initially possible.

Why is loss of measurement precision important? After all, there are different statistical tests designed for use with different levels of measurement. So what difference does the level of measurement make? In fact, the distinction between interval level and ratio level measurement is relatively unimportant in the selection of a statistical test. Many books on data analyses use the term *interval/ratio* to note the presence of either level of measurement, or they use the term *interval* to denote either. But measuring a variable in a way that produces only nominal level or ordinal level data when interval level or ratio level data were possible can result in a real loss. It can fail to generate sufficient evidence to support a research hypothesis, even though the relationship between the variables may be a real one. The resulting data analyses may result in a Type II error. Had interval or ratio level measurement been produced (and thus a different test used), that same relationship might have been statistically significant and the null hypothesis rejected.

The use of a measuring instrument that yields lower-level data (i.e., nominal, ordinal) automatically precludes the use of all statistical tests that require interval or ratio level data. This would not be problematic except, as we shall see, those statistical tests that require interval or ratio level data for one or more variables are some of the best statistical tests for identifying true relationships between variables (avoiding Type II errors). They are some of the most powerful tests.

Some tests (the more powerful ones) also have additional requirements that go beyond simply the level of measurement of variables. For example, they may require that a nominal level variable be dichotomous or even binary (Chapter 1) or that it must have more than two value categories. Or, there may be the requirement that any interval or ratio level variable must be either discrete or continuous. Whatever the measurement requirements of a test, they must be met, or another test should be selected. Fortunately, there is a test for any set of circumstances.

Desirable Amount of Statistical Power

Statistical power is the ability of the statistical analysis to correctly reject the null hypothesis—that is, its ability to correctly detect a true relationship between variables. Another way to think of the power of statistical analysis is its ability to avoid committing a Type II error.

Based on their mathematical computations, some statistical tests are inherently more powerful than others; that is, all other conditions being equal, some tests are better than others at detecting a true relationship between variables. Some may allow us to justify the rejection of the null hypothesis, whereas less powerful tests applied to the same data set under the same conditions would not allow us to reject the null hypothesis. As previously noted, the most powerful tests have more demanding conditions for their use than the less powerful ones.

As presented in Chapter 3, where appropriate, the standard deviation is preferable to the range as an indicator of variability, and the mean is a more precise indicator of central tendency than is the median or mode. Why? Both the mean and the standard deviation require computations using every case value within the variable's distribution and are therefore more precise. Less precise measures such as the trimmed mean, interquartile range, or range do not use every case value in their final computation. Thus, they offer less precise descriptions of the distribution of a variable.

The same principle applies in understanding the concept of statistical power as it relates to the respective power of different statistical tests. All other factors being equal, more powerful tests tend to be those that use all the values for all cases in their computations (directly or indirectly) rather than, for example, the ranks assigned to cases or the frequencies for different nominal-level value categories of a variable. Thus, they take full advantage of the greater precision in measurement that is available. Not surprisingly, the more powerful a statistical test, the more complex its formula.

Avoiding Type II Errors. Chapter 5 examined ways to reduce the likelihood of committing a Type I error. But Type II errors also need to be avoided. All tests possess a certain inherent power based on their mathematical formulas. But any test can be made more or less powerful by the conditions related to its use. There are five conditions that relate to the power of a statistical test and how it affects the likelihood of making a Type II error.

   1. *The actual strength of the relationship between variables that exists within the population.* This is the issue of effect size—the amount of influence that the independent variable exerts on the dependent variable (Chapter 5). If two variables are strongly related, we are almost certain not to miss their relationship in our statistical analysis (commit a Type II error), no matter what statistical test we use. If the relationship is very weak (and some weak relationships between variables may still be of interest), the likelihood of making a Type II error is much greater, no matter what statistical test we use. Unfortunately, we cannot influence the actual strength of the relationship between variables; all we can hope to do is to get a good estimate of it. We compute and report effect size so the reader of a report can put a finding of statistical significance into perspective.

   2. *The likely amount of sampling error in sample data, which is a function of the amount of variability of a variable in a population.* In examining the relationship between variables with larger standard deviations (more variability) among their values, we are more likely to commit a Type II error than when examining relationships between variables with smaller variability. Statistical testing will be less powerful. This is because with larger variability in a population, sampling error is likely to be greater; it is easier for samples to vary more from their populations than in populations where case values are relatively similar to each other. With a greater likelihood of sampling error, we are less likely to reject the null hypothesis, even when variables really are related, and thus run a higher risk of committing a Type II error.

   3. *The predetermined statistical rejection level (e.g., .01, .05, .10) that is used with the test.* At the beginning of a study, we could select a higher rejection level than the conventional .05. As noted in Chapter 5, however, there must be justification for doing this (usually within the literature). [If, for example, we decide to use the rejection level of .10 as the cutoff point at which we will reject the null hypothesis, we can decrease the likelihood of missing a true relationship between variables in our sample that also exists in the population. Thus, the likelihood of committing a Type II error is reduced and our statistical analysis is made more powerful.] As also noted in Chapter 5, however, this will increase the likelihood of committing a Type I error.

   4. *Whether a one-tailed or two-tailed research hypothesis was used.* In the previous chapter we saw how the use of a one-tailed research hypothesis will produce a single, larger rejection region than when a two-tailed research hypothesis is used and will thus also decrease the likelihood of committing a Type II error. The rejection region (see Figures 6.4 and 6.5) will be twice as large as either of the two rejection regions when a two-tailed research hypothesis is used (see Figure 6.3). But, as we will recall from Chapter 6, there is no rejection region (critical value) at all if the relationship is found to be in the direction opposite to that expressed in a one-tailed research hypothesis. If that is the case, we can only conclude that we failed to find support for the one-tailed research hypothesis.

   5. *The likely amount of sampling error in sample data, which is a function of the size of the research sample used.* Selecting larger samples makes statistical tests more powerful. Conversely, selecting smaller samples makes statistical tests less powerful. When larger samples are used, "the long run" is approximated. The law of averages states that larger samples contain less sampling error than smaller samples. Thus, larger samples are more likely to be able to dismiss sampling error as the cause for a relationship between variables in them, and thus we are more likely to be able to reject the null hypothesis. With larger samples we are unlikely to miss a true relationship (commit a Type II error).

   To summarize the conditions that affect statistical power: A statistical analysis is less likely to produce a Type II error (it is more powerful) if:

1. The true relationship between variables is strong rather than weak
2. The variability of the variables is small rather than large
3. A higher (e.g., .10 rather than .05) rejection level is used
4. A one-tailed research hypothesis is used, and the direction of the relationship between the two variables is correctly predicted
5. The sample used is large rather than small

What We Can and Cannot Control.   We cannot adjust the actual strength of a relationship between variables—it is a given. For the same reason, we cannot affect the amount of variation that exists among the values of a variable in its population.

   In relation to the third factor, while we have the capacity to adjust the rejection level used (e.g., to use .10 instead of .05 as the cutoff point), that would come at a cost. By reducing the likelihood of committing a Type II error, we increase the likelihood of committing a Type I error.

   We could also decrease the likelihood of making a Type II error by using a one-tailed rather than a two-tailed research hypothesis, but this may not be an option. The literature usually dictates whether it is justifiable to predict the direction of a relationship between variables.

   That brings us to the fifth factor in statistical power—sample size. It is the factor affecting power, over which we generally have the greatest control. Selection of a sample size may be constrained by various ethical and practical considerations. However, if we have the freedom to select a sample size of our choosing, we can perform a procedure that will tell us what sample size is optimal for our statistical analysis.

Statistical Power Analysis.   In data analyses, more powerful is not always better, since a statistical test that is too powerful can identify relationships between variables that may be statistically significant but very weak or otherwise meaningless. But a statistical test that is not powerful enough to detect a true relationship between variables also can be problematic. Using such a test can cause us to fail to identify a potentially valuable relationship between variables. Especially if the true relationship is relatively weak (but still of interest), it may be that a more powerful data analysis should be used or that the conditions under which it is used should be changed, usually by increasing sample size.

What we need is the optimum amount of statistical power. We want it to provide an acceptably low probability of risk for committing both Type I and Type II errors. We need a reasonable balance between the two. **Statistical power analysis** allows us to determine what sample size would constitute the right amount of power for our data analysis or, if a statistical test has already been conducted, to draw conclusions about whether it was not powerful enough (or too powerful) for what we were hoping to learn from it.

Tests of statistical inference (such as those discussed in subsequent chapters) allow us to determine the *p* value or the probability of mistakenly rejecting a true null hypothesis (committing a Type I error). In contrast, a statistical power analysis allows us to estimate the probability of committing a Type II error, given the statistical test used and the conditions under which it is used. Statistical power analyses are very complicated mathematical procedures that are beyond the scope of this text. However, the reader should be aware that tables have been developed that allow us to estimate the likelihood of committing a Type II error based on the rejection level used, the effect size (the estimated strength of the relationship between the variables in the population), and the sample size. These are three of the five factors that affect statistical power that were discussed in the previous section of this chapter. It is possible to use these tables to select a sample that will generate just enough statistical power to reduce the likelihood of making a Type II error to an acceptably low level, while not adding unnecessary cost to the research study. Conducting a statistical power analysis to select the optimal size research sample helps avoid (1) selecting a sample that is larger than needed, thereby unnecessarily increasing the cost of the study, and (2) inadvertently conducting a study with a sample that is so small that there is virtually no probability that statistical significance will be achieved, even though the variables really are related.

If we have no choice in the matter of sample size and the only available sample is relatively small, the tables can be used to suggest if it is worthwhile to conduct the study in the first place. They may suggest that, given the estimated strength of the relationship between the variables (effect size), there would be a very high probability of committing a Type II error with the small available sample. Perhaps the statistical power generated by the analysis would not be enough to provide support for the existence of the relationship, even though it may exist. We might attempt to generate more power by increasing the usual .05 rejection level to .10 or even .20. But that might make the probability of committing a Type I error unacceptably high.

Even after data have been analyzed, statistical power analyses can perform a second valuable function. Let us assume that we find insufficient statistical support to be able to reject the null hypothesis—the relationship between variables is not statistically significant. So we fail to reject the null hypothesis. But, as always, an error might have occurred, in this case a Type II error. If a statistical power analysis is used, the probability of committing a Type II error can be reported along with the finding of nonsignificance. For example, the research report might read, "There was a lack of statistical support for the research hypothesis ($p > .05$)." However, a statistical power analysis revealed that there was a .35 probability of committing a Type II error. This is useful information. It admits that the statistical testing used had relatively low statistical power. It puts the finding of nonsignificance in better perspective. It may suggest the advisability of replicating research studies with larger samples to explore further whether a Type II error might have occurred and whether the relationship between variables might exist after all.

Robustness of Tests Being Considered

In everyday English, power and robustness mean something very similar. They do, however, have very different meanings when used in statistical analyses. As we have just discussed, the power of a statistical analysis is its ability to detect a true relationship between variables. **Robustness** is the degree to which a specific statistical test produces accurate findings when one or more of its assumptions is not met. Robustness of a test is relative; every test is more or less robust. A relatively robust test is one that produces reasonably accurate results even if one or more of the assumptions for its use cannot be fully met.

As noted earlier, all statistical tests require certain conditions for their use, usually called *assumptions*. Assumptions most often relate to the sampling methods used, the shape of the distribution of one or more variables within the population, the amount of variability, and/or the level of measurement of one or more variables.

The *t* tests described in Chapter 11 are good examples of robust tests. Two of their assumptions are that, in examining the relationship between variables, any dependent variables should be at the interval or ratio level of measurement and should be normally distributed within the population. When *t* tests are used with variables that are somewhat skewed, however, the results are still quite accurate. A certain amount of flexibility about the usual assumption of a normal distribution is common among many other tests that are regarded as relatively robust.

PARAMETRIC AND NONPARAMETRIC TESTS

There are two general categories of statistical tests—*parametric* and *nonparametric*. **Parametric tests** require that:

1. At least one variable (usually the dependent variable) should be at the interval or ratio level of measurement
2. The dependent variable should be normally distributed (in the population); if samples are drawn from different populations and then compared, the distributions of the variable in these different populations are required to have equal or near-equal variances
3. Cases should be selected independently—that is, they are randomly selected from a population and, if an experimental design was used, also randomly assigned to experimental and control groups

Some additional requirements apply to specific parametric tests. Some tests allow us to waive one or more of the above three requirements. A test's special requirements are listed in more advanced statistics books, often along with a statement about its robustness, that is, what assumption(s) of the test, if any, can be waived (and to what degree). Generally, if the mean and the standard deviation are appropriate descriptive statistics for summarizing a study's findings, parametric statistics may be appropriate for examining the relationships between variables.

Nonparametric tests have fewer assumptions. They are designed for research situations in which one or more conditions for the use of parametric tests cannot be met. They do not require a normal distribution of the dependent variable in the population from which the sample was drawn. Some nonparametric tests are intended for independently drawn samples; others are not. The number of samples, the number of cases in each sample, and the presence or absence of "ties" (cases with the same value of a variable) also are important factors in selecting the most appropriate nonparametric test from the many that exist.

Most nonparametric tests require only nominal or ordinal level data, but some are more demanding, requiring greater measurement precision. As a group, nonparametric tests are less powerful than parametric tests. That is, they would be more likely to result in Type II errors than parametric tests if used with the same data set under the same conditions.

Because nonparametric tests generally are designed to be used with nominal or ordinal level data (or interval and ratio level data that are not normally distributed), they are often ideally suited to social work research. As noted earlier, many dependent variables cannot be assumed to be at the interval or ratio levels of measurement. Many also are dichotomous (e.g., success/failure; rehospitalization/non-rehospitalization; passage/nonpassage of legislation; employment/unemployment of clients).

Nonparametric tests should not be regarded as a second-best choice designed for situations in which criteria for parametric statistics cannot be met, however. They have some distinct advantages over parametric tests and often are the best tests for addressing our statistical needs. A nonparametric statistic, for example, is especially useful when one or more of the following three conditions exist:

1. Samples have been compiled from different populations, and we wish to compare the distribution of a single variable within each population
2. Variables are at the nominal level of measurement, or value categories of the variables allow for only the rank ordering of responses (ordinal level of measurement)
3. Very small samples (e.g., as small as 6 or 7) are all that are available for study

Fortunately, the relative lack of power of nonparametric tests sometimes can be compensated for, at least in part. As noted above, increasing sample size increases the power of any statistical test. When that can be done, nonparametric tests can be made just about as powerful as their parametric counterparts with the use of sufficiently large samples.

In many situations where nonparametric tests are appropriate, two or more tests could potentially be used, but they are likely to require different size samples. As a general rule, the test that uses the larger sample is likely to be the more powerful one.

If we anticipate the need for more power in testing (such as when we anticipate that a relationship between variables may be weak but still worth trying to document), we should consider the possibility of drawing a larger sample and using a test that is designed for use with larger samples.

MULTIVARIATE TESTS

A research hypothesis may indicate that we need to examine more than just the relationship between two variables (bivariate analysis). We may need to examine the complex relationship among three or more variables in order to attempt to sort out how they are interrelated. In that case, a selection must be made from among the more mathematically complicated tests—multivariate analyses.

There are dangers in using a series of bivariate statistical analyses to test the relationships between a large number of independent and dependent variables. Examining so many possible combinations of variables can easily result in a Type I error by causing us to stumble onto a spurious (not real) relationship. The laws of probability would tell us that if we examine many different pairs of variables that are not related, in some of them sampling error will lead us to reject the null hypothesis and erroneously conclude that they probably are related. That is one reason why we need to understand the principles behind multivariate analyses and to have a familiarity with them. They can reduce the likelihood of Type I errors.

There are situations where a multivariate analysis is the logical choice. Multivariate analyses are consistent with the multiple causation and systems theories of human behavior that dominate much social work literature. Like these theories, they allow us to attempt to sort out the complex interaction of variables that exist within practice and research milieus. For example, they allow us to sort out the complex relationship among rates of alcoholism, illegal drug usage, unemployment, and family violence, where the relationships are not simple cause-and-effect ones.

Multivariate analyses differ from bivariate analyses in two important ways. First, as already stated, they examine the relationship among three or more variables. Second, and more importantly, they examine the relationship among the variables simultaneously.

Suppose we wish to examine the relationship among the independent variables *per capita income* and *rates of child abuse* and the dependent variable *incidence of violence in schools* within various cities. Two bivariate analyses might look at (1) the relationship between *per capita income* and *incidence of violence in schools*, and (2) the relationship between *rates of child abuse* and *incidence of violence in schools*. By contrast, a single multivariate analysis, using a single procedure, would look at the total picture, including how income and rates of child abuse might be related and how all three variables might be related as a group. The brief descriptions of several multivariate tests in the chapters that follow will give some insight into their theoretical underpinnings and in what data-analysis situations they are especially helpful.

DECIDING WHICH TEST TO USE

The final selection of a statistical test or tests entails both (1) reference to the overall purpose of the research study, and (2) an assessment of the nature of the data that are to be analyzed. A series of questions might be asked:

1. Did the study seek to find support for one or more causal relationships (and was the design supportive of demonstrating support for them), or was the goal to learn if there was support for a relationship of association or correlation?
   a. Should analysis of data examine the relationship between two variables (bivariate analysis), explore the relationships among three or more variables (multivariate analysis), or both?
   b. What would be the consequences of making either a Type I or Type II error, and how do they suggest the appropriate amount of statistical power for data analyses?
2. Do the data support the use of parametric tests or are nonparametric tests best suited to data analyses?
   a. For each independent (or predictor) variable:
      i. What level of measurement is it?
      ii. Was it dichotomous or did it have more than two values or value categories? If the latter, is the variable considered discrete or continuous?
      iii. If interval or ratio level, is it considered normally distributed within the population?
   b. For each dependent (or outcome) variable:
      i. What level of measurement is it?
      ii. Was it dichotomous or did it have more than two values or value categories? If the latter, is the variable considered discrete or continuous?
      iii. If interval or ratio level, is it considered normally distributed within the population?
   c. If one or more confounding variables need to be statistically controlled, what measurement level are they, how are they distributed, and so forth?
   d. What sampling methods (random or nonrandom) were used in selecting research samples?
   e. If more than one test could be used, which one has the greatest potential to directly answer the research question or questions?

Deciding whether a parametric or a nonparametric test is indicated is perhaps the most important first step in narrowing the list of possible tests. The primary focus is on the level of measurement of key variables and, if a variable can be considered interval or ratio level, its distribution.

In this book, we have included two charts (Appendix A) that can be used as general guides for beginning the process of selecting a statistical test when conducting statistical analyses. They should be regarded as just a place to start, however, because they focus primarily on levels of measurement (Box A.1) of the variables and the number of variables in the analyses (Box A.2) and do not address any additional assumptions of the tests. All of the tests (both parametric and nonparametric) that are listed in Appendix A are ones we are likely to encounter in social work research studies. They are discussed in the chapters that follow.

Even the question of which test can be used with which level of measurement is not answered the same way by all researchers and statisticians. For example, although parametric tests traditionally are believed to require interval or ratio level data for the dependent variable, some people argue that parametric tests can be used with ordinal level data when the intervals within the ordinal data are approximately equal. Thus, the decision about whether it is acceptable to use ordinal level data with parametric statistical tests requires a close review of the data and of others' opinions about the robustness of a specific parametric test. There is consensus that the relationship between nominal level variables can be examined with the use of nonparametric statistical tests only.

There are a number of comprehensive books on statistical test selection, many of which are available in college and university libraries. Some books present highly detailed flowcharts for use in selecting statistical tests given various assumptions about a study's research design and the level of measurement of variables.

There are numerous other sources that describe how to select statistical tests. In fact, many of them are free of charge and easily accessed on the Web. The sites listed below are examples of sites that describe how to select statistical tests, once the level of measurement of key variables has been determined:

> http://www.ats.ucla.edu/stat/mult_pkg/whatstat/default.htm
> http://www.whichtest.info/index.htm
> http://www.graphpad.com/www/Book/Choose.htm
> http://www.richmond.edu/~choyt/supportingdocs_spring05/handout_stattests.doc
> http://sahs.utmb.edu/pellinore/intro_to_research/wad/sel_test.htm
> http://members.aol.com/statware/pubpage.htm
> http://www.graphpad.com/Downloads/InStat3Mac.pdf
> http://ndt.oxfordjournals.org/cgi/content/abstract/3/1/91
> http://bmj.bmjjournals.com/collections/statsbk/13.html
> http://science.uwe.ac.uk/MathsStats/material/expt_design/overview.pdf
> http://www.stat.ucla.edu/~dinov/courses_students.dir/Applets.dir/ChoiceOfTest.html
> http://www-users.cs.umn.edu/~ludford/Table%20of%20Contents.htm
> http://www.nd.edu/~rwilliam/xsoc592/lectures/x62.pdf

MORE ABOUT GETTING HELP

This chapter has focused on the process involved in selecting a statistical test to analyze the relationship between or among variables. It has introduced the complicated task of selecting the most appropriate statistical test or tests for hypothesis testing and noted some of the issues that need to be considered when selecting a test from the many that exist. It has not provided the answer to the question, "What statistical test should I use given my specific research situation?"

Recent advances in computer technology have made it even easier to select a test and to address other related issues, such as the best sample size to use. Statistical software programs use the information provided by the researcher—for example, the level of measurement of the independent and dependent variables, the shape of their distributions, the statistical power desired, and the sampling method used—to suggest which statistical test(s) is (are) most appropriate.

Computers cannot tell us what meaningful research problems to pursue or what hypotheses to test (not yet, anyway). They cannot tell us how to conceptualize, operationalize, design, implement, and gather data to test our research hypotheses. For now, these tasks are left to us. Computers can, however, quickly and effortlessly produce frequency distributions and attractive graphs that accurately describe our sample or population. They can calculate measures of central tendency and variability in a matter of seconds. They can also tell us the likelihood that sampling error produced a relationship between two or more variables in the data set (the likelihood of a Type I error if the null hypothesis were to be rejected). But even with computer-assisted statistical test selection and high-speed number crunching, we still need to know how to interpret the findings and decide if they are truly meaningful. If we conclude that they are meaningful, we still need to decide how to apply them to social work practice.

Consultation with experts can assist in the task of research design and statistical analysis. In schools and departments of social work and in many social service organizations throughout the world, there are people who know a lot about statistical analyses. They can help us if we know what questions to ask and how to ask them, and if we can comprehend and respond appropriately to the questions they ask.

Because so many statistical tests are available, even the experts cannot be knowledgeable about all of them. In fact, probably only a few dozen tests are commonly used in social work research, another group is seen occasionally in the literature, and a third group consists of a large number of relatively obscure tests designed for use in unique situations. Widespread access to computerized data analyses has resulted in some changes in this mix. Of course, new tests are also continuing to be developed.

THE PROCESS OF HYPOTHESIS TESTING

1. *State the research hypothesis(es).* Label the independent and dependent variables. State how each variable is conceptualized and operationalized.

Remember: The research hypothesis guides the entire conceptualization and operationalization process. In addition, it helps determine the best research design to use in an effort to rule out alternative explanations that could explain an apparent relationship between variables. Research hypotheses, if appropriate, should be supported by theoretical assumptions derived from a literature review.

A research hypothesis can be one-tailed or two-tailed (and, less frequently, in its "no relationship" form). The research hypothesis is not statistically tested; it is either indirectly supported or not supported by testing its corresponding null hypothesis.

2. *For any research hypothesis, state the corresponding null hypothesis.* Conceptualize how the data would look if the null hypothesis were, in fact, correct.

Remember: The null hypothesis states that any relationship between the variables in the sample is the work of sampling error. It covers all outcome possibilities that are not explicit in the research hypothesis. Thus, if a one-tailed research hypothesis states that the level of job satisfaction for medical social workers has increased significantly over the last 4 years, the null hypothesis includes the possibilities that job satisfaction has not changed and also that it has decreased.

If the null hypothesis can be rejected, support is present for the one-tailed or two-tailed research hypothesis. Hypothesis testing is a process of indirect proof. We never directly prove that the research hypothesis is correct; rather, if the null hypothesis can be rejected, the one-tailed or two-tailed research hypothesis (the alternative hypothesis) is supported only indirectly. In those rare instances where there is a "no relationship" research hypothesis (predicting no relationship between variables), support for the research hypothesis is achieved if the statistical analysis does not allow the researcher to reject the null hypothesis.

3. *Specify the statistical rejection level to be used.* If any level other than .05 is to be used, specify the justification for its use. Which type of error, Type I or Type II, are we more interested in seeking to avoid, and why?

Remember: This step entails determining the consequences of erroneously rejecting the null hypothesis or erroneously not rejecting it. The possibility of Type I errors can be reduced (among other ways) by setting a low rejection level (e.g., .01, .025, .05) rather than a higher one (e.g., .10, .15), which would reduce the likelihood of a Type II error. A statistical power analysis can help us estimate the latter.

4. *State all assumptions about the data and how they were collected.* What levels of measurement are assumed to exist? Which variables are assumed to be normally distributed? What specific sampling methods were employed? How large are the samples?

Remember: We must know the level of measurement for each of the variables to be analyzed. The method by which the sample is drawn, sample size, and the way our variables are distributed in the population also affect the choice of which statistical test to use.

5. *Describe the most relevant characteristics of the sample and/or population. Select and compute one or more inferential statistical test(s) to test the research hypothesis.* Is each test used appropriate for the conditions described in Step 4? Is a consultant to be used in the selection of the tests? Is computation of the test to be computer assisted? If so, what statistical software package will be used? Conceptually, how will each test generate a *p* value?

Remember: The statistical test used does not determine the degree to which rival hypotheses or design flaws (e.g., measurement error and sampling bias) may have helped create an apparent relationship between variables in a research sample. It only determines the likelihood that sampling error played a role in the study's findings.

6. *Determine whether the relationship between variables is statistically significant.* Is the probability (*p* value) smaller than the predetermined rejection level? If a one-tailed research hypothesis was used, is the direction of the relationship that was found the same as stated in the hypothesis? If so, are we reasonably certain that other factors (e.g., rival hypotheses, design flaws) did not produce the relationship between the variables within the sample? If so, it probably is safe to reject the null hypothesis and to conclude that a true relationship between the variables exists within the population.

Remember: We can never be totally certain that sampling error did not produce an apparent relationship between variables. When we reject the null hypothesis, we are saying only that we are reasonably certain that the apparent relationship is a real one, but we might still be wrong—we may have drawn an atypical sample because of sampling error.

7. *Determine whether each statistically significant relationship is meaningful.* To what degree did sample size contribute to statistical significance? How strong is the absolute relationship between the variables (effect size)? How surprising are the study's findings? How useful are they for the social work practitioner, educator, or researcher? To what extent would we feel safe in generalizing the findings beyond our sample and the population from which it was drawn (the issue of external validity)?

Remember: These decisions require a thoughtful combination of ethics, common sense, convention, and practice expertise. They must be addressed before a study's findings are implemented in social work practice.

CONCLUDING THOUGHTS

This chapter, along with Chapters 5 and 6, discussed various aspects of two related activities that are a central focus of most social work research—inference and hypothesis testing. Chapter 7 focused on the process of selecting the most appropriate statistical test to determine if there is support for a research hypothesis.

The chapters that follow present a description of statistical tests that have been widely used in social work research for many years and promise to remain popular. They are versatile and suitable for many types of data-analysis situations. The emphasis will be on understanding what they do and what their results mean rather than on the mathematics of their computations. In today's professional environment, we usually can leave that job to computers.

STUDY QUESTIONS

1. How can the use of an inappropriate statistical test harm the credibility of a research study?
2. How might a researcher's use of an inappropriate test ultimately have a negative effect on services to clients? Discuss. Provide an original practice example in your discussion.

3. How does the rule of the instrument sometimes lead to the selection of an inappropriate statistical test?
4. What factors related to sampling methods help determine which statistical test is appropriate?
5. What two characteristics of a variable also affect which statistical test should be used?
6. How does the operationalization of a variable performed before data are even collected serve to limit (or expand) which statistical test or tests can be used? Provide original examples in your discussion.
7. What do we mean when we say that one statistical test is more powerful than another? What is statistical power analysis, and why is it a useful counterbalance to inferential statistical analysis? What do we mean when we say that one test is more robust than another?
8. What factors affect the statistical power of a test?
9. How is it possible for a test to be too powerful? What problems can a too-powerful test create?
10. How is it possible for a test to be not powerful enough? What problems can a test that is not powerful enough create?
11. What three general assumptions must be met for a parametric test to be used?
12. Why are nonparametric tests particularly useful in many social work research projects? How can we make them more powerful?
13. In what ways do multivariate analyses differ from bivariate analyses? Why are they less likely to cause a researcher to commit a Type I error?

8

Correlation

The results of bivariate correlation analyses are extremely useful for interpreting research data. They can answer three questions:

1. What is the actual strength and direction of the relationship between variables within the sample studied?
2. How much of the variation in values of one variable is related to the variations in values of the other variable?
3. What is the probability that the relationship between variables within any given sample is due to sampling error?

Frequently, two or more variables within in a research study have neither been introduced nor manipulated in any way by the researcher. But they may appear to co-vary within the sample; that is, certain values of one variable tend to be found with certain values of a second variable.

As noted in Chapter 1, researchers generally use the labels *independent variable* and *dependent variable* to describe the relationship between variables in a research hypothesis. However, in this chapter and the next one, we will use their relative counterparts, *predictor variable* and *outcome variable*, because, as we shall discuss, covariance is not in itself sufficient evidence that the values of *one* variable actually produced the values of a second variable.

USES OF CORRELATION

Correlation analyses are versatile. For example, they can be used for developing and refining some forms of data-collection instruments, such as scales or indexes. They also are used to examine the reliability (consistency) of measurement instruments when, for example, the instruments are used with different populations, under different conditions, or at different times. In fact, the different methods for assessing reliability described in research methods books (e.g., interrater reliability, parallel-forms reliability, test–retest reliability, coefficient alpha) depend on the concept of correlation.

Teachers use correlation analyses to evaluate the reliability of multiple-choice or true–false tests. They may want to know the correlation between how individual students answered each question (who answered the question correctly and who did not) and how these specific students performed overall on the test. It is one indicator of a good question when students who had the highest overall grades on the test were less likely to miss the question than students who had the lowest overall grades on the same test. Correlation can thus help conclude whether a test question is a good one and should be counted or discarded in determining final student grades on the test. As with all types of correlation analyses, however, such analyses only tell us about the reliability of a test question. And, as we know, reliability is not enough to guarantee a question's validity; that is, it does not assure that the question really measures what it purports to measure.

Correlation analyses are also widely used for descriptive purposes. With the use of data collected from a research sample (or from an entire population), they provide a numerical summary of the relationship between or among variables. It might be useful for the reader of a research report to know, for example, that within a sample of employees in a human service agency, there was a high negative correlation between the variables *employees' ages* and *number of claims for disability insurance.* This knowledge might be valuable, even though such a correlation may not be typical or representative of all human service agencies.

Correlation analyses can also be used for inference, that is, to determine the probability that a correlation between variables found within a sample may be a real one that exists within the population from which the sample was drawn. We have chosen to discuss correlation at this point in this book because correlation analyses can be used for description as well as for inference. Thus, it forms a useful bridge between the discussion of descriptive statistical analyses in the early chapters and the discussion of inferential statistical tests in the chapters that follow.

SCATTERGRAMS

When used for descriptive purposes, a correlation analysis between two variables (and not more than two) can be displayed in a **scattergram.** The graphs in Chapter 2 displayed how many times each value occurred for a single variable (frequencies) within a sample or population. But scattergrams simultaneously portray the values for only *two* variables (for each case). They can thus begin to suggest the presence (or absence) of a relationship between the two variables.

If 23 clients, for example, completed a standardized self-administered measuring instrument that measures the variable *per-capita income* and also completed a standardized self-administered instrument that measures the variable *client satisfaction with social work services,* a scattergram could easily portray each person's score on both variables (i.e., *per-capita income, satisfaction with social work services*) with a single dot. The scattergram would have 23 dots—not 46—one to represent each of the 23 cases and their combination of measurements for the two variables. Scattergrams can be used to:

1. Suggest a possible relationship between variables
2. Graphically report relationships that have already been demonstrated to exist through the use of other statistical analyses
3. Identify and present patterns of possible relationships between variables that may exist within certain subsamples of a larger data set, but that might have gotten lost or canceled out when the entire data set was first analyzed. For example, when the data are first analyzed, the correlation between *per capita income* (first variable) and *client satisfaction with services* (second variable) may not be statistically significant among a large sample of clients with widely varying incomes. But when the same data are displayed using a scattergram, a fairly strong positive correlation (one that is likely to be statistically significant) may be apparent within, for example, the $12,000–$14,999 income range.

Like most of the other graphs presented in Chapter 2, scattergrams use two perpendicular lines (i.e., a horizontal *x* axis and a vertical *y* axis). Unlike the other graphs, however, scattergrams do not use the *y* axis to plot and display frequencies. As can be seen in Figure 8.1, the values of the first variable (predictor) are plotted along the *x* axis and the values of the second (outcome) variable along the *y* axis.

The values for the predictor and outcome variables for a scattergram do not need to not have identical intervals. For example, values for the predictor variable *number of siblings* can be marked off at equal intervals of one unit, and the values for the outcome variable *assertiveness score* can be marked off at equal intervals of five units.

How might a scattergram suggest a possible relationship between two variables? Suppose that we are interested in studying the relationship between the two

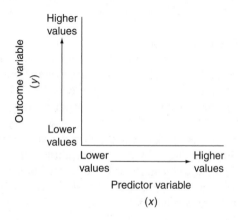

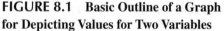

FIGURE 8.1   Basic Outline of a Graph for Depicting Values for Two Variables

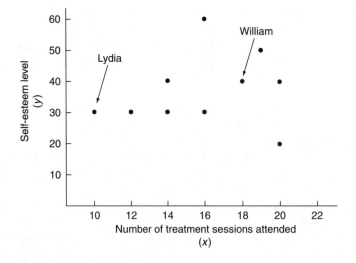

FIGURE 8.2   Scattergram: Number of Treatment Sessions Attended and Self-Esteem Level

variables, *number of treatment sessions a client attended* (predictor variable) and *client's self-esteem level* (outcome variable). We might hypothesize that among clients being treated for problems related to low self-esteem, there will be a positive association between current self-esteem levels and number of treatment sessions they attend; that is, the more treatment sessions clients attended, the higher their self-esteem scores, and vice versa. We could randomly select 10 cases, for example, and could display the number of treatment sessions attended (the predictor variable) and the clients' self-esteem scores (the outcome variable) in a scattergram such as Figure 8.2.

Each dot in Figure 8.2 represents an individual client's number of treatment sessions attended (*x* axis) and self-esteem level (*y* axis). Ten dots on the graph represent the case sample (*N* = 10). Notice that, for example, Lydia attended 10 treatment sessions and had a self-esteem level of 30; William attended 18 sessions and had a self-esteem level of 40.

Correlation analyses are most often used to describe the degree to which a **linear** relationship exists between variables in a sample or population. The fact that the dots in Figure 8.2 are scattered somewhat randomly (rather than falling in a straight line sloping upward *or* downward from left to right) suggests that the correlation between the two variables is far from a perfect linear one (in which every dot would fall on a straight line).

The absence of a strong linear relationship between the two variables suggests little support for the research hypothesis about the variables' relationship with one another. If the data in Figure 8.2 had suggested a stronger linear correlation between the two variables, it might have been productive to use additional statistical analyses to see if there was statistical support for the research hypothesis.

PERFECT CORRELATIONS

An example of a **perfect linear correlation** between a predictor variable and a criterion variable can be seen in Table 8.1. The table displays the hypothetical measurements of two variables, *client's motivation for treatment* and *client's level of functioning.* For each client there is a pair of values—the value of the predictor variable (motivational level for treatment) and the corresponding client value of the outcome variable (functioning level). Note in Table 8.1 that if, prior to data collection, a one-tailed research hypothesis had been formulated (i.e., "Clients with higher motivational levels for treatment will have higher functioning levels than clients with lower motivational levels and vice versa"), the data would lend support for the hypothesis.

A relationship between the two variables in Table 8.1 is evident because, without exception, higher motivational levels for treatment are associated with higher levels of functioning and vice versa. Floyd, for example, scored lowest on both motivational level for treatment (a value of 1) and functioning level (a value of 2). Jane scored second lowest on both levels (values of 2 and 3, respectively), and Lynne scored highest on both (values of 10 and 11, respectively). This perfect relationship also can be depicted in a scattergram, such as the one presented in Figure 8.3.

In Figure 8.3, each dot represents a pair of scores for one person. If connected, the dots would form a straight line—indicating a perfect linear correlation. The relationship between the two variables contained in Figure 8.3 could not be stronger, because each one of the client's paired scores falls along a straight line. Figure 8.4 is an example of a perfect negative correlation. The correlations reflected in Figure 8.3 and 8.4 are equally strong, because, in both figures, the dots fall in a straight line.

The relationship between the two variables displayed in Figure 8.3 can be described as positive. In a positive correlation, high values of *x* are associated with high values of *y,* and low values of *x* are associated with low values of *y.* Note that the line connecting the dots runs from lower left to upper right on the graph.

TABLE 8.1 Motivation for Treatment and Level of Functioning ($N = 10$)

Name	Motivational Level (X)	Functioning Level (Y)
Floyd	1	2
Jane	2	3
Robert	3	4
Sue	4	5
Herb	5	6
Bill	6	7
Margareta	7	8
Ann	8	9
Dorothy	9	10
Lynne	10	11

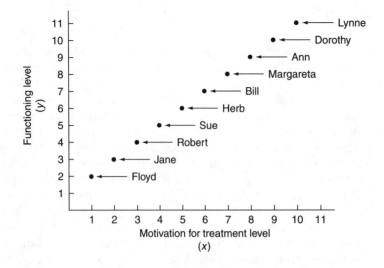

FIGURE 8.3   Scattergram of a Perfect Positive Correlation between Two Variables: Motivation for Treatment and Functioning Levels (from Table 8.1)

When the correlation between variables is negative (as in Figure 8.4), high values of one variable are associated with low values of the second variable and vice versa. The line connecting the dots runs from upper left to lower right on the graph. Figure 8.4 suggests that higher clinical stress levels (predictor variable) are associated with lower functioning levels (outcome variable) and vice versa.

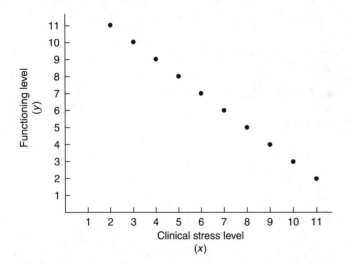

FIGURE 8.4   Scattergram of a Perfect Negative Correlation between Two Variables: Clinical Stress and Functioning Levels

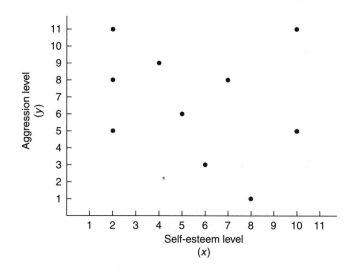

FIGURE 8.5   Scattergram of No Correlation between Two Variables: Self-Esteem and Aggression Levels

NONPERFECT CORRELATIONS

Figure 8.5 displays hypothetical data in which there is no perceivable relationship between the two variables of *self-esteem* and *aggression*. In other words, we could not say that the more (or less) self-esteem that clients possess, the more (or less) aggressive they are (at least in this sample anyway).

Virtually all relationships between variables reflect some degree of correlation, ranging from barely discernable to nearly perfect. Any correlation within this range is referred to as a **nonperfect correlation.** Figure 8.6 is a scattergram illustrating a nonperfect positive correlation between the variables *number of treatment sessions attended* and *clients' attitudes toward their peers.* The correlation is positive, but it is not a perfect positive correlation, like the one reflected in Figure 8.3.

Figure 8.6 shows that three clients were seen only once by a social worker, but one client (Sue) scored a 2 on the Attitudes toward Peers Scale, another (Robert) scored a 4, and a third client scored a 6. So, the relationship between the two variables is far from perfect, even though the paired values represented by dots fall in an overall positive direction (lower left to upper right).

INTERPRETING LINEAR CORRELATIONS

The dots within scattergrams can fall in a variety of patterns other than a straight line. They can form a U shape, a J shape, a series of waves (cyclical correlation), or a line that is curved like either an arch or an upside-down arch (**curvilinear** correlation). Any clear pattern in a distribution of dots indicates the presence of a relationship between two variables.

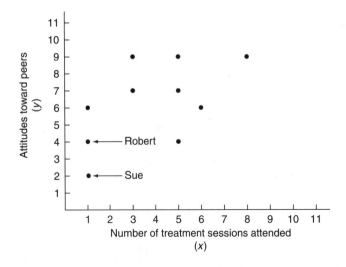

**FIGURE 8.6   Scattergram of a Nonperfect Positive
Correlation between Two Variables: Number of
Treatment Sessions Attended and Attitudes toward Peers**

Observing the pattern in which the dots in a scattergram fall is useful for understanding and drawing tentative conclusions about relationships between variables. It
also tells us whether it is appropriate to use certain tests of statistical significance. The
statistical tests in this chapter, for example, should be used only when variables are
linearly correlated. They should not be used to examine relationships between variables that may be correlated, but not in a linear way.

Scattergrams are one way of displaying the paired values for two variables in any
given data set. A more efficient way of displaying the relationship between two
interval-level or ratio-level variables is to use a correlation coefficient. A **correlation
coefficient,** expressed as the lowercase italicized letter *r,* provides a numerical indicator of both the strength and the direction of the relationship between variables.

Understanding Correlation Coefficients

As Figure 8.7 shows, correlation coefficients range between −1.0 (perfect negative) at one
extreme to +1.0 (perfect positive) at the other extreme, with 0.0 (no linear correlation) at
the midpoint. (If the correlation is positive, the + sign is generally not used, but is
implied.) The closer the numerical value of the correlation coefficient is to either

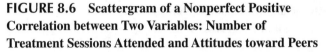

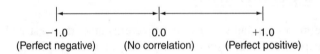

FIGURE 8.7   The Range of Correlation Coefficients

extreme, the stronger the linear relationship between the two variables. A coefficient of .72, for example, is closer to a perfect correlation than coefficients of either −.60 or .60 and therefore suggests a stronger correlation than either of the other two.

The closer the coefficient is to the middle of the range, the weaker the relationship between the two variables. A correlation coefficient that is close to 0 suggests that the linear relationship is very weak.

Whether a correlation coefficient is positive or negative indicates the direction of a relationship between the variables. The correlation coefficient (r) between a social worker's skill level and years of professional social work experience, for example, might be $r = .45$, a positive relationship. The correlation between skill level and level of apathy regarding one's work might be $r = −.35$, indicating a negative relationship; that is, persons who are most apathetic and uninvolved in their work are likely to be less skillful and vice versa.

The sign within a correlation coefficient ($−$ or $+$) should be interpreted only as an indicator of the direction of a relationship between variables. Thus, if a correlation coefficient is negative (that is, preceded by a minus sign), this does not mean a negative value in the usual mathematical sense. It merely indicates that, to the extent suggested by the value of the correlation coefficient, lower values of one variable tend to be found with higher values of the other variable, and vice versa.

If more than just a few bivariate correlation coefficients are reported as descriptive statistics within a research report, reporting them in tabular form may be helpful to the reader. A table designed for this purpose is called a **correlation matrix.** It lists all variables in a column on the left side and repeats them in a row along the top. Figure 8.8 is an example of a correlation matrix that displays the correlation between several interval level and ratio level variables. The reader can find the direction and strength of a correlation between any two variables by noting the correlation coefficient that appears in the matrix where the row in which the first variable appears intersects with the column headed by the second variable.

Very Strong Correlations

The discovery of a very strong correlation (positive or negative) between variables is not always a useful research finding. Moderately strong correlation coefficients or

FIGURE 8.8 **Correlation Matrix: Correlation between Selected Demographic Variables among Clients in XYZ Agency ($N = 109$)**

	Age	Education	# Siblings	Income	# Children
Age	1.00				
Education	−.23	1.00			
# Siblings	−.10	−.30	1.00		
Income	.39	.67	.06	1.00	
# Children	.24	.45	.38	.25	1.00

even those that are relatively weak may have greater potential to contribute to our body of knowledge than very strong ones. Why? A very **strong correlation** may describe a relationship between variables that is pretty obvious. In some human services agencies, for example, we probably could demonstrate a nearly perfect positive correlation between direct service workers' years of employment and the total number of clients they have seen. But such a correlation would be neither meaningful nor surprising.

Often, a very strong correlation exists because the two variables are nothing more than two measurements of the same variable. For example, this might explain the finding of a near-perfect positive correlation, say .93, between scores on an anger scale and scores on a hostility scale. The same interpretation might apply if a research study examined the relationship between assertiveness and timidity. Data analysis might produce a correlation coefficient of, say, −.95. Is this an important finding? Probably not. A logical interpretation might be that timidity and assertiveness are really opposite sides of the same variable.

A perfect correlation provides still another extreme example of this principle. If we performed a correlational analysis among a group of social work students for the variables *number of classes missed* and *number of classes attended* over the course of a semester, we would produce a perfect negative correlation coefficient (−1.0). This would not be surprising, because classes missed and classes attended are indicators of the same variable, *class attendance*.

What is the utility of very high correlation coefficients? It lies primarily in the area of research design. Very high correlation coefficients can demonstrate reliability (consistency) and thus are a necessary (but not sufficient) indicator of validity. A very high correlation between a college admissions test and subsequent grade point averages, for example, is an indication of the test's predictive validity—its ability to accurately predict academic success.

Other types of validity also can be indicated by the presence of very high correlation coefficients. For example, using a sample of clients, a very high positive correlation between their scores on a newly developed scale designed to measure antisocial attitudes and their number of arrests for antisocial behaviors is evidence of the new scale's concurrent validity.

Very high correlation coefficients also can be used in the construction of a scale. A very high correlation coefficient, for example, between responses to Item 16 on the first draft of a scale designed to measure homophobia and responses to Item 24 on the same scale suggests that the two items may be measuring the same indicator of the variable. In the future, one item could be deleted to make the scale shorter, or both can be left in, with one serving as a kind of reliability check on the other.

As should be obvious by now, a correlation coefficient indicates both the strength and the direction of the relationship between two variables. But, as we first noted in Chapter 5, if the coefficient is squared (r^2), we can learn much more. The new number (r^2) is a measure of association. It indicates the proportion of the variation in one variable that can be accounted for or is related to the variation in values of the other variable.

An r of .30, for example, describing the correlation between number of treatment interviews and self-esteem levels means that 9 percent ($.30^2 = .09$ or 9%) of the variation in self-esteem levels is related to the variations in number of treatment interviews. The other 91 percent ($100\% - 9\% = 91\%$) of variation in self-esteem levels remains unaccounted for and is related to other variables.

In interpreting a correlation coefficient, it is important not to treat it as if it were equivalent to ratio level data or to make statements that in any way give this impression. A correlation coefficient of .80, for example, does not suggest a correlation that is twice as strong as a correlation coefficient of .40. At least in one sense—its ability to account for the amount of variation in the outcome variable that is related to the variation in the predictor variable—a correlation of .80 describes an association *four times* as strong ($.80^2 = .64; .40^2 = .16; .64/.16 = 4$). When correlation coefficients are as strong as $+.80$, there will be few exceptions to the pattern of relationships between values of one variable and values of the second variable; that is, virtually all high values of the first variable will be found in cases with high values of the second variable, and vice versa. A weaker correlation coefficient (such as $+.40$) will have a much higher percentage of cases that reflect a relationship between variables opposite to the overall direction of the association.

Correlation Is Not Causation

What a correlation coefficient cannot do is tell us whether the values of the outcome variable have been caused by the values of the predictor variable. Unlike a research experiment in which we introduce or manipulate the independent variable, a correlational analysis generally is used to examine the pattern of a relationship between variables where the variations in the predictor variable are beyond our control—we neither introduced nor manipulated them. The natural variations were simply observed, often after the fact, along with these of the outcome variable. Thus, any interpretation of correlation that implies causation is incorrect.

Many variables tend to co-vary; they could thus be demonstrated to be correlated. Any statement suggesting causation, however, might be ludicrous. A few examples include (1) a positive correlation between ice-cream sales and drowning rates, (2) a positive correlation among geographical areas between Bible sales and whiskey sales, and (3) a positive correlation between highway speed limits and traffic fatalities. The correlation between the predictor variable and the outcome variable in each of these examples is easily explained (at least in part) by the presence of one or more other variables. For example, temperature, per capita income, and fuel costs (as well as the related miles driven), respectively, would help explain any linear correlations between the pairs of variables.

There are many different ways in which the presence of one or more other (confounding) variables can affect the correlation of two variables. For example, other variables can precede and cause both to co-vary. They can even make two related variables appear to be more closely related than they really are, or they can make them appear to be less related.

To summarize, correlation is necessary but not sufficient for proof of causation. This means that where causation exists between variables, those same two variables will always be correlated. Just because two variables co-vary, however, is no reason to believe that the different values of one produce the different values of the other.

There may be many other possible explanations for a correlation between them besides a cause–effect relationship.

Sometimes the ways in which other variables cause two variables to co-vary is less obvious. We all have heard media exhortations to young people to complete high school and, if possible, to go to college. The appeal usually includes correlation data about the relationship between the variables *educational level* (predictor variable) and *lifetime earnings* (outcome variable). A statement is made that the farther people go in school, the more money they will make over their lifetimes. A cause–effect relationship between the two variables is implied. The correlation between educational level and lifetime earnings may be undeniable. Can it be interpreted to mean that staying in school will automatically increase one's earning potential? No!

The outcome variable *lifetime earnings* may be strongly correlated with other predictor variables, such as *motivation, intelligence, personality,* and *socioeconomic status of parents.* All these variables might reflect a stronger correlation with lifetime earnings than *education level.* They may be more likely to contribute to both high levels of education and to lifetime earnings.

The complex interaction of variables that relate to lifetime earnings argues against any statement implying causation, despite the fact that a correlation with many different variables could be demonstrated to exist. All other things being equal (and when does this ever occur?), the high-school diploma or college degree might give a person an edge in being financially successful. However, this is not a conclusion that can be drawn from only a simple correlation between only two variables *educational level* and *lifetime earnings.*

Using Correlation for Inference

As noted earlier, correlation can be used for inference—testing the likelihood that an apparent relationship between variables in a sample may be the work of sampling error. How large an *r* do we need to conclude that we can safely reject the null hypothesis and be able to claim statistical support for the position that two sample variables may also be related within their population? It should come as no surprise that it depends on the size of the sample.

It also should come as no surprise that for a relationship between variables to be considered statistically significant, a correlation coefficient must be larger than the corresponding correlation coefficient at some predetermined rejection level (referred to as a **critical value**). Unless previously stated and justified, the .05 rejection level is used as the reference point for determining whether we can claim statistical significance for a relationship between variables.

The table of critical values of *r* (Table 8.2) illustrates the minimum strength of the correlation coefficient required to achieve statistical significance at various rejection levels and with various samples sizes. With a sample of 11 individuals, for example, a correlation coefficient of ±.6021 is required with a two-tailed research hypothesis to reach statistical significance at the .05 rejection level (±.7348 at the .01 level) and thereby to permit rejection of the null hypothesis. Of course, other alternative explanations for a relationship between them (besides sampling error) should have been adequately controlled for. With a sample size of 102 cases, however, rejection of the

Table

Critical Values of r

TABLE 8.2   Critical Values of *r*

	Level of Significance for a One-Tailed Test				
	.05	*.025*	*.01*	*.005*	*.0005*
	Level of Significance for a Two-Tailed Test				
N	*.10*	*.05*	*.02*	*.01*	*.001*
5	.8054	.8783	.9343	.9587	.9912
6	.7293	.8114	.8822	.9172	.9741
7	.6694	.7545	.8329	.8745	.9507
8	.6215	.7067	.7887	.8343	.9249
9	.5822	.6664	.7498	.7977	.8982
10	.5494	.6319	.7155	.7646	.8721
11	.5214	.6021	.6851	.7348	.8471
12	.4973	.5760	.6581	.7079	.8233
13	.4762	.5529	.6339	.6835	.8010
14	.4575	.5324	.6120	.6614	.7800
15	.4409	.5139	.5923	.6411	.7603
16	.4259	.4973	.5742	.6226	.7420
17	.4124	.4821	.5577	.6055	.7246
18	.4000	.4683	.5425	.5897	.7084
19	.3887	.4555	.5285	.5751	.6932
20	.3783	.4438	.5155	.5614	.6787
21	.3687	.4329	.5034	.5487	.6652
22	.3598	.4227	.4921	.5368	.6524
27	.3233	.3809	.4451	.4869	.5974
32	.2960	.3494	.4093	.4487	.5541
37	.2746	.3246	.3810	.4182	.5189
42	.2573	.3044	.3578	.3932	.4896
47	.2428	.2875	.3384	.3721	.4648
52	.2306	.2732	.3218	.3541	.4433
62	.2108	.2500	.2948	.3248	.4078
72	.1954	.2319	.2737	.3017	.3799
82	.1829	.2172	.2565	.2830	.3568
92	.1726	.2050	.2422	.2673	.3375
102	.1638	.1946	.2301	.2540	.3211

Source: From Table VII of R. A. Fisher and F. Yates, *Statistical Tables for Biological, Agricultural, and Medical Research,* published by Longman Group, Ltd., London (previously published by Oliver and Boyd, Ltd., Edinburgh) and by permission of the authors and publishers.

null hypothesis is possible with a relatively weak correlation ($\pm.1946$ at the .05 level and $\pm.2540$ at the .01 level). How can this be?

As noted in Chapter 7, increasing sample size increases statistical power. It is more likely that sampling error will cause two variables to appear to be related with a smaller sample than with a larger one. With larger samples, a relationship, even one that appears quite weak, is far less likely to be due to sampling error. If there were no true relationship between variables, the law of averages (the long run) should have taken effect with the use of a large sample—any early pattern of a relationship should have disappeared as new cases were added to it.

PEARSON'S *r*

A correlation can be computed using many different statistical formulas. The most commonly used one results in a **Pearson's product moment correlation coefficient,** or simply Pearson's *r.* It is a parametric test and its assumptions require that both the predictor and outcome variables be at the interval or ratio levels of measurement and be normally distributed within the population.

Computation and Presentation

A Pearson's *r* can easily be calculated with the aid of a computer. Box 8.1 is provided for readers who wish to see the mathematical foundations of the *r* formula. It uses ratio level data on the number of spouse-abuse reports (the predictor variable) and the number of child-abuse reports (the outcome variable). The raw data are listed in the *x* and *y* columns in Table 8.3. Notice how the predictor variable and outcome variables could easily be reversed. This would make the number of spouse-abuse reports the outcome variable and the number of child-abuse reports the predictor variable.

When the results of hypothesis testing using a correlation analysis such as Pearson's *r* appear in a research report, a short narrative description is usually included to elaborate on its meaning. The text might read like this:

> Among the 30 clients participating in the research study, the correlation between the number of treatment interviews they completed and their self-esteem levels was $r = .72$, $p < .01$ (one-tailed hypothesis). Thus their self-esteem levels were positively correlated with the number of times they were seen by the social workers.

Or the text may be:

> The correlation between the predictor and outcome variables for the 30 clients was $r = .72$, $p < .01$ which indicates the presence of a statistically significant positive correlation between the two variables.

Example: Verbal Participation among Female Group Members.   Leon is a social worker in a family service agency. He leads several treatment groups of female adolescents. He recently became aware of the wide variation in verbal participation among

BOX 8.1
Pearson's Product Moment Correlation Coefficient

Hypothesis: There is a positive association between the number of spouse-abuse reports and the number of child-abuse reports.

Null Hypothesis: There is no association ($r = 0$) between the number of spouse-abuse reports and the number of child-abuse reports.

Predictor Variable: Number of spouse-abuse reports—ratio level.

Outcome Variable: Number of child-abuse reports—ratio level.

Observed Frequencies: See Table 8.2.

Correlation Coefficient Formula:

$$r = \frac{N\Sigma XY - (\Sigma X)(\Sigma Y)}{\sqrt{[N\Sigma X^2 - (\Sigma X)^2][N\Sigma Y^2 - (\Sigma Y)^2]}}$$

where:
r = Correlation coefficient
N = Number of cases
ΣXY = Sum of xy column
ΣX = Sum of x column
ΣY = Sum of y column
ΣX^2 = Sum of x^2 column
ΣY^2 = Sum of y^2 column

Substituting values for letters:

$$r = \frac{(5)(1305) - (88)(59)}{\sqrt{[(5)(1790) - (88)^2][(5)(1031) - (59)^2]}}$$

$$= \frac{1333}{\sqrt{(1206)(1674)}}$$

$$= \frac{1333}{\sqrt{(2018844)}}$$

$$= \frac{1333}{1420.86}$$

$$= .94 \text{ (correlation coefficient)}$$

Presentation of Results:

$$r = .94, p < .01$$

Conclusions: The null hypothesis is rejected and the one-tailed research hypothesis is supported. In short, there is a statistically significant association between the number of spouse-abuse reports and the number of child-abuse reports. r^2, is $(.94)^2$ or .88. This indicates that 88 percent of the variance in the number of child-abuse reports can be explained by the number of spouse-abuse reports.

TABLE 8.3 Number of Spouse-Abuse and Child-Abuse Reports in Five County Social Services Offices

Office Number	Spouse-Abuse Reports (X)	Child-Abuse Reports (Y)	X^2	Y^2	(XY)
Office 1	30	25	900	625	750
Office 2	20	15	400	225	300
Office 3	12	10	144	100	120
Office 4	15	9	225	81	135
Office 5	11	0	121	0	0
Totals	88	59	1790	1031	130

group members. Although virtually all members responded when spoken to, a few never made any unsolicited comments. Over a period of several weeks, Leon privately asked some of the nonverbal members why they rarely spoke in the group sessions.

Of the seven members he asked, five had essentially the same answer—each was an only child in her family and had been taught by her parents that it was not her role to initiate communication. Leon then asked three of the most verbal adolescents, those who tended to dominate group discussions, how many siblings they had. Their responses were six, seven, and nine respectively.

Based on his very limited inquiries, Leon began to speculate on a possible relationship between the predictor variable *number of siblings in the family* and the outcome variable *number of unsolicited comments* in group treatment. He conducted a quick literature review to learn about such phenomena as social traits of only children, communication patterns among siblings, and variations in verbal participation in female adolescent treatment groups. Some of the literature seemed to confirm his rather unscientific observation that female adolescents with more siblings are more likely to volunteer comments than those with fewer siblings. He decided that he had sufficient justification for a one-tailed research hypothesis:

> Among female adolescents in treatment groups, there will be a positive correlation between number of unsolicited comments and number of siblings.

It was a policy in Leon's agency to videotape group treatment sessions for use in staff supervision. He received permission from the agency's administrator and the adolescent clients and their parents to use the videotapes from all his group treatment sessions to test his hypothesis. He operationally defined a case as being a female adolescent who attended at least 75 percent of group sessions over a 4-month period. Thirty-seven clients met this criterion. Leon developed an operational definition for the variable *unsolicited comments*. An unsolicited comment was judged to have been made only if both Leon and a colleague (who viewed the tapes independently) agreed that it met that definition.

Leon totaled the number of unsolicited comments for each case and then divided by the number of sessions the client attended. This number provided the average number of unsolicited comments per session (the outcome variable) for each case. Case values for the predictor variable, *number of siblings* were acquired from the agency's intake forms.

Leon used a statistical software package and his personal computer to analyze the data. He entered a pair of measurements (number of siblings and average number of unsolicited comments per session) for each case. Using Pearson's *r,* he achieved a correlation of .34 ($p < .025$). Leon knew that this meant that if he were to claim a relationship between the predictor and outcome variables, he would be on reasonably safe ground, assuming that something else (besides sampling error) had not produced the relationship between them within his sample. What's more, the correlation was in the direction that he had hypothesized it would be, that is, positive. Leon concluded that he had support for his one-tailed research hypothesis.

Leon was realistic about his findings. He had, for example, relied on a convenience sample and used only his own cases. Many potential design flaws and other variables that might have affected his findings could have been present. Perhaps Leon had been a less effective facilitator with group members from small families who may have been less comfortable in group situations. Leon also recognized that the .34 correlation coefficient between the two variables was really not that strong in an absolute sense. Less than 12 percent of the variation in number of comments was associated with the variable *number of siblings* ($.34^2 = .12$). That left approximately 88 percent of the variation unexplained.

Leon's findings, even though they were far from conclusive, were certainly not without value. He summarized them in a weekly staff meeting for other social workers. His colleagues provided a critique of his research methods and identified several problems that if eliminated would improve the design if he chose to replicate his study.

Leon and the other social workers who ran adolescent groups decided to make some adjustments to their practice methods based on Leon's preliminary findings. They also agreed to evaluate the changes after 6 months.

1. Staff would use the variable *number of siblings* (available on intake forms) to create more homogeneous groups among new clients. They felt that placing the most verbally assertive members (those with more siblings) in groups together would keep them from intimidating other group members who were less assertive. In turn, some of the members who the social workers believed to be less assertive (those with fewer siblings) might become more active and assertive when assigned to groups with persons more like themselves.

2. In other groups, new members from families with many siblings would be viewed as at risk to dominate discussions. Likewise, new members with no or few siblings would be viewed as at risk to be reticent to volunteer comments. This perception would affect the way in which the social worker would approach the role as facilitator with the more heterogeneous groups.

3. In all groups, leaders would facilitate discussion around such areas as attitudes toward the presence or absence of siblings, parental attitudes toward children's assertiveness, and so on.

Example: Worker Employment and Error Rates   Tanya is an administrator in a county department of social services. When she was hired, her agency's error rate for eligibility determinations for financial assistance applications was among the highest in the state. She assumed that the problem was related to the inadequate training of workers. She quickly took steps to increase training for all workers who had been employed by the agency for less than 6 months. She also required all senior workers who were not full-time supervisors to perform at least three eligibility determinations a week. To her surprise, 1 year after she implemented these decisions, the error rate had nearly doubled.

Tanya and her supervisor were very concerned about the new error-rate figures. Tanya wondered if her efforts to address a problem might possibly have made it worse. Why was increased training of newer workers, combined with greater use of more experienced personnel, associated with a dramatic increase in erroneous eligibility determinations?

In discussing this paradox with a staff member, Tanya began to speculate on what may have gone wrong. There had been a series of major changes in federal eligibility requirements over the past few years. Tanya had asked her senior workers to do more eligibility determinations because she thought that they would make fewer errors. They were not given additional training, however, to update them on the newer eligibility requirements. In fact, the use of senior workers who had not been retrained may have been a major contributor to the increased error rate.

Tanya did not wish to make another administrative decision that might not help the problem—or might make it even worse. If she were to recommend future changes, she could not rely solely on a hunch. She intended to have data to back up her hunch.

Tanya decided to examine the correlation between worker experience and error rate using data already available in the agency's management information system. Because she was interested in explaining differences in error rate this became her outcome variable; worker experience became her predictor variable. Based on her previous experience, a brief literature review, and conversations with colleagues, she formulated a one-tailed research hypothesis:

There will be a positive correlation between years of worker employment and error rate.

Tanya used her personal computer to analyze the data. For each of 42 workers currently doing eligibility determinations under her supervision, she entered a pair of values—number of years of employment and average number of identified errors per 100 cases (the last 100 reviewed).

The correlation between the variables *years of employment* and *error rate* was $-.21$ ($p > .05$). Even if the p value had been less than .05, Tanya would not have been able to claim statistical support for her hypothesis. Why? The correlation within her data set was negative—the correlation was in the opposite direction to what she predicted in her one-tailed research hypothesis.

At first, Tanya was disappointed with her findings. The negative correlation suggested that the most senior workers in her sample had actually made fewer mistakes than those with less experience, not at all what she had expected. But she quickly reminded herself that the lack of support for her hypothesis did not mean that no new knowledge had been generated. In fact, her findings helped her to shift her focus away from past work experience and/or lack of recent training of senior workers as factors in the recent rise in error rates.

She then recalled that in her haste to reduce the error rate, she also had implemented another change—newer staff were given expanded training in making eligibility determinations. Perhaps the problem had been made worse by the introduction of the training for newer staff. Tanya knew that more training did not guarantee that workers would be better prepared to do their jobs. She began to question whether the training was accomplishing its goals. She decided that she would

1. Design and implement an evaluative study of the current training for new eligibility workers
2. Continue to give senior workers increased responsibility for eligibility determinations and encourage them to assist newer workers in learning their jobs
3. Report her research findings to her superiors, informing them of her approaches to the problem (Steps 1 and 2).

NONPARAMETRIC ALTERNATIVES

Sometimes we cannot meet the assumptions of a parametric statistical test like Pearson's *r*, but we still wish to compute a correlation coefficient. This is possible using various nonparametric tests that require only ordinal level data (or interval or ratio level data that are skewed). They are commonly used in situations where, if normally distributed interval or ratio level data were present, Pearson's *r* would be used. Two of the most commonly used such tests are so similar that they may be considered almost interchangeable. They are **Spearman's rho** and **Kendall's tau.**

Spearman's Rho and Kendall's Tau

Like Pearson's *r*, Spearman's rho and Kendall's tau produce a correlation coefficient that is either positive or negative and that has a numerical value between -1.0 and 1.0. But whereas Pearson's *r* uses the actual case values for each of two variables in its computation, rho and tau are calculated using only the ranks of research participants (or objects) for each of the two variables. For example, the two nonparametric tests could examine the association between the ordinal level variable *motivation* and another ordinal level variable, *socioeconomic class,* among all cases in a research sample. One case may rank first in motivation, but tie for third in socioeconomic class. Another may have ranked fifth on both variables, another second on the first and seventh on the second, and so on.

Like most statistical tests, rho and tau are available on many statistical software packages. They can, of course, be computed by hand as well. If this is done, however, two factors must be considered in determining which specific variation of their formulas should be used: (1) the size of the sample and (2) the number of ties (more than one case sharing a ranking for a variable) present within the raw data set.

The two nonparametric tests possess about the same statistical power; that is, they are about equal in their ability to detect the presence of a real correlation between variables (but less powerful than Pearson's *r*). When both Spearman's rho and Kendall's tau are computed with the use of the same two variables within the same raw data set, they generally produce slightly different correlation coefficients, but very similar *p* values.

Example: Caregiver Willingness to Receive Hospice Services and Longevity of Patients.

Meredith is a social worker in a hospice program that provides services to terminally ill people and their caregivers. After working with hundreds of cases, it seemed to her that people whose caregivers readily accepted hospice services were more likely to live beyond their projected date of death than those whose caregivers were more reluctant to use the services based on these observations. Meredith decided to test the following one-tailed research hypothesis:

> There is a positive correlation between caregivers' willingness to receive hospice services and the longevity of their patients.

Meredith tested the null form of her hypothesis by conducting a small study using the nine patients and their caregivers who were referred for hospice services during the month of June. At the time of the initial interview, she and a social work student who observed the interview independently rated each caregiver and then categorized them as very reluctant, somewhat reluctant, or eager to receive services. Then, following the death of each patient, Meredith noted whether the patient died before, at about, or after the time of death the patient's doctor had projected when the patient was referred for services.

Meredith analyzed the data on the nine patients and examined the relationship between the predictor variable *caregiver's willingness to receive hospice services* and the outcome variable *longevity of the patient* with the use of Spearman's rho. She noted that her sample was small and that there were several ties in the rankings she compiled for the two variables, so she used the appropriate formula for these conditions.

The formula produced a correlation coefficient (*r*) of .24 (*p* > .05). By glancing at Table 8.3, it can be seen that, with only nine cases, she needed a minimum correlation coefficient of .5822 to achieve statistical significance at the .05 level.

Based on her statistical analysis, Meredith concluded that she could not reject the null hypothesis and claim statistical support for her research hypothesis. She decided that her hypothesis may have been wishful thinking. Just in case her hypothesis had been correct, however, she decided to test it again using a larger number of cases, all cases active in her agency over a 1-year period.

CORRELATION WITH THREE OR MORE VARIABLES

Bivariate relationships frequently need further explication. They can also be misleading. We are unlikely to explain how long a hospice patient survives, for example, based solely on data from the variables *caregiver willingness to receive services, patient diagnosis, number of family members in the home,* or any other single variable. Both a systems perspective and other theories of multiple causation argue that many variables work together to affect a single variable such as longevity, a human behavior, or an attitude. A better understanding of how variables are related can often be improved by including more than two variables at one time in a data analysis (multivariate analysis).

Partial *r*

In some situations, there is one variable that simply cannot be ignored if we are to understand the relationship between the predictor and outcome variables. For example, in order to assess a possible correlation between the variables *age* and *amount of charitable contributions to a family service agency,* it is only logical to consider also a third variable, *yearly income.* This third variable cannot be controlled, either before or during the study but it can be controlled statistically after the data have been collected.

A relatively simple statistical test, **partial *r*,** is very helpful in this type of situation. Data on all three variables can be entered into the partial *r* formula (via a computer) and a correlation coefficient can be obtained between any two of the variables, whereas the influence of the third is controlled by making mathematical adjustments in actual case values.

With the use of partial *r,* we are able to determine how large (and statistically significant) a correlation between age and amount of charitable contributions to a family service agency would be if the variations in yearly income were not a factor in their relationship (it was statistically equalized). A useful by-product of this analysis would be correlation coefficients reflecting the correlation between *yearly income* and *amount of charitable contributions to a family service agency* (controlling for *age*) and between *age* and *yearly income* (controlling for *amount of charitable contributions*).

A variation of the nonparametric Kendall's tau also can be used when the assumptions of the parametric partial *r* cannot be met (normally distributed interval or ratio-level variables). It is called **Kendall's partial rank correlation coefficient.** Like partial *r,* it is most useful when there is one potentially confounding variable that cannot be controlled by the research design. It thus represents an obvious rival hypothesis for explaining the variations in values of the outcome variable—that is, it (rather than the predictor variable) may explain the variations, or it may be causing the values to co-vary.

Partial *r* and Kendall's partial rank coefficient can help us to determine if a relationship between variables in a research sample or population is **spurious,** that is, is one that can be explained away by some other phenomenon such as rival hypotheses or confounding variables. For example, a relationship between two variables may disappear when a third variable is controlled, thus helping us to avoid a Type I error. Of course, any test that statistically controls for a third variable may also produce two other results: (1) the relationship between the original two variables may be weaker, but still statistically significant; or (2) it may be even stronger.

Multiple *R*

A more sophisticated type of correlation analysis is available for situations in which we are interested in examining the correlation between an outcome variable and several predictor variables working in combination with one another. **Multiple correlation (Multiple *R*)** looks at a whole set of predictor variables together in order to determine the degree to which their combined variations correlate with different values of the outcome variable. It thus can be used to help identify the best set of predictor variables that relate to different values of the outcome variable. It might tell us, for example, which interval level or ratio level demographic variables might collectively reflect the highest correlation with a variable such as rate of homelessness, incidence of spouse abuse, or sense of alienation. An at-risk population consisting of people with a certain combination of the right characteristics might thus be identified.

Multivariate correlation analyses such as Multiple *R* often are superior to bivariate analyses both for describing the characteristics of a sample or subsample and for testing hypotheses. They can easily examine the complexity of the interaction of three or more variables in a way that bivariate analyses such as Pearson's *r* or even partial *r* cannot. They also help us avoid stumbling onto spurious relationships that result simply from trying many combinations of bivariate analyses until, because of a highly unlikely amount of sampling error, one reflects a statistically significant correlation.

How does Multiple *R* extend our understanding of the relationship among variables? What if, for example, two or more predictor variables reflect a high correlation with the same outcome variable? We would have a better chance of explaining the variation in the outcome variable if we could look simultaneously at those two (or more) predictor variables and their correlation with the outcome variable.

In sum, Multiple *R* determines the degree to which a group of predictor variables correlate with the outcome variable. However, finding the best combination of predictor variables to do this is a fairly complicated process.

Example: Social Work Students' Scores on a Statistics Exam.   Suppose that we want to find out how well several predictor variables might correlate with a social work student's score on a standardized statistics examination (the outcome variable). We might, for example, use four interval level or ratio level predictor variables: (1) *number of statistics courses taken,* (2) *age,* (3) *undergraduate GPA,* and (4) *score on the mathematics section of the SAT.* Let us assume that all four predictor variables all are normally distributed.

Let us also say that the bivariate correlation between these variables and the outcome variable are, respectively, .45, .26, .51, and .74. To find out which two of these variables might be the best pair to explain the different scores that occur on the statistics examination and how well they would, in combination, explain the variation, we could not simply identify the two largest correlation coefficients and add them together. Why not? For one thing, adding .51 and .74 would produce a correlation coefficient greater than 1.00—and that is impossible. But more importantly, any two of the predictor variables (or three or all four of them) will share some of the same covariance with the outcome variable, so adding them together would be redundant. In other words, part of their bivariate correlation with the outcome variable will contribute nothing new to explaining the variation in values of the outcome variable;

one predictor variable would account for some of the same variation as others. That is because the four predictor variables, in addition to having some correlation with the outcome variable, also have some degree of correlation with each other.

Continuing with our example, we would expect a fairly high correlation between any two of the predictor variables *number of statistic courses taken, age, undergraduate GPA,* and *score on the SAT mathematics section.* Thus, the correlation between each of these variables and the outcome variable would not explain how much of the variation of the outcome variable is unique to that predictor variable. In fact, two predictor variables that are highly correlated with each other are unlikely to add much to our ability to explain variation in the outcome variable beyond what either one alone could have done. As noted earlier in this chapter, if they are nearly perfectly correlated (close to $r = +1.00$ or $r = -1.00$), they are probably just two measurements of the same variable; the use of both at the same time would be of little value.

Multiple R sorts out the degree to which any predictor variable alone accounts for the variation in the outcome variable. It produces what is referred to as a **beta weight** for each predictor variable. **Beta weights** essentially are partial correlations and are based on (1) the correlation coefficient between each predictor variable and the an outcome variable and (2) the correlation coefficients among the various predictor variables. By using both of these, Multiple R identifies the **unique variance** within the correlation between a given predictor variable and an outcome variable—that is, the variation in the outcome variable associated with that predictor variable that is not already accounted for by some other predictor variable. That is its beta weight.

Even though a given predictor variable might have the highest bivariate correlation coefficient with the outcome variable (as in the case of the SAT mathematics score in our example), this is no guarantee that its beta weight will also be higher than that of the other predictor variables. If it is highly correlated with the other predictor variables, its beta weight actually may be relatively low. Conversely, a predictor variable with a fairly low correlation with the outcome variable may have a relatively high beta weight.

Our example used only four predictor variables. But we probably could identify many more interval level or ratio level variables that might be expected to correlate fairly highly with scores on a standardized statistics examination. Multiple R can be used with a large number of predictor variables. Unless we have a considerably larger number of cases than we have predictor variables, however, we can be led into making too much of the correlation coefficient thus produced. It might be quite high just based on the high ratio of variables to cases. To avoid this problem, Multiple R should be used only when the number of cases is substantially larger than the number of predictor variables to be included in the statistical analysis.

Variations of Multiple *R*

There are variations of Multiple R, referred to as stepwise procedures, that can be very useful and are available in most statistical software packages. One of these, referred to as the **step-up procedure,** involves a rank ordering of the predictor variables by their beta weights. First, the predictor variable that contains the most unique correlation with the outcome variable (the highest beta weight) is identified. Then, the predictor variable with the next highest beta weight is added to see how much the multiple correlation coefficient is affected.

The process can continue with other predictor variables added (in order of their beta weights) until a point of diminishing returns—that is, until those predictor variables are reached that are of little value in accounting for any sizable additional variance within the outcome variable. The process allows us to narrow the list to only those predictor variables that are most important in explaining the variation of the outcome variable.

Another procedure, referred to as the **step-down procedure,** works in a similar way, but in the opposite direction. It begins with all the predictor variables and eliminates them one by one, starting with the one with the lowest beta weight. Predictor variables previously omitted can be added back along the way to see how the multiple correlation coefficient is affected. Like the step-up procedure, the step-down procedure allows us to winnow down the list of predictor variables to a relatively small number that is most useful in explaining the variation in the values of the outcome variable.

As mentioned throughout this book, there is a form of statistical analysis for just about any situation. There is yet another situation when still another type of correlation analysis is appropriate. As we know, Multiple R is used to obtain the correlation between one outcome variable and a group of predictor variables (sometimes called a **derived variable**). Another procedure, called **canonical correlation,** takes correlation even further. It is used to simultaneously examine the correlation between a weighted group of predictor variables (a derived predictor variable) and a weighted group of outcome variables (a derived outcome variable). The procedure is used when the outcome variable is somewhat abstract and cannot be adequately measured by using scores for any single variable.

For example, if we wanted to examine the relationship between a fairly abstract outcome variable such as *interpersonal skills on the job* and certain demographic characteristics, we might first ask workers to evaluate their co-workers on several different outcome variables that are believed to be indicators of the concept, such as *cooperation, communication ability, friendliness, helpfulness,* and so on. The weighted group of scores on these variables could then be correlated with another weighted group of scores on such predictor variables as *education level, years of work experience, number of siblings,* and so on, with canonical correlation used to produce a Multiple R.

We would then be able to evaluate the Multiple R thus produced (or any other one produced by the procedures described above) as to its strength and direction, using the same criteria that are used in evaluating the bivariate correlation coefficients produced by Pearson's r. All correlation coefficients, no matter what statistical procedure produced them, are interpreted the same way, as previously described.

OTHER MULTIVARIATE TESTS THAT USE CORRELATION

As should be evident by now, correlation is a generic concept based on covariance. It relies on the assumption that when certain values of one variable are found together in consistent patterns with certain values of a second variable, there may be a relationship between the variables—they share something in common. We now present an overview of two somewhat specialized multivariate techniques that have been widely used since computer analyses of data has become available in most academic and practice settings. They are **factor analysis** and **cluster analysis.** Both employ a form of correlation analysis to complete a task that is useful to researchers.

Factor Analysis

Researchers use factor analyses to perform several different tasks. One common use is to reduce the length of a measuring instrument such as a scale or index by eliminating items (or questions) that are redundant, that is, that measure the same indicator of a variable more than once.

The first draft of a measurement scale or index often is quite long. It contains many items that are believed to be indicators of the variable being measured. After a newly developed scale or index has been administered to a group of people, a factor analysis on the completed instruments can be performed. The results would reveal to what degree peoples' responses to one item correlate with their responses to other items. Why would this be useful to know? How would it suggest which items are redundant? When two or more items consistently produce the same responses from the same individuals, they may be assumed to be measuring the same indicator (redundancy). Items that produce dissimilar responses from the same individuals may be assumed to be measuring different indicators of the variable (no redundancy).

For example, in a scale that measures the variable *attentiveness in class,* one item might ask how frequently a student has fallen asleep in class. Another item might ask how often the student yawns in class. If, in a large sample of students, there is a strong pattern (positive correlation) of responses wherein individual students almost without exception respond the same to both items, it may be assumed that the two items measure the same indicator of attentiveness and are thus redundant. If, however, individual students tended to give different responses to the two items, we might conclude that they measure two different indicators of attentiveness.

By examining correlation among responses to items, a factor analysis groups the items into factors (which can be thought of loosely as indicators or derived variables). For example, it might list four different items in one factor because responses to them were similar among individuals. This would indicate that all four items probably are measurements of the same factor. We could then look at the four items themselves to determine what they have in common.

Returning to our previous example, a factor analysis might suggest that the four items that ask about falling asleep, yawning, head nodding, and resting one's head on one's hand constitute one factor. We might label it something like "physical manifestations of attentiveness." We may then decide that any one of the items is sufficient and the other three can be deleted, or we may wish to leave two, three, or all four of them in the next version of the scale as a kind of subscale. Similar options would also exist for the other factors that were identified by our factor analysis.

Factors derived from a factor analysis are independent of other factors—each measures a different indicator or derived variable. This does not mean, however, that an individual item will show up in only one group of items (a factor). The same item may be a part of two (or even more) factors.

The issue of how many items to retain is complicated. Among other considerations, we may ask how long a measuring instrument can be before respondents refuse to complete it. Researchers sometimes elect to retain two or more items from the same factor as a reliability check; that is, to see if an individual is responding consistently and thus honestly. If so, responses to the items should be identical or nearly identical.

A factor analysis also assists in the creation of equivalent forms of the same instrument, a desirable characteristic of a scale or index. One item selected from an identified factor can be used in one form and another item from the same factor in another form of the scale or index. It should not matter which specific item or items is present in a form, so long as all the factors are represented in all forms of the instrument. Then, no matter which form of the instrument a person completes, the measurement of the variable should be the same.

There are a number of other features of factor analyses that allow us to construct the exact measuring instrument we require. For example, factors can be refined using a process called **factor rotation.** Although the process is complicated and has many different variations, all of them are designed to help us develop more precise meanings of the factors within any given data set.

A second practical use of a factor analysis, in addition to instrument construction, is for the preliminary screening of large groups of variables prior to multiple regression or discriminant analysis (both discussed in the next chapter). With the use of a factor analysis, redundant predictor variables (those that emerge as part of the same factor as other variables) can be identified. It may then be possible to eliminate all but one, thus making the job of either type of analysis less complicated.

A factor analysis has many practical uses in fields such as business and marketing. A restaurant owner may do a factor analysis of customers' food preferences to try to identify menu items that are redundant (i.e., may appeal to the same customers). Once identified, some of these items can be eliminated and replaced with others that have the potential to broaden the restaurant's clientele base without offering more menu alternatives.

Marketing managers sometimes perform factor analyses to determine what factors lead people to buy a certain product. Then they develop magazine advertisements based on the results of their analyses. The advertisements are written carefully to avoid redundancy (the same factors) while covering all identified factors.

How might a social worker use factor analyses for making everyday, practical decisions? Client follow-up study data could be analyzed and the results examined to determine which factors constitute the variable *client satisfaction.* Then staff development sessions could be used to build in all of these factors while not engaging in unnecessary redundancy (overkill). Or, annual performance evaluations of staff could be analyzed to identify factors that supervisors deem important to good performance. Then, these factors could be emphasized in orientation sessions for new staff or, if the criteria being used seem inappropriate, they could be discussed with supervisors and the need for changes emphasized.

Factor analyses can be helpful in improving many forms of evaluation in social work. For example, they can (and should) be used to refine measuring instruments used by students to evaluate their instructors. Their use might help limit a tendency to place disproportionate weight on such factors as niceness or the ability to entertain.

Cluster Analysis

Whereas a factor analysis performs the task of clustering items into factors, a **cluster analysis** is used primarily to cluster similar cases together. A cluster analysis often is performed prior to hypothesis testing. It makes hypothesis testing possible by creating the value categories of a variable when none previously existed. Cluster analyses create subsamples of cases based on the fact that cases in each subsample have similar measurements (values) of the various indicators of some variable. Thus, the cases are similar to each other, but different from cases in other subsamples.

We might use a cluster analysis, for example, to attempt to create groups of cases with similar religious beliefs based on their beliefs about a divine being, the existence of life after death, and so forth. After the cluster analysis, each group formed would probably contain some persons who belong to the same religious denomination, but also people who belong to different denominations as well as people with no formal religious affiliation. A member of a group may have the same religious affiliation as a member of another group, but their religious beliefs would be different. After the groups have been formed, we could then test a hypothesis about the relationship between religious beliefs and, for example, attitudes about some social issue.

Cluster analyses can be used in many ways by social workers. Often the similarity of people's attitudes, beliefs, values, or behaviors is more important to understanding them than their label or diagnostic category. It might be useful, for example, to use a cluster analysis to create subsamples of psychiatric patients based on their reports of self-defeating behaviors, rather than upon their DSM category. Then we could test a hypothesis about the relationship between the type of self-defeating behaviors exhibited and, for example, whether patients will attempt to avoid taking prescribed medications. We could also simply use the clusters or groups thus formed to constitute several homogeneous treatment groups that might have therapeutic goals quite different from each of the other groups.

CONCLUDING THOUGHTS

This chapter presented a few of the many uses of correlation. As noted, correlation is used to design research studies, to refine data-collection instruments, to describe the relationship between and among variables in a population or sample, for inference testing, and even to create value categories to facilitate subsequent hypothesis testing. All correlation analyses produce a correlation coefficient that describes the strength and direction of a relationship, the covariance that exists between and among variables. The coefficient can be squared to gain an estimate of the amount of variation in the outcome variable attributable to the variation in the predictor variable or, when using Multiple R, to two or more predictor variables in concert.

We pointed out the effect that sample size has on statistical significance when using correlation analyses and why a correlation coefficient may be statistically significant while really quite weak. Even when a statistically significant correlation coefficient is obtained, the correlation may not be strong enough to represent a meaningful finding. It should also be remembered that the value of a correlation coefficient must be assessed with the use of common sense and knowledge of social work practice. A statistically significant, relatively low correlation coefficient may represent a meaningful finding in one study if it advances knowledge, but a relatively high correlation coefficient in another study may be relatively unimportant. Identifying no association

($r = 0$) between variables that are believed to be related may represent the most important finding of a study!

Chapter 9 builds closely on the concepts contained within this chapter. It examines simple linear regression and another important product of statistical analyses that we have only briefly mentioned up to this point, prediction.

STUDY QUESTIONS

1. What can a scattergram portray that other graphs cannot? What does each dot in a scattergram depict?
2. Construct hypothetical data on the variables *number of siblings* and *mother's highest school grade completed* for members of your class. Create a scattergram similar to Figure 8.3 to portray your data. Does the scattergram suggest that the two variables are related? If so, in which direction?
3. Why do we use the terms *predictor variable* and *outcome variable* rather than the terms *dependent variable* and *independent variable* in discussing correlation analyses?
4. In a correlation coefficient, what do the sign and the number each reflect?
5. What do we mean by *linear correlation*? Provide examples of variables that might be correlated in a nonlinear way.
6. What does r^2 tell us about the relationship between variables? Provide examples in your discussion.
7. Interpret each of the following hypothetical values for r. $r = -.45$; $r = +.45$; $r = +1.0$; $r = -1.0$.
8. Fill in the blanks to complete the following sentences:
   Correlation coefficients range from _____ to _____. A correlation coefficient suggests the _____ and the _____ of the relationship between variables. A correlation coefficient of _____ indicates a perfect positive relationship; _____ indicates a perfect negative relationship; and _____ indicates that there is no linear correlation between variables.
9. What are two nonparametric tests that can be used to examine correlation when the assumptions of Pearson's r cannot be met?
10. What do we call a type of correlation analysis that examines the correlation between two normally distributed interval level or ratio level variables while controlling for the effects of a third variable? How can it detect a spurious relationship between variables?
11. What do we call the multivariate form of a correlation analysis discussed in this chapter?
12. What does it mean when we say that one predictor variable is redundant when we use this type of analysis? What do we call the procedures for adding or subtracting predictor variables based on their ability to help explain variations in values of the outcome variable?
13. Find an article in a professional social work journal that used multiple correlation as the method of data analysis. What were the predictor variables? What conclusions did the author generate from the study? Do you feel the study was relevant to your future practice? Why? What other predictor variables could the author have used?
14. When using multiple correlation, why can we not simply add together the individual bivariate correlation coefficients between two predictor variables and the outcome variable to find their combined correlation with the outcome variable? Explain.
15. Describe at least two ways social workers can use factor analysis.
16. Why would a cluster analysis sometimes be a better way of grouping cases than such commonly used value labels as liberal and conservative? Provide an example.

CHAPTER

Regression Analyses

As presented in the previous chapter, a correlation coefficient (expressed as an *r* value) provides an overall picture of the relationship between two variables—its strength and direction. As we know, with sample data, we use the laws of probability to determine if this relationship is strong enough so that we can feel reasonably safe in concluding that the relationship probably was not due to by sampling error.

Another, related procedure, simple linear regression, takes a correlation between variables a step farther. For any case within the population, simple linear regression is used to predict (with varying degrees of accuracy) the value of the outcome variable based on the value of the predictor variable.

WHAT IS PREDICTION?

In statistical analyses, prediction has a meaning similar to that of everyday usage. Specifically, it refers to determining (without measuring) what the specific case value an outcome variable is most likely to be. When we refer to prediction, the different values of the outcome variable may occur in the future, or they may already have occurred. Thus, prediction might entail, for example, using the number of hours that Jolene studied for an exam on Sunday night (the predictor variable) to produce a best guess as to either (1) what her grade will be on an the exam on Monday (one outcome variable) or (2) how many hours she spent in social activities on Sunday night (a second outcome variable).

Understanding statistical prediction involves many of the statistical concepts discussed in the previous eight chapters. The mean and standard deviation (Chapter 3), the normal distribution (Chapter 4), and correlation (Chapter 8), for example, are all important to understanding prediction.

Suppose we want to predict the score of a new client named Joe on a standardized life-skills measuring instrument following a 12-week life-skills training course for people with developmental disabilities. The instrument is administered in the program at 6 weeks (midprogram) and 12 weeks (termination). It produces scores that range from 0 (very poor life skills) to 100 (excellent life skills).

To predict Joe's most likely score following completion of the course, we would have to rely on some data that we already know. If the only datum that we have is the mean life-skills score at completion for all people who have completed the course, this mean (e.g., 82) would be our best estimate for predicting Joe's final life skills score at the end of 12 weeks.

A prediction based on only a group's mean would provide a rather crude estimate. But we can do better. To improve the prediction, we might look to other data for help. Suppose we also know Joe's individual score from his 6-week assessment and the group's mean score after 6 weeks. We can use these data to make a more informed prediction about what Joe's final score is likely to be at 12 weeks.

Let us say, for example, that Joe's life skills score at 6 weeks was 79 and that the group's mean score at 6 weeks was 75. The distribution in Figure 9.1*a* shows that Joe scored 4 points higher than the group's mean at the 6-week assessment period. Thus, it would be reasonable to suggest that Joe would also score higher than the group's mean at the 12-week assessment period (presented in the distribution in Figure 9.1*b*).

Without any additional information about Joe or the program, we can statistically improve the accuracy of the prediction by considering the correlation between the scores at the 6-week and 12-week assessment periods. As we know from Chapter 8, the correlation coefficient (r) between the two variables would help by telling us (roughly) how accurate our prediction will be. If the correlation is equal to 0.0, data from the 6-week assessment will not help us predict scores at the 12-week assessment. However, if our correlation is $+1.0$ or -1.0, then we could use the data from the 6-week assessments to make perfectly accurate predictions about the 12-week assessments.

Understanding how **perfect predictions** are made requires an understanding of standard deviations and the normal distribution. Suppose there is a perfect positive linear correlation ($r = +1.0$) between the scores at the 6-week assessment and the scores at the 12-week assessment. Thus, a person's position within the group at the 6-week assessment period would correspond perfectly to his or her position within the group at the 12-week assessment period.

For example, if one person's score was 1.0 standard deviation above the group's mean score at the 6-week assessment period, then her score at the 12-week assessment period would also be 1.0 standard deviation above the group's mean score. If another person's score was 1.5 standard deviations below the group's mean score at the 6-week assessment period, then his score at the 12-week assessment period would also be 1.5 standard deviations below the group's mean score. By using the means and the standard deviations for the two distributions of the variable at the 6-week and 12-week assessment periods and the z-score formula (Chapter 4), we could compute exactly what every individual's score theoritically should be.

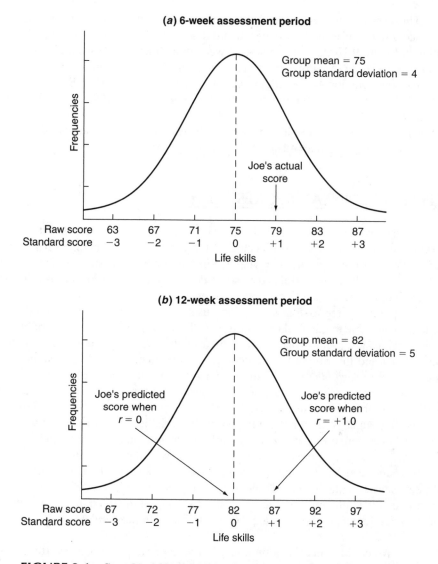

FIGURE 9.1　Standard Normal Distributions for Life Skills at 6-Week and 12-Week Assessment Periods

Take a closer look at Figure 9.1*a* and *b*. They show both the raw scores and the standard scores for the 6-week and 12-week assessment periods. The standard deviation for the 6-week assessment period is 4, because the raw scores change by increments of 4 along the base of the 6-week distribution. This being the case, Joe would have scored 1.0 standard deviation above the mean for the 6-week assessment on the standard normal distribution (75 + 4 = 79). If the correlation between 6-week and 12-week assessment scores was 1.0, we would know that Joe should have the same relative position on both normal distributions.

Thus, to predict Joe's score at the 12-week assessment period, we would find the raw score that corresponds to one standard deviation. As can be seen from the distribution in Figure 9.1*b*, Joe's predicted 12-week assessment score would be 87. It is 1.0 standard deviation (5) above the mean (82) for the 12-week scores.

As noted previously, perfect predictions are rare in the real world. Comparing the normal distributions for two variables that have a less-than-perfect correlation is not as straightforward as when $r = +1.0$ or -1.0. When the correlation between two variables is less than perfect, which is almost always the case, we can use simple linear regression analysis to help make predictions.

WHAT IS SIMPLE LINEAR REGRESSION?

As stated at the beginning of this chapter, simple linear regression makes it possible to predict (with varying degrees of accuracy) the value(s) of an outcome variable from a known value(s) of a predictor variable. Simple linear regression can be performed when two variables are correlated to some degree and the relationship is a linear one (positive or negative) as reflected on a scattergram.

Simple linear regression is especially useful in experimental research designs in which we are able to manipulate or introduce the value of the predictor variable. When these designs are used, it may be possible to demonstrate that the predictor variable actually caused the value of the outcome variable. (The terms *independent variable* and *dependent variable* might be more appropriate if this were the case.)

Simple linear regression can also be used in the types of research situations we more commonly encounter in social work—where we can only select and measure (but not introduce or manipulate) the predictor variable. How would this work? First we would measure both a predictor variable and an outcome variable within a data set. Then, with the use of simple linear regression, we would produce an equation describing the numerical relationship between the measurements of the two variables within the data set. The equation could then be used to predict (with some degree of accuracy) the value of the outcome variable for a case that was not included in the data set, based on its measurement (value) of the predictor variable. For example:

1. We could collect data on *undergraduate grade point average* (the predictor variable) among graduate students in a social work class and their *current graduate grade point average* (the outcome variable). With the use of simple linear regression, we could then produce an equation describing the numerical relationship between the measurements of the two variables within our data set. If another student (Katlyn) joined the class later, we could use the equation to predict her current graduate grade point average from her undergraduate grade point average.

2. We could use a data-collection instrument to measure both *number of prior felony arrests* (the predictor variable) and *hostility toward authority figures* (the outcome variable) among a randomly selected group of clients currently on probation. With the use of simple linear regression, we could then produce an equation describing the numerical relationship between the measurements of the two variables within our

data set. When another client (Edward) enters the system, we could use the equation to predict his hostility toward authority figures from his number of felony arrests.

3. We could use the records from an extended-care facility to compile data on *age at admission* (the predictor variable) and *number of visitors they received the first month* (the outcome variable) among current residents of the facility. With the use of simple linear regression, we could then produce an equation describing the numerical relationship between the measurements of the two variables within our data set. When another client (Simeon) enters the facility, we could use the equation to predict the number of visitors he is likely to receive the first month, based upon his current age.

Two important products of simple linear regression are a regression equation and a regression line that graphically reflects the equation. Before we discuss what they are and how they are used, however, we will first look at how to formulate a research question for a simple linear regression analysis and the limitations of simple linear regression.

Formulating a Research Question

A simple linear regression is an extension of a correlation analysis of the relationship between two normally distributed interval level or ratio level variables. It is meaningful only if the relationship between the variables has been found to be statistically significant and the correlation between them is fairly strong. When performing a simple linear regression, it is not necessary to restate the research and null hypothesis, because the null form of the research hypothesis—that there is no relationship between the outcome and predictor variables—will already have been tested and rejected with the use of Pearson's *r*.

Instead of restating the research hypothesis, we typically formulate a research question to specify what we hope to learn from a simple linear regression. It asks how knowing the value of a predictor variable will improve our ability to predict the value of an outcome variable. The following are research questions drawn from our earlier examples that can be answered with the use of a simple linear regression analysis:

Research Question:

How much does knowing a student's GPA in undergraduate school help to predict the student's GPA in graduate school?

Research Question:

How much does knowing the number of previous felony arrests help to predict an individual's degree of hostility toward authority?

Research Question:

How much does knowing a client's age help to predict the number of visitors the individual will have the first month after admission?

Limitations of Simple Linear Regression

A simple linear regression analysis produces an equation, called a **regression equation.** With the use of the equation, we can predict (with some degree of accuracy) the value of an outcome variable (Y) for a particular case by knowing the value for the case's predictor variable (X). The major benefit is that we can predict the most likely measure for a case's outcome variable without actually measuring it, if we just know the measurement for a case's predictor variable.

There are limitations to what we can legitimately do with the use of simple linear regression. We cannot make predictions about measurements of the outcome variable for cases whose values for the predictor variable are either larger than the largest X value or smaller than the smallest X value in the sample data that was the basis for the computation of the equation. Suppose, for example, that the predictor variable *number of hours of vigorous exercise per week* was used to predict the value of the variable *attitude toward obese persons.* If the sample on which the regression equation was computed included individuals who exercised between 2 and 15 hours per week, then no matter how strong the correlation, we could not use the equation to predict attitude toward obese persons for individuals with less than 2 or more than 15 hours of vigorous exercise per week. We will never know if the correlation exist's at all beyond the limits of our sample data.

Other statistical limitations of simple linear regression are the same as for Pearson's *r.* Both Pearson's *r* and simple linear regression require interval level or ratio level data, and both assume normal distributions of the predictor and outcome variables (see Chapter 8).

COMPUTATION OF THE REGRESSION EQUATION

Another example will show how to compute a simple linear regression equation. Suppose that, using a random sample of seven female clients, we have tested the research hypothesis that there is a positive correlation between educational attainment (predictor variable) and assertiveness (outcome variable). Educational attainment was measured by recording the last year of school completed, and assertiveness was measured by the completion of a self-report standardized measuring instrument that measures assertiveness. The correlation between the variables in our hypothetical study was $+1.00$, a perfect positive correlation. Even with our small sample, that strong a correlation is very unlikely to be the work of sampling error, we have rejected the null hypothesis and concluded that we have statistical support for our research hypothesis.

The measurements of the two variables (i.e., *educational attainment, assertiveness level*) are presented in Table 9.1. If we study the data in Table 9.1, we can make a number of observations. For all cases, the measurement of Y, the outcome variable (*assertiveness level*), is greater than for X, the predictor variable (*educational attainment*). A closer look at Table 9.1 reveals that for each case, Y is more than twice the value of X. In fact, in all seven cases, Y is exactly $2(X) + 5$. We can now express the relationship between the two variables as a regression equation:

$$Y' = 5 + 2(X)$$

TABLE 9.1   Educational Attainment and Assertiveness Levels ($N = 7$)

Name	Educational Attainment (X) (Predictor Variable)	Assertiveness Level (Y) (Outcome Variable)
Rochelle	9	23
Carny	12	29
Belinda	6	17
Amanda	8	21
Maria	11	27
Ky	15	35
Ruth	13	31

This equation is just a variation of the usual equation for a straight line, which is written as $Y = a + b(X)$. However, in a regression equation, the notation Y' is used to denote a predicted value (not an actual one). If we plotted the data contained in Table 9.1 with the use of a scattergram and connected the dots as in Figure 9.2, we would have a perfect straight line reflecting the perfect positive correlation between the two variables.

As Table 9.1 portrays, Rochelle has 9 years of education (X) and has an assertiveness level of 23 (Y). Thus, the regression equation reflects (exactly) the relationship between her education level and her assertiveness score: $Y' = 5 + 2(9) = 23$. Unlike what we would be likely to find in the real world (a less-than-perfect correlation), the equation $Y' = 5 + 2(X)$ holds true for the other six women as well. The general equation produced by simple linear regression analysis is:

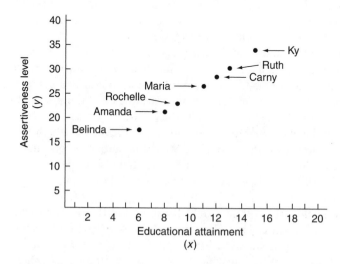

FIGURE 9.2   Scattergram of Educational Attainment and Assertiveness Levels (from Table 9.1)

$$Y' = a + b(X)$$

where:

Y' = the predicted Y value from a particular X value

a = the point where the regression line would intersect the y axis, the constant

b = the slope of the line, where the amount of change in Y is directly related to the amount of change in X, the regression coefficient

x = a selected value of the predictor variable used to predict the value of the outcome variable

Hand computations of regression equations are lengthy processes, especially for large data sets. With the help of a computer and almost any statistical software package, however, simple linear regression analyses take very little time. Most software packages also are programmed to display the data within a scattergram showing dots for all cases, the correlation coefficient (r), and the regression equation. For those who wish to see how a regression equation is calculated, Box 9.1 has been provided. It uses the data displayed in Table 8.2 in Chapter 8.

MORE ABOUT THE REGRESSION LINE

The regression line is a straight line of best fit for a given set of data. It is presented mathematically (the regression equation) or graphically on a scattergram. The values in Table 9.1 as illustrated in Figure 9.2 reflect a perfect positive correlation ($r = +1.0$), but it is far more likely that the actual data in our example would look more like those in Table 9.2 and Figure 9. 3. They reflect a less-than-perfect linear correlation between the variables *educational achievement* and *assertiveness level*.

A single straight line cannot be drawn through the seven dots in Figure 9.3, because the correlation between the two variables displayed is not a perfect one (it is neither $+1.0$ nor -1.0). If we used a computer to compute Pearson's r for the data, we would learn that $r = +.76$ for the two variables in Figure 9.3. But to be able to predict the most likely assertiveness level for a woman not among the seven cases based on our knowledge of her educational level we would need to do more than just compute this correlation. We would need quotes produce the line with the best possible fit—one, and only one, line that would pass through "the center of the dots," hitting as many dots as possible while not missing the others by "too much."

How can we find this line? What would its slope be; that is, how vertical (as opposed to horizontal) would it be? We could draw several lines through what appears to be the center of the distribution of dots, but it would be hard to determine from just a visual examination which line would be the best fit. Some lines would hit some dots but miss others; some would be more vertical, others more horizontal.

BOX 9.1
The Least-Squares Regression Equation

Problem: What is the least-squares regression equation ($Y' = a + b[X]$) for the data in Table 8.2?

Predictor Variable: Number of spouse, abuse reports—ratio level.

Outcome Variable: Number of child abuse reports—ratio level.

Slope Formula:

$$b = \frac{N\Sigma XY - (\Sigma X)(\Sigma Y)}{N\Sigma X^2 - (\Sigma X)^2}$$

where:
b = Slope
N = Number of cases
ΣXY = Sum of xy column
ΣX = Sum of X column
ΣY = Sum of y column
ΣX^2 = Sum of x^2 column
ΣY^2 = Sum of y^2 column

Substituting values for letters:

$$b = \frac{(5)(1305) - (88)(59)}{(5)(1790) - (88)^2}$$
$$= \frac{1333}{1206}$$
$$= 1.11 \text{ (slope)}$$

y-Intercept Formula:

$$a = \overline{Y} - b\overline{X}$$

where:
a = y intercept
Y = Mean of Y column
bX = Slope times mean of X column

Substituting values for letters:

$$a = \frac{59}{5} - (1.11)\left(\frac{88}{5}\right)$$
$$= 11.8 - (1.11)(17.6)$$
$$= 11.8 - 19.5$$
$$= -7.7 \text{ (y intercept)}$$

Presentation of Results:

$$Y' = -7.7 + 1.11(X)$$

Conclusion: A slope of 1.11 means that for every unit change in X (for every increase of 1 unit in the number of spouse abuse reports), there was a change of 1.11 units in Y (the number of child-abuse reports increased by 1.11). Note from Box 8.1, $r = .94$.

TABLE 9.2   Educational Attainment and Assertiveness Levels ($N = 7$)

Name	Educational Attainment (X)	Assertiveness Level (Y)
Rochelle	9	20
Carny	12	21
Belinda	6	14
Amanda	8	25
Maria	11	21
Ky	15	28
Ruth	13	30

The Least-Squares Criterion

The dots above and below the line represent actual, paired values for both variables. The line that we would seek for the data in Figure 9.3, its regression line, is a line of predicted values (Y'). Notice how the actual values above the line are predicted by the line to be lower than they actually are and the values below the line are predicted by the line to be higher than they actually are. This is basic to understanding simple linear regression. Unless the correlation is perfect, it does not provide perfectly accurate predictions, only "best guesses."

A regression analysis obtains a regression line; that is, it determines the equation reflecting its slope and where it would intercept the *y* axis—by using what is referred to as the **least-squares criterion.** No matter where we drew a straight line in Figure 9.3

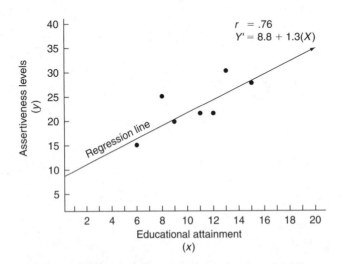

FIGURE 9.3   Scattergram of Educational Attainment and Assertiveness Levels (from Table 9.2)

we would miss some of the dots. The vertical distance between each of the respective dots and that line could be measured, however. Then each of these distances (referred to as deviations) could be squared and their squares added together (totaled). The sum of the squared deviations from the regression line would be different depending on exactly where we drew the line—some would be larger; some would be smaller. The least-squares criterion asserts that the best regression line is a line that produces the smallest sum of squared deviations from it.

Fortunately, there is a much easier way to arrive at a regression line for a data set than by trying an almost infinite number of lines, determining their sum of squared deviations, and then selecting the one with the least squares. It involves the computation of a regression equation. Box 9.1 presents the mathematical formula to calculate the slope and the point of the y intercept for any pair of interval level or ratio level variables.

The formula generates the linear equation for the regression line that we are seeking; that is, the least-squares line. The components of the equation are summarized in Box 9.2. Both the *a* value (where the line intercepts the y axis) and the *b* value are likely to be fractions, not whole numbers, as in our first example, in which a perfect correlation existed. For example, the computer-generated equation for the regression line shown in Figure 9.3 is $Y' = 8.8 + 1.3(X)$.

The Regression Coefficient (b).   In a regression equation, the **regression coefficient** (*b*) is the slope of the regression line. (Slope as used here has essentially the same meaning as it does when we refer to the slope of a hill; that is, the proportional relationship between vertical rise and horizontal distance.) In a regression equation, *b* is the amount and direction of change in *Y* for each unit of change in *X*. If *b* is positive, as *X* increases, *Y* will increase at a specific constant rate. If *b* is negative, as *X* increases, *Y* will decrease at a specific constant rate. Likewise, as *X* decreases, *Y* will increase at a specific constant rate. The *b* value suggests the rate of change in the value of *Y* (the outcome variable) for each unit of change in the value of *X* (the predictor variable).

The slope of the regression line (*b*) indicates exactly where, between the vertical and horizontal axes, the line would fall. High *b* values reflect lines that are nearly vertical; low *b* values reflect lines that are nearly horizontal.

The regression coefficient (*b*) within a regression equation is closely related to the correlation coefficient (*r*) for the two variables. But, unlike the value of *r*, which always ranges between +1.0 and −1.0, the value of *b* may be any number. Also, as we have suggested, *r* and *b* will always correspond in terms of positive and negative values. If *r* is negative, *b* is negative; if *r* is positive, *b* is positive.

After the data are entered into a computer program and a regression analysis is completed, the computer output will usually display both the correlation coefficient and the regression equation. The *b* value for Figure 9.3 is 1.3; it is shown in the upper right-hand corner of the figure. Because it is a positive number, this means that for each unit increase in *X*, *Y* increases 1.3 points. Thus, for each 1-point increase in educational attainment, we can predict that a person's assertiveness level will be 1.3 points higher. An actual assertiveness level can be predicted to be the education attainment times 1.3, plus the value of *a*.

The y Intercept (a).   Most statistical software packages also display the starting point for the line. The starting point is the **y intercept,** the point **at which** the regression line, if extended beyond the sample data as in Figure 9.3, would cross the *y* axis and become negative (if that is theoretically possible). This is the point that might represent the predicted value of *Y* when *X* equals 0. In our example, then, the predicted assertiveness score of a woman with 0 years of education would be 8.8. Of course, it would be theoretically impossible to have a negative number of years of education.

As noted earlier, however, we should not predict the assertiveness level of a woman with 0 years of education with the use of simple linear regression, because our sample data on which the regression equation was developed did not include anyone with less than 6 years of education. Because we did not actually study women with very little or no formal education, we have no way of guessing what the assertiveness level of such a woman might be. It might, in fact, be quite high. In other words, the relationship between the two variables may not be completely linear if women with all possible levels of education had been studied.

Statistical software packages draw the correct regression line in a scattergram and also show the place where it crosses the *y* axis. The value of *a* can be positive or negative. A positive *a* value tells us the regression line will meet the *y* axis at a value above 0; a negative *a* value indicates the regression line (extended, if necessary) would cross the *y* axis at a value below 0.

Predicted Y (Y′).   (Y') is the estimated score for an outcome variable for a given value of its corresponding predictor variable. We can predict the value of an outcome variable for a single case by computing Y' for any value of *X* that falls within the range of scores that were used to produce the regression equation. In the upper right-hand corner of Figure 9.3 we can see the regression equation $Y' = 8.8 + 1.3(X)$. The *X* component of the formula is any specific value of *X* for which we wish to predict a *Y* value. The following are two calculations for the

---

BOX 9.2
The Components of a Regression Equation ($Y' = a + b(X)$)

Y' = the predicted value of *Y* for a case with a known measurement of *X*.

a = the point where the regression line would intersect the *y*-axis; often, the predicted value of *Y* if *X* were zero.

b = the slope of the regression line; an indication of how vertical or horizontal the line is; the number of units of change in *Y* for each unit of *X*.

X = a value of the predictor variable (for a case) that can be used to predict the value of the outcome variable.

predicted *Y* values of two different cases when we substitute specific values for *X* (13 and 6, respectively):

Calculation 1:

Let us determine *Y'* by substituting 13 for *X:*

$$Y' = a + b(X)$$
$$= 8.8 + 1.3(13)$$
$$= 8.8 + 16.9$$
$$= 25.7 \text{ (predicted value of Y when } X = 13)$$

Calculation 2:

Let us determine *Y'* by substituting 6 for *X:*

$$Y' = a + b(X)$$
$$= 8.8 + 1.3(6)$$
$$= 8.8 + 7.8$$
$$= 16.6 \text{ (predicted value of } Y \text{ when } X = 6)$$

The two *X* values of 13 and 6 were arbitrarily chosen. They could have been any numbers within the range of the distribution of *X* within the sample studied. What do the *X* and *Y'* values mean? When *X* is 13, the predicted value of *Y* is 25.7 (Calculation 1); when *X* is 6, the predicted value of *Y* is 16.6 (Calculation 2). Thus, a client who has an educational attainment of 13 is predicted to have an assertiveness level of 25.7, and a client with an educational attainment of 6 is predicted to have an assertiveness level of 16.6.

An alternative approach to predicting the value of *Y* involves using the actual regression line as presented in a scattergram. We could find, for example, the exact value ($X = 13$) along the *x* axis of the scattergram in Figure 9.3. Next we could run a vertical line straight up until we reach the regression line. Then we could draw a straight horizontal line to the left until we touch the *y* axis.

Note that we hit the same *Y'* as predicted in the equation above ($Y' = $ about 25.7). This method of prediction is not nearly as precise as using a regression equation. It does provide a visual understanding of the data, however, and can be used as a quick check on a result obtained mathematically. We could use the same method to check the value for *Y'* when $X = 6$ to verify that our math was correct. Box 9.2 summarizes the meanings of the components of a regression equation.

Interchanging *X* and *Y* Variables

The example conceptualized years of education as the predictor variable (*X*) and assertiveness level as the outcome variable (*Y*). We could have conceptualized the relationship between the two variables the other way around. Assertiveness could be thought of as the predictor variable and years of education as the outcome variable. As emphasized earlier, labeling variables as predictor and outcome variables needs to make theoretical and logical sense. In this instance, we could build a logical case for a relationship between the two variables in either direction.

In computing the correlation between two variables, the correlation coefficient would be the same regardless of which variable we label the predictor variable and which we label the outcome variable. The predictor and outcome variables are not interchangeable in a regression analysis, however. If we enter years of education into our computer as the predictor variable and assertiveness as the outcome variable, we get one result (the regression equation above). But if we enter assertiveness as the predictor variable and years of education as the outcome variable, we get a different regression equation. We must be clear which is intended as the predictor variable and which is intended as the outcome variable (as stated in the research question). We must then be careful to input our data so as to reflect this understanding if we hope to get the regression equation that we seek.

INTERPRETING RESULTS

How valuable is a prediction that can be made from a regression line? The answer depends on the strength of the correlation between the two variables. When the correlation is very weak (e.g., approaching 0.0), there is no point in even calculating the best-fitting straight line to make predictions about the value of the outcome variable. The predictions would be wrong much more often than they would be correct. When a correlation is strong, however, the line can be used for predictive purposes with reasonable accuracy. Thus, there is a direct relationship between the magnitude of r and the accuracy of predictions.

The formula in Box 9.1 clearly shows how correlation is directly related to simple linear regression. As r decreases (e.g., approaches 0.0), the accuracy of prediction using simple linear regression decreases; as r increases (e.g., approaches $+1.0$ or -1.0), the accuracy of prediction increases.

Presentation of Y'

The presentation of Y' is straightforward. The regression equation $Y' = 3.5 + 6.8(X)$, for example, could be stated in words as "for every unit increase in X, there will be a 6.8 unit increase in Y." Using the variables *client's educational attainment* (X) and *assertiveness levels* (Y), this would read, "for each 1-year increase in a client's educational level, her assertiveness level will increase by 6.8 points."

The Standard Error

An indicator referred to as the **standard error** can provide an estimate of how well the regression equation can predict values of the outcome variable from known values of the predictor variable. When $r = +1.0$ or -1.0, all dots on a scattergram will fall exactly on the regression line. In this case, the standard error equals 0.0. The closer the standard error is to either $+1.0$ or -1.0, the more confident we can be that the regression equation will give us accurate predictions. The further r is from being perfect (as it approaches 0.0), the more errors will be made in making predictions of Y using the regression equation. When $r = 0.0$, the standard error would be at its maximum and the regression equation would be of no value whatsoever in predicting a value of an outcome variable from a known value of its predictor variable.

Using Regression in Social Work Practice

Although the primary function of regression is prediction, it is sometimes combined with the results of a correlation analysis to add additional information to hypothesis testing. We will examine two hypothetical examples to see how this can be done.

Example: Socializing with Family Members and Life Satisfaction. Shondra is a social worker in a family service agency. Over the last year, she saw 80 clients for counseling related to depression. During this time, she formed the impression that the clients who seemed most depressed had little time to spend socializing with family members. She also noticed that clients who had a considerable amount of time to spend socializing with family members did not seem as depressed as most other clients. Shondra decided to do a small-scale research study to see if she could find statistical support for her observations.

Shondra wanted to determine how well information about the amount of time a client spent socializing with family members would improve her ability to predict the client's life-satisfaction level. Her predictor variable was *the amount of time the client spent socializing with family members during the previous week* (X), and her outcome variable was the *client life-satisfaction level* (Y).

Over the next several months, Shondra had all 50 new clients complete a standardized self-report measurement instrument that measures life satisfaction at the interval level. She also asked how many hours they had spent socializing with family members during the previous week (ratio level). The life-satisfaction instrument produces scores ranging from 0 (lowest level) to 200 (highest level).

Shondra entered the pairs of measurements for the two variables (one pair per case) into her personal computer and selected simple linear regression from the drop down menu. The Pearson's r, regression equation, and p level produced for the data were as follows:

$$r = .70$$
$$Y' = 1.49 + 4.69(X)$$
$$p < .0005$$

Shondra studied the above findings. The relatively high $(+.70)$ correlation coefficient (r value) and the statistically significant p value indicated that the regression analysis was justified and might produce fairly accurate predictions for values of the outcome variable. She computed r^2 and noted that the amount of time clients spent with family members was related to a fairly sizable amount of the variation of their life satisfaction levels ($.70^2 = .49$, or 49%).

Based on the regression equation generated, a slope (*b*) of 4.69 indicated that for each unit of increase in *X*, there is an increase of 4.69 units in *Y*. For each additional hour spent socializing with family members, for example, there was an average increase of 4.69 points on the life-satisfaction instrument (a decrease in depression).

Shondra could use her findings to predict a future client's life satisfaction by knowing how many hours the client had spent socializing with family members during the week. She realized that her findings probably could not be generalized to other clients with different problems (i.e., those with a presenting complaint other than depression) and perhaps not even to other clients being treated for depression in other settings. She also knew that she could not predict the life-satisfaction levels for clients who had spent more or less time with family members during the week than those clients in her original 50-case sample.

After completing her study, Shondra saw her 51st client, David, who came to the agency to be counseled for depression. During their first interview, David told Shondra that he had spent 15 hours socializing with family members during the previous week. Shondra computed David's predicted life-satisfaction score (Y') as follows:

$$
\begin{aligned}
Y' &= 1.49 + 4.69(15) \\
&= 1.49 + (70.35) \\
&= 71.84 \text{ (predicted value of } Y \text{ when } X \text{ equals 15)}
\end{aligned}
$$

To test how accurate her prediction had been, Shondra had David complete the life-satisfaction instrument and obtained his actual score. She compared his actual score (i.e., $Y = 73$) to his predicted score ($Y' = 71.84$) and was pleased to find that they were close.

Example: Worker's Caseload Size and Number of Sick Days Taken.   Josie is an administrator in a child protection agency. With recent cutbacks in funding, caseloads have increased for her staff. In the past, her child-protection workers typically managed a caseload between 30 and 40 clients. More recently, workers were assigned to as many as 60 active cases. Josie noticed that since caseload size had increased, there also seemed to be an increase in sick days taken by her workers.

Josie wondered if the size of a worker's caseload might be a good predictor of the number of sick days that the worker would take. The predictor variable for her correlation and simple linear regression analysis was *caseload size,* and the outcome variable was *number of sick days taken.* Both variables were measured at the ratio level.

To shed some light on her research question, Josie reviewed employee records over the past year. There were 22 frontline child protection workers on staff during the year. She reviewed their employee records and randomly selected a 1-month period for each worker. She noted the workers' average caseload size and the number of sick days taken during that month.

After entering the data into her personal computer, Josie performed a simple linear regression analysis and printed the results. The printout contained the following:

$$r = .76$$
$$Y' = -6.8 + .25(X)$$
$$p < .0005$$

Josie noted a statistically significant ($p < .0005$) strong correlation coefficient ($r = +.76$). Based on the strong correlation, Josie was confident that her regression equation could generate reasonably accurate predictions. The direction of the relationship between the two variables was also positive, exactly what she had expected. She noted that the regression coefficient (*b*) of .25 meant that for every unit change in *X*, there is an increase of .25 in *Y*. In other words, for every additional case added to a worker's caseload, the number of sick days a worker is likely to take would increase by .25.

Josie could use her findings to predict the number of sick days that a given worker might be expected to take in a month. She knew, however, that her study's findings might be useful for prediction only among those workers in her agency whose caseload was no smaller or larger than those contained in her sample of 22 cases.

Josie used her regression equation to predict how many sick days a worker named Roberto, who had a caseload of 43, would be likely to take for the month:

$$Y' = -6.8 + .25(43)$$
$$= -6.8 + 10.75$$
$$= 3.95, \text{ rounded to 4 (predicted value of } Y \text{ when } X \text{ equals 43)}$$

Josie's best guess was that Roberto would take 4 days of sick time during the month.

REGRESSION WITH THREE OR MORE VARIABLES

Not surprisingly, simple linear regression has its multivariate counterpart, **multiple linear regression.** Multiple correlation and multiple linear regression have many similarities and are closely related. They have both theoretical and actual differences, however.

In theory, all correlation analyses (including Multiple *R*) are designed to analyze data where we have no control over the distribution of the variables (random variables) in the population. We can only measure the predictor and outcome variables retroactively, after they have already been distributed among cases or objects. Consequently, a correlation coefficient is supposed to be no more than an indication of how these variables co-vary naturally—that is, without our interference. No matter how high the correlation coefficient produced, in theory it is presumptuous to imply that the predictor variable in any way caused the variations in the values in the outcome variable.

In contrast, linear regressions were designed for situations in which an experimental research design is in place—where we either introduced or directly manipulated the predictor variables. That is the way regression was designed to be used. In reality, regression analyses are now also used in many situations for which we have only random variables whose distributions are beyond our control, and correlation is sometimes used with experimental designs. This generally causes no major problems, so long as we are confident that the measurement of the predictor variables is accurate and other assumptions about their distributions are met.

In those relatively rare situations in which experimental research designs are employed and normally distributed interval level or ratio level predictor and outcome variables exist, regression analyses (simple or multiple) are the statistical procedures of choice. If the predictor variables are really randomly distributed (that is, their distribution is outside the control of the researcher), either correlation or regression analyses can be used, but correlation is really the more correct of the two.

Multiple linear regression even can be used with nominal level or ordinal level predictor variables. We do this by creating dummy variables (see Chapter 1) from a single nominal level or ordinal level variable. The variable *marital status,* for example, is at the nominal level of measurement and often contains five different value categories (e.g., currently married, separated, divorced, widowed, never married).

By creating four dummy variables, this nominal level variable could become four ratio level variables, with the value of 0 representing a state of no measureable quantity for each of its values. Thus, one dummy variable could be currently married (0 = no; 1 = yes); a second could be separated (0 = no; 1 = yes); a third could be divorced (0 = no; 1 = yes); and a fourth could be widowed (0 = no; 1 = yes).

In this way, a group of four dummy variables (one less than the number of value categories used for the nominal level variable *marital status*) can be added to a multiple linear regression analysis as four predictor variables. Why not five? A person who has values of 0 for the first four dummy variables has never been married. To include "never marriedness" as another dummy variable would be redundant (the same data) and will produce misleading results when a multiple linear regression analysis is performed.

As noted in Chapter 8, Multiple R produces a correlation coefficient that tells us the degree of correlation between a group of predictor variables and the outcome variable. When squared (R^2), it can tell us what percentage of the variation in values of the outcome variable can be explained by the group of predictor variables. Multiple linear regression does even more. The use of a multiple regression equation helps us estimate the actual value of an outcome variable, knowing the corresponding values for two or more predictor variables.

A regression equation produced by a multiple regression is longer—but no more complicated to interpret—than one produced by a simple linear regression. A main advantage of a multiple regression analysis is its ability to simultaneously examine the relationship of two or more predictor variables (or *X*s) with the outcome variable. Let's go back for a moment and revisit Shondra's simple regression problem where she identified her predictor variable as *the amount of time the client spent socializing with family members during the previous week* (*X*) and her outcome variable as *client life-satisfaction level* (*Y*).

As we might have guessed by now, life satisfaction is a complex concept that is likely affected by much more than just a person's social time with family. Suppose, for

TABLE 9.3 Multiple Regression Results that Predict Life-Satisfaction Levels from Client Variables

Variable	*B*	*S.E.*	*β*	*t*	*p*
Time with Family	3.90	1.15	.39	3.38	.001
Number of Living Parents	2.05	0.68	.20	3.01	.004
Number of Living Siblings	0.73	0.48	.16	1.18	.126
Intercept	22.68				

$F (3,46) = 4.33, p < .009$, Multiple $R = 4.69$, $R^2 = .220$, Adjusted $R^2 = .169$

example, that after reading a few research articles Shondra decides to include the variables *number of living parents* and *number of living siblings* as two additional predictor variables in her regression analysis. Shondra's new regression equation would contain three predictor variables, and each X would use subscripts to denote the differences among the variables. Her multiple regression equation might look like this:

$$Y' = 22.68 + 3.90(X_1) + 2.05(X_2) + .73(X_3)$$

Predicted Life-Satisfaction Score	Intercept	Time with Family	Number of Living Parents	Number of Living Siblings

Table 9.3 illustrates how Shondra might report her regression results as a table in the context of the results section of her report.

What if Shondra had wanted to include a nominal level variable that she thought is related to life satisfaction, for example, *employment status,* as one of her interval or ratio level variables? Table 9.4 illustrates how she would report her regression results in a table after creating three dummy variables for the variable.

TABLE 9.4 Multiple Regression Results that Predict Life Satisfaction Levels from Client Variables with Three Dummy Variables for Employment Status

Variable	*B*	*S.E.*	*β*	*t*	*p*
Time with Family	3.90	1.15	.39	3.38	.001
Number of Living Parents	2.05	.68	.20	3.01	.004
Number of Living Siblings	.73	.48	.16	1.18	.126
Employment Status					
Employed Full-time					
Employed Part-time	−.69	.62	.09	−1.18	.126
Retired, Other	−.80	.87	.07	−.919	.363
Unemployed	−1.93	.72	.14	−2.69	.011
Intercept	22.68				

$F (5,44) = 4.31, p < .008$, Multiple $R = 4.59$, $R^2 = .219$, Adjusted $R^2 = .167$

Note that the overall number of predictor variables used in Shondra's analysis has increased. Consequently, Shondra's regression equation would also change to include all her predictor variables. Shondra's new regression equation might look like this:

$$Y' = 22.68 + 3.90(X_1) + 2.05(X_2) + .73(X_3)h - .69(X_4) - .80(X_5) - 1.93(X_6)$$

| Predicted Life-Satisfaction Score | Intercept | Time with Family | Number of Living Parents | Number of Living Siblings | Employed Part-Time | Retired Other | Unemployed |

In addition to producing an equation, a multiple linear regression analysis tells:

1. Whether an apparent relationship between the predictor variables and the outcome variable in a research sample is likely to be the work of sampling error (the *p*-value)
2. The strength and direction of the relationship between variables (the correlation coefficient)
3. How accurate the regression equation is likely to be as a predictor of values of the outcome variable (the strength of the correlation)

A multiple linear regression also provides an assessment of the relative value (i.e., respective contributions) of different predictor variables for predicting values of the outcome variable. The formula for multiple linear regression is similar to that of simple linear regression, but not surprisingly, it is more complex. Like the formula for Multiple *R,* it takes into consideration the fact that the predictor variables are not only correlated with the outcome variable, they are also correlated to a greater or lesser degree with each other. We could not just add up their individual prediction powers, because some of the prediction power of one predictor variable duplicates the power within another predictor variable.

The regression counterpart of Multiple *R*'s beta weights are referred to as **beta coefficients.** Like beta weights, they reflect the relative importance of a predictor variable in predicting the value of the outcome variable, given which other predictor variables were present in the equation.

There are other similarities between Multiple *R* and multiple linear regression. Stepwise procedures help us select the smallest possible number of predictor variables while not sacrificing too much in our ability to predict. Like Multiple *R,* this can be accomplished by using either a step-down or step-up procedure—that is, by systematically dropping or adding different predictor variables. Statistical software packages can quickly provide the best (in terms of prediction of the outcome variable) combination of predictor variables (whatever number we choose) that will produce the best multiple linear regression equation.

Like all types of statistical analyses, multiple linear regressions can produce results that, if we are not careful, can lead us into Type I or Type II errors. Several assumptions for their use must be met. An advanced statistics text can help explain and thus avoid such undesirable phenomena as collinearity (two highly correlated predictor variables that can distort the results of an analysis), self-fulfilling prophecies, and regression to the mean.

OTHER TYPES OF REGRESSION ANALYSES

There are many types of regression analyses. We will introduce two that appear in social work literature: discriminant analysis and logistical regression.

Discriminant Analysis

In social work research and practice, we often wish to learn how best to predict the value categories of a nominal level (or ordinal level) outcome variable such as *recidivism* (i.e., will abuse again, will not abuse again), *rehospitalization* (i.e., will be rehospitalized, will not be rehospitalized), or *employment* (i.e., will remain employed, will not remain employed) with the use of several interval level or ratio level predictor variables. We may want to identify that group of interval level or ratio level predictor variables that will do the most accurate job of predicting the value category for the outcome value of a given individual, or we may simply wish to know how people in one value category differ from those in the other categories. Because the outcome variable is only at the nominal or ordinal level, multiple regression cannot be used. In such situations, discriminant analysis is appropriate.

In the previous chapter we described a statistical procedure (cluster analysis) to create homogeneous groups of cases. **Discriminant analyses,** in contrast, begin with groups that are believed to be essentially homogeneous. They comprise the value categories of the outcome variable. Discriminant analyses can be used, then (1) to try to better predict what value category (of the outcome variable) a person will fall into based on his or her measurement of certain predictor variables, and (2) to identify how people who fall into the one value category differ from people in each of the other value categories.

A discriminant analysis works in a way similar to other types of multivariate analyses. It creates a derived variable (in this case called the discriminant function) from the weighted values of several predictor variables. Stepwise variations of the procedure are also available.

When one is conducting discriminant analyses, the outcome variable can be dichotomous, as in previous examples, or it can contain three or more value categories. Suppose the standardized self-report measurement that Shondra used to assess *life-satisfaction level* for her clients produced a result that put clients into one of three possible categories: (1) suicidal, (2) acceptable, and (3) very satisfied. She could use discriminant analysis: (1) to determine what group of interval level or ratio level predictor variables might be most helpful in predicting her client's level of life satisfaction, or (2) to try to identify those variables (e.g., income, marital status, or other factors) that might distinguish clients who fall into each of the three categories of life satisfaction. Table 9.5 displays a sample of how Shondra might report the results of her analysis using a matrix in the context of the results section of her report.

A table such as Table 9.5 is refered to as a **confusion matrix.** Using the data that were analyzed, it displays the type and number of errors that a given group of predictor variables might have produced. It does this by displaying both the number of cases that actually were in a given value category of the nominal level (or ordinal level) outcome variable and the number that a discriminant analysis would have predicted to

TABLE 9.5 **Classifying Level of Life Satisfaction** (*N* = 50)

	Predicted Group Membership							
	Very Satisfied		Acceptable		Suicidal		Total	
Actual Group Membership								
Life Satisfaction Category	*n*	*%*	*n*	*%*	*n*	*%*	*N*	*%*
Very Satisfied	**30**	93.8	2	6.3	0	.0	32	100.0
Acceptable	1	20.0	**4**	80.0	0	.0	5	100.0
Suicidal	1	7.7	0	.0	**12**	92.3	13	100.0

92.0% of actual grouped cases correctly classified (30 + 4 + 12 = 46/50)

be there. It thus provides the likely number of prediction errors in any direction if a certain group of predictor variables were used and allows us to judge whether that number is acceptably low.

Although discriminant analyses are closely related to multiple regressions, in a statistical sense they are less powerful than multiple regressions (there is more likelihood of a Type II error) because the outcome variable is only nominal or ordinal level. Discriminant analyses should not be used when both predictor and outcome variables are at the interval or ratio level. Why throw away measurement precision and statistical power unnecessarily?

Logistic Regression

Logistic regression is still another procedure (actually a group of statistical procedures) that is commonly used for prediction. It is used to predict the likelihood that a given value category of a dichotomous outcome variable will occur. The prediction is based upon the measurements of one or more predictor variables of any level of measurement.

Dichotomous outcome variables are common in social work research, particularly in outcome research or evaluation. For example, consider the many dichotomous outcome possibilities for research studies related to adolescents. Do adolescents commit crimes or not? Do they drop out of school or not? Do adolescents in foster care return home or not? Do adolescent females get pregnant or not? These dichotomous situations are best defined as an event and a non-event, something we can also think of as simply a yes-or-no situation. In other words, the two value choices for the outcome variable are mutually exclusive choices.

Logistic regression is conceptually similar to other forms of statistical analyses described in this chapter. Its formula results in an equation that allows us to predict the likelihood of a given value category of the outcome variable—usually the category identified as the problem for a given case or person. Using it, Shondra could, for example, compute a logistic regression equation that tells her the probability that a given client has attempted suicide. Because her criterion variable consists of only two choices (i.e., suicide attempted, suicide not attempted), she could also learn the probability of the non-event by calculating the probability of the event. It will be 1.0 minus the probability of the event occurring. For example, if the probability of her client having attempted suicide is .19, the probability of her *not* having attempted suicide will be .81 (1.0 − .19 = .81).

Logistic regression is similar to linear regression and to discriminant analysis in that they all attempt to predict the value or value category of the outcome variable. But there are fewer assumptions for its use. One of the critical assumptions of linear regression, for example, is that the relationship between the predictor and outcome variables is characterized by a constant change. In describing the relationship between *life-satisfaction levels* and *amount of time spent with family*, we would hypothesize a linear relationship between the two variables only if, for example, we believed that for every extra hour of time spent with family, client life-satisfaction levels increase by a certain amount.

Of course, such a scenario of constant change is rare in the real world. Consider the relationship between the *amount of time clients socializing with family members* (*X*) and whether or not *they* have *attempted suicide.* In the real world, the probability of the event (i.e., attempted suicide) may be affected very little (say 1%) by 3 hours or more per week of time spent socializing with family members, but may change quite a bit (say, 5%) for clients who spend less than 5 minutes per week socializing with family. In this scenario then, the relationship between time spent socializing with family and attempting suicide is nonlinear. Shondra would use logistic regression in this situation or others where she believed that two variables were related but in nonlinear fashion.

When logistic regression is used, the results as presented in a table of a report are similar to the presentation of linear regression results. For example, Table 9.6 illustrates how Shondra might report her logistic regression findings as a table in the

TABLE 9.6   Logistic Regression Results That Predict the Likelihood of Clients Attempting Suicide from Client Variables

Variables	B	S.E.	Wald	df	P	Odds Ratio
Time with Family	1.000	.016	10.116	1	.001	.95
Annual Salary	.000	.000	.534	1	.465	1.000
Currently Married	.090	1.233	.005	1	.942	1.07
Constant	−3.105	1.705	3.318	1	.069	22.312
−2 Log Likelihood (intercept)			59.30			
−2 Log Likelihood			26.34			
Model Chi Square			32.91	3	.000	
Goodness-of-Fit Chi Square			1.48	8	.993	
Pseudo R^2			.48			

context of the results section of her report. Note that Shondra's logistic regression table (Table 9.6) and her linear regression table presented earlier (see Table 9.3) both present regression coefficients (*B*) and their standard errors (*S.E.*). Instead of reporting the results of an *F* test, as was the case with her linear regression results in Table 9.3, this time Shondra displays the Wald test statistic (see Table 9.6).

The Odds Ratio column in the table gives critical information about the likelihood of a client having attempted suicide given the values of the predictor variables in the table. In short, Table 9.6 reveals that *time with family* is the only predictor variable showing a statistically significant relationship with the outcome variable (i.e., *attempted suicide*). An odds ratio of less than 1.0 corresponds with a decrease in values of the outcome variable. For example, the odds ratio of .95 for *time with family* indicates that for every one unit increase of time spent with family, the odds of having attempted suicide are multiplied by .95, which is a 5 percent $(1-.95)$ decrease. Having information about clients' annual salaries or marital statuses, on the other hand, does not assist Shondra in predicting which of her clients have attempted suicide and which clients have not.

The reader may have noted several additional statistics located at the bottom of Table 9.6, and may even have guessed that they are comparable to those reported at the bottom of the linear regression table (see Table 9.3 and 9.4). Discussions of these statistics are beyond the scope of this book. Suffice it to say that all regression analyses are accompanied by statistics that tell us how accurate the regression equation (or model) will be at predicting the outcome variable, and the statistics reported at the bottom of Table 9.6 suggests that Shondra's logistic regression model is a good one.

CONCLUDING THOUGHTS

This chapter presented a brief overview of simple linear regression and several related procedures that are used for prediction, an extension of correlation. Based on the correlation between variables within a data set, they produce an equation that enables us to predict the value of an outcome variable if we know the value of one or more predictor variables for a given case.

Simple linear regression is a useful technique when a reasonably strong linear correlation exists between two normally distributed interval level or ratio level variables. When there is only a weak correlation between the two variables, or the correlation is strong but not linear, creation of a simple linear regression equation is an exercise in futility. It does little to enhance our ability to predict a value of the outcome variable by knowing the value of a predictor variable.

Chapter 9 also presented a brief overview of three related multivariate procedures, multiple regression, discriminant analysis, and logistic regression. Unlike multiple regression, which requires all variables to be interval or ratio level, the criterion variable can be only nominal or ordinal level when discriminant analysis is performed, and both the predictor and outcome variables need be only nominal level to perform logistic regression.

STUDY QUESTIONS

1. What can simple linear regression do that correlation cannot do? Provide examples in your discussion.

2. What statistical insights discussed in earlier chapters are critical to an understanding of simple linear regression? Describe how they relate to it.

3. Explain why it is not necessary to state a research or null hypothesis when using simple linear regression. What alternative to restating a hypothesis do researchers commonly use when performing simple linear regression analysis?

4. Using examples drawn from social work practice, discuss why it is not a productive use of time to use regression when the correlation coefficient between two variables is low. Draw two scattergrams to illustrate your point, with one scattergram showing a low correlation and the other showing a high correlation. Discuss the two scattergrams in relation to simple linear regression.

5. What do we mean when we say that the predictor and outcome variables are not interchangeable for statistical purposes when we perform a simple linear regression? What implications does this have when we program a computer to conduct a simple linear regression analysis?

6. In your own words, explain why you think we should not predict Y when an X value is below the minimum or above the maximum value used in generating Y.

7. Describe two situations in which you believe that it would be appropriate to perform a regression analysis in a social service agency with which you are familiar. How would the results have the potential to help the agency?

8. For each of the two major examples of the use of simple linear regression in this chapter, discuss additional methodological limitations (in addition to those mentioned) that might serve to depreciate the statistical findings. You may wish to consult a book on social work research methods and review the section on threats to internal validity.

9. What type of research situations would be especially suited to the use of multiple linear regression? Give an example of how a social work practitioner might use it to predict the amount of some client behavior.

10. Which form of multivariate analysis is designed to help predict the value of an interval level or ratio level outcome variable from the measurements of two or more interval level or ratio level predictor variables that have been introduced or manipulated by the researcher?

11. Describe how dummy variables can be used to perform a multiple linear regression using a nominal level predictor variable. Provide an example.

12. How do step-up and step-down regression differ from each other? Describe how each works.

13. What are two different ways in which social workers can use discriminant analysis to learn more about people who participate in hate crimes against minority groups?

14. Why is logistical regression especially useful for social workers who wish to know the probability that a problem will occur for a specific client? Provide an example.

10

Cross Tabulation

Cross tabulation is a process of placing raw data into a simple table so they can be analyzed. It is associated with several related statistical tests that analyze the relationship between nominal level variables. The best known of these is the chi-square test of association.

THE CHI-SQUARE TEST OF ASSOCIATION

The chi-square test of association is often referred to simply as chi-square. No nonparametric statistical test (and probably no other statistical test) is better known than chi-square. Research articles using chi-square analyses appear frequently in the professional literature. Because we feel comfortable with the test, we are more likely to read research reports that use it than those that employ less widely known and understood statistical tests.

A major reason for the popularity of chi-square is that it requires only nominal level measurement of the dependent and independent variables. Thus, it is especially well suited for social work research situations. We often want to know, for example, if there is a relationship between certain variables and treatment effectiveness. The independent variables that may be related to treatment effectiveness often are only at the nominal level. They might be, for example, the type of intervention provided (e.g., individual treatment, group treatment), the highest degree completed by the social worker (e.g., BSW, MSW), or various demographic characteristics of the client (e.g., marital status, gender, religious affiliation, ethnicity, sexual orientation, type of disability).

More often than not, measurement of the dependent variable (treatment success) produces only a nominal level variable (e.g., found employment, did not find employment; abused again, did not abuse again; was rehospitalized, was not rehospitalized).

Sometimes in social work research studies both the independent and dependent variables are at the nominal level and have yes/no or other dichotomous value categories. A small research study, for example, might measure whether a piece of social legislation passed *or* did not pass in different states and whether the local chapters of the National Association of Social Workers supported *or* did not support the legislation. Another study could examine whether there is an association between whether candidates for local offices were elected (*or* not) and whether (*or* not) they had taken a pro-choice position on the issue of abortion.

Simply put chi-square is a statistical test of association between variables. Thus, except in those rare situations where a ridged experimental design was used, even if a chi-square test demonstrates support for a relationship between variables, it is not appropriate to claim that the different value categories of the independent variable caused the different value categories of the dependent variable. We can only state that a strong pattern or clustering of value categories is found to exist—certain value categories of one variable tend to be found where certain value categories of the other variable are also present. Like all inferential statistical tests of significance, chi-square can determine whether an association between two nominal level variables within sample data is so strong that sampling error is an unlikely explanation of the association.

A simple hypothetical example illustrates how chi-square works. Suppose that we want to find out if there is a relationship between one nominal level independent variable, *type of treatment* (i.e., group, individual), and one nominal level dependent variable, *client outcome* (i.e., success, failure), within a large alcoholism counseling program. Based on a review of professional literature and previous practice observations, we feel justified in formulating the following one-tailed research hypothesis:

> Alcohol-addicted clients in group treatment are more likely to abstain from alcohol for 2 months than clients in individual treatment.

The corresponding null hypothesis for our one-tailed research hypothesis would be as follows:

> There is no relationship between the type of treatment that clients who are addicted to alcohol receive and whether they abstain from alcohol for 2 months.

The null hypothesis would assert that although it may seem (within a sample) that successful treatment is more likely to occur among clients who received group treatment than among those who received individual treatment, there is not a real relationship between the variables within the population from which the sample was drawn. Any difference in success rate within the sample is likely to be due to sampling error.

When a one-tailed research hypothesis is stated and we are planning to use the chi-square test to determine if it is safe to reject its null hypothesis, it is helpful to display the research hypothesis in the form of a dummy table. A **dummy table** shows where we would expect to find a disproportionately large number of cases if the results of the chi-square test support the rejection of the null hypothesis. In our example, we would expect to find a relatively large number of cases in group treatment who

TABLE 10.1   Dummy Table:
Type of Treatment by Client Outcome

Type of Treatment	Chart Outcome		
	Success	**Failure**	**Totals**
Group	*		
Individual		*	

abstained from alcohol (success) and a relatively large number of cases in individual treatment who did not abstain (failure). This is reflected in the placement of the asterisks in the body of Table 10.1. A dummy table created at the time a one-tailed research hypothesis is formulated can later assist in the interpretation of a study's findings.

To conduct the study, we could randomly select a sample of 100 cases ($N = 100$) from the 300 outpatient clients who are currently being seen for alcohol-dependency problems. We could then ask each of their social workers to tell us for each one of our sample clients (1) whether the client was in individual *or* group treatment and (2) whether the client abstained *or* did not abstain from alcohol for the previous two-month period.

Type of treatment would have two possible value categories—group and individual. Client outcome also would have two possible value categories—success and failure. (Success would be operationalized as at least 2 months of alcohol abstention.) Thus, there are four possible combinations of value categories that could be recorded for each client, with every client falling into one, and only one, of the following four classifications:

1. Group treatment and client success
2. Group treatment and client failure
3. Individual treatment and client success
4. Individual treatment and client failure

Suppose, for example, that the 100 clients were distributed among each of the four categories as follows:

1. Group treatment and client success (40 clients)
2. Group treatment and client failure (20 clients)
3. Individual treatment and client success (15 clients)
4. Individual treatment and client failure (25 clients)

Observed Frequencies

The above data, (i.e., 40, 20, 15, 25) are now placed into what is called a cross-tabulation table. The data in the four **cells** of Table 10.2 are the actual number of clients who possessed each combination of value categories for the two variables.

TABLE 10.2   Observed Frequencies:
Type of Treatment by Client Outcome (*N* = 100)

| | *Client Outcome* | | |
Type of Treatment	Success	Failure	Totals
Group	40 (*a*)	20 (*b*)	60
Individual	15 (*c*)	25 (*d*)	40
Totals	55	45	100

Such a table (also referred to as a chi-square table, cross-break table, or contingency table) is constructed with the use of the variable labels, value categories, and frequencies drawn from the data.

The areas where the frequencies (i.e., 40, 20, 15, 25) are placed are called **cells.** Table 10.2 contains two dichotomous (two-value category) variables: *type of treatment* and *client outcome;* thus, it has four cells. It is, of course, possible to have nominal level variables with more than two value categories. The cross-tabulation table would then have more rows and columns and thus more cells.

By convention, small italicized letters (e.g., *a, b, c, d*) are used to refer to the respective cells. As can be seen from Table 10.2, they are lettered left to right, starting with the top row, then going to the next row, and so on.

In the far right-hand column of Table 10.2, the totals for each row (adding across) are entered. Likewise, the totals for each column (adding down) are entered on the bottom line. These row and column totals are called *marginals* (**marginal totals).** They indicate the total number of cases that were observed to possess a given value category for each variable: group treatment (60), individual treatment (40), success (55), and failure (45). The grand total of cases (*N*) in the sample entered in the bottom right-hand corner (100). Note that the sum of the row totals equals the grand total, as does the sum of the column totals.

Because the variables are at the nominal level of measurement, there is no logical sequence in which they should appear in a table. In our example, it would have been equally correct to place individual treatment above group treatment or to place failure to the left of success. By convention, however, we display the dependent variable in the columns and the independent variable in the rows, as seen in Table 10.2. If neither variable is clearly one or the other, it makes no difference which variable's value categories run across the top of the table and which run down the side.

Once the data have been placed in a cross-tabulation table (e.g., Table 10.2), we can compare the outcomes of clients who received group treatment with outcomes of clients who received individual treatment. Such a comparison, however, cannot be easily accomplished using only the observed frequencies as contained in Table 10.2. We cannot simply compare the raw number of clients who had successful outcomes with group treatment (40) directly with the raw number of clients who had successful outcomes with individual treatment (15) and conclude that group treatment is better just because 40 is larger than 15. We would naturally expect to have more successes among

TABLE 10.3   Percentages of Clients:
Type of Treatment by Client Outcome ($N = 100$)

	Client Outcome		
Type of Treatment	**Success**	**Failure**	**Totals**
Group	66.7	33.3	100.0
Individual	37.5	62.5	100.0

those clients in group treatment than among those in individual treatment because more clients (60) were in group treatment and fewer (40) were in individual treatment.

It is possible to compensate for the difference in the number of cases in the two subsamples (individual versus group) by using percentages. Percentages equalize the sizes of groups. Using percentages, we can demonstrate, for example, that 66.7 percent of the 60 clients who received group treatment had successful outcomes, compared with 37.5 percent of the 40 clients who received individual treatment and had successful outcomes. Table 10.3 is a percentage table for the observed data contained in Table 10.2.

If the percentages in cells *a* and *c* and the percentages in cells *b* and *d* had been exactly the same, we would have no reason to believe that the variables are related. The percentages in the cells in Table 10.3 are quite different, however, and thus may not be due to sampling error. They seem to suggest that among clients who are alcohol dependent, type of treatment and treatment success may be related. Yet, at this point, it is difficult to know whether the apparent relationship is only related to sampling error. The null hypothesis would argue that a 29.2 percentage point difference (66.7% − 37.5% = 29.2% points) is not really that large. But is it? How much of a percentage point difference is needed to rule out sampling error as the "real cause" of the apparent relationship between the two variables? Percentages alone cannot answer this question.

Expected Frequencies

In order to answer the question, we need to introduce the concept of expected frequencies. **Expected frequencies** are the frequencies we would expect to occur most often in an infinite number of samples if the null hypothesis were correct—that is, if there was no real relationship between the two nominal level variables. Unlike observed frequencies, which reflect actual data collected (e.g., Table 10.2), expected frequencies are hypothetical numbers; they are derived with the use of simple mathematics from the marginal totals in a cross-tabulation table.

To understand expected frequencies, return to Table 10.2. Let us see how the expected frequencies for a cell are obtained. Look first at cell *a,* which contains the 40 clients who were in group treatment and who had successful outcomes.

The expected frequency for any cell is based on the two marginal totals that correspond to that cell, that is, the total for the row in which the cell appears and the total for the column in which the cell appears. For cell *a* in Table 10.2, for example, these two marginal totals are 60 and 55, respectively. For cell *b*, they are 60 and 45, respectively. For cell *c*, they are 40 for the row total and 55 for the column total, and for cell *d*, they are 40 and 45.

The expected frequency for any given cell is computed by multiplying that cell's row total by its column total and then dividing by the grand total for the table or the sample size (*N*). We can express this as a formula:

$$E = \frac{(R)(C)}{N}$$

where:

$E =$ Expected frequency in a particular cell
$R =$ Marginal total for the row in which the cell appears
$C =$ Marginal total for the column in which the cell appears
$N =$ Total number of cases in the data analysis

With the use of the formula, we can determine the expected frequency for each cell:

$$\text{cell } a = \frac{60 \times 55 = 3300}{100} = 33$$

$$\text{cell } b = \frac{60 \times 45 = 2700}{100} = 27$$

$$\text{cell } c = \frac{55 \times 40 = 2200}{100} = 22$$

$$\text{cell } d = \frac{45 \times 40 = 1800}{100} = 18$$

Table 10.4 displays the expected frequency for each of the four cells in parentheses next to the corresponding observed frequency. Note that there is only one set of marginal totals because they are the same for both the observed frequencies and the expected frequencies.

TABLE 10.4   Observed and Expected Frequencies: Type of Treatment by Client Outcome (*N* = 100)

Type of Treatment	Client Outcome				Totals
	Success		*Failure*		
	Observed	**Expected**	**Observed**	**Expected**	
Group	40	(33)	20	(27)	60
Individual	15	(22)	25	(18)	40
Totals	55		45		100

Chi-square compares the observed frequency for each cell with its respective expected frequency. It uses a formula to produce a chi-square value, which is directly related to the size of these differences. Larger differences between the observed and expected frequencies produce larger chi-square values and vice versa. We will look at how a chi-square value is calculated and interpreted with the use of the data in Table 10.4. Before we do this, however, we will introduce the concept of degrees of freedom and how it relates to a given chi-square value.

Degrees of Freedom

If we were to study the chi-square formula carefully (Box 10.1), we could see why the size of the differences between observed and expected frequencies is not the only thing that generates larger chi-square values. The likelihood of obtaining a smaller or larger chi-square value is also affected by the size of the cross-tabulation table on which it is computed, that is, by the number of rows and columns it contains and, more specifically, by the number of cells in the table.

The larger the table, the more likely it is to have a large chi-square value. Why? The more cells in a table, the more cells available to contribute to the chi-square value and the higher that value is likely to be, even if the difference between individual pairs of observed frequencies and expected frequencies is quite small. Thus a chi-square value must be evaluated in relation to the size of the table from which it was computed. A large chi-square value in itself may not suggest a real relationship between two nominal level variables within the population. It could have been generated by a large table with many cells, each contributing a small amount (because of small differences) to that value. Conversely, a smaller chi-square value may still reflect a real relationship between variables if the table that produced it had relatively few cells to contribute to its value.

The **degrees of freedom** (*df*) for any cross-tabulation table is the number of rows minus 1, times the number of columns minus 1. With the use of this formula, Table 10.2 (which is referred to as a 2 × 2 or 2-by-2 table because there are two value categories for each of its two variables) has 1 degree of freedom (as will all 2-by-2 tables). A 3-by-3 table would have 4 degrees of freedom $(3 - 1) \times (3 - 1) = 4$, a 2-by-3 table would have two degrees of freedom $(2 - 1) \times (3 -) = 2$, and so on. As can be seen in Table 10.5, larger degrees of freedom (tables with more cells) require larger chi-square values to achieve statistical significance at the same rejection level (e.g., .05) than smaller degrees of freedom (i.e., tables with fewer cells). Thus, degrees of freedom is a way of correcting for the number of cells that contribute to the chi-square value.

Using Chi-Square

With easy access to computer software programs, a chi-square analysis is rarely undertaken with pencil and paper anymore. When it is, there are seven fairly simple steps:

1. Place the observed frequencies into a cross-tabulation table, and add the marginal totals.
2. Compute the expected frequencies, and add them to the table.

BOX 10.1
The Chi-Square Statistic (Without Yates Correction Factor)

Research Hypothesis: Clients who received group treatment are more likely to abstain from alcohol than clients who received individual treatment.

Null Hypothesis: There is no difference between the type of treatment clients received and whether they abstained from alcohol.

Independent Variable: Type of treatment—nominal level (group versus individual).

Dependent Variable: Client outcome—nominal level (success versus failure).

Observed Frequencies: See Table 10.2.

Expected Frequencies Formula: $E = \dfrac{(R)(C)}{(N)}$

where: E = Expected frequency in a particular cell C = Total number in that cell's column
R = Total number in that cell's row N = Total number of cases

Substituting values for letters:

Cell a: $E = (60)(55)/100 = 33$ Cell c: $E = (40)(55)/100 = 22$
Cell b: $E = (60)(45)/100 = 27$ Cell d: $E = (40)(45)/100 = 18$

Chi-Square Formula: $\chi^2 = \sum \dfrac{(O - E)^2}{E}$

where: χ^2 = Chi-square value E = Expected frequency
O = Observed frequency Σ = Sum of (for all cells)

Substituting values for letters:

$$\chi^2 = \overset{\text{cell } a}{\frac{(40 - 33)^2}{33}} + \overset{\text{cell } b}{\frac{(20 - 27)^2}{27}} + \overset{\text{cell } c}{\frac{(15 - 22)^2}{22}} + \overset{\text{cell } d}{\frac{(25 - 18)^2}{18}}$$

Degrees of Freedom Formula: $df = (r - 1)(c - 1)$

where: df = Degree of freedom
r = Number of rows
c = Number of columns

Substituting values for letters:

$$df = (2 - 1)(2 - 1)$$
$$= 1 \text{ (degree of freedom)}$$

Presentation of Results: $x^2 = 8.24$, $df = 1$, $p < .005$

Conclusions: The null hypothesis is rejected and the one-tailed research hypothesis is supported. In short, clients who received group treatment had statistically significant better outcomes than clients who received individual treatment.

TABLE 10.5   Critical Values of χ^2

df	Level of Significance for a One-Tailed Test					
	.10	.05	.025	.01	.005	.0005
	Level of Significance for a Two-Tailed Test					
	.20	.10	.05	.02	.01	.001
1	1.64	2.71	3.84	5.41	6.64	10.83
2	3.22	4.60	5.99	7.82	9.21	13.82
3	4.64	6.25	7.82	9.84	11.34	16.27
4	5.99	7.78	9.49	11.67	13.28	18.46
5	7.29	9.24	11.07	13.39	15.09	20.52
6	8.56	10.64	12.59	15.03	16.81	22.46
7	9.80	12.02	14.07	16.62	18.48	24.32
8	11.03	13.36	15.51	18.17	20.09	26.12
9	12.24	14.68	16.92	19.68	21.67	27.88
10	13.44	15.99	18.31	21.16	23.21	29.59
11	14.63	17.28	19.68	22.62	24.72	31.26
12	15.81	18.55	21.03	24.05	26.22	32.91
13	16.98	19.81	22.36	25.47	27.69	34.53
14	18.15	21.06	23.68	26.87	29.14	36.12
15	19.31	22.31	25.00	28.26	30.58	37.70
16	20.46	23.54	26.30	29.63	32.00	39.29
17	21.62	24.77	27.59	31.00	33.41	40.75
18	22.76	25.99	28.87	32.35	34.80	42.31
19	23.90	27.20	30.14	33.69	36.19	43.82
20	25.04	28.41	31.41	35.02	37.57	45.32
21	26.17	29.62	32.67	36.34	38.93	46.80
22	27.30	30.81	33.92	37.66	40.29	48.27
23	28.43	32.01	35.17	38.97	41.64	49.73
24	29.55	33.20	36.42	40.27	42.98	51.18
25	30.68	34.38	37.65	41.57	44.31	52.62
26	31.80	35.56	38.88	42.86	45.64	54.05
27	32.91	36.74	40.11	44.14	46.94	55.48
28	34.03	37.92	41.34	45.42	48.28	56.89
29	35.14	39.09	42.69	46.69	49.59	58.30
30	36.25	40.26	43.77	47.96	50.89	59.70
32	38.47	42.59	46.19	50.49	53.49	62.49
34	40.68	44.90	48.60	53.00	56.06	65.25
36	42.88	47.21	51.00	55.49	58.62	67.99
38	45.08	49.51	53.38	57.97	61.16	70.70
40	47.27	51.81	55.76	60.44	63.69	73.40
44	51.64	56.37	60.48	65.34	68.71	78.75
48	55.99	60.91	65.17	70.20	73.68	84.04
52	60.33	65.42	69.83	75.02	78.62	89.27
56	64.66	69.92	74.47	79.82	83.51	94.46
60	68.97	74.40	79.08	84.58	88.38	99.61

Source: From Table IV of R. A. Fisher and F. Yates, *Statistical Tables for Biological, Agricultural, and Medical Research,* published by Longman Group, Ltd., London (previously published by Oliver and Boyd, Ltd., Edinburgh) and by permission of the authors and publishers.

3. Compare the observed frequencies with the expected frequencies for each cell with the use of the chi-square formula.
4. Compute degrees of freedom for the cross-tabulation table.
5. Go to the appropriate line for the degrees of freedom in a critical values of chi-square table (see Table 10.5), and see where the chi-square would fall (between which two numbers).
6. Go to the number to the left of where the chi-square value would fall.
7. Go to the top of the column in which that number appears and obtain the approximate *p* value with the use of the line corresponding to the type of research hypothesis used (one-tailed or two-tailed). The probability that sampling error may have produced the relationship between the two variables can now be described as less than ($<$) that approximate *p* value.

The formula needed to compute a chi-square statistic (Step 3 above) is the general formula contained in Box 10.1. It is appropriate for any cross-tabulation table containing more than four cells. In fact, if there are only four cells, as in our example, we should adjust the formula slightly by reducing the absolute difference between the observed and expected frequencies by .5 for each cell before squaring it (referred to as the **correction for continuity** or, sometimes, the **Yates correction factor**). This is a mathematical correction designed to avoid the slightly inflated chi-square value (such as that in Box 10.1) that the uncorrected general formula produces when used with 2 × 2 tables.

In order to illustrate the basic chi-square formula, we did not use the correction for continuity in Box 10.1. However, the chi-square values displayed in the 2 × 2 tables elsewhere in this chapter were derived with the use of the corrected formula.

Today, any statistical software program and many calculators have the capacity to calculate a chi-square value almost instantaneously. The formula for chi-square along with the formulas for expected frequencies and degrees of freedom are all programmed. Once we have entered the data for the cases in our research sample, we would then select cross-tabulation (or, in some cases, chi-square) from the menu. The displayed results would include the chi-square value, the degrees of freedom, and the associated *p* value for the data.

In our example, we would learn that the chi-square value for the data contained in Table 10.2 is 8.24 (without using the correction for continuity) and that it is reduced to 7.11 when the Yates formula is used. With one degree of freedom, the *p* value for the data, using either formula, was less than .005.

Presentation of Findings

The actual presentation of findings of a chi-square analysis is straightforward. First, the cross-tabulation table (containing observed frequencies) is displayed. The actual chi-square value derived from the analysis of the data (χ^2), the degrees of freedom (*df*), and the probability that sampling error might have produced the observed frequencies (*p*) are placed at the bottom of the cross-tabulation table as in Box 10.1:

$$\chi^2 = 8.24, df = 1, p < .005$$

Interpreting the Results of a Chi-Square Analysis

Because we did not specify and justify the use of a different rejection level, the traditional .05 rejection level would be used as the cutoff point for determining whether or not to reject the null hypothesis. The p value that was produced by our chi-square analysis was $< .005$, much less than .05. The mathematical probability that sampling error produced the results is less than 5 times out of 1000. So we could safely reject the null hypothesis.

Can we now say that we have statistical support for our one-tailed research hypothesis? Not quite yet. Chi-square is just a statistical test; it has no way of knowing what we predicted in our one-tailed research hypothesis. It simply checks to see if the difference between the observed and expected frequencies is large enough that it probably is not the work of sampling error.

In our example, a large chi-square value and a corresponding low p value would have occurred if clients in group treatment had a much better record of alcohol abstinence, than clients in individual treatment. However, they also would have occurred if the better record had been among clients in individual treatment. Our chi-square analysis told us only that the variables probably are related; it did not (and cannot) tell us if the direction of that relationship was what we hypothesized.

To find out if we have statistical support for our one-tailed research hypothesis, we could now compare the dummy table (Table 10.1) that we created to represent our one-tailed research hypothesis with Table 10.4. We would ask, "Where are the disproportionately large observed frequencies?" (A disproportionately large observed frequency is one that is larger than its expected frequency.) Are they in the cells where we predicted they would be (*a* and *d*), or are they in the opposite cells (*b* and *c*)?

The disproportionately large observed frequencies are in cells *a* and *d* in Table 10.4, just where we predicted they would be. Thus, we can now reject the null hypothesis and claim statistical support for our one-tailed research hypothesis. However, the disproportionately large observed frequencies had occurred in cells *b* and *c* (where clients in individual treatment who abstained from alcohol and clients in group treatment who did not are displayed), we could not claim support for our research hypothesis. In that case, we would have reason to believe that the variables are related, but in the opposite direction to that we predicted.

Having demonstrated a statistically significant association between the variables in the hypothesized direction, we are still a long way from concluding that clients who are alcohol dependent should be put into group treatment. True, the difference between the percentages of abstinence in our two subsamples was pretty substantive (66.7% for group treatment versus 35.7% for individual treatment). Before we can claim that we have uncovered a relationship between the two variables we would want to be very sure that the alternative explanations for a real relationship between them (besides sampling error) did not produce the apparent relationship between the variables.

Perhaps, for example, most of the substance-abuse workers in the agency were hired because they are especially adept at working with groups and they have less skill in individual counseling, or perhaps there was an unwritten policy that all clients with the most severe alcohol problems are assigned to individual treatment. Either fact might explain the relatively high rate of success among clients in group treatment.

The most we can say about our finding of a statistically significant relationship between the variables is that most likely the variables really are associated, at least in the agency from which the sample was drawn. We cannot say with certainty, however, why this relationship occurred, nor can we predict if it will be found again in different agency settings with different staff training, agency policies, type of group or individual treatment used, and so forth. Maybe we are on to something, but only replication and other research studies—perhaps using more powerful research designs and more powerful statistical analyses—will provide evidence that our original one-tailed research hypothesis is, indeed, correct.

Meaningfulness and Sample Size

When we see that a chi-square test has demonstrated the presence of a statistically significant relationship between variables, it is easy to be impressed, but we need to look carefully at the sample size (N) that produced it. Like other statistical tests, a chi-square analysis can identify a statistically significant relationship between variables, but it may be a statistically significant weak relationship that is of little or no practical value.

A continuation of the example we have been using will demonstrate this point. Suppose that we tried to replicate the results of our earlier research study. This time, a sample of 200 clients being treated for alcoholism was followed over a 2-month period. The results of the second study are displayed in Table 10.6.

When a chi-square test is computed for the data in Table 10.6, $p > .10$ (for a one-tailed research hypothesis), because the likelihood that chance might have produced the difference between the observed and expected frequency for these data is relatively large, we would lack sufficient statistical support to be able to reject the null hypothesis (i.e., .10 is larger than .05).

Because the evidence in support of our one-tailed research hypothesis is now conflicting, we might want to repeat the study for a third time, this time with a very large sample. Let us suppose that we used data on 10 times more clients, 2,000 clients. The data from this third study are displayed in Table 10.7.

TABLE 10.6   Observed Frequencies and Percentages: Type of Treatment by Client Outcome ($N = 200$)

| Type of Treatment | Client Outcome | | | | | |
| | Success | | Failure | | Totals | |
	Frequency	Percentage	Frequency	Percentage	Frequency	Percentage
Group	30	60.0	20	40.0	50	25
Individual	80	53.3	70	46.7	150	75
Totals	110		90		200	

$\chi^2 = .429$, $df = 1$, $p < .10$ (direction predicted)

**TABLE 10.7   Observed Frequencies and Percentages:
Type of Treatment by Client Outcome ($N = 2,000$)**

| Type of Treatment | Client Outcome | | | | | |
| | Success | | Failure | | Totals | |
	Frequency	Percentage	Frequency	Percentage	Frequency	Percentage
Group	300	60.0	200	40.0	500	100
Individual	800	53.3	700	46.7	1500	100
Totals	1,100		900		2,000	

$\chi^2 = 4.29$, $df = 1$, $p < .025$ (direction predicted)

A close look at Tables 10.6 and 10.7 reveals that the percentages of the 2,000 clients in the respective cells in Table 10.7 are exactly the same as those within the comparable cells in the sample of 200 cases in Table 10.6. In both hypothetical studies, 60 percent of clients in group treatment abstained from drinking compared with 53.3 percent of clients in individual treatment. Both 2×2 tables have 1 degree of freedom. But the chi-square values are very different. The value is 10 times larger in the study using the larger sample than in the one using the smaller sample.

The p value also is very different (less than .025 with the sample of 2,000, compared with greater than .10 with the sample of 200). The relationship between the variables is not statistically significant when the data in the study with 200 cases are used, but it is statistically significant in the study with 2,000 cases. If we had used 20,000 clients, the chi-square value would be 42.9; if we had used 200,000 clients, it would be 429, and so on. Because the percentages within the tables did not change, the strength of the association would be identical in each instance, but the chi-square values would be very different.

There is a logical reason why we would be more likely to be able to reject the null hypothesis when larger samples are used even though the percentages are the same the analysis is more powerful. When smaller samples are used—the short run mentioned in the discussion of the role of probability in hypothesis testing in Chapter 5—a difference of 6.7 percentage points (60.0% − 53.3% = 6.7% points) may well have been the work of sampling error. With the much larger samples, the law of averages (the long run) should have taken over; any differences in success for the two types of treatment should have disappeared as more and more cases were added if no real relationship between type of treatment and treatment success existed. The fact that a 6.7 percentage point difference still exists for the very large sample suggests that the relationship between the variables may be a real one.

How would we interpret the results of our three hypothetical studies comparing clients in group treatment with those in individual treatment? In two of them (those with samples of 100 and of 2,000), clients in group treatment had a higher success rate than clients in individual treatment, and the differences in success rate were statistically significant (very unlikely to be the work of sampling error). The research hypothesis was supported. So, should we conclude that group treatment really is more effective for treatment of the problem than individual treatment? Not yet. In the study with a sample of 200, clients in group treatment had a higher success rate too, but the difference was not statistically significant (the probability of it being attributable to sampling error was relatively large). The null hypothesis could not be rejected. Should we then conclude that type of treatment really makes no difference, just because the difference was not statistically significant in this one study? No, that would not be justified either.

On another level it is hard to ignore the finding that, in all three studies, clients in group treatment had a higher success rate than those in individual treatment. That in itself would be unlikely if the two types of treatment are equally effective—right? Group treatment may be more effective, but any such conclusion drawn from looking at the findings from the three studies can only be tentative—as findings always are in scientific research. However, there is another point that can be made here. Making sense of the results of statistical testing with the use of data drawn from one study can be complicated enough (especially if all alternative explanations for a relationship between variables have not been controlled). However, when research is replicated with different sized samples and the results of statistical testing differ somewhat among the studies (as they usually do), interpreting the results can get really complicated!

Reporting the Strength of a Relationship.   It is helpful to report the strength of a relationship between variables (effect size) along with the results of a statistical analysis. Then the readers of a report can draw their own conclusions about whether they should allow the findings to influence their own practice or research in any way. Including actual percentage differences is one way to do this when a chi-square test has been used. Reporting a related measure of association is another. When a chi-square analysis is performed with the use of a statistical software package, related indicators often are displayed as part of the results of the data analysis. Some of the better known ones are **phi, Yule's Q, lambda,** and **Cramer's V.** Each is designed for a specific data-analysis situation. For example, *Q* is designed for use with two dichotomous variables, is easily computed by hand, and produces a correlation coefficient that can be used to describe the strength of the relationship between variables, but it should not be used if one of the cells has an observed frequency of 0.

Although both phi and *V* produce a correlation coefficient that can be squared (r^2) to suggest the amount of variation in the dependent variable that is associated with the variation in the independent variable, phi should be used if both variables are dichotomous and *V* if one or both variables contain more than two value categories. If both variables are at the ordinal level (and chi-square often is still the test of choice in such situations), still other measures of association (for example, *gamma* or one of the nonparametric tests of correlation introduced in Chapter 8) can be used to report the strength of the relationship between the variables. Reporting the appropriate measure of association along with chi-square values and *p* values helps put research findings into perspective. It is especially recommended if very large sample sizes are used, because statistical significance is so likely that it can be almost meaningless as a research finding.

Restrictions on the Use of Chi-Square

We must know what an expected frequency is and how it is calculated in order to understand the important concept that the chi-square statistic compares observed frequencies with expected frequencies. But it is also useful to know how to calculate an expected frequency so that we can determine if we should be using the chi-square statistic at all.

The chi-square statistic is not appropriate for all the analyses of the relationship between two nominal level variables. Its formula will not produce accurate results and it, therefore, should not be used if either of two situations exists:

1. When, in a 2 × 2 (four-cell) table, at least one cell has an expected frequency of less than 5.
2. When, in a table that is larger than 2 × 2, more than 20 percent of the cells have expected frequencies of less than 5, or any cell has an expected frequency of 0.

A handy check on whether there is a problem with small expected frequencies in any cross-tabulation table can be performed by locating the cell with the smallest expected frequency. To do this, locate the row with the smallest marginal total and the column with the smallest marginal total. The cell with the smallest expected frequency is at the intersection of that row and column. The cell's expected frequency can be determined with the expected frequency formula. If an expected frequency in a 2 × 2 table is 5 or more, it is safe to use the chi-square statistic. If the expected frequency is less than 5, chi-square should not be used.

In larger tables, additional checks have to be made to see if the second "no-go" situation exists. (If a computer software package is used, a warning generally appears if all expected frequency requirements have not been met.) If there are problems, it may still be possible to use a chi-square test by combining adjoining cells to form a table with fewer cells with sufficiently large expected frequencies. This process, called **collapsing,** should be done with the use of common sense and logic and in a way that does not discard any more data than absolutely necessary. Value categories of a variable that are thus combined should possess a strong logical similarity to each other.

An Alternative: Fisher's Exact Test

If, in examining the relationship between two dichotomous variables, the expected frequency size requirements for the use of the chi-square test cannot be met, **Fisher's exact test** is an alternative test. Like chi-square, it is used with two independent subsamples. The independent subsamples may have resulted from the random sampling of cases that have been categorized as falling into two identifiable groups, such as gender (e.g., male, female) or marital status (e.g., married, not married). Or they may be the experimental and control groups to which cases were randomly assigned in a classic experimental research design.

Because Fisher's exact test can only analyze data using a 2 × 2 contingency table (four cells), if there are more than two value categories of either (or both) of the variables, it is necessary to first collapse the data into a 2 × 2 table (making both variables dichotomous). This results in a loss of available measurement precision, so if feasible, it might be preferable to enlarge the size of the research sample so that the requirements for the use of chi-square can be met.

Using Chi-Square in Social Work Practice

Major changes in the delivery of social work services may have a positive or a negative effect on the lives of clients. Changes based on findings derived from a chi-square analysis alone can be especially risky. After all, as we have noted, the identification of a statistically significant relationship between variables with the use of a chi-square test is usually just evidence of association; a causal relationship cannot be implied.

Like any type of statistical analysis, chi-square can also suggest relationships between variables that are spurious. They might disappear if the influence of other variables is controlled in some way. For this reason, chi-square analyses are sometimes best used to tentatively identify associations between variables and to formulate critical questions that can subsequently be answered through more high-powered statistical analyses.

Example: Discharge Planning and Readmission. Amelia is a social worker in a state inpatient hospital. Her main duty is to do readmission intake interviews with patients with prior hospital admissions. Over the past 5 years, she observed what appeared to be a disproportionately large number of patients who were readmitted to the hospital who had been previously discharged to live with their relatives. Knowing that her social work colleagues doing discharge planning also made frequent use of boarding homes for discharged patients, she wondered why she was not seeing more readmissions of patients who were discharged to boarding homes. She wondered if there might not be a relationship between patients being readmitted (or not readmitted) to the hospital and the place to which they had been discharged (boarding home versus relatives).

Amelia read all the available related literature. She then designed and implemented a small-scale research study that would gather data to see if she had support for her one-tailed research hypothesis:

> Patients discharged to boarding homes will have a lower rate of readmission to the hospital than patients discharged to live with their relatives.

Amelia received permission from her supervisors to select a 10 percent random sample of all files of patients discharged during the previous 18 months. Using a simple data-collection instrument that she constructed, she gathered data on a wide variety of demographic variables on the 148 patients (10% of 1,480 patients = 148 patients) who were discharged to boarding homes and the 250 patients (10% of 2,500 patients = 250 patients) who were discharged to relatives. Her total sample (N) was 398 patients (148 + 250 = 398).

Table 10.8 displays the findings from Amelia's data analysis. What did she learn from them? From her general knowledge of hypothesis testing, she knew that $p < .01$ meant that the differences between the observed and expected frequencies probably were not

TABLE 10.8   Readmission to Hospital by Discharge Status (*N* = 398)

Discharge Status	Readmission?		Totals
	Yes	No	
Boarding Home	25	123	148
Relatives	71	179	250
Totals	96	302	398

$\chi^2 = 6.113$, $df = 1$, $p < .01$ (direction predicted)

due to sampling error; the likelihood that sampling error produced the relationship between the variables within her sample was less than 1 percent. She thus was able to reject the null hypothesis and conclude that there was a statistically significant relationship between the variables.

Amelia also knew that when a one-tailed research hypothesis is tested by a chi-square test, it is necessary to determine whether a statistically significant relationship between variables is in the predicted direction, either by looking for the cells where disproportionately large observed frequencies occurred or by examining percentages. With the use of Table 10.8, Amelia was able to determine that approximately 17 percent (25 of 148) of patients discharged to boarding homes had been readmitted to the hospital, compared with 28 percent (71 of 250) of those discharged to relatives. These two percentages were consistent with the direction of her hypothesis; patients discharged to boarding homes were less likely to be readmitted than patients discharged to relatives.

Before Amelia drew any conclusions about the meaningfulness of the statistical significance between the variables, she knew that she must acknowledge the limitations of her research design. The validity of the data in the patient records might be a problem; in addition, there might be other factors relating to bias. There was also a long list of other variables that might have affected readmission of the patients in her study. They included patient diagnosis, length of first hospitalization, availability of aftercare services, patient's use of medication, and a myriad of other factors that she had no reason to believe were proportionally represented in the two groups (boarding home/relatives) of patients.

What did her findings really tell Amelia about the relationship between the setting to which patients are discharged and their readmission? The goal of a chi-square analysis is to acquire evidence for or against the existence of an association between variables. Determining if the relationship was a causal one was not a possibility from the beginning, due to the absence of an experimental research design. What Amelia learned was that, for whatever reasons, patients who were discharged to boarding homes from her particular hospital were not as likely to be readmitted as those patients who were discharged to relatives.

Amelia also gathered data on patient diagnosis and length of first hospitalization. She could examine the relationship among these other variables and the dependent variable as well, with the use of the appropriate statistical analysis. The patients' records might have yielded insights into still other variables that went into the decision to live with relatives or in a boarding home; these data could be used to enhance the results of her analysis and to shed more light on her original findings.

Given all the limitations that tempered the interpretation of Amelia's findings, it might seem that they were of little value. The likelihood of the existence of many other variables that might have affected whether a patient was readmitted would seem to discount the utility of the findings for social work practice. Yet, despite a less-than rigorous research design and the use of a relatively low-powered nonparametric statistical analysis, several possible practice implications emerged.

Knowing (even without fully understanding why) that patients discharged to boarding homes in Amelia's hospital are less likely to be readmitted than patients discharged to relatives could be valuable to her social work colleagues doing discharge planning. Patients discharged to live with relatives could be perceived (for whatever reason) as being at higher risk of readmission. Based on her findings in Table 10.8, Amelia began to ask certain questions:

1. Should I try to find boarding home placements for more of my clients?
2. Should I endeavor as a professional social worker to work toward the creation of more boarding home facilities?
3. Should I endeavor to provide additional sources of support for patients going to live with relatives in order to reduce the likelihood of their being readmitted?

These applications of the research findings are still only questions. None of them indicates that Amelia or the other social workers at her hospital should make drastic modifications in their service delivery methods without careful consideration and, what is more important, without additional research studies.

Example: Legislators' Voting Patterns and Tax Issues.   Juan is a social worker employed by a legislative committee. He is attempting to assist in the passage of an increase in the state sales tax, which will provide additional revenues for public education. As part of his job, he recently began gathering demographic data on state legislators. He hoped to gain insight into why they might favor or oppose the proposed tax increase.

After he had examined available data and hearsay on 30 legislators, it seemed to Juan that legislators who favored the bill tended to have children currently attending public schools; legislators who were on record as not supporting the bill tended not to have children currently in public schools. Juan wondered whether he could find statistical support for a relationship between the nominal variables *support (or nonsupport) of the bill* and *use (or nonuse) of public schools.*

After a discussion with committee members and a review of the literature available on legislators' voting patterns on various tax issues, Juan concluded that he could justify formulation of a one-tailed research hypothesis:

> Legislators who currently have children attending public schools are more likely to support the bill than are legislators who do not have children currently attending public schools.

TABLE 10.9   Legislators' Support for Tax Bill by Whether They Use Public Schools (N = 125)

	Support for Bill?		
Use Public Schools?	**Yes**	**No**	**Totals**
Yes	39	36	75
No	21	29	50
Totals	60	65	125

$\chi^2 = .834$, $df = 1$, $p > .10$ (direction predicted)

Juan continued to gather data on the state's legislators, but he made a special effort to learn about and systematically record data on his two variables. He identified 160 legislators who had publicly stated support for or opposition to the tax bill. Of these, he obtained sufficient current biographical data on 125 (78 percent) to conclude with reasonable certainty whether or not they were currently sending their children to public schools. Table 10.9 presents Juan's findings.

Juan was somewhat disappointed by the findings of his chi-square analysis, yet he was grateful that he had not relied on his subjective hunches in his presentation to the legislative committee. If he had, he might have misled the committee members.

With 1 degree of freedom and a one-tailed research hypothesis, Juan knew his chi-square value should have been at least 2.71 (see Table 10.5) in order to reject the null hypothesis at the customary .05 rejection level. It was only .834. He lacked sufficient evidence to conclude that the legislators' use or nonuse of public schools for their children was associated with their voting preference on the tax bill (which was his original one-tailed research hypothesis).

Perhaps other variables were more closely associated with whether they favored the bill—for example, their voting record on all tax bills, their perceptions of the fairness of a sales tax versus other sources of revenue, a partner who was teaching in the public school system, and so on. Juan also knew that these other variables may have helped obscure the presence of a relationship between the variables whose association he had tested.

The lack of statistical support for Juan's one-tailed research hypothesis in no way negated the value of his study. He avoided drawing an erroneous conclusion based on inadequate evidence that might have resulted in an inappropriate lobbying strategy. Portraying the motivation of legislators who opposed the bill as self-serving would have been a mistake. Juan could now spend his time more efficiently by pursuing other avenues to gain insight into the legislators' positions on the proposed tax.

CROSS TABULATION WITH THREE OR MORE VARIABLES

In the example used earlier in this chapter, we were seeking to document the existence of an association between the variables *type of treatment* and *client success*. Suppose we repeated the research study with the use of 100 clients and again used chi-square to analyze the data. The observed frequencies for this hypothetical study are displayed in Table 10.10.

TABLE 10.10 Observed Frequencies:
Type of Treatment by Client Outcome ($N = 100$)

	Results		
Type of Treatment	**Success**	**Failure**	**Totals**
Group	15	35	50
Individual	25	25	50
Totals	40	60	100

$\chi^2 = 3.376$, $df = 1$, $p > .05$ (direction predicted)

Despite the presence of a statistically significant association between the variables, we may wonder if a third (confounding) variable, for example, *gender*, may explain why clients in group treatment appear to do better than those in individual treatment. We would like to somehow control for the effects of this third variable to get a better picture of the true relationship between type of treatment and client outcome.

One way to explore the effect of the third variable might be to divide our sample into its two subcategories, male and female. We could then construct two separate tables—one for female clients and one for male clients. We could use the chi-square test with each of the two subsamples to see if the relationship between type of treatment and client outcome held up within each of the subsamples. But there would be a better and more efficient way to accomplish the same purpose, the use of **multiple cross-tabulation tables.** It is possible to examine the association between two nominal-level variables while controlling for a third variable (which is then called a **control variable**) while using a single cross-tabulation table. Multiple cross-tabulation tables can be used to spread the cases in the original cross-tabulation table (e.g., Table 10.10) among a larger number of cells. (This is the opposite of the process of collapsing described earlier.) Two or more variables are displayed along one axis or even along both axes. Table 10.11 is a multiple cross-tabulation table using the same data that were used in Table 10.10, only in Table 10.11 a third variable, gender, has been added.

TABLE 10.11 Observed and Expected Frequencies:
Type of Treatment and Gender of Client by Client Outcome ($N = 100$)

		Client Outcome				
		Success		Failure		
Treatment	**Gender**	**Observed**	**Expected**	**Observed**	**Expected**	**Totals**
Group	Male	7	(10)	18	(15)	25
Group	Female	8	(10)	17	(15)	25
Individual	Male	13	(10)	12	(15)	25
Individual	Female	12	(10)	13	(15)	25
Totals		40		60		100

$\chi^2 = 4.334$, $df=3$, $p. > .05$ (direction predicted)

Notice that the chi-square values in Table 10.10 and 10.11 are similar—the one in Table 10.11 is actually a little larger. But the *p* values displayed in Tables 10.10 and Table 10.11 (< .05 and > .05, respectively) are different. Before the variable *gender* is introduced, we would be able to reject the null hypothesis (using the .05 rejection level), but after it is introduced, we cannot. How can we interpret this phenomenon? It may mean that the relationship between *type of treatment* and *client outcome* is a spurious one or is so weak that the introduction of gender has obscured it in the sample studied.

Problems with Sizes of Expected Frequencies

It is not always possible to control for one or more variables with the use of multiple cross-tabulation. When data are spread out in larger cross-tabulation tables, size requirements for expected frequencies for using chi-square sometimes cannot be met.

In Table 10.11, the 100 cases are distributed among eight cells. The expected frequencies of the eight cells would thus be smaller than the expected frequencies of the four cells in Table 10.10. The expected frequencies are, however, over 5 in a sufficiently large percentage (more than 80 percent) of the cells to justify the use of the chi-square test. This happened only because the number of cases in group and individual treatment were equal; there were an equal number of males and females, and the overall number of successes and failures were similar. If the cases had not split so evenly into the value categories, the expected frequencies may have been less than 5 in more than 20 percent of the cells. Then we could not have used the chi-square test.

Because the use of multiple cross-tabulation tables spreads the cases into a larger number of cells, such tables can be used only when relatively large samples are available and cases break fairly evenly among value categories of the variables. Even then, if at least one examined variable has been measured in a way that results in a large number of value categories, the value categories may have to be collapsed so that the cross-tabulation table has fewer cells (and sufficiently large expected frequencies) before we can use the chi-square test.

Only the expected frequency size requirement of the chi-square test prevents the more frequent use of multiple cross-tabulation tables for examining the effect of other variables on the relationship between variables. Theoretically, several variables could be combined along the left of the table and several more could be combined along its top. To do this, however, a very large sample would be required, larger than is found in most social work research studies.

Effects of Introducing Additional Variables

As in the above example, the original association between variables will sometimes disappear when a third variable is controlled. Other times, the relationship between the two original variables will appear stronger when a third variable is controlled. In such instances, the third variable, called a **suppressor** or **obscuring variable,** may cause us to underestimate the actual strength of the association between the two variables.

When a third variable is introduced, a third result also may occur. The relationship between the first two variables may remain statistically significant. But it may be significant in one direction with one or more value categories of the third (control) variable and significant in the opposite direction in its other value categories. When this happens, it is usually not possible to summarize the findings easily; the relationship between the independent variable and dependent variable has to be described for each value category of the control variable. The third variable is said to further specify the relationship between the first two variables, and it is therefore called a **specifying variable.**

The many possible effects of the introduction of one or more additional variables to a statistical analysis remind us of the complexity of most relationships among variables. It is because of this complexity that we should exercise extreme caution in drawing conclusions about the effect of one variable on another or even about their association. A statistically significant relationship between variables can still be a spurious one. All that statistical significance tells us is that the relationship is unlikely to be due to sampling error.

SPECIAL APPLICATIONS OF THE CHI-SQUARE FORMULA

Other statistical tests also rely on cross-tabulation and the chi-square formula to determine if the relationship between variables is statistically significant. Two of them—**McNemar's test** and the **median test**—are sometimes found in the professional literature.

McNemar's Test

One special application of the chi-square test, **McNemar's test,** also called the *test for the significance of changes,* is popular in research situations that employ a one-group pretest–posttest research design. The test entails two measurements of a dichotomous nominal level variable with the use of a single research sample. It could be used, for example, to determine if an educational program on the life experiences of Bantu refugees was associated with a desired change in attitudes about them among community members who attended an educational program (the intervention).

In social work practice and research we often wonder whether an intervention (the independent variable) can be demonstrated to be associated with desirable changes in the dependent variable. The McNemar's test offers the opportunity for at least a preliminary insight into this question. It can tell us if the amount of change that occurred in the desired direction in a research sample was statistically significant or likely to be due to sampling error.

Example: Attempting to Influence Parents. Chester is a school social worker. He requested time to address a meeting of a parents' group to present arguments for hiring four additional school social workers for the district, a proposal currently being considered by the school board. Chester believed that parents would reflect a positive change in their attitudes following his presentation.

Because Chester predicted that his presentation would be associated with a positive change in parents' thinking on the issue, he formulated a one-tailed research hypothesis:

After my presentation, more parents will reflect positive attitudes about hiring additional social workers than they had before my presentation.

Just prior to his presentation to the parents' group, Chester gave a sheet of paper and a pencil to each parent. On the paper, he asked each parent to include a five-digit identifying number and to indicate if he or she was in favor of hiring the four additional social workers. Immediately after his presentation, he once again gave all parents a sheet of paper and a pencil and asked them to supply the same identifying number and to again indicate if they were in favor of hiring the additional social workers. Based on pretest and posttest data supplied by the parents, Chester classified each parent into one of four mutually exclusive categories:

1. Favored before, favored after
2. Favored before, did not favor after
3. Did not favor before, favored after
4. Did not favor before, did not favor after

Chester placed his raw data into a 2 × 2 cross-tabulation table (Table 10.12). He then used the basic chi-square formula (with a correction for continuity) to compute a chi-square value. He checked the table of critical values (see Table 10.5) to see whether he had statistical support to reject the null hypothesis.

In Table 10.12, the totals on the right side represent the numbers of parents for and against the proposal before (pretest) Chester's presentation (32 and 18, respectively). The totals along the bottom of the table represent the numbers for and against it after (posttest) the presentation (16 and 34, respectively).

The numbers within the body of the table (its four cells) represent individual cases, as they do in any cross-tabulation table. The 50 cases (parents) were distributed among the table's four cells based on a pair of measurements—whether or not each parent favored the proposal before the presentation and whether or not he or she favored the proposal after it. Thus, for example, if Ms. Aguilar favored the proposal

TABLE 10.12   Significance of Change Analysis (McNemar's Test): Positions on Proposal before and after Chester's Presentation

Before Presentation	After Presentation		Total
	For	**Against**	
For	6 (*a*)	26 (*b*)	32
Against	10 (*c*)	8 (*d*)	18
Totals	16	34	50

$\chi^2 = 5.58$, $df = 1$, $p < .01$

before Chester's presentation, but opposed the proposal after his presentation, she would be one of the 26 cases in cell *b.* Or if Mr. Owens was against the proposal before his presentation and was still against it after the presentation, he would be one of the 8 cases in cell *d.*

The McNemar's test focuses on cells in which change is reflected, in this case, cells *b* and *c,* where parents changed their position. (Cells *a* and *d* contain parents who did not change their position.) When using McNemar's test, the null hypothesis is that some change would be likely to occur with some cases but whatever change occurred probably would be about equal in both directions. These changes would theoretically cancel each other out, and the number of parents favoring or opposing the proposal to hire more social workers would remain about the same after the presentation as they were before it.

Using the McNemar's test, the null hypothesis can be rejected only if a large percentage of the changes that occurred were in one direction (larger than what sampling error normally would be expected to produce). This is reflected in a statistically significant *p* value (usually, $p < .05$). In addition, if a one-tailed hypothesis had been formulated (as was the case in Chester's study), most of the changes must be in the direction predicted. In Chester's study, they were in the opposite direction, that is, from support for the proposal to hire more social workers to opposition to it. Thus, despite a *p* value of $< .01$, Chester could not reject the null hypothesis and claim statistical support for his one-tailed research hypothesis.

Only 14 parents failed to change their positions (cells *a* and *d*). But of the 36 who changed them (cells *b* and *c*), only 10 moved from negative to positive (cell *c*), whereas 26 (cell *b*) who had previously favored the proposal opposed it after the presentation. Chester speculated on the meaning of these findings. Had he said something to turn off the parents? Why had so many of them changed in a negative direction following his presentation? Before he gave any more presentations to parents' groups, he planned to review carefully what he had said and how he had said it.

In sum the McNemar's test is used in research situations that involve a dichotomous nominal level dependent variable that is measured twice for the same sample of cases. Because it is ideal for many one-group pretest–posttest research designs that evaluate practice intervention methods, it can be a useful test for the social work researcher or practitioner.

The Median Test

The median test is another related statistical procedure that is useful in situations in which one variable (usually the dependent one) is at the ordinal, interval, or ratio level, but badly skewed. It is designed to assess the likelihood that the value categories of the other dichotomous nominal variable (e.g., experimental group, control group) are sufficiently different from each other in regard to the ordinal, interval, or ratio variable to warrant the rejection of the null hypothesis.

The median test is relatively simple. Scores are first rank ordered, and the median for all scores is computed. Values that fall at the median are dropped or added to one group or the other. Then the number of values or value labels above and below the median are tabulated for both categories of the dichotomous nominal level variable, and the frequencies are placed in a cross-tabulation table.

Because it uses the median as the cutoff point, the median test divides the sample into two equal-sized subgroups (half above the median and half below the median) based on measurements of the variable. With larger samples (30 or 40 or more total cases) that also reflect a reasonably even split in the number of cases in a dichotomous nominal level variable (two subsamples), the expected frequencies may be large enough to justify the use of the chi-square test to complete the data analysis. When the total number of cases (both groups) is small, Fisher's exact test is substituted to see if the relationship between the two variables is statistically significant.

The median test is based on the assumption that if the two groups are not really different or if they reflect differences that can be attributable to sampling error, each will have approximately the same percentage of cases above and below the median of the ordinal level, interval level, or ratio level variable. A clustering above the median by one group and below the median by the other group may indicate a real relationship between the two variables, depending on the strength of the pattern and the degree to which other alternative explanations have been ruled out.

Example: Understanding Reluctance to Undergo Amniocentesis.   Beulah is a social worker employed in a genetic counseling center. She observed that less than half of pregnant women over 40 years of age who were referred for amniocentesis (a medical procedure that determines if a fetus has certain genetic problems) followed through with the referral. She noticed what she thought might be a factor related to this phenomenon. It seemed to her that women who did not follow through on the referral tended to have more children; those who did follow through seemed to have fewer children. Thus, she formulated a one-tailed research hypothesis:

> Women with more children are less likely to complete a referral than those with fewer children.

Beulah drew a random sample of 100 ($N = 100$) case records that documented referral for amniocentesis. She recorded for each (1) the number of children in the family at the time of the referral, and (2) whether the client completed the referral. The variable *number of children* is at the ratio level of measurement. Beulah knew, however, that the variable is positively skewed. Thus, she decided to use the median test. She computed the median for the variable number of children in her sample (2.14). She then grouped the data into four cells of a contingency table (Table 10.13) based on where each case fell in relation to the two-category nominal-level dependent variable (i.e., did not complete referral, did complete referral) and the ratio-level independent variable *number of children* (i.e., above the median, below the median).

The criteria for size of expected frequencies for the chi-square test were met for (the smallest, cell *c*, was 5.76), so she completed her statistical analysis with the use of the formula for chi-square (using the correction for continuity). Her initial one-tailed research hypothesis was confirmed by the median test—women with more children were less likely to complete a referral than those with fewer children. She speculated on her findings, wondering whether the possible birth of a child with Down syndrome, for example, was of less concern in larger families because additional child-care help was available from older siblings. She decided to pursue this possible explanation.

TABLE 10.13   Median Test Data: Completion of Referral for Amniocentesis and Number of Children (*N* = 100)

| Completion of Referral | Number of Children (MD = 2.14) | | Total |
	Above Median	Below Median	
No	28 (*a*)	12 (*b*)	40
Yes	22 (*c*)	38 (*d*)	60
Totals	50	50	100

$\chi^2 = 9.375, df = 1, p < .005$

This example is a little unusual for use of the median test in that the independent variable is at the ratio level of measurement, but badly skewed and the dependent variable is nominal and dichotomous. More typically, it is the dependent variable that is at the interval or ratio level of measurement, but skewed, whereas the independent variable (e.g., type of treatment) is nominal level and dichotomous.

All too frequently, researchers observe that the criteria for use of a parametric test (for example, one or more normally distributed interval level or ratio level variables) cannot be met and immediately turn to chi-square. The median test takes better advantage of the level of measurement precision that is available. The median test at least treats a skewed interval level, ratio level, or ordinal level variable as being more than nominal. Chi-square treats all variables as if they were at the nominal level of measurement. To use chi-square in such situations increases the risk of a Type II error in drawing conclusions about a relationship between variables.

Like the McNemar's test, the median test has no formula of its own. It really would be more accurate to describe both not as tests but as procedures for assigning cases into the cells of a contingency table. Then the formula for chi-square, or Fisher's exact test, can be applied to produce a *p* value.

CONCLUDING THOUGHTS

Most of this chapter was devoted to the widely used chi-square test of association. The fact that it requires only nominal level data for both variables means that it is ideally suited to many of hypothesis-testing needs in our profession. Unfortunately, there are certain errors commonly made in its use. They usually entail making too much of a finding of statistical significance by (1) implying that the relationship is one of more than just association, (2) overestimating the importance of findings that reflect weak relationships between variables where a finding of significance was virtually inevitable because of the use of very large samples, or (3) failing to consider that the association may be a spurious one and thus not attempting to control for other variables that may be creating a false impression about the relationship that has been identified.

Still another common error is made when the chi-square test is used when one or both variables are at the ordinal, interval, or ratio level of measurement. When this happens, the test treats different values as if they are only differences in kind (value categories); it ignores the fact that they reflect quantitative differences in the variable. Unless both variables are only at the nominal level of measurement, there is very likely to be a better (often a more powerful) statistical test that can and should be used. We presented an overview of one of these, the median test. Others were presented in the previous chapter and still others will be discussed in Chapter 11.

STUDY QUESTIONS

1. Why is the frequent use of chi-square in social work research both good and bad? How is the test particularly well suited to social work research?
2. What do the numbers in each of the cells in a cross-tabulation table mean?
3. What is a dummy table, and what does it reflect?
4. Can chi-square ever tell us whether one variable causes variations in the second variable? Explain.
5. What are expected frequencies, and how are they used in chi-square testing?
6. How do degrees of freedom affect whether a chi-square value of a given size (e.g., 10.00) will be considered statistically significant?
7. What are the minimum expected frequency requirements for the use of chi-square? What other nonparametric alternative is available when the expectation for a 2-by-2 table cannot be met?
8. What is the final step in the process for determining if chi-square has demonstrated support for a one-tailed research hypothesis? Provide examples.
9. How can cross-tabulation (chi-square) be used to examine the relationship between variables while controlling for the effect of a third variable? How can this detect the presence of a spurious relationship between variables?
10. What is a useful test that examines whether the change in a nominal level variable in a single group of cases is statistically significant?
11. Why is the median test preferable to chi-square when one variable is interval or ratio level but badly skewed?

t Tests and Analysis of Variance

In social work research and practice, we frequently have reasonably precise measurements of the dependent variable. Examples of common dependent variables in social work research are *client self-esteem, public attitudes toward welfare recipients, marital satisfaction,* and *clinical depression,* to name just a few. Thanks to the work of researchers over the years, many standardized self-report measuring instruments to measure these variables now exist. Many of them can be assumed to generate interval level data that approximate a normal distribution in the population on which they have been developed.

Other variables, such as *number of appointments missed, number of stated oppositions to a proposed social service program,* or *amount of illegal drugs consumed,* often are normally distributed at the interval or ratio levels of measurement by their very nature. Thus the mean is an appropriate measure of their central tendency and the standard deviation is an appropriate measure of their variability (see Chapter 3).

In our research hypotheses, the independent variable is often at the nominal level of measurement. It may be, for example, *type of treatment intervention, gender of the social worker, ethnicity of the social worker,* or some other variable that can only be measured by grouping cases into different value categories. Often, the research sample available for a study is small; large samples are not common in social work research, particularly in clinical situations.

The three conditions briefly described above—one nominal level independent variable, one normally distributed interval level or ratio level dependent variable, and relatively small random research sample(s)—are ideally suited to a family of related statistical procedures: (1) **t tests** and (2) **simple analysis of variance (or simple ANOVA).**

THE USE OF *t* TESTS

In many social work research studies, the dependent variable is measured within either a single sample or two samples. In a single-sample situation, for example, we may wish to know if the sample really differs greatly from its population in relation to the dependent variable—that is, how typical is it? On the other hand, in the two-sample situation, we may wish to know if measurements of the dependent variable differ greatly between the two samples in relation to the dependent variable—that is, are the two samples really all that different from one another in relation to the dependent variable?

The various *t* tests are based on something called the *t* **distribution of means.** There is actually a different *t* distribution for each sample size under 30. As sample sizes approach $N = 30$, they start to look more and more like a normal distribution curve.

Both normal distributions (Chapter 5) and sampling distributions (Chapter 6) rely heavily on knowledge of the amount of variation (standard deviation) of a variable in the population. With this knowledge, it is possible to compute a confidence interval that can then be used to determine just how large (or small) a sample mean would be required in order to achieve statistical significance—that is, to conclude with reasonable certainty that the difference between the sample's mean and its population's mean is unlikely to be due to sampling error.

But what if the amount of variation in the population is not known? This is true for many dependent variables that we attempt to influence. We are unlikely to know, for example, a population's standard deviation for variables such as number of unsafe sexual contacts per month in a given community or weekly number of bullying incidents within a middle school. Then we must rely on the *t* distribution. It allows us, based on measurements of the variable in a sample and the size of that sample, to compute a confidence interval for interval level and ratio level variables whose standard deviations in the population are unknown.

Because *t* tests are classified as parametric, they are designed for use in situations where the dependent variable is at the interval or ratio level and normally distributed. They are, however, quite robust; that is, if we use them with interval level or ratio level variables that are only somewhat skewed, they produce findings that are still quite accurate.

Misuse of *t*

As with the chi-square test, the popularity of *t* tests sometimes can lead to their misuse. The tests are familiar to us, easily understood, and relatively nonthreatening. Consequently, there may be a tendency to want to use them in situations in which they are inappropriate and in which other, more appropriate tests should be used. Two common misuses are (1) totally ignoring the shape of the distribution of the interval-level or ratio-level dependent variable in the population and (2) using the "shotgun" approach to data analyses.

If an interval or ratio level variable is badly skewed within the population, other tests (such as the nonparametric alternatives discussed later in this chapter) should be used in place of *t* tests. The credibility of research findings would be seriously jeopardized if *t* tests were used.

A second common misuse of two types of *t* tests (the two-sample independent and dependent *t* tests) involves calculating a large number of the tests using a single dependent variable and a long list of dichotomous independent variables. In some particularly glaring examples of this shotgun approach to data analyses, researchers have run hundreds of tests with little basis in the professional literature for believing that any of the independent variables might be related to the dependent variable. To their delight, this fishing expedition has produced a statistically significant relationship between a few of the independent variables and the dependent variable.

Findings of a few statistically significant relationships between variables when a large number of pairs of variables have been tested should not be surprising. In fact, we would probably be more surprised if none of the relationships between the variables proved to be statistically significant. Probability theory alone suggests that we will uncover one or more spurious relationships this way. It is nothing more than the mathematical principle that "with an infinite number of monkeys, an infinite number of computers, and an infinite amount of time, some monkey, sometime, somewhere, will write a Pulitzer Prize winning novel."

Expressed another way, by trying enough combinations, a researcher is almost certain to stumble onto one of those rare times that sampling error caused two variables to be strongly related within a research sample, even if the variables really are unrelated. Statistically examine the relationship between 100 different pairs of variables that have no relationship to each other whatsoever, and the laws of probability tell us that the most likely result is that perhaps 4 (4 is less than 5) of the combinations will reflect a statistically significant relationship at the .05 rejection level. Making too much of a "finding" from such a misuse of a statistical analysis can result in a Type I error, because the results are unlikely to be replicated in a second pair of samples. In situations in which there is reason to believe that many different independent variables may be related to the dependent variable, multivariate statistical tests that are specifically designed for such situations should be used.

Of course, the two common misuses of two-sample *t* tests that we have just described can occur when other inferential tests are used, too. For example, we can mistakenly use Pearson's *r* (Chapter 8) when one or both variables reflects a skewed distribution in the population. Or we could use a series of 100 bivariate chi-square tests (Chapter 10) and then make far too much of what might be a spurious relationship when a statistically significant relationship is found between a few of the pairs of variables.

THE ONE-SAMPLE *t* TEST

The **one-sample *t* test** is used when a research study employs only one randomly selected sample. It compares the mean of an interval level or ratio level variable in a sample with its estimated population mean. The formula for the test produces a *t* value, which is then compared with a table like Table 11.1 to find the *p* value, the likelihood that sampling error might have produced the sample mean of the dependent variable, given the size of the sample that was employed. When a computer is used, the output displays both the *t* value and the corresponding *p* value, along with the degrees of

TABLE 11.1   Critical Values of *t*

	Level of Significance for a One-Tailed Test					
	.10	.05	.025	.01	.005	.0005
	Level of Significance for a Two-Tailed Test					
df	.20	.10	.05	.02	.01	.001
1	3.078	6.314	31.821	31.821	63.657	636.619
2	1.886	2.920	4.303	6.965	9.925	31.598
3	1.638	2.353	3.182	4.541	5.841	12.941
4	1.533	2.132	2.776	3.747	4.604	8.610
5	1.476	2.015	2.571	3.365	4.032	6.859
6	1.440	1.943	2.447	3.143	3.707	5.959
7	1.415	1.895	2.365	2.998	3.499	5.405
8	1.397	1.860	2.306	2.896	3.355	5.041
9	1.383	1.833	2.262	2.821	3.250	4.781
10	1.372	1.812	2.228	2.764	3.169	4.587
11	1.363	1.796	2.201	2.718	3.106	4.437
12	1.356	1.782	2.179	2.681	3.055	4.318
13	1.350	1.771	2.160	2.650	3.012	4.221
14	1.345	1.761	2.145	2.624	2.977	4.140
15	1.341	1.753	2.131	2.602	2.947	4.073
16	1.337	1.746	2.120	2.583	2.921	4.015
17	1.333	1.740	2.110	2.567	2.898	3.965
18	1.330	1.734	2.101	2.552	2.878	3.922
19	1.328	1.729	2.093	2.539	2.861	3.883
20	1.325	1.725	2.086	2.528	2.845	3.850
21	1.323	1.721	2.080	2.518	2.831	3.819
22	1.321	1.717	2.074	2.508	2.819	3.792
23	1.319	1.714	2.069	2.500	2.807	3.767
24	1.318	1.711	2.064	2.492	2.797	3.745
25	1.316	1.708	2.060	2.485	2.787	3.725
26	1.315	1.706	2.056	2.479	2.779	3.707
27	1.314	1.703	2.052	2.473	2.771	3.690
28	1.313	1.701	2.048	2.467	2.763	3.674
29	1.311	1.699	2.045	2.462	2.756	3.659
30	1.310	1.697	2.042	2.457	2.750	3.646
40	1.303	1.684	2.021	2.423	2.704	3.551
60	1.296	1.671	2.000	2.390	2.660	3.460
120	1.289	1.658	1.980	2.358	2.617	3.373

Source: From Table III of R. A. Fisher and F. Yates, *Statistical Tables for Biological, Agricultural, and Medical Research,* published by Longman Group, Ltd., London (previously published by Oliver and Boyd, Ltd., Edinburgh) and by permission of the authors and publishers.

freedom for the sample size that was used. With t tests, degrees of freedom adjust for the sample size that produces a t value. For the one-sample t test, the degrees of freedom are the number of cases in the sample minus one.

The one-sample t test is used for two different purposes: (1) to determine whether a sample is sufficiently representative of its population in relation to some variable for use in a research study (a design issue) and (2) to test hypotheses (for inference).

Determining if a Sample Is Representative

When using the one-sample t test to evaluate the representativeness of a sample in relation to an interval level or ratio level variable, we generally hope *not* to be able to *reject* the null hypothesis. Why? If we get a high p value such as .10, .50, or even .75, this provides support for the position that any difference between the two means is so small that it is very likely to be due to sampling error—that is, our sample is indeed representative of its population.

For example, suppose we want to conduct a simple research study to examine the relationship between the variables *age* and *job satisfaction level* among child-protection social workers (using Pearson's r). We have been told by the program's director that we can draw only a small random sample ($N = 25$) of workers, because we need to conduct extensive interviews with them. We would like the sample to be representative of the population of all child-protection workers in relation to what logically may be an intervening interval level variable, *size of a worker's caseload*. We have been told by the director that the average caseload for all child-protection workers is normally distributed and is about 50 cases.

We could draw the sample of 25 and then use the one-sample t test to compare the sample's mean caseload size with the population's mean caseload size of 50. If the results of our analysis suggest that the difference between the two means is likely to be the work of sampling error (say, $p > .50$), we would not reject the null hypothesis. The sample would be not all that different, probably close enough to be considered representative of its population in regard to the variable *size of worker's caseload*. We would proceed to interview the 25 cases in the sample.

If, however, a one-sample t-test analysis compared our sample's mean with its population's mean and concluded that the difference between the two means was not likely to be the work of sampling error ($p < .05$), we would reject the null hypothesis. From this, we could conclude either (1) that our sample and its population really are different in regard to the variable *size of caseload* or (2) that the director gave us misinformation about the estimated average caseload size in the population.

If we were to proceed to the interviewing stage of the study with a sample that may be different from its population, we would jeopardize our ability to generalize our study's findings to the population from which the sample was drawn. It might be better to draw two or three more random samples and repeat the statistical analysis using the one-sample t test. If the other samples all produce a relatively large p-value (we cannot reject the null hypothesis) and their means are similar, it is probably safe to use one of them for our study and conclude that the first sample was just a fluke. However, if repeated sampling continues to generate p values of $< .05$ and the means are all similar, it is altogether possible that the director gave us misinformation because, with samples of 25, most samples should have mean caseloads quite close to the population mean. The average caseloads in the samples, especially if they are quite similar to each other, may indeed be representative of the true population and therefore any one of them may be appropriate for use.

Hypothesis Testing

When we use the one-sample *t* test to attempt to gain support for a one-tailed or two-tailed research hypothesis, we hope to demonstrate that our sample is so different from its population in regard to an interval level or ratio level dependent variable that the difference is not likely to be due to sampling error. Thus, we hope to be able to reject the null hypothesis.

A one-sample *t* test can determine if an intervention may have made a real difference. We could, for example, select a random sample of clients with low frustration tolerance (as measured by a standardized scale) and offer a supplemental treatment to them (such as a special workshop on frustration management). We could then measure their frustration tolerance levels and compare their mean frustration tolerance level with the estimated mean frustration tolerance level of all clients who have a similar diagnosis with the use of a one-sample *t* test.

The one-sample *t* test also can be used for hypothesis testing when one is using nonexperimental research designs. Suppose, with child-protection caseworkers used as research participants, we hope to demonstrate statistical support for our belief that child-protection workers in our county agency do better overall on the state licensure examination than most other child-protection caseworkers. Our one-tailed research hypothesis would be stated as follows:

> Social workers at ABC county office score higher than their peers on the state licensure examination.

We could collect the scores from all 25 of our workers who took the examination during the past 5 years and, with the use of the one-sample *t* test, compare their mean score with the mean score of all child-protection workers who took the examination during the past 5 years. Perhaps our sample's mean score did turn out to be higher than the population's mean. That alone would not be sufficient to lend support to our one-tailed research hypothesis.

The question remains, was it that much higher? Would we be safe in concluding that our sample's higher mean score was not just due to sampling error? The results of a one-sample *t*-test analysis would answer this question. It would result in both a *t* value and a corresponding *p* value, which would be based on the *t* value and the appropriate degrees of freedom. If we had used .05 as our rejection level, a low *p* value (i.e., $p < .05$) would support a decision to reject the null hypothesis and would lend support for our one-tailed research hypothesis. A higher *p* value (i.e., $p > .05$) would support a decision not to reject the null hypothesis. It would suggest that the difference between the two mean scores is probably just the work of sampling error and that there is no reason to believe that, in the long run, our child-protection workers would tend to score higher on the examination than the population.

**TABLE 11.2   Reporting Results of One-Sample
t Analyses: State Licensure Examination Scores**

Research Participants	Mean	Difference
Sample (*n* = 25)	85.42	85.42
Population (*N* = 100)	80.42	−80.42
		5.00

$t = 2.620, df = 24, p < .01$

Presentation of Findings

With the use of our example, Table 11.2 shows how the findings of one-sample *t* tests are presented in a research report. It displays the population mean (80.42), the mean of the research sample (85.42), the number of cases in the research sample and in the population (25 and 100, respectively), the *t* value (2.620), the degrees of freedom (24), and the corresponding *p* value ($p < .01$).

Where did these numbers come from? The *t* value was derived from the formula for a one-sample *t*, which is quite complicated. A *t* value generated by the formula is actually the number of standard deviations above (if it is positive) or below (if it is negative) the mean of a *t* distribution of samples of a certain size, that is, with a certain number of degrees of freedom. In our example, the *t* value generated by the formula was 2.620, and the degrees of freedom were 24 ($25 - 1 = 24$). If we look at the table of critical values for *t* (Table 11.1), we can see that the minimum *t* value for rejecting the null hypothesis when using a one-tailed research hypothesis and a .05 rejection level is 1.711 (24 degrees of freedom). Our mean fell above the mean of the *t* distribution's mean as predicted, 2.620 standard deviations above it. It was well into the rejection region for a one-tailed test when using the .05 rejection level. So why do we say we that our *p* value was $<.01$ rather than $<.05$? Because 2.620 is even greater than 2.492, the critical value of *t* for the .01 rejection level with a one-tailed research hypothesis. Thus $<.01$ is a more accurate description of the results of our analysis than $<.05$.

By glancing at Table 11.2, we can see that the 25 workers who took the examination in ABC county scored, on the average, 5 points higher than the population ($N = 100$) as a whole. This means that a 5-point difference would happen because of sampling error less than 1 time out of 100 with this size sample and the mean for the scores in the research sample.

A Nonparametric Alternative: Chi-Square Goodness of Fit

There is a useful alternative to the one-sample *t* test, the **chi-square goodness-of-fit test** (often referred to as simply goodness of fit). It performs the same two functions when the dependent variable is only nominal level.

Unlike the one-sample *t* test, goodness of fit does not compare the sample's mean with its population's mean. It is, of course, impossible to compute a mean with nominal level data. Unlike other uses of chi square (Chapter 10), it does not compare observed frequencies of cases with certain combinations of values with their expected frequencies. What the goodness-of-fit test does, however, is compare the *percentage* of cases in a given value category of a nominal level variable for a sample with the known percentage of cases in that variable's value category in its population.

For example, say we estimate that the percentage of left-handed people in a specific population is 12 percent. We could use a chi-square goodness-of-fit test to determine if the percentage of left-handed people in a sample drawn from this population differs significantly from that in the population—that is, from 12 percent.

Based on sampling distributions (Chapter 6) and how other statistical tests work, we would probably not be surprised if the percentage of left-handed people in our sample of 25 was, say, 11 percent or 13 percent. We would not expect the difference between either of these two sample percentages and the population's 12 percent to be statistically significant. We would not expect to be able to reject the null hypothesis, which would state that any difference between the percentages is probably just due to sampling error. After all, if nothing unusual were going on, we would expect our sample to contain about the same percentage of left-handed people as contained in the population from which it was drawn, and either 11 percent or 13 percent is very close to 12 percent.

But what if the percentage of left-handed people in our sample was, say, 5 percent or 19 percent? Then we would need help to determine whether to reject the null hypothesis—that is, to determine the likelihood (*p* value) that sampling error might have produced the percentage of left-handed people in a sample of this size.

With the use of the chi-square formula (Chapter 10), the chi-square goodness-of-fit test can compare our sample's percentage of left-handed people with its population's known percentage of left-handed people. A *p* value is produced, which then tells us the likelihood that the percentage of left-handed people in the sample could have been due to sampling error. The degrees of freedom are always one less than the number of value categories of the single variable ($2 - 1 = 1$ in this example).

How might we use this test? We probably would not care if a sample had a disproportionate number of left-handed people in it. But we might want (1) to determine whether a sample drawn is sufficiently representative of its population in relation to some potentially confounding nominal level variable for use in a research study (a design issue) and (2) to test hypotheses (for inference). The chi-square goodness-of-fit test can do either of these. They are the same tasks that a one-sample *t* test performs with the use of interval level or ratio level data.

Example: Assessing the Representativeness of a Research Sample—Family Support and Longevity.   Mable wanted to examine the correlation between an independent variable *number of living siblings* and a dependent variable, *length of client survival* among the residents of a large long-term care facility. Her literature review, however, had suggested that gender may be a confounding variable in the relationship between the independent and dependent variables. With the use of case files, she drew a simple random sample of 50 ($N = 50$) residents from the facility's population of 1,000 ($N = 1,000$).

Mable determined from the home's weekly census that its percentage of females was 72 percent (720 women). Before she conducted a statistical analysis with the use of Pearson's *r*, she wanted to know if her random sample (which consisted of 37 females, or 74% females) could be considered representative of the home's population for the potentially confounding variable *gender*. Thus, she hoped to be unable to reject the following null hypothesis:

> The percentage of females in the research sample does not differ significantly from the percentage of females in the population from which the sample was drawn.

To accept or reject her null hypothesis, Mable used the chi-square goodness-of-fit test to compare her sample's percentage of females (74%) with the home's actual percentage of females (72%). The test produced a *p* value of >.05. Thus, she was not able to reject the null hypothesis—the percentage difference between her sample (74%) and its population (72%) was relatively small (2 percentage points) and may well have been attributable to sampling error. In other words, her sample was sufficiently representative of the population for the variable *gender*. She went on to conduct her primary data analysis, assured that if she found a relationship between the independent variable and the dependent variable, at least it did not occur because the sample contained a disproportionately large number of females. Table 11.3 illustrates how Mable might report her finding as a table in her report.

Example: Involvement in the Political Process. Max works for a community agency located in his precinct, a very low socioeconomic neighborhood in the inner city. One of his agency's goals is to get local residents more involved in the political process in order to work for better public services. Recent election data revealed that only 22 percent of eligible voters in the inner city voted in the last several county council elections. Max selected a random sample of 100 eligible voters in his precinct from voter registration lists and visited all of them in their homes. He stressed the importance of voting in the next month's county council election. After the election, he determined that 35 of those he had visited, or 35 percent, had voted, while the overall percentage within the precinct remained constant at 22 percent.

TABLE 11.3 Comparison of Gender Distribution in the Population versus the Sample

	Percentage of Residents	
	Female	*Male*
Population of care facility	72%	28%
Study Sample	74%	26%

$x^2 = .49, df = 1, p > .05$

TABLE 11.4   Percent of Voters in the Population versus the Sample ($N = 100$)

	Voted in Election	Did Not Vote
Electoral Population	22%	78%
Study Sample	35%	65%

$x^2 = 4.53$, $df = 1$, $p < .05$

Max used the chi-square goodness-of-fit test to determine the probability that the difference between the voting percentage in his sample of 100 people (35%) and the usual percentage of those voting within the population (22%) was due to sampling error. After all, there was a 13-point percentage difference (35% − 22% = 13% points).

The results of his analysis were that the probability (p) of a difference of that magnitude occurring with a sample of 100 just because of sampling error was very low ($p < .05$). Max believed that he could safely reject the null hypothesis. Apparently, his sample was really different in its voting record following his intervention. He was hopeful that his home visits had made the difference, and that it was not just the work of some alternative explanation. Table 11.4 illustrates how Max might present his finding as a table in the context of the results section of his report.

THE DEPENDENT *t* TEST

The **dependent *t* test** is also called the paired-groups *t* test, matched-groups *t* test, dependent-groups *t* test, or correlated-groups *t* test. Unlike the one-sample *t* test, a dependent *t* test does not compare a sample's mean for an interval level or ratio level variable with its population's mean. It does, however, compare mean scores from two samples. The two samples may be two different but related samples (naturally related or matched in some way) that are both measured once, or the same sample measured on two separate occasions.

Use with Two Connected (or Matched) Samples Measured Once

In this application of the dependent *t* test, research participants or cases are matched in some way and put into two distinct samples, or groups. The two samples may consist of, for example, two groups of people who are naturally similar in some way, such as twins, or two groups of people that have been deliberately matched in relation to one or more variables (often, potentially confounding ones) so that both samples are believed to be comparable. Once the samples are thus constituted, we could, for example, administer a treatment intervention to one of the samples (but not the other) and use the dependent *t* test to see if there is a statistically significant difference between the two samples in relation to an interval level or ratio level variable, such as life satisfaction. (Degrees of freedom are the total number of measurements of the dependent variable minus 1.)

Example: A Support Group for Neglected Children.   Erin works in a family agency. Many of the clients that the agency serves are children who are victims of parental neglect. In the past, only individual and family counseling services were offered to children and their families. Although it appeared that these services were helpful in reducing the number of future incidents of neglect, they did not seem to have much effect on some of the emotional problems of the children. Specifically, many of the children seemed to remain shy and withdrawn.

Erin wanted to try something different—a support group for preadolescent victims of neglect. Her supervisor was supportive of her idea and agreed to help her set up the group and to find the time to run it. However, a condition of this agreement was that Erin would evaluate the group's effectiveness and that she would only be allowed to offer it again if it were found to be effective.

Many of the children in the agency who had been neglected were sibling groups who had shared the same life experiences. From each sibling group, Erin randomly selected one child to be in her support group and another to be in a control group. Thus, the two groups were considered "matched"—they were similar in relation to a number of variables that might correlate with shyness (confounding variables). Only one child in each family participated in the support group, but all children in the families continued to receive the usual services along with their parents. After she had run the group for eight weeks, Erin administered a standardized scale that measured shyness to the 10 group members and also to their 10 siblings in the control group. Then she entered her data (the scores on the scale) into her computer and ran the dependent *t* test. It compared the mean scores of the two groups and (with the use of a one-tailed research hypothesis) produced the following results: $t = 2.14$; $df = 19$; $p < .025$. Because .025 is only half of .05 and the children in her group had the lower mean shyness scores (the relationship between variables was in the predicted direction), Erin concluded that she could safely reject the null hypothesis. She had found statistical support for the effectiveness of her group in reducing shyness. However, she realized that, among other explanations, the extra time and attention provided to the children in the group (rather than the group experience itself) might have helped to produce their lower level of shyness.

Use with One Sample Measured Twice

When the dependent *t* test is used with a single sample consisting of the same people measured at two different times, we have what is called a **one-group pretest–posttest research design.** Suppose we wanted to test the effectiveness of a smoking cessation program. We could draw a random sample of clients who smoke and ask them to record the average number of cigarettes they smoked 1 day before enrolling in a smoking cessation program (pretest). We could record the number of cigarettes they smoked the day after they completed the program (posttest). We then could compare the mean number of cigarettes the group smoked 1 day before the program with the mean number they smoked 1 day after the program. If we were able to reject the null hypothesis, we would also want to rule out the possibility that something else may have created the relationship between variables within the research sample. The time lapse between the day on which the data for the pretest were collected, for example, and the day on which the data for the posttest were collected (and what may have occurred for

TABLE 11.5   Child-Rearing Skill Scores for Pregnant Teenagers before and after a Child-Rearing Skills Workshop ($N = 22$)

Pretest	Posttest	Difference
4.8	5.8	1

$t = 2.53$, $df = 21$; $p < .01$

our participants in the interim) may be a more plausible explanation than the intervention for any reduction in cigarette smoking.

To use another example, suppose we wished to attempt to find support for the following one-tailed research hypothesis:

> Pregnant teenagers will have increased knowledge of child development after they undergo a child-development workshop.

A 5-day child-rearing skills workshop could be offered to 22 pregnant high-school students. The group's mean child-rearing skills score could be calculated before the workshop (pretest) and after it (posttest).

Table 11.5 provides an example of how the results of this hypothetical research study might be displayed. Notice that the students had a pretest mean score of 4.8 and a posttest mean score of 5.8. The difference between the two means was 1 point (5.8 − 4.8 = 1). This 1-point difference is statistically significant at the .01 level with 21 degrees of freedom (the number of pairs of scores −1 for the dependent *t* test). This means that a 1-point difference would happen because of sampling error less than 1 time out of 100 with this size sample even if the workshop had no real effect on child-rearing skills. Thus, we can reject the null hypothesis and, if all other competing explanations for the apparent relationship can be ruled out, we can claim support for our one-tailed research hypothesis.

A Nonparametric Alternative: Wilcoxon Sign

Sometimes we find ourselves with two related samples (naturally or through matching) and measurements of a dependent variable that are more than ordinal level but not quite interval level measurement. The measurements can be rank ordered based on the absolute amount of the variable that they contain. This is frequently the case with newly developed measuring instruments that measure attitudes, perceptions, or beliefs. Sometimes the amorphous nature of the concept being measured prevents us from claiming that the values we assign reflect precise intervals—that is, equal difference in quantity of the variable.

The **Wilcoxon sign test** is useful in those situations in which, for example, we know that a score of 65 on an anxiety scale reflects more anxiety than a lower score of 60, and where we also believe that this difference is greater than the difference in anxiety between, say, scores of 62 and 60. If this latter determination can be made, we would be throwing away available measurement precision if we were to look at only the direction of difference (more, less, or the same) between pairs of related cases that constitute two subsamples.

In using the Wilcoxon sign test to evaluate the relative effectiveness of two forms of social work intervention, an assumption is made: If the form of intervention used makes no difference, there will be essentially no difference in regard to the dependent variable among the cases in one group and the cases in the other group (the null hypothesis). Specifically, the null hypothesis would state that, for either of the two matched groups, the sum of the overall ranks of positive cases (cases with higher scores than their counterparts in the other group) will equal the sum of the ranks of negative cases (cases with lower scores than their counterparts in the other group).

The ideal situation for using the Wilcoxon sign test involves the use of perfectly matched pairs of cases. Because this is rarely possible, however, cases are usually matched based on a pretest measurement of one or more of the most likely intervening variables.

Once matched pairs are identified, one member is randomly assigned to one group; the second goes to the other group. After the intervention, the Wilcoxon sign test examines the direction and amount of difference between each. In the process, the differences between pairs are themselves rank ordered (without regard to direction). If the preponderance of differences suggests higher scores for one group and the greatest differences are also among those cases, the Wilcoxon sign test is likely to suggest a statistically significant difference between the two groups. The stronger the pattern, the more likely the null hypothesis can be rejected and vice versa.

Example: Counseling Effectiveness of Student Volunteers. Katie is a social work counselor in a student health center. Over the years, she has wondered whether college students having social adjustment problems benefit more from counseling by untrained student volunteers (peers) or by professional social work staff. With the use of standard intake screening measurements over a 1-month period, she identified a group of prospective clients who were all diagnosed as having moderate social adjustment problems. Before assignment for counseling, she identified 15 matched pairs (matched on such key variables as *gender, grade-point average,* and the like) and randomly assigned one member of each pair to be seen by a student volunteer and the other member to be seen by a social worker. After six 1-hour counseling sessions, all clients were administered a standard measuring instrument that measured the dependent variable *social adjustment.*

The measuring instrument, which Katie considered to be an indicator of college students' social adjustment, was deemed to be capable of generating the ordinal-plus level data required for use of the Wilcoxon sign test. Data were compared for each pair, and the direction and amount of the differences were noted. The differences were then rank ordered without regard to the direction of the difference.

Katie was pleased to learn that almost all of the students who were seen by the social workers scored much better on the measuring instrument than did those seen by student volunteers. She analyzed her data with the use of the Wilcoxon sign test. It allowed her to reject the null hypothesis ($p < .05$). Table 11.6 illustrates how Katie might present her finding as a table in the context of the results section of her report.

TABLE 11.6   Comparison of Adjustment Scores for Students Seen by Social Workers versus Volunteers

	N (%)	Z	p
• Pairs where student seen by social worker has *lower* adjustment score than student seen by volunteer	2 (13%)	− 2.45	.014
• Pairs where student seen by social worker has *higher* adjustment score than student seen by volunteer	13 (87%)		
• Pairs where student seen by social worker has *same* adjustment score than student seen by volunteer	0 (0%)		
Total Number of Pairs. . . .	15		

Katie was, of course, not ready to discount student volunteers as effective counselors based on this single small-scale research study. She wondered, however, whether student volunteers might benefit from closer supervision by social work staff or whether they might be used more effectively with students having other problems. She also decided to replicate her study, using another standardized measurement of social adjustment, to see if consistent findings would be obtained.

THE INDEPENDENT *t* TEST

Another variation of the parametric *t* test, the **independent *t* test,** is especially useful in research studies that employ experimental or quasi-experimental research designs. Like the dependent *t* test, it also compares the means of two samples. But to use the independent *t* test correctly, the two samples must be independently drawn from a population—that is, the random selection of one case does not increase or decrease the likelihood of any other case being selected. This is not the case when the dependent *t* test is used.

The two groups do not have to contain an equal number of cases, which often is the situation in social work evaluations of treatment effectiveness (see Appendix A). Often two subsamples (e.g., clients in group treatment, clients in individual treatment) are unequal in size. Even in experimental research studies where it is considered ethical to randomly assign an equal number of cases to two subsamples, clients are likely to drop out of treatment before the study is completed. Any resulting discrepancy between the sizes of the two subsamples presents no problem for the independent *t* test. The formula for the test automatically controls for it.

When the independent *t* test is used, the two samples often consist of cases with one or the other measurement of a dichotomous independent variable (e.g., *Intervention A or Intervention B; female therapist or male therapist*). In experimental research designs, the two samples would consist of cases randomly assigned to either the experimental group (Sample 1) or the control or comparison group (Sample 2).

With the use of the formula for the independent *t* test, mean scores of the two samples are compared to produce a *t* value and a corresponding *p* value. On the basis of sampling error, the means of the two samples are almost certain to be somewhat different. The independent *t* test examines the amount of that difference and determines how likely sampling error is to have produced it if, in fact, the variables are unrelated.

If the difference turns out to be so small that sampling error is a likely explanation for this difference, the *p*-value will be relatively high and the null hypothesis cannot be rejected. We can conclude that the difference between the means of the two groups is too likely to be a function of sampling error and does not reflect a real relationship between the independent and dependent variables.

On the other hand, if the results indicate that the difference is large enough that it is very unlikely to be the work of sampling error (a low *p* value), we can reject the null hypothesis and conclude that the difference observed in the sample may indeed reflect a real relationship between the variables. Sampling error will have been effectively discounted as a possible explanation for the apparent relationship between them.

As should be evident by now, with small samples such as those often used in social work research, even a fairly large difference between two means may be due to sampling error—that is, it may not be statistically significant. Conversely, even small differences between means may suggest a real relationship between variables if the samples are quite large. As with the other *t* tests, degrees of freedom are a way of examining differences in means within the two groups while factoring in the size of the sample that produced them. For the independent *t* test, the degrees of freedom are the total number of cases in both samples, minus 2. With the use of the *t* value produced by the *t* test and the appropriate degrees of freedom, we can determine if the difference between the means of two independently formed groups is sufficiently large that sampling error alone is unlikely to have produced it. Generally, we conclude that this is the case when the corresponding *p* value (described as level of significance in Table 11.1) is $< .05$.

If data have been computer analyzed, the *t* value, the degrees of freedom for our data, and *p* value are all displayed, along with, among other results, the actual means for each of the two groups. A comparison of the means is a good indicator of effect size—that is, how much difference the independent variable really may have made in a tightly controlled experiment. If the actual difference in the means is quite small but statistically significant (as can easily happen with larger samples), then common sense and practice knowledge might lead us to conclude that the time, effort, and money required for any changes in our practice might not be justified.

Example: Treatment of Marital Problems. Rose is a social worker in a large family service agency. In her agency's orientation procedure, she was taught that the best format for marital counseling is to see both the husband and wife together. Five years ago, she treated 20 couples, all of whom could only be seen individually (husband *or* wife) because of their work schedules. She was surprised to observe that although they were never seen as couples after their initial interviews, all 20 couples seemed to make excellent progress in solving their marital problems.

Over the years, Rose saw more and more couples on an individual basis. Because she believed she was having good client outcomes, she encouraged six of her colleagues to also counsel couples with marital difficulties by seeing them separately rather than together. The other social workers were also pleased with their clients' progress.

Rose was not ready to conclude that the individual-counseling format was really preferable to couples counseling without conducting some research on the issue. She decided to see if she could find statistical support for her hunch that couples seen individually make better progress toward solving their marital problems than couples seen together.

As Rose began to search the social work literature, she found considerable support for the position that marital satisfaction is best enhanced when couples are treated in counseling together, not individually. But as she ventured into the literature from other fields, such as psychology and pastoral counseling, Rose found a fair amount of support for the belief that success in marital counseling may be more likely to result from individual counseling. A reason sometimes given is that clients tend to discuss areas of dissatisfaction more readily and candidly when the spouse is not present.

Rose concluded that the professional literature was conflicting. She felt that her own observations, however, and those of her colleagues were sufficient to tip the balance enough to justify a one-tailed research hypothesis:

Among couples receiving marital counseling for 10 weeks, those seen individually will reflect higher levels of marital satisfaction than those seen together.

Rose designed a small-scale research study to see if she would find support for her one-tailed research hypothesis. She received permission from the agency director and her clients to randomly assign new clients who requested marital counseling during a 3-month period to either individual counseling or couple counseling. In a research sense, the clients were randomly assigned to one of two groups. All six social workers who had previously used, and were experienced with, both couples counseling and individual counseling participated as counselors in Rose's study.

Beginning the next month, every other couple seen at intake was assigned to one of the six social workers to be seen together for counseling, 50 minutes per week; the remaining couples were assigned to be seen individually for 25 minutes each per week. Those who could not agree to this arrangement were also seen but were not included as research participants in the study.

The counseling method (i.e., individual, couple) was the independent variable. The dependent variable, *marital satisfaction,* was measured after 10 consecutive weeks of counseling with a widely used standardized measuring instrument. The measuring instrument produces interval-level data.

Fourteen couples were randomly assigned to individual counseling sessions, and 14 were assigned to be seen as couples. Twelve couples assigned to individual counseling completed 10 weeks of treatment, and 13 in couples counseling completed 10 weeks of treatment. After all 25 couples completed the marital satisfaction measuring instrument, Rose took the score for each partner and averaged it with that of his or her spouse to get a couple score.

Then she computed the mean couple score of those who were seen individually (experimental group) and compared it with the mean couple score of those who were seen together (control group) with the use of the independent *t* test. The variable *marital satisfaction* has been found to be normally distributed, so Rose felt justified in using this test for her statistical analysis. She was attempting to determine whether the difference between the mean scores for the two groups was sufficiently large to allow her to reject the null hypothesis. She hoped to be able to conclude that a real relationship between the two variables was the likely explanation for any difference in the mean marital satisfaction scores of the two groups of clients.

The *t* value for Rose's data was 1.312. From a table of critical values of *t* (Table 11.1), she learned that she needed a minimum *t* value of 1.714 to be able to reject the null hypothesis at a rejection level of .05, a sample of 25 (23 degrees of freedom), and a one-tailed research hypothesis.

Rose noted that if she were to reject the null hypothesis based on the analysis of her data, she would have slightly more than a 1 in 10 (10%) probability of committing a Type I error (1.312 is slightly smaller than 1.319). Thus, she lacked statistical support for her one-tailed research hypothesis. Table 11.7 illustrates how Rose might present her finding as a table in the context of the results section of her report.

Rose observed that the clients who had participated in individual counseling had, in fact, scored somewhat worse in marital satisfaction, on the average, than did the clients seen together. She studied her findings some more. She then realized that her lack of demonstrated support for her research hypothesis reflected a useful finding in and of itself. Her inability to reject the null hypothesis could be interpreted to mean that it makes little difference which counseling method is used. Perhaps client convenience should play a larger role in determining which format should be used.

Rose also wondered how she could have been mistaken. The findings from her study were inconsistent with her previous impressions. She wondered whether, in the past, she and the other social workers had perhaps merely perceived their individual counseling clients as doing better because of their surprise at how much progress they made using a counseling format that was not believed to be as effective.

Of course, Rose also wondered whether her initial one-tailed research hypothesis might still be correct (she had committed a Type II error). Perhaps the true relationship between the independent variable and the dependent variable had been hidden by

TABLE 11.7   Marital Satisfaction Score by Counseling Method

Counseling Method	*Number of Couples*	Marital Satisfaction Score[a]	
		Mean	*Standard Deviation*
Individual	12	72	11
Couple	13	75	12
Total	25		

[a]Marital satisfaction scale 0 (low) to 100 (high), $t = 1.312$, $dt = 23$, $p < .05$

biased measurements or the influence of rival hypotheses (e.g., the social workers' greater experience with couple counseling). As she thought about it, Rose concluded that additional studies employing more rigorous research designs were indicated.

In the interim, before further research studies could be conducted, Rose wondered what practical use she could make of her findings. She presented the results of her study at the next agency staff meeting. She was able to draw implications for social work practice within the agency. As frequently happens in social work research, her research study generated more questions than answers. These questions, however, served to focus the staff's attention on potentially productive areas of inquiry. Based on her findings, Rose and other staff members began to ask the following questions:

1. Because type of counseling (individual or couple) may have little or no effect in enhancing marital satisfaction, should continued attempts be made to encourage clients to enter couple counseling if they resist or if it causes a scheduling difficulty for them?
2. Should funds be allocated for a staff development program to enhance the social workers' use of individual counseling in treatment of marital problems?
3. Should the staff develop a single treatment model that combines individual and couple counseling, or should the professional staff members be allowed freedom to select the counseling format they prefer to use?

These three questions, along with others, range from issues that affected the individual social work practitioner to those that are related to agency policies. The principal value of Rose's study was to call into question certain previously unchallenged practices and to encourage the staff either to justify or to discard them based on further examination.

Like the other tests that we have discussed, independent *t* can be used to answer a variety of questions that a social worker might have. The examples that follow illustrate how it can do much more than evaluate the effectiveness of practice intervention.

Example: Study Guide for the State Merit Exam.

Dave has developed a new study guide to help social workers prepare for the state merit exam. To evaluate the effectiveness of such a study guide, he randomly selected 15 of the 30 social workers who planned to take the exam the next month and provided them with a copy of it. He asked them to spend part of their study time each night using the guide as instructed.

The 15 social workers who used the guide could be regarded somewhat loosely as the experimental group; the remaining 15, who did not use it, could be regarded as the control group. After all 30 social workers took the state merit exam, their results were compared. Dave compared the mean exam score of the 15 social workers who used the guide (the experimental group) with the mean exam score of the 15 social workers who did not use it (the control group).

In comparing the means for the two groups with the use of the independent *t* test, Dave found a statistically significant ($p < .05$) relationship between the two variables. Table 11.8 illustrates how he might report his findings in the context of the results section of his report.

TABLE 11.8 **Exams Scores for Study Guide Users and Nonusers**

		Exam Score				
Used Study Guide?	*N*	*Mean*	*SD*	*Difference*	*t*	*P*
Yes	15	71	13	13	2.43	<.05
No	15	58	14			
Total	30					

What Dave learned provided answers to several questions:

1. Is the mean difference between the two groups large enough to allow me to reject the null hypothesis? (Yes.)
2. How confident can I be that the difference was not due to sampling error? (At least 95 percent confident.)
3. Is the difference in the direction that I predicted, that is, did those using the study guide do better on the exam than those who did not use it? (Yes.)
4. Does the data analysis suggest that the use of the study guide might help other social workers taking the state merit examination, not just those in the experimental group? (Yes.)

Dave knew, however, that there are other possible explanations for his research finding. Perhaps, for example, the guide merely served to remind the social workers to prepare for the exam. Consequently, they may have put more time and energy into studying than did those in the control group. Maybe the guide itself was of no direct help at all.

Even if other possible alternative explanations could be ruled out (in addition to sampling error), another question still would have to be addressed: Is the relationship between the variables a meaningful one? Did the size of the difference in the mean scores on the exam, for example, justify the purchase price of the guide for social workers planning to take the exam?

The answer to this question, like others related to the practical value of any research findings, might be a difficult one, even a very individual one. For example, suppose that Dave had found that the people in his study who used the study guide scored an average of 5 points higher on the exam than those who did not use it. Remember, first, that the average score in each of the two groups was calculated by a group of scores that may have ranged widely. A few social workers in his experimental group might have done quite poorly on the exam, perhaps worse than if they had not used the study guide. So, just because the group did better on the exam overall, there is no guarantee that Phil and Marylea will do better if they use it; one or both might do worse. In addition, not only is assuming that the study guide might increase scores by an average of 5 points a big assumption at this point, but 5 points might not be as meaningful for one person as for another. For Kim, it could be the difference between failing or passing; it might be meaningless for Greta, who would easily pass without the study guide. Of course, the cost of the study guide and the different financial situations of individuals would also factor into whether an average difference of 5 points would be more or less meaningful for any one individual.

Example: Staff Turnover.   Antonia is the director of social services for a large state health agency. In her professional role, she oversees social work services offered in the 50 district offices throughout the state. It was recently brought to her attention that her agency was having a serious problem with social work staff turnover. A preliminary examination of agency data revealed that the problem was statewide and appeared to be normally distributed among the 50 district offices.

Antonia spoke with the personnel officer responsible for conducting exit interviews with employees leaving the agency. At first he preferred not to suggest possible reasons why so many social workers were resigning. But after Antonia assured him that she did not plan to ask him to identify workers who made complaints to him, he volunteered that the reasons given by many of the social workers for leaving appeared to be amazingly similar. He recalled that many of them seemed totally frustrated with their lack of autonomy in decision making. Although they recognized that in some professional and administrative matters the final decision had to be made by their supervisors, they saw no reason why many other decisions could not be made by them and their fellow professionals through a more democratic process.

Antonia thought about what she had been told. Although her first inclination was to be annoyed with the district supervisors for their apparent autocratic approach to decision making, she quickly realized that she had to take much of the responsibility for their supervisory styles. She herself was autocratic when it came to decision making. Because it seemed to work so well for her, she had regularly encouraged her supervisors to be more autocratic. Apparently, the supervisors were responding to Antonia's message that an autocratic management style is a sign of good supervision.

Antonia knew that she needed an objective way to determine whether management style was related to staff turnover. She did not want to merely trust the impressions of the personnel officer without further data. She might need to help all her supervisors become more democratic in delegating decision making, but she did not want to do so until she could be reasonably certain that a relationship existed between the two variables.

Antonia decided to conduct a small-scale research study to see if she would find support for the following one-tailed research hypothesis:

> There will be a lower rate of staff turnover in units where a democratic decision-making style is used than in units where a more autocratic style is used.

Antonia knew that management literature stressed the use of quality circles as a promising way to solve some administrative problems by arriving at decisions via the group process. Antonia had been considering the use of quality circles anyway and saw this as a good time to try them. Quality circles seemed to her to be a good way to create a more democratic approach to decision making in the district offices.

Antonia randomly selected 10 districts to serve as her experimental group. She then provided release time to the 10 district supervisors to attend an out-of-state workshop on the use of quality circles. She told the supervisors that she expected them to implement quality circles in their districts, and she requested a report on their methods of implementation to ensure that this had been done. They were asked not to share their experiences with other district supervisors.

At the same time, Antonia randomly selected 10 other districts as her control group. These district supervisors were given no additional training and no new instructions on how they should handle decision making in their district offices.

After 1 year, Antonia computed a mean rate of turnover for districts in the experimental group and for those in the control group. She had two value categories of the dichotomous nominal level independent variable *decision-making environment* (i.e., use/nonuse of quality circles). Her dependent variable (*staff turnover rate*) was considered ratio level. The situation seemed to be well suited to the use of the independent *t* test to determine whether there might be statistical support for her one-tailed research hypothesis.

Antonia compared the mean turnover rate for the two groups with the use of the independent *t* test. The mean turnover rate of the experimental group was lower than the mean turnover rate of the control group, exactly as she had hypothesized. The *t* value was 1.992. She concluded that there were 18 degrees of freedom (10 + 10 = 20; 20 − 2 = 18). With the use of a table like Table 11.1, she noted that, for the row corresponding to 18 degrees of freedom, the *t* value from her statistical analysis fell between 1.734 and 2.101. She moved to the left (1.734) and observed that it was in the column headed by .05 for one-tailed tests and .10 for two-tailed tests. The *p* value corresponding to her data under the one-tailed research hypothesis was therefore less than .05. Table 11.9 illustrates how Antonia might present her finding with the use of a table in the results section of her report.

From her knowledge of statistics, Antonia knew that she had found support for her research hypothesis. She knew that if she were to reject the null hypothesis, she would have less than a 5 percent probability of committing a Type I error.

Because her study had been very limited in scope, Antonia was reluctant to view her findings as an unequivocal endorsement of the expanded use of quality circles (or other more democratic methods of decision making) as a way to reduce staff turnover. She recognized that it would be precipitous on her part to proceed to implement her

TABLE 11.9   Staff Turnover Rate by District Office

Decision-Making Environment	*N*	*Mean*	*SD*	*Difference*	*t*	*P*
With quality circles	10	.21	11	.06	1.992	<.05
Without quality circles	10	.27	12			
Total	20					

findings based solely on a finding of statistical significance. Her study's research design had certainly not eliminated the two alternative explanations (i.e., rival hypotheses, design bias) as possible explanations for the difference between the two staff turnover rates.

Certain methodological questions remained. How much did the opportunity to go out of state for training, for example, positively affect the morale of the supervisors in the experimental group? Perhaps the break from their regular duties put them in a better mood and thus they were more inclined to be more considerate of their workers. If so, this may have been a better explanation than the implementation of quality circles for their lower mean staff turnover rate. Or did the workers view the supervisors in the experimental group as more considerate simply because they made an effort to try something new (a kind of Hawthorne effect)? If so, this might have been a major factor in the lower mean turnover rate.

Despite the fact that Antonia's findings would have to be viewed as tentative, she was still able to use them both to better understand the problem of staff turnover and to begin to address it through her actions. In light of her findings, she asked herself the following six questions:

1. How can I avoid unintentionally communicating to the district supervisors that I expect them to adopt my autocratic management style?
2. How can I help district supervisors identify decisions that are more appropriately made using the democratic process? How can I make them feel more comfortable using this process?
3. How can I help district supervisors identify decisions that are inappropriate for the democratic process (e.g., personnel matters)?
4. What use of the democratic process, besides quality circles, would help social workers feel that they have more input into decisions if they possess the necessary expertise?
5. Would it be advisable to send all district supervisors to quality circle training out of state?
6. What further research studies can be designed to provide additional support for the finding that democratic decision making may be associated with lower staff turnover?

After thinking about these six questions and others that emerged from her study, Antonia discussed her ideas for implementing her findings with social work administrators in other large social service agencies. She then settled on a plan of action.

At the next meeting of all district supervisors, Antonia shared the findings of her research study. She reiterated her support for the use of staff authority in certain situations but also stated her belief that social workers at all levels are professionals and need to be involved in decision making. She emphasized that she believed that overreliance on autocratic supervisory approaches can hurt morale and, even more important, does not take advantage of the expertise of other staff in addressing problems.

She supported these contentions by asking a former district supervisor of the experimental group to use part of the next supervisors' meeting to teach all the supervisors (including herself) the basic principles of quality circles. In the meeting, the other 9 district supervisors who had used quality circles were asked to share their experiences as well.

Antonia was convinced that district supervisors should share decision making in certain situations with their respective workers. In another meeting, she emphasized this belief to the supervisors. Consistent with it, she allowed them to decide individually whether they preferred to receive training in quality circles so as to implement that technique in their district offices or to develop their own plans (with her approval) for introducing ways to increase democratic decision making among their supervisees.

Finally, Antonia set aside time to develop a more comprehensive and larger-scale study of staff turnover. This study would examine factors other than approaches to decision making that the literature suggests are related in some way to staff morale and turnover. She hoped that the findings from this larger-scale study could ultimately be generalized to other social work settings and that a report of the findings would have the potential for publication in a professional social work journal.

Nonparametric Alternatives: *U* and K-S

Several nonparametric options are available if all of the conditions for independent *t* tests cannot be met. Two of the better known ones are the Mann-Whitney U test and the Kolmogorov-Smirnov two-sample test. A third, the median test, was discussed in Chapter 10.

The **Mann-Whitney *U* test** (hereafter called *U* test), is used with a dichotomous nominal level independent variable and an ordinal level, interval level, or ratio level dependent variable that need not be normally distributed (as required for use of the independent *t* test). Like the independent *t* test, the *U* test determines whether the differences between two independent subsamples with respect to the dependent variable are the work of sampling error.

The *U* test is ideally suited for research studies involving two small independent subsamples consisting of the two different measurements of a dichotomous independent variable. Like the independent *t* test, it is frequently used in experimental and quasi-experimental research situations to determine whether a treatment given to an experimental group, but not to a control group, appears to produce different results.

Like the independent *t* test, the *U* test does not need two groups of identical size (or subsamples). The same formula is used with very small samples (under eight) or larger ones, but we must be careful in interpreting results to use the table of critical values (not included in this book) that is designed to adjust for sample size.

A *U* test is easily computed. It is based on the assumption that a good indicator of the difference between the two groups is the number of cases in one group that fall below each respective score of the other group when all scores are rank ordered.

The logical premise underlying *U* is that the presence of a disproportionate number of higher scores drawn from one group and of lower scores drawn from the other group probably suggests that, on the whole, the two groups really are different in regard to the dependent variable. The *U* test is a mathematical way of determining whether this pattern is sufficiently strong to reject the null hypothesis, which would state that scores from the two groups will be pretty much evenly distributed when all scores are rank ordered to form an array.

Example: Use of co-Workers in Counseling. Shanti is a social worker employed by a large corporation. During July he had 17 referrals of workers identified as having attitude problems on the job. He asked each of their supervisors to name another worker at the same level whom they would describe as having a very good attitude who might participate with him when the problem worker was being counseled. Seven of the supervisors complied with his request; the other 10 did not.

Shanti saw all 17 workers (7 with their co-workers and the other 10 alone) for five sessions. After the fifth interview, he asked their supervisors to complete a standard-ized measuring instrument that measures an employee's attitude toward work. He then rank ordered the scores of all 17 workers and used the U test formula to see if he would find support for his one-tailed research hypothesis:

> Members in the experimental group (those receiving counseling with a coworker participating) will have higher job attitude scores than members in the control group (those receiving the usual counseling involving only the supervisor).

Shanti quickly noted that three of the top four attitude scores were achieved by members in the experimental group. However, as he examined the data in more detail, he noticed that two of the lowest scores also came from experimental group members. The U test produced a p value $> .10$; it did not support a decision to reject the null hypothesis. Table 11.10 illustrates how Shanti might present his finding with the use of a table in the results section of his report.

Even if the U test had achieved statistical significance, alternative explanations for a true relationship (e.g., lack of random assignment to groups, the effect of other vari-ables) could not have been ruled out because of the lack of rigor of Shanti's research design. Shanti decided to tighten up the design and to pursue his inquiry further by using a larger randomly selected sample.

The **Kolmogorov-Smirnov two-sample test** (hereafter called the K-S test), has some similarities with the median test discussed in Chapter 10 as a procedure for assigning cases to cross-tabulation tables prior to using the chi-square or Fisher's exact tests. But K-S compares more than just central tendency data, that is, where scores fall in relation to the median. It compares (between two samples) the dispersion, skew-ness, and other characteristics of the distribution of values of an ordinal level variable or a skewed interval level or ratio level variable. To express this another way, it

TABLE 11.10 Employee Attitude by Co-Worker Role in Supervision

Co-worker Participated in Sessions	N	Mean Rank[a]	Mann-Whitney U	p
Yes (Experimental Group)	7	18.7	14.6	>.10
No (Comparison Group)	10	15.3		
Total	17			

[a]Employee attitude; higher scores reflects better attitudes

compares the entire shape of the distribution of the dependent variable in one sample with the shape of its distribution in the other sample.

The K-S test is based on the assumption that if two subsamples are randomly drawn from the same population and the null hypothesis is correct, the overall shape of the distribution of the ordinal level variable (or skewed interval level or ratio level variable) should be the same for the two subsamples. If differences in the distribution of the variable are considerable, they probably are not just the work of sampling error. They may indicate a real relationship between the independent and dependent variables. Thus, the K-S test is a way of determining whether the differences in the distribution of the values of the ordinal level variable (or skewed interval level or ratio level variable) are large enough to rule out sampling error and to reject the null hypothesis.

K-S relies on cumulative frequencies (Chapter 2) to compare the two distributions and to identify at what points in an array of measurements of the dependent variable they differ or are similar to each other. It focuses on the point or points at which the cumulative frequency difference between the two subsamples is the largest. If the dependent variable is interval or ratio level, it might, for example, focus on the fact that a life-satisfaction score of 50 falls at only the 65th percentile in the experimental group, but it at the 95th percentile in the control group. If the dependent variable is only ordinal level, the K-S test compares the cumulative frequencies for intervals in the variable (e.g., what percent of cases were rated either not improved or slightly improved for the control group versus the experimental group). K-S is equally useful for analyzing the relationship between variables when the independent variable falls naturally into two value categories (rather than being assigned to them by the researcher, as occurs in an experiment).

Example: Referral for Fraud Investigations. Roosevelt is a county director in a state public welfare agency. Several of his African American workers had complained that Caucasian workers seemed to have excessively suspicious attitudes toward some of their African American clients. Specifically, they told him that they believed that the African American clients who were being seen by Caucasian workers were assumed by them to be liars and cheats.

No valid and reliable measuring instrument for the variable *suspicious attitudes* was immediately available. Roosevelt concluded, however, that the variable *number of referrals for fraud investigation* was an acceptable way to operationalize the variable. Although an exact count of referrals was possible, when used as an indicator of suspicious attitudes (the real dependent variable), ordinal measurement of the variable was all that could be claimed.

Roosevelt compiled a count of fraud referrals for each worker during the previous 3 months. Referrals ranged from 0 to 23. He then assembled a cumulative frequency distribution for African American workers and for Caucasian workers (the two value categories of the independent variable), with the use of eight intervals of number of referrals (for example, 0–2, 3–5, 6–8, and so forth) as his ordinal level value categories. The decision to use eight intervals was made in an effort to conserve some of the precision of measurement available (using only two or three intervals would throw away too much data) while not cutting too thin.

With the use of the K-S test, Roosevelt compared the cumulative frequencies for the dependent variable of one group of workers (African American) with that of the other group (Caucasian) and identified the interval at which the cumulative frequency distributions were most different from each other. He learned that, in fact, there was little real difference between the two groups for the measurement of the variable, at least not enough to rule out sampling error and to be able to reject the null hypothesis ($p > .50$).

Although Roosevelt did not totally discount the complaints of the African American workers, because a better method of operationalizing the dependent variable might have revealed an attitudinal difference, he concluded that he lacked sufficient evidence to confront his Caucasian workers about what some of his fellow African American workers perceived as a problem. He chose instead to remind all his staff about the need for nonjudgmental attitudes while gathering necessary data about clients.

The K-S test is useful in looking at the relationship between an ordinal level dependent variable (or skewed interval level or ratio level variable) and a nominal level dichotomous independent variable when just a comparison of central tendency may be insufficient. By examining the whole distribution of values of the dependent variable, we get a fairly complete picture of the similarity or difference between two subsamples.

A variation, the **K-S one-sample test**, works similarly, except that it compares the distribution of a variable within a sample with another, theoretical distribution of the variable. Thus, it should be regarded as another nonparametric alternative (along with the chi-square goodness-of-fit test) to the one-sample *t* test.

Another test, the **Wald-Wolfowitz runs test,** goes even further than the K-S test in that it identifies some of the more subtle differences in distributions of a variable that the K-S test does not detect. Still another nonparametric alternative, the **Moses test of extreme reactions**, is the test of choice for those relatively rare research studies where the presence of a treatment in the experimental group (but not in the control group) might be predicted to create extreme, opposite reactions in the experimental group. For example, a very confrontational form of intervention might make some clients in a group much more assertive; it might make others in the group much less assertive. It might seem that the intervention had no effect (these opposite reactions would cancel each other out) if we were to use tests that rely on a comparison of central tendency (such as the median) or one that simply compares rankings in the two groups (such as the Mann-Whitney *U* test) to compare the experimental and control groups. If we used the Moses test, however, we would be less likely to be misled by the results of our data analysis.

A Multivariate Alternative: T^2

Sometimes, we are interested in determining if there is a statistically significant relationship between a dichotomous independent variable and a set of interval/ratio level dependent variables. The dependent variables may be related in some way. For example, in an outcome program evaluation (see Appendix A) of a child-abuse prevention program, we might want to know if the program's three objectives (increased knowledge of the "shaken baby syndrome," increased knowledge of child development, and improved anger management) were achieved through clients' completion of the program. To accomplish this, we might turn to the **Hottelling's T^2 test.**

Hottelling's T^2 is very versatile; it can be used all of the ways that t can be used. Continuing with our example, in a way similar to one-sample t, it could compare the means of the set of dependent variables for clients who completed the program with the same set of means for the population of at-risk clients who did not participate in the program (if these data are available). Or, in a way similar to the two-sample dependent t test, it could compare their set of means with the same set of means for either a group of matched clients who did not participate in the program or with measurements of their own set of means before they started the program (a before-and-after design). Or, in a way similar to the two-sample independent t test, it could compare their set of means with those clients who were also selected at random, but who were assigned to a control group.

SIMPLE ANALYSIS OF VARIANCE (SIMPLE ANOVA)

Simple analysis of variance, hereafter called simple ANOVA, is also sometimes called *one-way analysis of variance* because there is one independent variable and only one dependent variable. Like the independent t test, it is appropriate for examining the relationship between variables when there is a nominal level independent variable and a normally distributed interval level or ratio level dependent variable. But, unlike an independent t test, which requires the independent variable to be dichotomous (have only two value categories), simple ANOVA is used when the independent variable contains three or more value categories. As with an independent t test, the subsamples used in simple ANOVA need not be of equal size.

Simple ANOVA also can be used when the independent variable is at the interval or ratio level. Its values might reflect different levels or dosages of the variable. For example, in a social work research study, the independent variable might be *number of treatment interviews, length of hospitalization,* or *dosage of a medication.*

Although t tests produce a t value that can be compared with a table (i.e., Table 11.1) to determine whether it is justifiable to reject the null hypothesis, simple ANOVA produces an **F ratio** with its own table (not included in this book) that allows us to make this same determination. When computer software is used for data analyses, the displayed results of both t and simple ANOVA analyses include p values along with their respective t values or F ratios.

An example illustrates how simple ANOVA works. In a large psychiatric outpatient clinic, there are 20 people with the job title case manager. They all (theoretically, at least) perform the same case management functions, even though some are psychologists, some are social workers, and some are nurses by training. The case managers work on one of three teams. One is led by a social worker, one by a psychologist, and one by a psychiatric nurse. We want to know if there are differences in client satisfaction among the three teams. To attempt to find out, we formulate the following one-tailed research hypothesis:

Client satisfaction will be higher among clients served by the team led by a social worker than among clients served by the other two teams.

We could use a standardized measuring instrument that yields interval level or ratio level data to measure the dependent variable *client satisfaction*. Because there are three categories of the independent variable *professional discipline of team leader*—(1) psychologist, (2) social worker, and (3) psychiatric nurse—we could compare the three possible combinations of pairs of means (client satisfaction) with three independent *t* tests—that is, (1) psychologist and social worker, (2) psychologist and nurse, and (3) social worker and nurse. But, why conduct three separate statistical analyses when one will do nicely? Using simple ANOVA would tell us if any differences among the three mean client satisfaction levels are related to the discipline of the team leader. Specifically, simple ANOVA would tell us the probability (*p*), considering degrees of freedom (based on the size of the samples), that any differences in mean client satisfaction levels among the three teams might have been produced by sampling error.

Simple ANOVA would compare the mean client satisfaction level for each of the three subsamples (i.e., for each team) with the grand mean—the mean client satisfaction level for all clients studied. Thus, simple ANOVA examines how much the mean of each subsample (each individual value category of the independent variable) differs from the means of the other subsamples as well as from the grand mean. Simple ANOVA examines these differences (referred to as the between-groups variance) as well as the amount of variability of client satisfaction within each subsample (referred to as the within groups variance). Table 11.11 illustrates how ANOVA results might be presented with the use of a table in the results section of a research report.

Simple ANOVA is a powerful parametric test. It can easily identify relationships between variables that less-powerful statistical tests might miss. As a general rule, however, more-powerful tests also are more restrictive than less-powerful tests—that is, more conditions for their use must be met. Simple ANOVA is no exception.

In addition to the requirements of the other parametric statistical tests, simple ANOVA should be used only when the amount of variance for the dependent variable within each subsample is approximately equal. In our hypothetical study, we could not use simple ANOVA if, for example, the amount of variation in satisfaction among clients served by the team led by a social worker tended to be much greater than among clients served by either of the other two teams.

TABLE 11.11 Client Satisfaction Levels by Profession of Team Leader

Team Leader	N	Mean	SD
Social Worker	20	16.92	1.55
Psychologist	12	13.22	2.19
Psychiatric Nurse	18	10.40	2.57
Total	50	13.90	3.03

$F_{(2,47)} = 18.06, p < .000$

Additional Data Analyses

Simple ANOVA is regarded as a general or **omnibus test**; that is, it is designed to determine if there are any differences in the means of the dependent variable among the different values or value categories of the independent variable. Thus, the null form of research hypotheses involving simple ANOVA is always the same—"The means of the dependent variable are equal." The test is not designed to answer more specific questions such as:

- Is the mean for a certain value or value category of the independent variable significantly different from the mean of some other value or value category of the independent variable?
- Among which value categories did the most dramatic differences occur?
- Do all of the means differ from each other?
- Do some combinations of means differ from another mean or another combination of means?

The answers to these questions can be difficult to ascertain. Yet, they may be the very answers that we seek. Let us look at just the first question, probably the simplest one. We could find the answer to it by using a series of tests, if the comparisons can be considered independent of each other. Returning to our previous example, we might examine the relationship between *client satisfaction level* (the dependent variable) and three dichotomous independent variables whose value categories are (1) social worker and psychologist, (2) psychologist and psychiatric nurse, and (3) social worker and psychiatric nurse.

When the number of comparisons is relatively small and we have developed research hypotheses to support why they will be found to exist, it is permissible to conduct a series of independent two-group comparisons to see if we can find support for the research hypotheses and then return to the data to conduct simple ANOVA. This is known as **planned comparison** and may entail the use of a series of two-sample independent *t* tests followed by simple ANOVA under certain conditions (equal variance and equal sample sizes), or another related test if these conditions are not present.

What if there had been many different values or value categories of the independent variable or they are not considered independent of each other? For example, what if the independent variable had been *number of treatment interviews* or *medical diagnosis*? Could we just conduct many different two-group comparisons? We could, but we shouldn't. Earlier in this chapter we discussed why it is a misuse of *t* tests to go on a fishing expedition by, for example, using hundreds of dichotomous independent variables to see if any of them reflect a statistically significant relationship to some dependent variable. The likelihood of uncovering spurious relationships would be great; one or more Type I errors would be likely to occur. The same result could be expected if we were to use a long series of two-group comparisons to examine the relationships between many pairs of values or value categories of the independent variable and measurements of the dependent variable. Besides, the process would be very time consuming, as there would be so many possible combinations to explore. Multivariate analyses were developed to avoid these problems.

Suppose, however, that the number of values or value categories is relatively small (as in our example), but we had not developed research hypotheses about the relationships between the measurements of the independent variable and measurements of the dependent variable. However, we use simple ANOVA and it suggests that one may exist. Can we then go back and reexamine the data with the use of two-group comparisons? Yes, but the procedure is different, because it now entails **post hoc comparison**, that is, seeking statistical support for relationships that emerged from data analysis rather than having been hypothesized to exist. It uses a variety of specific procedures that are beyond the scope of this text. Two of the most widely used ones are Tukey's HSD method and the Scheffe test.

A Nonparametric Alternative: Kruskal-Wallis

As suggested earlier, the Mann-Whitney U test is useful for comparing the rankings of a skewed interval or ratio level variable within the two variable categories of a nominal level variable (a dichotomous variable). However, if there are more than two subsamples (value categories of the nominal level independent variable), there is a related nonparametric test, the **Kruskal-Wallis test,** a useful nonparametric alternative to ANOVA. It works very much like the U test, ranking all scores, sorting the rankings into subsamples, and then examining how many cases in other subsamples are ranked below each case in a given subsample (or value category). An extension of the median test (Chapter 10) also is sometimes used in situations in which we wish to examine the relationship between an independent variable (with more than two values or value categories) and an interval level or ratio level dependent variable that is skewed.

MULTIVARIATE ANALYSIS OF VARIANCE

There are several other forms of analysis of variance that involve examination of the relationship among three or more variables. We will mention them only briefly here, because they are a more appropriate topic for advanced courses in statistics.

There is a **multifactor** ANOVA (also called **factorial designs**), in which there are more than two independent variables, but still just one interval or ratio level dependent variable. The independent variables can be of any measurement level. The number of independent variables is often included in the title given to the analyses, for example, **two-factor** ANOVA or **three-factor** ANOVA.

There is also MANOVA (an acronym for multiple analysis of variance) that is used if there are two or more dependent variables. In **one-factor** MANOVA, there is one independent variable and two or more interval or ratio level dependent variables. In situations where one-factor MANOVA is used, a series of simple ANOVAs could be used instead. But to do so would fail to address the importance of the intercorrelation between or among the dependent variables, something that the formula for one-factor MANOVA takes into consideration.

Finally, there is **multifactor** MANOVA in which there are two or more independent variables as well as two or more interval or ratio level dependent variables. Table 11.12 summarizes the various major types of analyses of variance.

TABLE 11.12   The Major Categories of Analysis of Variance

Name	Independent Variable(s)	Dependent Variable(s)
Simple ANOVA	One—e.g., profession of team leader	One—e.g., satisfaction level of client
Multifactor ANOVA	Two or more—e.g., profession, age, and year of work experience of team leader	One—e.g., satisfaction level of client
One-factor MANOVA	One—e.g., profession of team leader	Two or more—e.g., satisfaction, functioning level, level of clinical depression of client
Multifactor MANOVA	Two or more—e.g., profession age, and years of work experience of team leader	Two or more—e.g., satisfaction functioning level, level of clinical depression of client.

CONCLUDING THOUGHTS

The family of related tests in this chapter are well suited to social work research. They are versatile and powerful. The *t* tests (for use with two means) and simple ANOVA (for use with three or more means) and their nonparametric alternatives are among the most commonly used tests for seeking support for research hypotheses in social work research and practice. Although these tests often are used in major research projects that have extensive funding and use sophisticated research designs, they also are valuable for answering everyday questions that social workers encounter.

As illustrated in this chapter and elsewhere in the book, although statistical findings that can be used in support of research hypotheses are of practical value at many different levels for the social work practitioner, a lack of statistical support for research hypotheses can be of equal value. If a research study is designed and implemented well and statistical testing is conducted correctly, we can advance the body of knowledge available to social work practitioners, whether statistical support for a research hypothesis is found or not. Hopefully, the previous chapters have contributed to readers' understanding of statistical analyses and increased the likelihood that such analyses will be used appropriately to advance knowledge in the profession of social work. Additional ways that they can be used to contribute to EBP will be discussed in Chapter 12.

STUDY QUESTIONS

1. What is the appropriate combination of levels of measurement of two variables for using either an independent *t* test or a dependent *t* test?
2. Why do the sample size and subsample size comparability requirements of the independent *t* test frequently make it ideally suited for social work research?

3. If with the use of the independent *t* test, the null hypothesis were correct, would the mean value of a variable in one sample be very similar to or very different from the mean value for that variable in the other sample?

4. What is a nonparametric alternative to the one-sample *t* test that might be used if the variable can be regarded as only nominal level?

5. What is a nonparametric alternative to the dependent *t* test that might be used if the dependent variable can be regarded as a little less than interval level?

6. What additional step is required in determining whether a *t* value that is statistically significant reflects support for a one-tailed research hypothesis?

7. Explain why a *t* test that does not result in a finding of statistical significance may still produce a finding that is useful for the social work practitioner. Provide an example.

8. Provide an original example of how one could use a one-sample *t* test to evaluate practice effectiveness in a social agency with which you are familiar.

9. Find an article in a professional social work journal that reports on the use of the dependent *t* test. What was the study's hypothesis? How did the author interpret the study's results? Do you feel the test was used appropriately? Why? What contribution did the article make to the profession's knowledge base?

10. What conditions for use of the Mann-Whitney *U* test make it particularly well suited for the individual practitioner who wishes to evaluate the effectiveness of a new treatment method? Provide an original example in your discussion.

11. What multivariate alternative to the *t* tests examines the relationship among a group of independent variables and a set of interval/ratio level dependent variables?

12. When would we use one-way ANOVA rather than the two-sample independent *t* test?

12

Other Contributions of Statistics to Evidence-Based Practice

In Chapter 1 we mentioned the importance of knowledge of statistics for deciding which of the many research studies that we encounter should influence our practice decision making. EBP requires us to be judicious in deciding which studies are credible and worthy of application and which, because of design flaws or misuse of statistical analyses, can be dismissed. Thus, in later chapters we examined the appropriate methods for statistically analyzing different types of social work research data in studies that examine a wide array of research questions. Most of the applications that were discussed and the examples that we provided described how statistical analyses should be used to summarize the characteristics of a data set (descriptive statistics) or to determine how safe it would be to conclude that two variables are related within a population from analyses of their relationship in a research sample (inferential statistics). These are the most common uses of statistical analyses—they are essential to basic research. However, there is another, specialized use of statistical analyses that we have only alluded to at several points. Statistical analyses are used to provide knowledge for EBP directly—they are used to help to decide whether the helping methods (interventions) employed by social workers are effective.

Evaluations of practice effectiveness (which can be broadly classified as evaluation research) occur at different system levels. In this chapter we will see how statistical analyses can be used for evaluating groups of studies that seek to learn if a particular type of intervention is effective with some client population. Then we will look at some ways that they can help to determine if a specific social program is effective. Finally, we will see how they can help us to learn if our individual practice is effective with a given client or client system. In discussing these different applications of statistics, we will rely mostly on statistical tests and methods already discussed, but introduce two new ones as well.

META-ANALYSIS

A **meta-analysis** is a specific type of research study in which reports of similar research studies are examined to answer a variety of questions. The questions can relate to research methodology (for example, What is the relationship between length of cover letters and response rate of surveys?). However, because our focus here is the relationship between statistics and EBP, we will focus on another common use—for answering questions about the effectiveness of methods of intervention. For example, meta-analysis can be used to answer questions such as, "How effective is aversive therapy in the treatment of people who are adjudicated sex offenders?" or, "Is reality therapy effective with people who are chronic abusers of prescription medication?" Thus, it tests the value of certain theories of intervention.

As is the case with the other methods for evaluating practice effectiveness that are discussed in this chapter, certain research terms that have universal meanings in more basic research have somewhat unique meanings in meta-analysis. They are summarized in Box 12.1.

BOX 12.1
Research Concepts and Their Most Common Meanings in Meta-Analysis

dependent variable = the amount of change in the problem addressed by the intervention

independent variable = the type of intervention

case = a report of a research study that examined the relationship between the independent and dependent variables

sample = the group of research reports that are examined

sampling error = generally not relevant, unless a sample of reports is picked at random from among a larger group of studies that meet the criteria for inclusion

sampling bias = an assumption because of a variety of factors; why the reports examined cannot be considered a representative sample.

In meta-analysis, a research report is the equivalent of a case in more traditional research. Thus, the data in a meta-analysis may consist of all of the studies that a researcher can locate which studied the effectiveness of some method of intervention for addressing some social problem or a problem of a particular group of people. More commonly, researchers put certain restrictions on which reports of studies will be included in the analyses. For example, they may decide to include only those that were full reports rather than journal articles or abstracts, those that are available in printed form rather than accessible only on the Internet, those that used one or more true control groups, those with a sample size of 30 or more, and so forth. Although such restrictions limit the number of studies in the sample, they have at least two advantages: (1) they help to eliminate studies that lack at least a minimum of design rigor, and (2) they increase the degree to which the studies are similar in their methodology or in some other important way.

In a meta-analysis, there is an inherent weakness in the sample of studies that are examined that cannot be avoided—the sample is neither random nor unbiased. It is not possible to select a random sample of studies that meet the necessary criteria because there is no "master list" of all such studies from which to draw one. The reports of some studies never get written or may never get published in a form available to researchers. They may simply sit in a file somewhere or their findings may have been discarded. Additionally, because findings that report statistically significant relationships between variables have historically had a better chance of being published than those in which one-tailed or even two-tailed research hypotheses have failed to gain statistical support, the studies available for a meta-analysis are likely to be a biased sample. What does this imply? The sample in a meta-analysis of the effectiveness of some form of intervention is likely to contain a disproportionately large number of studies in which an intervention was considered to be effective and a disproportionately small number of studies in which it was not effective. This can lead to a Type I error, if caution is not used.

In selecting a method of statistical analysis, the lack of random samples suggests that certain types of statistical tests, parametric ones, can be immediately ruled out for analyses of meta-analysis data. Another dilemma in selecting a method of data analysis relates to the fact that the studies, no matter how well matched they may be by setting certain criteria for their inclusion, still differ from each other in their methodologies. Should they then be treated as equal, with each "counting" equally in an overall evaluation of the effectiveness of some method of intervention? Or, should some be weighted more than others because they seem to contain more design rigor? This is a hard question to answer, because even decisions about the amount of design rigor in a study can sometimes have elements of subjectivity.

The most common statistical analysis used in a meta-analysis is one that discounts methodological differences and weights each study equally. It entails the use of the **mean effect size,** the average effect size among all of the studies included in it. As we discussed in earlier chapters, effect size is an indicator of the strength of a relationship between variables. Effect size is an estimate of the amount of variation in the dependent variable that is related to variation of the independent variable. It is not the same as a p value (the probability that a relationship between variables was produced by sampling error). As noted in previous chapters, it helps us to know if a statistically significant relationship is also substantive or meaningful.

To compute the mean effect size in a meta-analysis, researchers take the effect size of a relationship between the independent variable (the intervention) and the dependent variable (a measurement of the problem that the intervention addressed) as reported in each study. If it was not reported, they estimated it using tables constructed for this purpose. Then the effect sizes from all of the studies are averaged to produce the mean effect size.

How would this work? Suppose we wanted to conduct a meta-analysis to answer the research question, "Is reminiscence and life review (an intervention method believed to help people by providing structured reflection on the meaning of their lives) effective in improving the life satisfaction of older people who are living in long-term care facilities?" Following a preliminary search of the literature, we might conclude that we would have enough studies for inclusion if we were to limit our meta-analysis to studies that: (1) used reminiscence and life review as the primary method of intervention; (2) used either a control group or a pretest measurement of life satisfaction; (3) were available in written form in either research monographs or articles in refereed professional journals.

Although we might like to control for other confounding variables (such as *health status of research participants* or *professional discipline of those offering the intervention*), that could produce its own problems. First, it might narrow the meta-analysis to the reports of too small a number of studies. Second, even if the number of studies meeting the additional criteria were deemed adequate, it might limit the external validity (generalizability) of any findings about the effectiveness of the intervention.

Once the studies to be used are identified, we could either identify or estimate the effect size reported in each for the relationship between the two variables. Then we would average them, to get the mean effect size. As with any time the mean is used, outlying scores could cause problems. They can produce misleading findings, and sometimes are used as an argument against the use of the mean effect size. Suppose that, in examining 20 cases, 19 effect sizes are positive between the use of the intervention and improved life satisfaction and they fall in the range between .3 and .5. However, one effect size (in a study in which life satisfaction declined dramatically during the time that the intervention was offered) was high and negative, say, $-.8$. (The report might not tell us that the intervention was implemented incorrectly.) This one study would dramatically affect the mean effect size and lead us to believe that the intervention is not very effective, despite the fact that there was support for its effectiveness in most of the studies. In situations like this, it might be preferable to use another type of statistical analysis. Unfortunately, the ones that are available are quite complex and beyond the scope of this book.

Why not just use some of the nonparametric tests that we have already discussed? Even if the reports of the studies contain enough data to justify the use of some of them, the findings would be questioned for any number of reasons—for example, the lengths of the intervention may vary in the different studies, as well as the characteristics of research participants. The studies cannot be just combined as we might wish. Critics of meta-analyses point out the many problems of attempting to statistically analyze the reports of a group of studies that are not comparable with the use of traditional methods. This kind of analysis is not quite the equivalent of "comparing apples and oranges." However, it is comparable to taking a group of apples and oranges and treating them as if they were a homogeneous sample (which clearly they are not) for statistical purposes.

The mean effect size remains the best (if far from perfect) way to use statistics in meta-analyses. However, mathematicians and researchers are always designing new ways to analyze data. Perhaps in the not-too-distant future one or more better, yet simple ways will emerge. In the meantime, it is probably best to regard the results of statistical analyses as very tentative evidence of the effectiveness or ineffectiveness of certain types of intervention with certain problems. And that is still a contribution to EBP.

ANSWERS SOUGHT IN PROGRAM EVALUATIONS

An in-depth discussion of program evaluation is beyond the scope of this book. There are many good books and sections of books devoted to it. We will assume that the reader has at least a good general knowledge of what it is about, either from studying about it in other courses or through experience with it in organizational settings. We will focus on some ways that statistical analyses can be used as part of this important activity. Most program evaluations seek the answer to one of three basic questions:

1. Is the social service program needed or (in the case of an already existing program) still needed? (**needs assessments**)
2. Is the program functioning as it should be? (**formative evaluations**—sometimes called process evaluations)
3. Did the program achieve its objectives? (**outcome evaluations**)

NEEDS ASSESSMENTS AND FORMATIVE EVALUATIONS

Data collected in the process of conducting needs assessments and formative evaluations come from a wide variety of sources (e.g., social indicators, personal interviews with staff and/or clients, focus groups, key informants, direct observations). Most of the data are descriptive in nature. They can take many different forms (e.g., researcher's notes, direct quotations, numerical data, video- or audiotapes). The greatest need of the person conducting these types of program evaluations may be to make some sense of these data; that is, to synthesize them. Until that occurs, it is almost impossible to conclude whether a program is needed (for needs assessments) or if it is functioning as it should (for formative evaluations).

How can statistical analyses be of assistance? Descriptive statistics are sometimes helpful. The researcher might first condense the data into frequency distributions and graphs (Chapter 2), at least for those data that are in a form that lend themselves to their construction.

Correlation analyses are also sometimes used. For example, in a needs assessment designed to see if a proposed program is needed and, if so, how and where it should be implemented, it might be useful to use Pearson's *r* or its nonparametric alternatives to describe the strength and direction of the correlation between the variables *income level* and *attitudes toward proposed services* of potential clients. Similarly, chi-square or some other similar test might occasionally be used to demonstrate an association between certain variables. However, tests of inference would be rarely used. Although we might speculate on, or even predict, what will be found in general terms, usually research hypotheses per se are not stated. Thus, we would not expect hypothesis testing to be a major component of these forms of program evaluation, and there would be little need for tests of statistical inference.

OUTCOME EVALUATIONS

Outcome evaluations often have descriptive components. Some of their findings may consist of demographic profiles of the clients who were served by the program or its staff or a summary of how program funding was spent. Frequency distribution tables, graphs, measures of central tendency, and measures of variability are all effective ways to summarize and present these data.

Although description of various aspects of a program is almost always present in an outcome evaluation, it is usually not the central focus. What the reader of a report wants to know is, "was the program effective?", that is, to what degree did it achieve its outcome objectives? This suggests that an outcome study should be designed in such a way that it provides data that can be objectively analyzed to provide evidence of the degree to which the program was effective.

Hypothesis Testing in Outcome Evaluations

Determining if a program is effective is a complex process. Ideally, the design for an outcome evaluation is developed before a program gets under way, along with the program itself. The design consists of a combination of qualitative and quantitative research methods to acquire various perspectives on the merit, worth, or value of the program.

In focusing on program effectiveness, every effort is made to learn if benefits or other desirable changes among its clients are produced by the program or by something else. Thus, whenever it is ethically and logistically possible, confounding variables, rival hypotheses, and threats to internal validity are controlled. For example, clients may be randomly selected for a program in an effort to make them representative of their population. Or, clients may be randomly selected and assigned to the program and its control group in an effort to try to equalize the groups. However, even if it is possible to use a rigorous design such as the true experiment, there is still the question of sampling error. How certain can we be that what appear to be the achievements of the program are not really the work of sampling error? This question requires that we test the null hypothesis by using statistical tests of inference.

In some outcome evaluations, research hypotheses are formulated and stated. In others, they are not stated but are implicit in the program's goals and objectives. Whether they are stated or implicit, they can assume the usual three forms: two-tailed, one-tailed, or no relationship. One-tailed hypotheses are the most common—generally, it is believed that a program is better than other similar programs and/or that it will prove to be effective or it would not be initiated or funded in the first place. However, the other two types of hypothesis are more common than we might initially assume, especially when two or more programs are being compared.

When stated, the specific wording of a research hypothesis depends upon a number of factors, including: (1) the outcome objectives of the program, (2) the general design of the evaluation, and (3) whether the program is being evaluated on its own merits or is being compared with one or more other programs. However, it is possible to use a number of "templates" to illustrate the different general forms that hypotheses can take. For example, if the research design called for comparing the results of two similar programs, the dependent variable would be the amount of change in some problem for all clients who participated in their respective programs. The independent variable would be the program (say, Program *A* or Program *B*) in which clients participated. Thus, research hypotheses could be:

- *"Either Program A is more effective than Program B, or program B is more effective than program A."* (two-tailed)
- *"Program A is more effective than Program B."* (one-tailed)
- *"Program A and Program B are equally effective."* (no relationship)

We might expect that two similar programs will produce different results and simply we will want to learn which of the two is the most effective. Then a two-tailed research hypothesis would be appropriate. A one-tailed research hypothesis would be more appropriate if we believe it is justifiable to predict that one program will be more effective than the other. In either case, we would hope to be able to reject the null hypothesis; that is, to be able to conclude that any difference in the results of the two programs is large enough to be statistically significant—unlikely to be the work of sampling error. The lack of a statistically significant difference between the programs (or, in the case of a one-tailed hypothesis, a statistically significant difference but one in the direction opposite to that which was predicted) would constitute a lack of support for the research hypothesis.

What if the study had a "no relationship" research hypothesis? Then, support for it would be achieved if we were not able to reject the null hypothesis. For example, we might have hypothesized that a shorter or less expensive program will produce results that are the same as those of a longer or more expensive program. We would then be able to claim support for the research hypothesis if the results of the two programs were found to be similar enough that any differences in them were fairly likely to be the work of sampling error. A statistical test that generated a p value of $>.05$, perhaps much greater, would reflect such a finding.

An outcome evaluation may also focus on a single program and whether or not clients show a statistically significant improvement in relation to some problem (the dependent variable) following completion of the program. A one-group pretest posttest design might be used. In this type of design the independent variable is the time of measurement of the dependent variable (before and after program completion). Although one-tailed research hypotheses are used most frequently, any of the three forms may be used, depending on what was learned from a literature review, practice experience, and so forth:

- *Following completion of the program, "Clients' problems will either be improved or will get worse."* (two-tailed)
- *Following completion of the program, "Clients' problems will be improved."* (one-tailed)
- *Following completion of the program, "Clients' problems in the program will be unchanged."* (no relationship)

When evaluating the effectiveness of a single program using a true experiment, there is an experimental group (the program's clients) and a control group consisting of other clients who are potential participants who were not selected for the program. Clients are randomly assigned to be in one group or the other. If an experimental design is used, the possible research hypotheses would be:

- *Following completion of the program, "Either the clients in the program or the clients in the control group will show more improvement."* (two-tailed)
- *Following completion of the program, "Clients in the program will reflect more improvement than clients in the control group."* (one-tailed)
- *Following completion of the program, "There will be no difference in improvement between clients in the program and clients in the control group."* (no relationship)

Sometimes clients are selected at random to participate in a program to see if it successfully addresses some problem. The problem (the dependent variable) might be something that has been measured many times before, and we now have available population data for it. For example, if the variable is *marital satisfaction*, we might already know that the satisfaction scores of all clients in the population have a mean of 50 and a standard deviation of 12. An outcome evaluation design might seek to learn whether clients in the program differed from the population in relation to the dependent variable following completion of the program. The independent variable would be who provided the measurement of the dependent variable—the people who completed the program (the sample) or the population from which clients were drawn. Research hypotheses might be:

- Clients who complete the program will have a different level of the problem than the population. (two-tailed)
- Clients who complete the program will have less of the problem than the population. (one-tailed)
- Clients who complete the program will have the same level of the problem as the population. (no relationship)

BOX 12.2
Research Concepts and Their Most Common Meanings in Program Evaluations

dependent variable = the problem addressed by a program

independent variable = most frequently, (1) whether clients are in a program or its control group; (2) whether clients are in one program or another program; or, (3) whether clients have not begun or have completed the program.

case = most frequently, a client in a program or its control group(s)

sample = a series of observations of the program by the evaluator, the group of clients in a program or its control group(s), a group of staff members in a program, a group of people in a community, or some other group that provides data for a program evaluation.

sampling error = the natural tendency of any sample (even a random one) to differ from its population or for two samples drawn from the same population to differ from each other.

control group = a group of clients who do not participate in a program or the clients in some other program

experimental group = a group of clients who participate in a program

sampling bias = the systematic distortion of one or more samples for a variety of reasons

---

It would be highly unlikely that we would ever use the no relationship hypothesis in this type of situation or in the previous two examples. Two-tailed hypotheses would be almost as rare. One-tailed hypotheses are by far the most common form of hypothesis in outcome evaluations that focus on a single program.

As in meta-analyses some research concepts take on specialized meanings within the context of program evaluations. They are summarized in Box 12.2.

Statistical Analyses of Outcome Evaluation Data

As in all research studies, support for either a two-tailed or one-tailed research hypothesis would be found by statistically demonstrating that it would be reasonably safe to reject the null hypothesis ($p < .05$). When using a "no relationship" hypothesis, support could be demonstrated through statistical testing if it could be shown that the probability of sampling error having produced any difference in the outcome of the two programs is relatively high ($p > .05$).

What statistical analyses would be appropriate for testing the null form of any of the above research hypotheses? The family of *t* tests (or, if there are multiple program objectives, T^2) (discussed in Chapter 11) may be a good place to start if the assumptions for their use can be met. Suppose that clients were randomly assigned to be in one of two different programs (which we are comparing) or to either a program or its control group, and were not matched. Then we might use the two-sample, independent *t* test to compare the mean score of the dependent variable of clients in one group (sample) with that of those in the other group (sample). If a two-tailed research hypothesis had been used, we would find support for it if the test produced a small p value (usually $p < .05$), thus suggesting that the difference in the two means was unlikely to be the work of sampling error. Support for a one-tailed research hypothesis would be found only if the test produced a low p value (usually $p < .05$) *and* the higher mean score for the dependent variable was in the group where the hypothesis predicted it would be found. If the researcher had predicted that "one program is just as good as the other," or that "clients in the program will reflect no more improvement than those in its control group," support for this "no relationship" research hypothesis would be achieved only if the two-sample, independent t test produced a p value greater than .05.

If the conditions for the parametric, two-sample, independent t test were not met (for example, if measurements of the dependent variable produced only ordinal-level data or interval/ratio data that were known to be badly skewed), a nonparametric test should be used instead. The Mann-Whitney U test (described in Chapter 11) should be considered.

What statistical analyses would be appropriate for testing the null form of research hypotheses when the research design calls for evaluating a single program with the use of a pre-test and posttest design? Because we would be comparing the same individual clients' measurement of the dependent variable (e.g., "hostility," "assertiveness," "sexist attitudes") before participation with their measurements of it after completion of the program, the two-sample, dependent t test would be a possibility. If conditions for its use could not be met, we might first consider the nonparametric Wilcoxon sign test instead.

If population data estimates were available, we could compare the mean of the measurements of the dependent variable of clients following program completion with the population mean for the variable. That would suggest that the one-sample t test might be appropriate or, if its conditions cannot be met, the nonparametric alternative, chi-square goodness of fit.

The same tests of inference that we discussed in earlier chapters (and many others) are appropriate for program evaluations as well as for more traditional research studies. The same principles of hypothesis testing (Chapters 5 through 7) and the same conditions for the use of different tests also apply. Unfortunately, researchers conducting program evaluations in the past have often made many of the same mistakes in selecting statistical analyses that other researchers have made. For example, they have been known to use chi-square when they could have used more powerful tests that would have been more likely to provide support for a one-tailed or a two-tailed hypothesis. Others have used tests designed for small samples with very large samples, thus virtually guaranteeing statistical significance, even though the actual amount of improvement of clients in the program was minimal. Still others have used statistical tests with very small samples of clients in a program. Their statistical analyses were so lacking in statistical power (Chapter 7) that they could not possibly identify a true relationship between the independent and dependent variables. Their analyses could only result in a Type II error; that is, the conclusion that the program probably made no difference, even if it really was effective. As in other types of research studies, a statistical power analysis prior to data collection can help to avoid these kinds of problems.

ANSWERS SOUGHT IN SINGLE-SYSTEM RESEARCH

Individual practitioners also require feedback about their work. The most commonly used method for doing this is single-system research. As in the previous discussion, we will assume that readers have some familiarity with this important part of social work practice through their study of research methods and/or social work practice methods.

Single-system research is used to help social work practitioners to objectively evaluate the effectiveness of their services (interventions) in eliminating or reducing a problem of a client or client system. Single-system research designs consist of one or more A phases (during which a specific intervention is not offered) and one or more B-phases (during which the intervention is offered). An A phase is also sometimes referred to as a baseline; although this is only an accurate description with an A phase that occurs before the intervention is offered for the first time. Then, the A phase produces a true baseline, that is, a measurement of the usual pattern of the target problem (its frequency, duration, severity, and so forth) prior to providing the intervention. After it has been offered, any subsequent A phase is most likely to consist of a time during which the intervention is withdrawn following its use.

The most common statistical analyses of single-system data entail the comparison of a true baseline phase (A) with the first B phase (or, in the case of an AB design, the only B phase) during which the intervention is introduced. The dependent variable in single-system research is the target problem, often a client or client system behavior, perception or attitude that the social worker hopes to positively affect through the intervention. It is measured throughout all phases (A and B) of the study. The independent variable is the phase (A or B) in which the measurements of the dependent variable took place, that is, whether the dependent variable was measured during the A or the B phase. The specific meanings of research terms when used in single-system research are displayed in Box 12.3.

Specifically, data analyses involve a comparison of a sample of measurements of the dependent variable during the A phase with a second sample of measurements of the same variable taken during the subsequent B phase. For example, a social worker might determine how many times a 6-year-old boy fought with his sister each week during a 10-week baseline (A) phase when the particular intervention being tested (perhaps the weekly showing of a video reflecting consideration) was withheld ($n = 10$). Then a comparison of these data would be made with measurements with the number of times he fought with the sister each week during the 10-week (B) phase when the intervention was present ($n = 10$).

Hypothesis Testing in Single-System Research

Most often, research hypotheses in single-system research tend to be one-tailed. They reflect the belief that the intervention will be effective. The specific wording varies depending on the exact nature of the intervention and the target problem, but research hypotheses are generally something like this:

> *"When the intervention is present, a desirable change in the target problem will occur."*

BOX 12.3

Research Concepts and Their Most Common Meanings in Single-System Research

dependent variable = the target problem (and its pattern)

independent variable = the presence (B phase) or absence (A phase) of the intervention

case = a measurement of the dependent variable in either an A phase or a B phase

sample = the group of measurements of the target problem in either an A phase or a B phase

sampling error = normal fluctuation of the target problem; why the A phases and B phases may differ

control group = the sample of measurements of the target problem during an A phase

experimental group = the sample of measurements of the target problem during a B phase

---

Less-frequently, we might attempt to see if we can find support for a two-tailed research hypothesis. Perhaps we believe our intervention will produce a change in a target behavior, but we are unsure in which direction it will change, for example, we are unsure whether the presence of a co-therapist in a treatment group will increase or decrease group participation. We would not have a "no relationship" research hypothesis in single-system research studies. Why would we ever predict that our intervention will make no difference? If we really believed that it would not make a difference, it would be a waste of time (and unethical) to use it.

Statistical Analyses of Single-System Data

Many single-system designs, because of little available knowledge about a target problem and/or what might be an effective intervention to address it, are just descriptive or even exploratory. Thus, they tend to be simple, for example, AB, BAB, ABA. Logistical or ethical concerns may also preclude the use of some of the more complex research designs (those containing more than just two or three phases). Unfortunately, that eliminates those designs most likely to control for the effects of rival hypotheses (some variable other than the presence or absence of the intervention produced any change in the target problem) or the usual threats to internal validity that might obscure the true relationship between the independent and dependent variables.

If the research design used is only exploratory or descriptive, it is almost certain to contain inherent design flaws. Thus we can graph the data and conduct statistical analyses of them but, even if they suggest that the intervention might have been effective, conclusions can only be tentative at best. Statistical analyses (comparing measurements of the dependent variable during an A phase with those during a subsequent B phase) can tell us if the differences between the two sets of measurements is statistically significant; that is, unlikely to be the result of sampling error. But, that is all. It cannot tell us if this apparent relationship between the independent and dependent variables is a spurious one. We would have to interpret the findings as best we could, relying on our knowledge of social work practice, our knowledge of the client or client system, and our knowledge of research methods. For example, we might consider whether maturation, history, statistical regression to the mean, and so forth might have affected the dependent variable in some way.

Explanatory single-system research designs (for reasons previously mentioned) are relatively rare in social work. When they can be implemented, the process of data analysis is: graph the data, "eyeball" them to see if there appears to be any support for the research hypothesis, and, if so, conduct appropriate statistical analyses to determine if there is statistical support for it. However, because explanatory designs do a better job than exploratory or descriptive designs of controlling for rival hypotheses, sampling bias, and so forth, more definitive conclusions regarding the effectiveness of an intervention can be drawn than when exploratory or descriptive designs are used.

There are 3 basic assumptions in statistical analyses of single system data (in addition to those central to all statistical testing). They are:

1. The A (baseline) phase is an accurate representation of the dependent variable and its variability.
2. The same pattern of variations would continue after the A phase if the intervention were not implemented.
3. Any difference between the pattern of the dependent variable in the A and subsequent B phases may (dependent on the research design employed) be attributable to the presence of the intervention during the B phase.

Using Familiar Statistical Tests

It is possible to analyze the data in a single-system study with the use of some of the methods described earlier in this book. Some of the tests that entail cross tabulation (Chapter 10) sometimes can be used. If the dependent variable is only at the nominal level, a table can be constructed and the chi-square test (Chapter 10) can be used. For example, if the dependent variable is *compliance with medication* (yes or no), the table might look like Table 12.1.

TABLE 12.1 Cross-Tabulation Table for Single-System Data Analysis: Caleb's History of Medication Compliance ($N = 30$)

Complete Compliance	Phase		*Totals*
	A	*B*	
Yes	6	9	15
No	9	6	15
Totals	15	15	30

If the measurement of the dependent variable produces interval or ratio level and the variable is believed to be normally distributed, the two sample independent *t* test (Chapter 11) sometimes can be used. The mean can be computed for measurements during the A phase and also for measurements in the subsequent B phase. Then the two sample means can be compared with the use of the test. When the conditions for the two-sample independent *t* test are present, it can be ideal. However, the fact that the two samples are not really randomly selected and that other criteria do not appear to be met generally preclude its use.

If the data are at the interval or ratio level but skewed, Mann-Whitney *U* (Chapter 11) can be used. Another possibility is the median test (Chapter 10). How could we use it? Suppose that we are attempting to see if some new form of intervention is effective in reducing the number of instances of verbal abuse that occur between a couple we are counseling. We could ask the couple to count up and report each week the number of times that abuse occurs during an phase A (baseline) and during a subsequent B phase (when she offers the intervention). We could then compute the median number of times that abuse occurred during the entire time (both A and B phases) and place the data into a cross-tabulation table such as Table 12.2. Then we could use the chi-square test or, if the conditions for its use cannot be met, Fisher's exact to see if any difference in the dependent variable between the two phases is statistically significant.

Two Other Popular Tests

There are two other statistical analyses, the two-standard-deviation method and the proportion/frequency method that are widely used among social work practitioners conducting single-system research. (The validity of a third popular one, the celeration line method, has been called into question, so we will not present it here.) The popularity of these tests is attributable, at least in part, to the fact that they are (a) simple to compute, and (b) well suited to the measurements of the dependent variable found in many examples of single-system research.

The **two-standard-deviation method** is most appropriate when (a) measurements of the dependent variable is at the interval or ratio level, and (b) when graphed, during a baseline phase, they are relatively flat; that is, they do not vary too widely. Measurements of the target problem should vary somewhat, but they vary randomly around some central point (the mean of the measurements).

TABLE 12.2   Median Test Data: Number of Instances of Verbal Abuse by Day for the Smiths ($N = 56$)

	Phase		
Number of Days (MD = 5.3)	*A*	*B*	*Totals*
Above Median	20	8	28
Median or Below	8	20	28
Totals	28	28	56

The test relies heavily on concepts that we discussed in earlier chapters. Central to its understanding is the normal distribution (Chapter 4), and the percent of cases that will fall a given number of standard deviations from the mean when a variable is normally distributed. In Chapter 6 we illustrated the rejection regions for two-tailed and one-tailed research hypotheses. (It might be helpful here to refer back to those figures.) The rejection level for a two-tailed research hypothesis fell 1.96 standard deviations from the mean. Thus, a measurement that varies by as much as 2.0 standard deviations from the mean would occur rarely (less than 5 percent of the time). If a one-tailed research hypothesis were used, the rejection region falls only 1.58 standard deviations from the mean. Thus, a measurement that falls 2.0 standard deviations from the mean (in the predicted direction) would be even more rare.

How are these facts applied with the two-standard-deviation method? Suppose our hypothesis is two-tailed. After plotting the data for both the A and subsequent B phases, we would first visually determine if there is support for the research hypothesis. If it appears that there might be a statistically significant difference in the target problem between the phases, then the following steps are used:

1. Calculate the mean and standard deviation for measurements in the A phase.
2. Draw two bands (usually dotted lines) horizontally on the graph through the A phase and extended through the B phase, one at the point two standard deviations above the mean and the other at the point two standard deviations below the mean.
3. Statistical significance ($p < .05$) is achieved if either: (1) the mean of all measurements in the B phase is outside either standard deviation band, or (2) any two consecutive measurements in the B phase fall outside the same standard deviation band.

Remember, the measurements of the dependent variable are just two samples taken at different times (i.e., A and B phases). Especially if they are relatively small, they might be expected to differ just because of sampling error. Thus, the two samples might be indicative of little more than the normal fluctuation of the dependent variable. So, how much difference between the A and B phases will it take before sampling error can be dismissed as the likely cause of the difference? The two conditions under which statistical significance are achieved (Step 3 above) with the use of the two-standard-deviation method have been determined for us by mathematicians with the use of the rejection regions of the normal distribution and the laws of probability. They tell us the point at which sampling error is very unlikely ($p < .05$) to have produced an apparent relationship between the independent and dependent variables.

Example: Simone's Math Homework. Jennifer wanted to test the null form of her one-tailed research hypothesis that her intervention (5 minutes spent in discussing technology careers during daily counseling sessions) would increase the amount of time that her adolescent client (Simone) spends doing her math homework. Jennifer asked Simone's mother to record how much time Simone spent doing her math homework on 10 consecutive school nights while Jennifer met with Simone, but did not offer the intervention (i.e., A phase). The measurements during this phase were

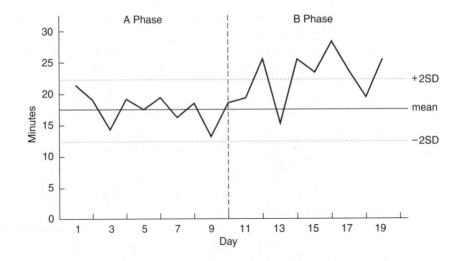

FIGURE 12.1   **Simone's Time Spent Doing Her Math Homework**

(respectively): 16, 22, 19, 14, 19, 16, 19, 16, 18, and 13 minutes. Simone's mother then continued to measure the dependent variable during the next 10 school nights (the B phase) during which Jennifer offered her intervention. This time the measurements were: 18, 19, 25, 16, 25, 23, 28, 25, 18, and 24 minutes. Jennifer plotted the measurements on a graph. She then calculated the mean and standard deviation for the 10 measurements in the A phase. The mean was 17.20 and the standard deviation was 2.48. She added two standard deviations to the mean of the A phase to find the location of the upper two-standard-deviation band: $17.20 + 2(2.48) = 22.16$. She subtracted two-standard-deviations from the mean to find the location of the lower two standard-deviation band: $17.20 - 2(2.48) = 12.24$. She added the two bands as shown in Figure 12.1, a graph known as a Shewart chart.

Jennifer then computed the mean for her measurements during the B phase. It was 22.10, a little less than 22.16, so she did not meet one of the requirements for rejecting the null hypothesis. However, as she examined the data in her graph, she noticed that she met the other one. There are four consecutive measurements above the +2-standard-deviation band (during days 15 to 18). Thus, the change in the dependent variable between the A phase and the B phase was in the predicted direction and was statistically significant, very unlikely to have been produced by sampling error. Of course, Jennifer would have to consider whether the positive change in Simone's behavior might have been caused by something else other than the intervention before she could jump to any conclusions about the intervention's effectiveness. Many other factors (threats to internal validity) besides her intervention may have produced the increase in the dependent variable.

Many target problems can only be measured at only the nominal level. Furthermore, many target problems are dichotomous; that is, they either occur or they do not occur. If the dependent variable is only at the nominal level of measurement and dichotomous, the **proportion/frequency method** can be used to test the null hypothesis. Assumptions underlying this method of statistical analysis are:

1. Desirable measurements of the dependent variable can be observed to occur a certain proportion of the time during a baseline (A phase).
2. If the intervention were not introduced after the A phase, desirable measurements of the dependent variable would continue to occur about the same proportion of the time (the same trend would continue).
3. If desirable measurements of the dependent variable occur a greater proportion of the time in the B phase, this may indicate that the intervention was effective.

What do these assumptions mean? Suppose that we want to see if we can increase the proportion of days in which a client (Lucille) is in full compliance with her medication regimen. We observe her over a period of time (or, perhaps, determine her past pattern of compliance from her medical record). We conclude that she normally takes her medication as directed about 40 percent of the time (proportion = .40). We thus can assume that, if we do not offer some intervention that we wish to try, Lucille will continue to take her medication about 40 percent of the time. If we offer the intervention over a period of time and Lucille's medication compliance goes up a considerable amount, say up to 60 percent, we may have support for the research hypothesis that our intervention will positively affect Lucille's medication compliance.

The steps in using the proportion/frequency method are:

1. Construct a graph of the baseline (A) phase and subsequent B phase.
2. Determine the proportion of measurements in the A phase that reflect the desirable measurement of the target behavior (often, either "yes" or "no").
3. Count the number of desirable measurements of the target behavior in the B phase.
4. Use a table of the Cumulative Binomial Probability Distribution to determine the minimum number of desirable measurements of the target behavior in the B phase that is required for statistical significance, given the number of measurements in the B phase.

The Cumulative Binomial Probability Distribution table is quite large and we were unable to include it here. However, it can be found in more advanced statistics books and in some research methods books. When using the proportion/frequency method, the number of measurements in the A and B phases can be different. Thus, an A phase need only last long enough to establish the usual pattern of the target problem and it can last as long as the social worker believes it might take for it to be effective.

Example: Karl's Attendance at Treatment Group.   A social worker (Stella) wanted to see if an intervention (showing an educational video), might improve Karl's attendance at treatment group. Stella kept a record of Karl's attendance over a 20-day period to form a baseline (A phase). During that time, Karl attended his group 6 times

A Phase (*n* = 20)   B Phase (*n* = 25)

Yes   * * * *   * *   * * * * * * * * * * *
No   ** * * ** **** ** **   ** ** * * * ** * * * **

Day   1——————————— 20   21 ——————————— 45

**FIGURE 12.2   Proportion/Frequency Graph:
Karl's Group Attendance (*N* = 45)**

(30% or .30). Then she entered the B phase of her intervention in which she showed an educational video at each group meeting. She constructed a graph of her research findings (Figure 12.2).

The B phase consisted of 25 group sessions. Karl attended 11 of these sessions (44% attendance). Clearly, this reflected improvement in his attendance. With the use of a Cumulative Binomial Probability Distribution table, Stella was able to determine that, with 25 measurements in the B phase and a proportion of attendance in the A phase of .30, Karl would have had to attend at least 12 sessions for the improvement in his group attendance to be statistically significant. The *p*-value for his observed frequency of attendance was .098, greater than .05. Thus, Stella was not able to reject the null hypothesis. The difference in Karl's attendance between the A and B phases was just too likely to be attributable to sampling error or his normal fluctuation in attendance.

CONCLUDING THOUGHTS

We began by stating the importance of EBP to social work practice. We explained how it is not an attainable goal unless a social worker has a thorough understanding of research methodology and statistics. We have devoted the early chapters of this book to providing the theoretical grounding in statistics that is needed to understand conceptually what statistical analyses are all about. In later chapters we introduced statistical inference and then we examined in some detail some of the statistical tests of inference that social workers are likely to encounter in their practice (as well as some less common ones), with emphasis on when they should and should not be used. Much of this content was designed to help the reader to become a critical consumer of research reports, specifically, their use of statistics. This is, of course, essential for EBP.

Chapter 12 helped to complete our discussion of statistics and its relationship to ESP. It focused directly on how statistical analyses can be used to help to determine which interventions are effective, that is, to help to accumulate evidence for use by EBP at several levels. We hope that we have been successful in both demystifying the topic of statistics and in helping to make EBP an achievable goal for the reader.

STUDY QUESTIONS

1. In a meta-analysis, why do we say that the sample is biased? Why is it not considered to be a random sample? How does that limit the type of statistical analyses that can be used?

2. What is the most common type of statistical analysis in a meta-analysis? Why do some people say the findings of individual studies should not receive equal weighting?

3. How do researchers conducting meta-analyses attempt to match the cases in their research sample? Do you think this gives their statistical analyses more credibility? Why or why not?

4. If you were conducting a meta-analysis on the effectiveness of support groups for relatives and friends of survivors of people who are recently deceased, what are some ways that you might go about it? How would you interpret the mean effect size for the data?

5. Why are tests of statistical inference rarely used in needs assessments or formative evaluations? Why are descriptive statistics more useful?

6. In an outcome evaluation that used a two-group, pretest–posttest design, what might be an appropriate statistical test to use if the measurement of the problem could be considered to be interval or ratio level and normally distributed within the population? Explain.

7. What if, instead, the problem could only be assumed to be at the ordinal level of measurement? Then what test of inference would be more appropriate?

8. Why is it generally incorrect to use a parametric test like two-sample independent t to compare a baseline A phase with a subsequent B phase? What conditions for its use are rarely if ever met?

9. Explain the relationship between the two-standard-deviation method and rejection regions? Why do we use two standard deviations rather than one or three standard deviations?

10. In the proportion/frequency method for analysis of single-system data, to what do the terms proportion and frequency refer? Why is the test appropriate in working with a child diagnosed as ADHD when the target problem is school attendance, but not appropriate if it is the variable *number of disruptive outbursts in the classroom*?

A

Beginning to Select a Statistical Test

In Chapter 7 we discussed how we might go about the process of selecting the most appropriate tests of statistical inference. Boxes A.1 and A.2 that follow are provided both to assist the reader in beginning this process and as a review and summary of the discussions in Chapters 8–11.

BOX A.1   Using Level of Measurement to Begin to Select a Bivariate Statistical Test

Parametric Statistical Tests			Nonparametric Statistical Tests		
Test	Dependent (Criterion) Variable	Independent (Predictor) Variable	Test	Dependent (Criterion) Variable	Independent (Predictor) Variable
—	—	—	Chi-square	Nominal	Nominal
—	—	—	Fisher's exact	Nominal	Nominal (two categories)
—	—	—	McNemar's	Nominal (before)	Nominal (after)
One-sample *t*	Interval/ratio	Nominal (sample/population)	Goodness of fit	Nominal	Nominal
Independent *t*	Interval/ratio	Nominal	Mann-Whitney *U*	Ordinal/skewed interval	Nominal
			Kolmogorov-Smirnov	Ordinal/skewed interval	—
Dependent *t*	Interval/ratio	Nominal	Wilcoxon Sign	Ordinal "plus"	(2 repeated measures)
One-way ANOVA	Interval/ratio	Nominal	Kruskal-Wallis	Ordinal/skewed interval	Nominal
Pearson's *r*	Interval/ratio	Interval/ratio	Spearman rho	Ordinal/skewed interval	Ordinal/skewed interval
			Kendall's tau	Ordinal/skewed interval	Ordinal/skewed interval
Simple linear regression	Interval/ratio	Interval/ratio	Logistic regression	Nominal	Nominal

BOX A.2   Some Bivariate Tests and Related Multivariate Tests

Bivariate Test	Multivariate Test
Chi-square*	Multiple contingency tables
Pearson's *r*	Partial *r*
	Multiple *R*
	Canonical correlation
	Factor analysis
	Cluster analysis
Kendall's tau*	Kendall's partial rank correlation coefficient
Simple linear regression	Multiple linear regression
	Discriminant analysis
	Logistic regression
Two-sample independent *t*-test	T^2
Simple, one-factor ANOVA	Multifactor ANOVA (Factorial designs)
	MANOVA
	One-factor MANOVA
	Multifactor MANOVA

Glossary

This glossary is designed as a general reference for the student of statistics. Many of the terms are discussed in detail in the text. Others that sometimes appear elsewhere in the statistical literature also have been included.

Absolute frequency distribution: A table that displays the frequencies for various measurements of a variable.

Acceptance region: The outcome of a statistical test that leads to the acceptance of the null hypothesis.

Allowance factor: Used in constructing confidence intervals, it is the distance (on the measurement scale) between the sample statistic and the limits of the interval. We both add and subtract the allowance factor to find, respectively, the upper and lower limits of the confidence interval.

Alpha error: See Type I error.

Alternative hypothesis: See research hypothesis.

Analysis of variance: A statistical technique by which it is possible to partition the variance in a distribution of scores according to separate sources or factors; a statistical measure to test the differences among the means of three or more groups; sometimes referred to as ANOVA.

ANOVA: The abbreviation for the statistical procedure known as analysis of variance.

Antecedent variable: A variable that precedes the introduction of the independent variable.

A priori probability: The probability of a future event calculated from prior knowledge of the number of possible outcomes and their relative frequencies.

Arithmetic mean: See Mean.

Axes: Reference lines that delineate the two (or sometimes three) dimensions of a graph; the horizontal and vertical lines in a graph on which values of a measurement or the corresponding frequencies are plotted.

Bar graph: A graphical technique of descriptive statistics that uses the heights of separated bars to show how often each score occurs; graphical representation of a frequency distribution table in which each measurement category is represented by a bar that extends to the appropriate distance in the frequency dimension; usually has spaces between bars to represent nominal-level data.

Beta coefficient: When using multiple regression, a mathematically derived indicator of the amount of prediction of the criterion variable that is attributable to any one predictor variable.

Beta error: See Type II error.

Beta weight: When using multiple R, a mathematically derived indicator of the amount of variation in the criterion variable that is attributable to any one predictor variable.

Biased sample: A sample selected in such a way that some members of the population are more likely than others to be picked for sample membership; if we wish to make generalizations about the population based on sample observations, it is desirable to avoid biased samples.

Bimodal distribution: A frequency distribution with two modes reflecting equal or nearly equal frequencies.

Binary variable: A dichotomous variable whose values are 0 (reflecting absence of any quantity of the variable) and 1 (reflecting presence of the variable).

Bivariate analysis: A statistical analysis of the relationship between two variables.

Box plot: A graph that reflects both the central tendency and variability of the distribution of a variable. In one of its most common variations, lines are used to indicate the five-number summary, that is, the minimum value, the 25th percentile, the median, the 75th percentile, and the maximum value.

Canonical correlation: A statistical procedure that simultaneously examines the correlation between a weighted group of criterion variables (a derived predictor variable) and a weighted group of outcome variables (a weighted criterion variable).

Causality: A relationship of cause and effect; the effect will invariably occur when the cause is present; causality is usually statistical; changes in the causal variable (independent variable) will, on the average, alter values of the affected variable (dependent variable).

Causal relationship: A relationship between two variables for which we can say that the presence or absence of one variable determines the presence or absence of the other or that values of one variable result in specific values of the other variable.

Cell: A compartment in a matrix or table, such as in a cross-tabulation table.

Central limit theorem: The assumption underlying mathematically derived sampling distributions. It states that for a skewed distribution of a variable in a population, the distribution of means from samples of fixed sizes drawn from the population will approach a normal distribution if the sample sizes are large (generally defined as more than 30). The sampling distribution will have the same mean as the population mean, and its variance will be the population variance divided by the sample size.

Central tendency: A typical value for a variable within a data set; one of several descriptive statistics used to reflect a middle value in an array of case values.

Chance: The probability of an event occurring because of some random variation; also referred to as sampling error.

Chi-square table: See Cross-tabulation table.

Chi-square test of association: A common statistical procedure used to analyze the association between two nominal-level variables. It is usually referred to as *chi-square*.

Class frequency: Number of observations falling in a class (referring to a frequency histogram).

Cluster analysis: A multivariate statistical procedure that, among its other uses, groups together cases that have similar measurements (values) in relation to certain variables.

Coding: The act of categorizing raw data into groups or giving the data numerical values.

Conceptualization: The first step in the measurement process, in which the researcher selects the variables to be measured; delineating the exact meaning of the independent and dependent variables.

Concomitant variation: The case in which two variables vary together; individuals who differ with respect to variable *x* will also differ with respect to variable *y*.

Confidence interval: A range of values within which we are willing to assert with a specified level of confidence that an unknown parameter value lies; computed from sample statistics, the width of the confidence interval depends on the rejection level stated, the sample size, and the variability in the sample.

Confidence level: The probability that a population parameter lies within a given confidence interval.

Confidence limits: Upper and lower boundaries of confidence intervals.

Confounding variables: Variables operating in a specific situation in such a way that their effects cannot be separated; they occur when the effects of an extraneous variable cannot be separated from the effects of the dependent variable; the effects of the extraneous variable thus confound the interpretation of research results.

Confusion matrix: A table that displays the type and number of errors that a given group of predictor variables have produced; a product of discriminant analysis.

Constant: A characteristic that has the same value for all individuals in a research study.

Contingency table: See Cross-tabulation table.

Continuous variable: A variable that may theoretically assume any value between two points on the measurement scale; it can thus have an infinite number of possible values between those points.

Control group: A group of people who do not receive the experimental treatment; a group used for comparison purposes; those people to whom no experimental stimulus is administered but who resemble members of the experimental group in all other respects; in an experimental research design, a group in which the independent variable is left unchanged; serves as a reference to compare the effect of manipulating the independent variable in the experimental group(s).

Control variable: A variable, other than the independent variable(s) of primary interest, whose effects we can determine; variable that has been controlled by the research design; a variable that is included in designs as an independent variable for the purpose of explaining (controlling) variation.

Correction for continuity: An additional step added to the formula for chi-square if there are only four cells (a 2-by-2 table) entailing the subtraction of .5 from the absolute difference between the expected and observed frequencies for each cell prior to squaring it. It is also known as the *Yates correction factor.*

Correlated *t* test: See Dependent *t* test. See also *t* test.

Correlated variables: Variables whose values are associated; values of one variable tend to be associated in a systematic way with values in the others.

Correlational analyses: Statistical methods that allow us to discover, describe, and measure the strength and direction of associations between and among variables; include the various techniques of computing correlation coefficients and regression analyses.

Correlation coefficient: A single statistic that indicates both the strength and direction of the relationship between two ordinal level, interval-level, or ratio-level variables; correlation coefficients have values between -1 and $+1$, with positive values indicating positive relationships and negative values indicating negative relationships; two commonly used correlation coefficients are Pearson's product-moment correlation coefficient (Pearson's *r*) and Spearman's rho.

Correlation matrix: A table used to display the correlations among three or more pairs of variables.

Covariance: The degree to which certain values of one variable tend to be found disproportionately with certain values of some other variable.

Criterion variable: The variable whose values are predicted from measurements of the predictor variable; another term for *outcome variable.*

Critical region: A set of outcomes of a statistical test that leads to the rejection of the null hypothesis.

Critical value: A value of a test statistic that demarcates the region of rejection and that is thus used as a criterion for statistical significance in hypothesis testing; the value of the statistic that marks the significance level.

Cross-break table: See Cross-tabulation table.

Cross-tabulation table: A table showing the joint frequency distribution of two or more nominal level variables; presents how often each combination of values of each variable occurs; the entries in the table show the number of observations falling into the cells.

Cumulative frequency distribution: A frequency distribution that gives the number of scores that occur at or below each value of a variable.

Cumulative frequency polygon: A frequency polygon that shows how often scores occur at or below each value of a variable.

Cumulative percentage distribution: A table that shows what percentage of scores occurs at or below each value of a variable.

Cumulative proportion graph: A graph in which one axis represents values of a variable and the other represents the proportion of the distribution that falls below those values (i.e., their cumulative proportions); when the data have been grouped, each point on the graph is plotted over the upper true limit of the interval it represents; each point thus represents the proportion of the observations falling at or below that interval.

Cumulative proportion table: A summary table of a group of observations that has one column listing values of a variable and another column indicating the proportion of the distribution that falls at or below each value; when the data have been grouped, the table lists intervals on the measurement scale rather than individual values.

Curvilinear correlation: A relationship between variables that, if displayed using a scattergram, would form one or more curves; a relationship between two variables that is not linear.

Data: The numbers or scores generated by a research study; the word *data* is plural.

Datum: Singular of *data*.

Degrees of freedom: A characteristic of the sample statistic that determines the appropriate sampling distribution; the number of ways in which the data are free to vary; the number of observations minus the number of restrictions placed on the data; a number related to the sample size in a way that depends on the particular statistical technique employed; in many statistical tests, degree of freedom, or *df*, is needed in order to determine the *p* value.

Dependent events: Events that influence the probability of occurrence of each other.

Dependent *t* test: A hypothesis-testing procedure used to decide whether the means within two dependent samples could have occurred by sampling error; sometimes referred to as a dependent-groups *t* test, correlated-groups *t* test, paired-groups *t* test, or matched-groups *t* test.

Dependent variable: The variable that we do not directly introduce or manipulate; after the different levels of the independent variable have been administered, all research participants are measured, in the same way, on the same dependent variable; a variable in which the changes are results of the level or amount of the independent variable(s); also, the variable whose variations are of most interest to the researcher; when used with correlation or regression, it is referred to as the outcome variable.

Derived variable: The correlation between one outcome variable and a group of predictor variables.

Descriptive data analyses: Methods used for summarizing and describing data in a clear and precise manner; strictly speaking, descriptive analyses apply only to the people (or objects) actually observed; methods for data reduction.

Design flaw: Any effect that systematically distorts the outcome of a research study so that the results are not representative of the phenomenon under investigation. Includes measurement error and sampling bias.

Deviation from the mean: The distance of a single score from the mean of the distribution from which the scores come.

Deviation score: The difference between the mean of a distribution and an individual score of that distribution; deviation scores are always found by subtracting the mean from the score; a positive value indicates a score above the mean; a negative value indicates a score below the mean.

Dichotomous variable: A variable that can take on only one of two values.

Direct relationship: A relationship between two variables in which high values of one variable are found with high values of the second variable and vice versa; also referred to as a positive relationship between variables or a positive correlation.

Directional hypothesis: A hypothesis stated in such a manner that the direction of the relationship between variables is hypothesized for the results; it uses a statistical test with only one region of rejection, that is, a one-tailed test; a directional test is called for only when certain assumptions can be made; because the region of rejection is located entirely at one end of the distribution in a directional test, fewer deviant values of the observed statistic will lead to rejection of the null hypothesis than in the nondirectional test with the same rejection level.

Directional test: See Directional hypothesis.

Discrete variable: A variable that can assume only a finite number of values.

Discriminant analysis: A form of multivariate statistical analysis that is used to classify cases into two or more values of a nominal or ordinal criterion variable based on measurements of a group of interval or ratio predictor variables.

Discriminant function: A derived variable created in multivariate discriminant analysis that represents the weighted values of several independent variables.

Dispersion: The amount that values of a variable tend to cluster around a measure of central tendency within a data set. It is alternately referred to as *spread* or *variability*.

Distribution: The pattern of frequency of occurrence of scores; the total observations or a set of data for a variable; when observations are tabulated according to frequency for each possible score, we have a frequency distribution.

Distribution-free method: A method for testing a hypothesis or setting up a confidence interval, for example, that does not depend on the form of the underlying distribution.

Distribution-free tests: A term referring to a large family of statistical tests that, in general, do not require assumptions about the precise shape of the population distribution; the population distribution of a variable need not be normal in shape and data need not be at least interval level; also called nonparametric tests.

Dummy table: A cross-tabulation table that contains asterisks to reflect where disproportionately large frequencies will be found if a directional hypothesis is supported.

Dummy variable: A variable that is created by converting a qualitative variable into binary variables.

Effect size: The percent of variance in the dependent variable that can be explained by the independent variable. The predicted effect size is one consideration (along with rejection level) in choosing a sample size that will result in the optimal statistical power for data analysis.

Empirical frequency distribution: A frequency distribution tabulated from data that have actually been collected (as opposed to a theoretical frequency distribution, which is constructed from theoretical or mathematical considerations).

Empirical sampling distribution: A sampling distribution generated by actually taking random samples and measuring each sample's characteristics.

Error of estimation: Distance between an estimate and the true value of the parameter estimated.

Error of measurement: In measurement, the extent of its inaccuracy.

Estimate: Number computed from sample data used to approximate a population parameter.

Estimator: Rule that tells us how to compute an estimate based on data contained in a sample; an estimator is usually given as a mathematical formula, as in regression analysis.

Expected frequencies: In the chi-square test, the frequencies of observations in different categories (cells) that would be most likely to appear if the null hypothesis were true.

Expected value: The long-run average of a random variable over an indefinite number of samplings.

Expected value of a statistic: The mean of a statistic's sampling distribution.

Experiment: A research study in which we have control over the levels of the independent variable and over the assignment of people or objects to different conditions.

Experimental group: In an experimental research design, the group in which the independent variable is manipulated or introduced.

Extraneous variable: See Intervening variable.

_F_ ratio: The between-group estimates of the variance of the sampling distribution of the mean divided by the within-group's estimate; the _F_ ratio can be viewed as a measure of the strength of a treatment effect.

_F_ statistic: A test statistic that is used to compare variances from two normal populations; used in analysis of variance.

Factor analysis: A statistical method for identifying certain factors or dimensions that exist in a data set.

Factorial designs: Variations of analysis of variance (ANOVA) that are used to examine the relationship among two or more independent variables and one interval or ratio dependent variable. Sometimes called _multifactor_ ANOVA.

Factorial experiments: Experimental research designs that look at the separate effects and interactions of two or more independent variables at the same time.

Factor rotation: A group of statistical procedures designed to develop more precise meanings of the factors created through a factor analysis.

Fisher's exact test: A nonparametric statistical test that can be used to examine the association between two dichotomous nominal level variables when the size requirement for expected frequencies for using chi-square cannot be met.

Five-number summary: A concise description of the distribution of the values of a variable in a sample or population. It consists of the minimum value, the 25th percentile, the median, the 75th percentile, and the maximum value. It can be portrayed graphically in a box plot.

Frequency: Number of observations falling in a cell or value category of a specific variable.

Frequency distribution: A table or graph that presents the number of times (frequency) with which different values of the variable occur in a group of observations; a technique of descriptive statistics that shows how often each score occurs.

Frequency polygon: A graphic technique of descriptive statistics that uses the height of connected dots to display the shape of the distribution of a variable; graph of a frequency distribution in which the horizontal axis represents different values of a variable and the vertical axis represents frequencies with which those values occur; in constructing a frequency polygon, a dot is placed over each value of the variable at a height corresponding to the appropriate frequency; the dots are then connected with lines to form a polygon.

Frequency table: In its simplest form, a two-column table with one column listing values of a variable and the other column listing the frequency with which the different values occur in a group of observations. Columns for percentages, cumulative percentages, and cumulative frequencies may also be included.

Goodness-of-fit test: A method of data analysis used to decide whether a sample with a given frequency distribution could have occurred by chance from a population with a known frequency distribution (or known percentage composition); a nonparametric statistical test that allows us to decide whether observed frequencies are essentially equal to or significantly different from expected frequencies.

Grouped cumulative frequency distribution: An extension of a grouped frequency distribution that shows how often scores occur at or below each interval.

Grouped frequency distribution: Table or graph in which frequencies are not listed for each possible value of the variable; rather, a frequency is listed for each of a number of intervals on the measurement scale; each interval is a range of values; all observations falling within the limits of the interval add to the frequency count for that interval; grouped frequency distributions are used most often when data represent observations on a continuous variable.

Grouped frequency histogram: A histogram that shows how often scores occur at given intervals.

Grouped frequency polygon: A frequency polygon that shows how often scores occur at given intervals.

Histogram: A graphic representation of a frequency distribution in which the horizontal line represents values of a variable and the vertical line represents frequencies with which those values occur; a bar is constructed over each value of the variable (or the midpoint of each interval, if the data are grouped) and extended to the appropriate frequency; the term *histogram* usually refers to such a graph for interval or ratio data, whereas the term *bar graph* usually refers to such a graph for nominal or ordinal data; a graphic technique of descriptive statistics that uses the heights of adjoining bars to show how often each score occurs.

Horizontal axis: The horizontal dimension of a two-dimensional graph; it usually represents values of the independent variable in frequency distributions; sometimes called the *x* axis.

Hotelling's T^2: A statistical test used to examine the relationship among a dichotomous independent variable and a set of two or more interval/ratio dependent variables.

Hypothesis: See Research hypothesis.

Hypothesis testing: A technique in inferential statistics in which we make a decision about the state of reality in the population; the decision consists of either accepting the state of reality proposed by the null hypothesis or rejecting the null hypothesis in favor of the research hypothesis; usually postulates a very specific set of conditions; a technique of inferential statistics that helps us decide whether research results are attributable to chance.

Hypothetical population: A statistical population that has no real existence but is imagined to be generated by repetitions of events of a certain type.

Independent samples design: An experiment in which people are assigned to different groups on a completely random basis; samples are drawn in such a way that the particular subjects chosen for one sample have no influence on which subjects are chosen for the other sample.

Independent *t* test: A statistical test used to decide whether two independent samples could have occurred by sampling error. See also *t* test.

Independent variable: The variable we believe to be associated with the different values of the dependent variable; the variable that is manipulated or introduced in a research study in order to see what effect differences in it will have on those variables proposed as being dependent on it.

Inferential statistics: Statistical methods that make it possible to draw tentative conclusions about the population based on observations of a sample selected from that population and, furthermore, to make a probability statement about those conclusions to aid in their evaluation.

Interaction: When the effect of one factor on a response depends on the level(s) of one (or more) other factor(s); the effect of one independent variable on another; the failure of one independent variable to remain constant over the levels of another; two treatments are said to interact if scores obtained under levels of one treatment behave differently under different levels of the other treatment.

Interquartile range: A statistic used as a measure of variability; the distance between the 75th and 25th percentiles; the interquartile range is more stable than the simple range and can be used with ordinal-level data; it does not, however, reflect the value of every observation in the group (as does the standard deviation); the median and interquartile range are often used together to describe the distribution of a variable, since both are based on percentiles.

Interval measurement: A measurement that, in addition to ordering scores, also establishes an equal unit so that distances between any two scores are of a known magnitude; a measurement in which objects, events, or processes are assigned to ordered categories that are separated by equal intervals; any measuring device that is capable not only of placing people (or objects) in their rank order on a characteristic but can also measure the differences between them in regard to that characteristic.

Intervening variable: A variable whose existence is inferred, but that cannot be manipulated; a variable that may affect just what influence (if any) an independent variable has on a dependent variable; also referred to as a confounding variable or an extraneous variable; when controlled for in a research design, it is known as a control variable. In its most specific usage, a variable that may have come between (in time) the introduction of the independent variable and the dependent variable and may thus have affected the latter.

Inverse relationship: A relationship between two variables in which high values of one variable are found with low values of the other variable and vice versa; sometimes referred to as a negative relationship or negative correlation.

Kendall's partial rank correlation coefficient: A nonparametric test designed to examine the correlation between two variables of at least ordinal level while controlling for a third variable of at least ordinal level.

Kendall's tau: A test producing correlation coefficient showing the strength and direction of a relationship between ranks of two variables in a number of paired observations; it can thus be used when one or both variables are at the ordinal level or when interval or ratio data are badly skewed; it is sometimes used as a quickly computed substitute for Pearson's *r*.

Kolmogorov-Smirnov one-sample test: A nonparametric test that compares the overall distribution of a sample with another theoretical distribution in relation to an ordinal or skewed interval or ratio dependent variable.

Kolmogorov-Smirnov two-sample test: A nonparametric test that compares the overall distribution of two samples in relation to an ordinal level or skewed interval level or ratio level dependent variable. It identifies the point at which the two samples reflect the greatest difference.

Kruskal-Wallis test: A nonparametric statistical test that can be used to examine the relationship between a nominal variable with more than two values and an ordinal level or skewed interval level or ratio level variable. It is a common nonparametric alternative to simple, one-way ANOVA.

Kurtosis: A quality of the distribution of a set of data dealing with whether or how much the data pile up around some central point; the quality of peakedness or flatness of the graphic representation of a statistical distribution.

Least-squares criterion: The principle that the best regression line is one that would result in the smallest sum of squared deviations from the line.

Leptokurtic distribution: A relatively peaked frequency distribution; a frequency distribution that is more concentrated around the mean than the corresponding normal distribution.

Level of confidence: A term used in constructing confidence interval estimates of parameter values to specify our confidence that the interval includes the parameter value; with the use of procedures for constructing a 95 percent confidence interval, for instance, we would enclose the true parameter value within its limits on 95 percent of such attempts; the higher the level of confidence, the wider the interval.

Level of measurement: Refers to the degree to which characteristics of the data may be modeled mathematically; the higher the level of measurement, the more statistical methods are applicable.

Level of significance: See Rejection level.

Limits of confidence intervals: The upper and lower values at the two ends of a confidence interval; in a symmetrical confidence interval, the limits are located one allowance factor above and below the sample statistic.

Linear correlation: A correlation between variables that if displayed using a scattergram would approximate a straight line.

Linear relationship: A relationship between two variables in which a straight line can be fitted satisfactorily to the points on the scattergram; the scatter of points will cluster elliptically around a straight line rather than around some type of curve.

Line of best fit: See regression line.

Lower confidence limit: Smaller of the two numbers that form a confidence interval; in frequency distributions where data have been grouped, it is the lower boundary of an interval on the measurement scale.

Mann-Whitney *U* test: A nonparametric test that is used to examine the relationship between a dichotomous nominal level variable and an ordinal level or skewed interval level or ratio level variable. It is a common alternative to the parametric independent *t* test.

MANOVA (multiple analysis of variance): A form of multivariate statistical analysis used to compare the means of two or more interval level or ratio level dependent variables across the value categories of a nominal level independent variable.

Marginals: The count of frequencies with which certain responses occur; in a cross-tabulation table, the row and column totals.

Matched pairs test: A statistical test for the comparison of two population means; the test is based on paired observations, one from each of the two populations; in the two-sample experiment, a procedure in which the entire subject pool is arranged in matched pairs, where pair members are similar (matched) on important characteristics; one member of each pair is then assigned to each group.

Matrix: A two-dimensional organization; each dimension is composed of several positions or alternatives; any particular score is a combination of the two dimensions as, for example, in a correlation matrix.

McNemar's test: A nonparametric test used to examine both the direction and amount of change in a group of cases in a pretest–posttest situation where the dependent variable is at the nominal level. It is sometimes called the *test for significance of changes*.

Mean: A term shared by several measures of central tendency (arithmetic mean, harmonic mean, geometric mean, and quadratic mean), all of which are computed with the use of the value of every observation in the data set; in a general sense, the mean is equivalent to the average of all of the values within a data set.

Mean deviation: Measure of variability, that is, literally the mean (absolute value) of the deviations about the mean.

Measure of central tendency: A single number that describes the location, or relative magnitude, of a typical score in a sample or population; synonymous with the term *average;* the mode, median, and mean are examples of central tendency.

Measurement: In the most general sense, the assignment of labels to observations according to a rule or system; in statistics, measurement systems are classified according to level of measurement and may produce data that can be represented in numerical form or in words; the assignment of numerals to objects or events according to specific rules.

Measurement error: A source of measurement distortion that can occur because of any of a wide variety of phenomena. It can be either systematic or random.

Measure of variability: A single number that describes how spread out a group of scores is in a sample or population; the range, variance, and standard deviation are examples of variability.

Measures of association: Indicators of relationship magnitude or the actual strength of the relationship between variables. The level of measurement of the independent and dependent variables is used to determine which of several measures of association can appropriately be used.

Median: A measure of central tendency defined as the point on the measurement scale where 50 percent of the observations fall above it and 50 percent of the observations fall below it; it thus coincides with the 50th percentile; it is useful in skewed distributions because it is not as sensitive as the mean to the presence of a few outliers (extremely high or low values); it requires at least ordinal level data.

Mesokurtic distribution: A frequency distribution that is neither excessively peaked nor excessively flat; the normal distribution is a mesokurtic distribution.

Midpoint of an interval: The value located halfway between upper and lower limits of an interval, found by adding upper and lower limits and dividing by two; when graphing or computing statistics from grouped data, the midpoint of each interval is sometimes used to represent all observations appearing in that interval.

Mode: A measure of central tendency; the most frequently occurring value in a distribution of scores (in grouped distributions, the midpoint of the interval with the highest frequency).

Moses test of extreme reactions: A nonparametric test designed for experimental situations in which it is believed that the introduction of the independent variable will produce extreme changes in the ordinal level dependent variable in one direction among some research participants and extreme reactions in the opposite direction among others.

Most powerful test: The statistical test that has the smallest probability of producing a Type II error.

Multifactor MANOVA: A form of multivariation analysis in which there are two or more independent variables and two or more dependent variables.

Multiple-group design: An experimental research design with one control group and several experimental groups.

Multiple linear regression: A multivariate statistical procedure that is used to predict the value of an interval or ratio level outcome variable using the values of two or more interval or ratio level predictor variables.

Multiple *R*: A form of multivariate statistical analysis that determines the amount of variation in an outcome variable that can be explained by the combined variation of a group of predictor variables.

Multivariate analysis: A statistical analysis of the simultaneous relationship among three or more variables.

Mutually exclusive events: In applications of probability theory, two or more events that cannot both happen on a single trial; on a single flip of a coin, for example, the events heads and tails are mutually exclusive.

Negatively skewed distribution: See Negative skew.

Negative relationship: The situation in correlational analysis in which high values of one variable tend to be associated with low values of another and vice versa; negative relationships are indicated by negative correlation coefficients.

Negative skew: A descriptive term applied to frequency distributions with many high values and few extremely low values; on a frequency polygon, negative skew produces a tail in the direction of low values—to the left; skewness in which the mean is less than the mode.

Nominal measurement: A measurement that simply classifies elements into two or more mutually exclusive categories, indicating that elements are qualitatively different but not giving order or magnitude; a measurement in which objects, events, or processes are assigned to categories having no inherent order; the level of measurement whose only requirement is that each observation falls in one, and only one, measurement category; also referred to as categorical measurement; it is the lowest level of measurement.

Nondirectional test: A statistical test with two regions of rejection, that is, a two-tailed test; the area under the sampling distribution curve equal to the rejection level is divided into two equal parts at each end of the distribution, creating two regions of rejection; an observed statistic in either region leads to rejection of the null hypothesis; a test used when we have not predicted the direction of a relationship between two variables.

Nonparametric tests: Usually refers to statistical tests of hypotheses about population probability distributions, but not about specific parameters of the distributions; a test that does not require a normal population distribution; a method for testing a hypothesis that does not involve an explicit assertion concerning a parameter; hypothesis-testing procedures that do not make stringent assumptions about population parameters.

"No relationship" research hypothesis: A form of research hypothesis in which the researcher expects and predicts that no statistically significant relationship between two variables will be found. It is sometimes referred to as the "null research hypothesis."

Normal distribution: A symmetrical bell-shaped curve that often arises when a trait is composed of a large number of random, independent factors; the curve possesses a specific mathematical formula.

Null hypothesis: A statement concerning one or more parameter(s) that is subjected to a statistical test; a statement that there is no relationship between the two variables of interest; the belief that any apparent relationship between or among variables in one or more research samples has been caused by sampling error; the hypothesis that is tested when seeking to gain statistical support for a one-tailed or two-tailed research hypothesis.

Obscuring variable: A third variable that may cause a researcher to underestimate the true strength of the relationship between the independent and the dependent variables. Also called a *suppressor variable.*

Observation: An objectively recorded fact or item of datum; statistics are usually applied to collections of observations. Also referred to as a case.

Omnibus test: A type of statistical test (such as simple ANOVA) that can determine only if there is a relationship somewhere among a group of variables, but cannot pinpoint which of the variables is related to which other variable.

One-sample *t* test: A hypothesis-testing procedure used to decide whether a mean of a variable within a sample could have occurred by sampling error.

One-tailed research hypothesis: A form of research hypothesis in which the researcher predicts that a statistically significant relationship between variables will be found and also predicts the direction of that relationship.

One-tailed test: See Directional hypothesis.

One-way analysis of variance: See Simple ANOVA.

Ordinal measurement: A measurement that classifies and ranks elements or scores; a procedure that is capable of rank-ordering individuals (or objects) on a particular characteristic but that cannot distinguish how different each is from the others; a measurement in which objects, events, or processes are assigned to ordered categories; the level of measurement above nominal but below interval; the data represent at least ordinal scale measurement if each observation falls into one, and only one, category and if observation categories can be rank ordered.

Origin: The point of a graph at which the x axis and y axis intersect.

Outcome: A possible result of an experiment or observation; in probability applications, the result of an experimental trial; see also Probability.

Outcome variable: The variable whose values can be predicted by values of the predictor value; sometimes called the criterion variable.

Outlier: An extreme value of a variable in a data set that is either larger or smaller than most other values in the variable's distribution.

Paired observations: An observation on two variables, where the intent is to examine the relationship between them; paired observations form the raw material of correlational analyses; recording both a person's height and weight and keeping both of those measurements associated with the same person constitute collection of a paired observation.

Parameter: A characteristic of a population determined from observations on every member of the population; population parameters of interest to us include the mean, range, median, standard deviation, and many others; also a characteristic of a mathematical relation whose value must be specified before the expression can be evaluated; a measure computed from all observations in a population.

Parameter estimates: Attempts to estimate the values of population parameters (e.g., the mean) from statistics computed on a sample selected from the population; estimates may consist of a single value (a point estimate) or a range of values (confidence interval).

Parametric tests: Statistical methods for estimating parameters or testing hypotheses about population parameters; a statistical test in which the null and research hypotheses are stated in terms of population parameter values; an example is the test for the significance of the difference between two means; procedures that make relatively stringent assumptions about population parameters.

Partial *r*: A test of correlation in which the relationship between two variables is examined while a third potentially intervening or extraneous variable is held constant.

Pearson's product-moment correlation coefficient: A correlation coefficient that specifies the strength and direction of a relation between two interval or ratio level variables; it is the most commonly used statistic in correlational analyses; also called Pearson's *r*.

Percent: Synonymous with *in 100* or the number of cases out of 100.

Percentage distribution: A table that displays the percentage of cases that were found to have each of the respective measurements of a variable.

Percentile: A point on the measurement scale below which a specified percentage of the group's observations fall; the 20th percentile, for instance, is the value that has 20 percent of the observations below it.

Percentile rank: A transformed score that tells us the percentage of scores falling at or below a given score.

Perfect relationship: A relationship between two variables in which the value of one variable is known if the value of the other variable is specified; a relationship, either direct or inverse, in which there is a perfect predictability between the two variables; when all points in the scattergram lie exactly on the regression line.

Pie chart: A graph that displays the frequency distribution of a variable as portions of a circle reflecting percentages of the whole.

Planned comparison: The planned use of additional analyses following the use of an omnibus test. It is based upon a belief in a specific relationship between variables.

Platykurtic distribution: A frequency distribution that has a relatively flat shape; a distribution that is less concentrated around the mean than the corresponding normal distribution.

Point estimate: A single value, produced by application of inferential methods to observations on sample members, that is our best guess of a parameter value.

Population distribution: A distribution of all the scores in a population; a collection of all observations identifiable by a set of rules; a designated part of a universe from which a sample is drawn; the complete group of potential observations.

Positively skewed distribution: See Positive skew.

Positive relationship: The situation in correlational analyses that exists when high values of the first variable tend to be associated with high values of the second variable, and low values of the first variable tend to appear with low values of the second; also referred to as a positive correlation.

Positive skew: A descriptive term applied to frequency distributions with many low values and a few extremely high values; on a frequency polygon graph, positive skew produces a tail in the direction of the positive values; skewness in which the mode is less than the mean.

Post hoc comparison: The unplanned use of one or more statistical test to examine relationships between variables subsequent to the use of an omnibus test such as simple ANOVA.

Power of test: See Statistical power.

Prediction: The estimation of scores on one variable from data about one or more other variables.

Predictor variable: The variable that, it is believed, allows us to improve our ability to predict values of the outcome variable.

Probability: A measure of likelihood; the number of outcomes in which an event can occur divided by the total number of possible outcomes; reported as a *p* value.

Probability distribution: For discrete random variables, the probability distribution is a relative frequency distribution; the relative frequencies associated with values indicate the probabilities of their occurrences.

Proportion: A fraction of one.

Proportion/frequency method: A statistical test commonly used in single-system research when the target problem is a dichotomous variable.

p **value:**   The mathematical probability that sampling error might have caused variables to be related in a research sample.

Quartile: A percentile that is an even multiple of 25; the 25th percentile is the first quartile, the 50th percentile is the second quartile (it is also the median), and so forth.

r^2**:**   The amount of variation in the outcome variable that can be explained by the predictor variable; an indicator of association.

Random measurement error: Measurement error that occurs in no particular pattern. It is harder to detect than systematic measurement error.

Random variable: A variable that can assume different values; there is a probability associated with occurrence of different values of the variable, and these probabilities constitute a probability distribution.

Random sample: A sample drawn from a population in such a way that all cases had an equal probability of being selected.

Range: Difference between the largest and smallest numbers of an array plus one; the distance between the highest and lowest values in a distribution (more accurately, the distance between the upper true limit of the highest value and the lower true limit of the lowest value); it is used as a measure of variability.

Ratio measurement: A measurement that, in addition to containing equal units, also establishes an absolute zero point within the scale; a measurement in which objects, events, or processes are assigned to ordered categories that are separated with equal intervals, and where the zero point is not arbitrary; the highest level of measurement; it is reached when each observation falls in one, and only one, category; when observation categories can be ordered; when there are equal intervals between adjacent categories on the measurement scale; and when a value of zero represents a zero quantity of the variable being measured.

Raw score: A numerical value assigned to an observation that is expressed in the original units of measurement; a score obtained directly by measuring some characteristic of a person, event, or process in a research study.

Regression analysis: A variation of a correlational analysis that makes possible prediction of the value of one variable from observations on another variable; these predictions are based on a collection of previously made paired observations on both variables; regression analyses require that the two variables be fairly strongly correlated and that the relation between them approximate a linear one.

Regression equation: A derived equation in the form of $Y' = a + b(X)$ that makes it possible to predict the value of an outcome value from a value of a predictor variable.

Regression line: A hypothetical line that goes through data points and that uses the method of least squares; one of two least-squares lines through a scatter plot of paired observations; each regression line constitutes the collection of predicted values for one of the variables; the straight line of best fit (usually according to the least-squares criterion) for a set of bivariate data; the line of best fit in a scattergram; mostly used to predict values of the y variable from values of the x variable.

Rejection level: The selected probability level at which the null hypothesis is rejected; the commonly used rejection level is .05; the probability of rejecting the null hypothesis when it is true; also called the alpha level.

Rejection region: A specific region of a normal curve that, when it contains a measurement from a sample, suggests that it is safe to reject the null hypothesis.

Relative frequency distribution: A table or graph that shows observation categories and the proportion of the group that falls within each value category—that is, the relative frequency of each category; the proportion of observations that falls in one category or interval; in probability applications, the relative frequency of an event is the proportion of trials on which the event occurs.

Reliability: The consistency of a measurement instrument.

Reliability coefficient: A measure of the consistency of a statistical test; there are several methods of computing a reliability coefficient, depending on the test and the specific situation.

Replication: Repetition of the same research procedures (usually by a second researcher) for the purpose of determining if earlier results can be duplicated; the collection of two or more observations under a set of identical experimental conditions.

Research hypothesis: A prediction of the relationship between two or more variables; when using one-tailed or two-tailed research hypotheses, the hypothesis to be supported if the null hypothesis is rejected; also called the alternative hypothesis.

Rival hypothesis: Theoretical alternatives for explaining the apparent relationship between the independent (or predictor) variable(s) and the dependent (or outcome) variable(s); other variables that might explain variations in the dependent (or outcome) variable(s).

Robustness: Refers to the property that certain hypothesis-testing procedures have of yielding accurate results regardless of whether all assumptions for the test are strictly satisfied.

Sample: A subset of the population under study; a subset of a population often used synonymously with *group* and *condition* when discussing research designs; sometimes referred to as a research sample.

Sample distribution: The frequency distribution of all observations in a sample; when a number of different samples are selected from one population, each sample will probably have a sample distribution slightly different from other samples.

Sample statistic: Characteristics of samples; statistics computed from observations on sample members; the mean of a sample is a sample statistic because only members of the sample contribute to its value; the mean of a population is a parameter (rather than a statistic) because all members of the population contributed to its value.

Sampling: A method of selecting members of the population for inclusion in a research study; strictly speaking, proper sampling procedures must be used if inferences about the population are to be made from sample statistics; two broad categories of sampling procedures are random (probability) sampling and nonrandom (nonprobability) sampling.

Sampling bias: Refers to the systematic distortion of a research sample. It can occur for any of a variety of reasons and produces a sample that is not representative of its population. Not to be confused with sampling error.

Sampling distribution: A theoretical distribution that can be specified for any statistic that can be computed for samples from a population; it is the frequency distribution of that statistic's values that would appear if all possible samples of a specified size were drawn from the population; it is the foundation of inferential statistics because it allows us to specify the probability with which different values of the statistic appear; it is assumed that a statistic computed from sample observations is one value from such a distribution.

Sampling error: Refers to the natural phenomenon whereby sample statistics tend to differ from population parameters; the degree to which the sample can be predicted to vary from the population in relation to some variable based on this phenomenon. Sometimes referred to as chance. Not to be confused with sampling bias.

Scattergram: A graphic representation of the relationship between two interval- or ratio-level variables; a two-dimensional graph in which each axis represents values of a different variable; paired observations on both variables are represented as dots on the graph; it may be used as a preliminary step in a correlational analysis or to portray in graphic fashion the strength and direction of a relationship between two variables; sometimes referred to as a scatter plot.

Scheffé test: One of several methods or conducting a post hoc comparison.

Score: A numerical value assigned to an observation; a case value.

Score interval: In a grouped frequency distribution, the range of observed values is divided into a number of score intervals; the frequency distribution table lists the number of observations that fall into each score interval.

Semi-interquartile range: Half the interquartile range, sometimes used as a measure of variability.

Sign test: Nonparametric statistical test used to compare the same sample at two different times.

Simple ANOVA: A statistical test used to decide whether two or more samples could have occurred by chance from populations with equal means.

Simple linear regression: A statistical procedure that produces an equation that makes it possible to predict the value of the criterion variable for a given value of the predictor variable.

Skewed distribution: A distribution in which more observations fall on one side of the mean than on the other side.

Skewness: A quality of the distribution of a set of data dealing with whether the data are symmetrically distributed around a central point.

Spearman's correlation coefficient: A correlation coefficient showing the strength and direction of a relationship between ranks of two variables in a number of paired observations; it can thus be used when one or both variables produce data at the ordinal level or when interval or ratio data are badly skewed; it is sometimes used as a quickly computed substitute for Pearson's *r;* also referred to as Spearman's rho.

Specifying variable: A third variable that can further explain a relationship between the independent and dependent variables that is statistically significant but that seems to exist in two different directions.

Spurious relationship: Not a real relationship that exists beyond the sample or samples in which it was identified. It can be explained away by the presence of rival hypotheses confounding variables or other phenomena.

Stability: The degree to which a statistic's value remains constant when it is computed for a number of different groups that are essentially alike but that differ in a few values; in inferential statistics, a stable statistic is one whose value remains stable from sample to sample when all samples are taken from the same population.

Standard deviation: A common measure of variability; it requires at least interval level data and reflects the value of every observation in the distribution; like other measures of variability, it is a single number whose size indicates the spread, or dispersion, of the distribution; a measure of variability that is the square root of the variance; it represents a specified distance along the baseline of a distribution curve.

Standard error: An estimate of how well a regression equation can predict values of the criterion variable from known values of the predictor variable.

Standard error of a statistic: The standard deviation of the underlying (sampling) distribution of the statistic.

Standard error of estimate: In the regression situation, the standard deviation of observed values around the regression line; the smaller the standard error of estimate, the more precisely we can predict scores of the criterion variable.

Standard error of the difference: Refers to the standard deviation of the sampling distribution of the difference for independent samples.

Standard error of the mean: The standard deviation of the underlying (sampling) distribution of the mean. It is the square root of the variance of the mean.

Standard normal distribution: The normal distribution with a mean of 0 and a standard deviation of 1.

Standard score: A score stated in units of standard deviation from the mean of the distribution; a negative score indicates a score below the mean and a positive score indicates a score above the mean; an individual observation that belongs to a distribution with a mean of 0 and a standard deviation of 1; any distribution of raw scores can be transformed into a distribution of standard scores without changing the shape of the distribution or the relative order or distances between members because the transformation to standard scores is linear; also referred to as a *z* score.

Statistical decision: Choosing between states of possible reality on the basis of probability considerations; hypothesis testing involves a statistical decision in which we either accept or reject the null hypothesis.

Statistically significant: Judged too unlikely to have occurred because of sampling error. However, other variables or conditions may have produced it.

Statistical power: The ability of a statistical test to reject the null hypothesis correctly; a test's ability to detect a true relationship between or among variables.

Statistical power analysis: A procedure for determining the likelihood of committing a Type II error given the size of sample(s) used, the statistical test of inference employed, and other factors.

Statistics: In comparison to the term *parameters,* statistics refers to the characteristics of a sample rather than to the characteristics of a population; in the context of descriptive statistics, measures taken on a distribution; in the context of inferential statistics, measures or characteristics of a sample; in a more general sense, the theory, procedures, and methods by which data are analyzed; the area of study that includes methods for producing and interpreting statistics; generally speaking, statistical methods are applied in an attempt to understand large masses of data, to discover and describe characteristics of the data that are not apparent from casual observation, and to describe characteristics of a group of observations rather than single observations.

Stem-and-leaf plot: A graph consisting of numbers that reflect the actual case values of all cases in a frequency distribution.

Structural variables: In data analyses, those characteristics formed by combining units from lower levels of analysis.

Suppressor variable: A third variable that may cause a researcher to underestimate the true strength of the relationship between the independent and dependent variables. Also called an *obscuring variable.*

Symmetrical distribution: A distribution in which, for every observation on one side of the mean, there is another observation at an equal distance on the other side of the mean; in a symmetrical distribution, the left half of the polygon (or histogram) is a mirror image of the right half; a distribution with a frequency polygon whose left and right sides will coincide if it is folded in the middle along a vertical line.

Systematic measurement error: Reliable (consistent) measurement of a variable that, for one of several reasons, produces measurements that are not valid.

Transformed standardized score: A score that allows us to tell at a glance where it falls in a distribution of scores; a standard score that has been transformed so that it now belongs to a distribution with any mean and standard deviation we wish; transformed scores are used most often in evaluating test scores.

Trimmed mean: A measure of central tendency calculated by first trimming a small percentage (usually 5%) of values off the upper and lower limits of an array of case values and then averaging the remaining values.

True control group: A control group composed of cases that were both randomly selected *and* randomly assigned to it and to the experimental group.

True limits of a number: The upper and lower points on the measurement scale that enclose all values of the variable actually represented by a number.

t **test:** A group of parametric tests that use the *t* distribution to examine the issue of inference; determines if there is a statistically significant difference between the means of two samples or between a sample's mean and its population's mean.

Tukey's HSD: One of several methods for conducting a post hoc comparison.

Two-standard-deviation method: A relatively simple statistical analysis often used in single-system research when the target problem is measured at the interval level and the measurements vary somewhat around a central point.

Two-tailed research hypothesis: A form of research hypothesis in which the researcher predicts that a statistically significant relationship between variables will be found but does not predict the direction of that relationship.

Two-tailed test: See nondirectional test.

Type I error: Error that occurs when the null hypothesis is rejected when a true relationship between variables does not exist; also called *alpha error.*

Type II error: Error that occurs when the null hypothesis is not rejected when a true relationship between variables exists; also called *beta error.*

Unbiased estimator: Estimator that has a probability distribution with the mean equal to the estimated parameter; an estimate of a parameter is said to be unbiased if its expected value is equal to the parameter.

Unbiased statistic: A statistic computed in a manner such that the mean of its underlying distribution is the parameter that the statistic estimates.

Underlying sampling distribution of a statistic: The distribution (usually theoretical) of all possible values of the statistic from all possible samples of a given size selected from the population.

Unimodal: Refers to a distribution with only one mode.

Univariate analysis: Statistical analysis of the distribution of values of a single variable.

Upper confidence limit: Larger of the two numbers that form a confidence interval.

Upper limit of an interval: In frequency distributions where data have been grouped, the upper boundary of an interval on the measurement scale.

Validity: The degree to which a measurement instrument accurately measures what it is supposed to measure.

Variability: Dispersion of a distribution; the extent to which values differ among themselves; variability is not the name of a specific statistic; rather, it is the term applied to the characteristic of dispersion.

Variable: A characteristic that takes on different values; any attribute whose value, or level, can change; any characteristic (of a person, object, or situation) that can change value or kind from observation to observation.

Variance: Measure of variability that is the average value of the squares of the deviations from the mean of the scores in a distribution; measure of data variation; the mean-squared deviation from the mean; the squared standard deviation, sometimes called the mean square.

Variation: Sum of the squared deviations about the mean; in some applications, variation is useful in its own right as a measure of variability; also called sum of squares.

Vertical axis: The vertical dimension of a two-dimensional graph; it usually represents frequency in frequency distributions, relative frequency in relative frequency distributions, and cumulative proportion in cumulative proportion graphs; when experimental results are graphed, it usually represents values of the dependent variable.

Weighted mean: The average of a group of scores that are weighted to reflect their different levels of importance. The weighted mean is widely used to compute student final grades when different graded exercises or examinations have been assigned different percentages of the course grade.

Wilcoxon sign: A nonparametric statistical test that examines the relationship between two "ordinal plus" variables in two matched case samples.

x **variable:** The variable plotted on the *x* axis of a scattergram and the predictor variable (used to predict the *y* variable) in regression; usually the independent variable in a research study.

Yates' correction factor: In computing the obtained chi-square statistic, a mathematical correction that should be applied when $df = 1$.

Yule's *Q*: One of several easily computed statistical tests often used for exploratory data analysis, that is, to determine if relationships between variables are sufficiently promising to examine, using more powerful forms of analysis.

***y* variable:** The variable plotted on the *x* axis in a scattergram and the predicted variable (predicted from the *x* variable) in regression; usually the dependent variable in a research study.

Zero relationship: The situation that exists when values of one variable are not related in any way to values of another variable; with a zero relationship, knowing the value of one variable gives us no indication of the value of the other; perfect zero relationships are represented by correlation coefficients of 0.

***z* score:** A transformed score that tells us how many standard deviations a score lies away from the mean in a distribution.

***z* test:** A hypothesis-testing procedure used to decide whether a given sample could have occurred by chance from a population with a given mean and known standard deviation.

INDEX